The Definitive Guide to Berkeley DB XML

Danny Brian

Apress®

The Definitive Guide to Berkeley DB XML

Copyright © 2006 by Danny Brian

ISBN-13: 978-1-59059-666-1

ISBN-13 (electronic): 978-1-4302-0220-2

Library of Congress Cataloging-in-Publication data is available upon request.

Printed and bound in the United States of America (POD)

Lead Editor: Matt Wade
Technical Reviewer: George Feinberg
Editorial Board: Steve Anglin, Ewan Buckingham, Gary Cornell, Jason Gilmore, Jonathan Gennick, Jonathan Hassell, James Huddleston, Chris Mills, Matthew Moodie, Dominic Shakeshaft, Jim Sumser, Keir Thomas, Matt Wade
Project Manager: Kylie Johnston
Copy Edit Manager: Nicole LeClerc
Copy Editor: Nancy Sixsmith
Assistant Production Director: Kari Brooks-Copony
Production Editor: Kelly Winquist
Compositor: Molly Sharp
Proofreader: Linda Seifert
Indexer: John Collin
Artist: April Milne
Cover Designer: Kurt Krames
Manufacturing Director: Tom Debolski

Distributed to the book trade worldwide by Springer-Verlag New York, Inc., 233 Spring Street, 6th Floor, New York, NY 10013. Phone 1-800-SPRINGER, fax 201-348-4505, e-mail orders-ny@springer-sbm.com, or visit http://www.springeronline.com.

For information on translations, please contact Apress directly at 2855 Telegraph Avenue Suite 600, Berkeley, CA 94705. Phone 510-549-5930, fax 510-549-5939, e-mail info@apress.com, or visit http://www.apress.com.

The source code for this book is available to readers at http://www.apress.com in the Source Code section.

For the late Darrel Danner
who taught me authenticity

Contents at a Glance

Contents

■CHAPTER 8   BDB XML with C++ 103

■CHAPTER 9   BDB XML with Python 125

About the Author

 **DANNY BRIAN** first began programming on the Apple IIe as a way to keep his fingers warm during the cold Minnesota winters. Games stole his attention early on, and several of his first game creations helped him (barely) pass his junior high classes. After a formal education in music, Danny became enamored with open source and he started a web software company. In the past decade, Danny has worked as a senior engineer for Norwest Bank, Ciceron Interactive, and NTT/Verio. At Verio, he spearheaded the adoption of XML technologies and architected the application framework for most of Verio's current web hosting products. Danny speaks frequently at the O'Reilly Open Source convention on a wide range of topics. In 2001, he was awarded the Damian Conway Award for Technical Excellence (Best of Show at OSCon) for two papers on Natural Language Processing. He was a columnist for *The Perl Journal*, with articles republished in the books *Games, Diversion, and Perl Culture* and *Web, Graphics, and Perl Tk* (O'Reilly, 2003). Danny holds the distinction of being the only human ever to grace the *TPJ* cover. (It was the last issue of that publication, too.)

Danny is an avid composer, having written several commissioned choral works, and frequently records and produces recordings of his piano improvisations. He also performs a stand-up mentalism act (mind-reading) for parties and adult gatherings. Danny's show does not include yachts or swords, and he does not belong to a magician's guild. Any more.

Danny is the founder of Conceptuary, Inc., a games startup company. He is presently neck-deep in work on the Glass Bead Network (at `http://glassbead.net`), which he insists will Change Everything. He lives in Woodland Hills, Utah, with his wife of 11 years, Marie, and their three children.

About the Technical Reviewer

 **GEORGE FEINBERG** is responsible for the technical direction, design, and implementation of Berkeley DB XML at Oracle Corporation (which acquired Sleepycat Software early in 2006). In the late 1990s, he was responsible for the design of the eXcelon XML database at Object Design. In addition to working with XML databases, George's background includes operating system kernel work at Hewlett-Packard and the Open Software Foundation, and a history of distributed file system projects.

Acknowledgments

I've been fortunate to work with first-class folks through all phases of this book, and I want to thank a few people for their contributions.

George Feinberg at Sleepycat/Oracle has the responsibility for the BDB XML architecture. He's also the primary contributor of community support for the product via the BDB XML mailing list and is a great source of general technical know-how (as readers who join the list will quickly learn). George's detailed review and suggestions (and answers to silly questions) have been invaluable to the production of this book, and I hope Sleepycat appreciates him and his product as much as they should. (Subtle, huh?) Thank you also to John Merrells for originating the product and for his early input on the book's contents. This book's subject is not academic for me because BDB XML plays a central part in my current life's work. I'm thankful to all those who have aided in its creation.

A hearty thank you to the staff of Apress. Thanks to Matt Wade for being so easy to work with and for making this project happen in the first place. Nancy Sixsmith and Kelly Winquist helped a great deal to make things read as well as they do. And thank you to Kylie Johnston for patient persistence; you're definitely the most organized and effective project manager I've worked with. Thanks also to the production staff: Molly Sharp, Linda Seifert, John Collin, and April Milne.

Thanks to Scott and Ryan for your support and encouragement (especially when the book interfered with The Project). Thank you to my family for your constant support and (albeit feigned) interest in my work: Mom, Dad, Larry, Cheryl; and my kids, Garron, Tess, and Annie.

My adorable wife deserves the most gratitude. For your unending patience, for your unquestioning approval of my thousand and one projects, for getting up every morning with the goombahs, and for being sincere in all you do   thank you Marie!

Introduction

Berkeley DB XML is exciting to me for multiple reasons. Text data is appealing (as you'll realize as you read *The Definitive Guide to Berkeley DB XML*), and I crave technologies that make it easy to work with. XML is attractive for its flexibility, XPath for its intuitive elegance, XSLT for its declarative nature, and so on. I know full well that XML didn't break new technical ground or invent something we didn't already have. I don't care about that. What XML *did* was to convince an industry to use it and to use it everywhere. Call it hype; call it The Man. The bottom line is that I now have an astonishing array of tools and technologies, all compatible, to work with data as I like.

Until recently, a database was the big missing link; I had to convert data to and from SQL to index it. Eventually, XML databases began to pop up. But even as they did, I was unhappy with their design: most were language-specific, some were just XML-to-RDB interfaces, many had proprietary or otherwise limited query languages, and so on.

Berkeley DB XML caught my eye for three reasons. First, it's Sleepycat, and I've been a big fan of Berkeley DB for a long time its ease of use, its simplicity, and its near-ubiquity. Second, it's embedded, which is one of my pet requirements on any project that doesn't *absolutely* need a database server (just ask my associates). And third, it has language API support for all the major programming languages. When version 2 came along with full support for the industry-standard XQuery language (which is so cool), it was ready for production use in my own sizable projects.

I doubt that many technical books get written if the author isn't excited by the subject matter. I want to assure you that this is the case for *The Definitive Guide to Berkeley DB XML*. I wanted this book to exist because BDB XML has made so much of my current work feasible and fun. I think it's an important piece of software that can dramatically improve how you work with data: how you store it, how you search it, and how you retrieve it. I think XQuery is a great domain-specific language that makes querying data er, enjoyable, if I dare say so.

That's what I think. And so I wrote the book I wanted to read on the matter.

Who This Book Is For

The Definitive Guide to Berkeley DB XML is for any developer who works with XML, whatever the application. I included an XML overview (Appendix A "XML Essentials") for developers who aren't necessarily familiar with XML. The early chapters address programmers who might be unconvinced of the benefits of either an embedded database or the benefits of XML itself, but there's also plenty of information there for any converts.

As long as I brought it up, rest assured that I'm not a *total* zealot. I think that most application technologies programming languages, markup languages, databases, data transports, query languages have their time and place. No one tool is good for everything some are great at some things, and all are horrible at least one thing. BDB XML is no different. I would never suggest that it should completely replace other data solutions, for example. That said, it has replaced many (but not all) of my own such systems, particularly in the area of document storage, and I am quite happy with the results.

The Definitive Guide to Berkeley DB XML is not an exhaustive treatment of XQuery, XML, or related technologies. This book instead pulls them together as used by Berkeley DB XML and gives you everything you need to know about them to work with it.

How This Book Is Structured

The Definitive Guide to Berkeley DB XML has four sections:

Preparation (Chapters 1..4): These chapters get you rolling by covering installation and a "getting started" tutorial chapter.

Details (Chapters 5..7): These chapters discuss the particulars of BDB XML, including its physical organization, its indexes, and its query interface.

APIs (Chapters 8..12): These chapters contain tutorials for individual languages, so consult the chapter for the language you intend to use. (The API reference in Appendix B, "BDB XML API Reference," can fill in any blanks for you.)

Utilities, beginner materials, and references (Chapter 13, "Managing Databases," and the appendixes): The rest of the chapters are extras, including a complete API reference for all languages, an XQuery reference, and an XML beginner's guide.

Chapter 1, "A Quick Look at Berkeley DB XML," provides a quick-fire, several-page look at the software and its functionality. This chapter should give you an idea of what BDB XML is all about.

Chapter 2, "The Power of an Embedded XML Database," is a lightweight (and opinionated) look at embedded databases and XML from an application architecture perspective. If you're not interested in design issues, skip it.

Chapter 3, "Installation and Configuration," details the steps to get BDB XML up and running. It's a painless process, but be sure to refer to the BDB XML documentation for completely up-to-date information.

Chapter 4, "Getting Started," is a tutorial to using BDB XML, focusing on the shell utility provided with the distribution. As such, it's a good practical starting point, regardless of which programming language you intend to use later.

Chapter 5, "Environments, Containers, and Documents," presents the building blocks of BDB XML. These core concepts are necessary for using the system, just as you need to understand tables to be able to use a relational database.

Chapter 6, "Indexes," describes various options for indexing your documents.

Chapter 7, "XQuery with BDB XML," teaches the XQuery language. It is a huge subject, but this chapter tries hard to touch on most of the points you'll want to know to write effective query expressions.

Chapter 8, "BDB XML with C++," offers a tutorial for using BDB XML from C++. All the other language APIs inherit the C++ interface, so it's a useful read for all developers.

Chapters 9 through 12 contain API tutorials for Java, Python, Perl, and PHP. I recommend that you jump to the chapter for your language of choice because the API chapters are largely redundant. These chapters do discuss language particulars, and each includes language-specific code examples. Note that not all languages that have BDB XML APIs are covered; APIs exist for Tcl and Ruby, but the concepts discussed are useful there, too.

Chapter 13, "Managing Databases," touches on some topics that are not in the scope of this book, including database backups and recovering.

Appendix A, "XML Essentials," is an XML overview for XML novices. It's also a decent summary of XML details for use by experienced XML programmers, with sections on XPath and the Document Object Model (DOM).

Appendix B, "BDB XML API Reference," is a complete reference for the BDB XML API for the languages covered in this book: C++, Java, Python, Perl, and PHP.

Appendix C, "XQuery Reference," provides a short list of all XQuery keywords and operators, supported functions, and data types.

Prerequisites

BDB XML is supported on both Unix and Windows, with support for many programming languages. Its recommended that you run the latest stable versions of compilers and languages with which you intend to use BDB XML.

At the time of writing, the current version of BDB XML is 2.2.13, but many details about the next release (2.3) have also been included. Versions prior to 2.2.13 might not have their quirks covered here, and code examples might not be compatible.

Downloading the Code

The source code for this book is available to readers at `http://www.apress.com` in the Downloads section of this books home page. Please feel free to visit the Apress website and download all the code there. You can also check for errata and find related titles from Apress. I have also created a quick reference card for BDB XML, available as a download from both the Apress and Sleepycat sites.

Contacting the Author

Danny Brian can be contacted at `danny@brians.org`, and you can visit his own sizable BDB XML deployment as part of the Glass Bead Network at `http://glassbead.net`.

CHAPTER 1

■ ■ ■

A Quick Look at Berkeley DB XML

Most developers, especially Unix programmers, are familiar with Berkeley DB (BDB). The embedded database has been an integral part of BSD-based distributions since 1992, which now include Linux and Apple OS X. Core open source projects such as sendmail, Subversion, MySQL, and OpenLDAP add valuable services atop BDB's key/value storage. Sleepycat the company that owns, develops, and supports BDB claims an installation base of more than two million. Google, Amazon.com, AOL, Cisco, Motorola, Sun, and HP are all companies that depend on the database as part of critical applications. In short, BDB is about as ubiquitous as software gets.

■**Note** In February 2006 Oracle acquired Sleepycat Software, pulling the most widely used open source database into its product offering. Oracle plans to continue development of Sleepycat's product line and support of its large customer base.

Because it wanted to move into the XML application space, Sleepycat (with the primary participation of John Merrells) developed BDB XML as a layer atop BDB. Today, BDB XML boasts a sophisticated query engine using XQuery with query plan optimization and flexible indexing. It also inherits the transaction features of BDB.

This chapter gives a brief overview of BDB XML for those familiar with the core concepts: embedded databases, XML, and XQuery. Later chapters examine these topics in more depth. The examples in this chapter make use of the BDB XML shell utility, but can be written in any of the programming language supported by BDB XML including C++, Perl, Python, Java, and PHP, all covered later in this book. (Tcl is also supported in the BDB XML distribution, but is not covered here.)

A Complete Example

For an illustrative example of exactly what BDB XML does, imagine that we have a collection of XML files for books that we intend to sell. A sample is shown in Listing 1-1.

Listing 1-1. *A Sample Book XML File,* 0553211757.xml

```
<book isbn="0553211757">
  <title>Crime and Punishment</title>
  <author id="923117"/>
  <publisher>Bantam Classics</publisher>
  <weight>9.3</weight>
  <pages>576</pages>
</book>
```

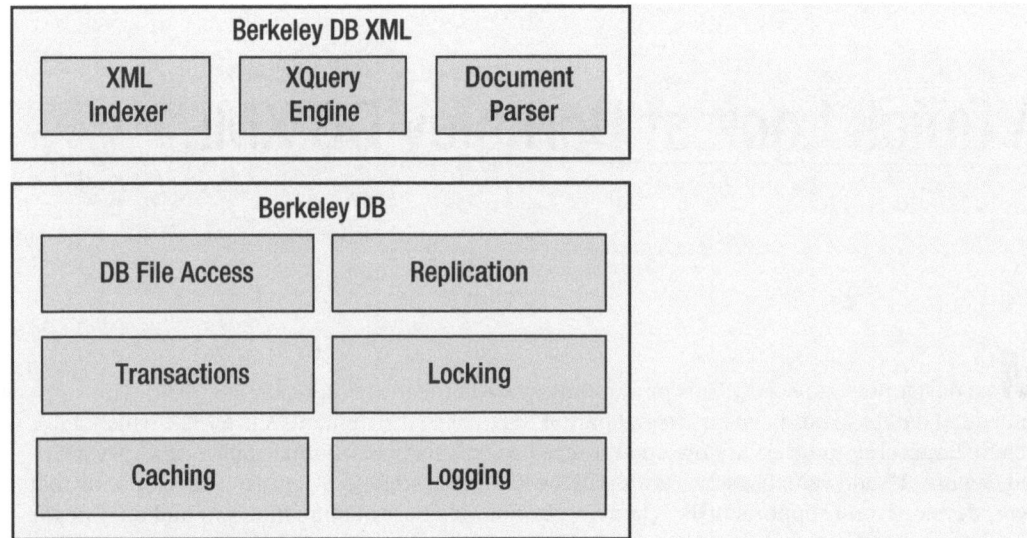

Figure 1-1. *Berkeley DB XML's features built upon Berkeley DB*

A collection of XML files exists for authors as well, as shown in Listing 1-2.

Listing 1-2. *A Sample Author XML File,* author-923117.xml

```
<author id="923117">
  <name>Fyodor Dostoevsky</name>
  <birthdate>November 11 1821</birthdate>
  <deathdate>February 9 1881</deathdate>
</author>
```

Clearly we aren't maintaining comprehensive information here, but we'll use these files to populate a BDB XML database.

Creating and Using a Database

Like BDB, a BDB XML database is a file on disk and is typically referred to as a *container.* Your application opens, reads, and writes to this file directly.

Assuming that we have these XML files in the current directory, the following example uses the dbxml command-line utility   available as part of the BDB XML distribution   to create a container, add to it an index, and populate it with the preceding book document.

```
dbxml> createContainer books.dbxml
Creating node storage container with nodes indexed
```

```
dbxml> addIndex "" title node-element-equality-string
Adding index type: node-element-equality-string to node: {}:title
```

```
dbxml> putDocument 0553211757.xml 0553211757.xml f
Document added, name = 0553211757.xml
```

Basically, we now have a database file, books.dbxml, containing a single document (with a name matching the filename, which is why we supplied it twice). The database has equality indexes for elements with the names isbn, title, and id.

Querying a Database

We can now query the database using XQuery, which in this case is close to looking like an XPath statement:

```
dbxml> query '
collection("books.dbxml")/book[title="Crime and Punishment"]
'
1 objects returned for eager expression
```

Typing print to the shell will display the resulting document in its entirety, which matches the document we added. Before going further, we'll add two more indexes to this container for attributes isbn and id:

```
dbxml> addIndex "" isbn unique-node-attribute-equality-string
Adding index type: unique-node-attribute-equality-string to node: {}:isbn

dbxml> addIndex "" id node-attribute-equality-string
Adding index type: node-attribute-equality-string to node: {}:id
```

Creating these indexes before the database becomes large avoids the overhead of indexing a more populated database.

Creating and Querying a Second Database

We want to use a second container to store the author information, so we'll do that next:

```
dbxml> createContainer authors.dbxml
Creating node storage container with nodes indexed

dbxml> addIndex "" id node-attribute-equality-string
Adding index type: node-attribute-equality-string to node: {}:id

dbxml> addIndex "" name node-element-equality-string
Adding index type: node-element-equality-string to node: {}:name

dbxml> putDocument author-923117.xml author-923117.xml f
Document added, name = author-923117.xml
```

We'd most likely populate this database with our author files programmatically by using one of the BDB XML APIs, but the shell is ideal for testing before implementation. We added the author document and created an index for the author id and name. We can perform more complex queries by using both containers; for example, a query to find all books written by an author by the name "Fyodor Dostoevsky" looks like this:

```
dbxml> preload books.dbxml

dbxml> query '
collection("books.dbxml")/book[author/@id =
    collection("authors.dbxml")/author[name="Fyodor Dostoevsky"]/@id]
'
1 objects returned for eager expression ...
```

In practice, we expect such queries to often be dynamic, with an author name submitted by a user, for example. And in a real application, a user having clicked "Dostoevsky" would give us the author's id, so we would use that for a query for all books by the author.

There is no real limit to the XML that can be stored or queried in a database. BDB XML enables the creation of indexes for documents' attributes and elements using a node's name. Indexes can be given data types to optimize certain queries, such as numeric and date types for range comparisons, and can enforce database uniqueness for the nodes they index. Because BDB XML uses XQuery as its query engine, you can build sophisticated queries that perform set computations, perform numeric and string processing, and even rewrite XML to another dialect.

Metadata

For the example here, there is a lot of data we want to associate with a book record, including the price and perhaps a sales ranking. This is data we expect to change frequently, and we'd rather not have to change our book XML to accommodate it (if, for example, the XML is data shared with resellers). BDB XML enables metadata to be added to documents in a container and indexed. This data gets queried by using the same XQuery expressions, meaning it will be available for the same query processing as if it were XML in the documents.

Here, we add a price metadata attribute to the book file we added previously and then add an index for it to the container:

```
dbxml> openContainer books.dbxml

dbxml> setMetaData 0553211757.xml '' price decimal 10.95
MetaData item 'price' added to document 0553211757.xml

dbxml> addIndex '' price node-metadata-equality-decimal
Adding index type: node-metadata-equality-decimal to node: {}:price
```

We added price metadata to our document with a value type price, which will help when we want to perform range queries   for example, to find products within a certain price range:

```
dbxml> query '
collection("books.dbxml")/book[dbxml:metadata("price") < 11.00]
'
1 objects returned for eager expression ...
```

Metadata can similarly be used to store dates, booleans, base-64 data, and even durations. In fact, BDB XML can contain metadata-only records as well (records with no XML content). You can even build a flat relational database with BDB XML by using just metadata and no XML! (Hopefully, this is not part of your planned application design because it discards most of the usefulness of the system.)

XQuery

As demonstrated, BDB XML uses XQuery for its query engine. XQuery in its entirety is not in the scope of this book, being an elegant yet comprehensive query and scripting language in its own right. (A chapter is dedicated to it, however.) Consider just the following query example; it queries for books by a given title (which has been stored in the variable $title), subqueries for the author name, and outputs the results with XML.

```
dbxml> query '
for $book in collection("books.dbxml")/book[title=$title]
    for $author in collection("authors.dbxml")/author[@id=$book/author/@id]
        order by $author/name
        return
            <author>{$author/name/string()}</author>
'
```

XQuery supports user functions, importing of XQuery files, and even network document queries. You can imagine some of the possibilities, and they're all available with BDB XML.

Conclusion

Where BDB XMLs power is derived from its flexible indexing and XQuery engine, its reliability lies in its design as an embedded API for use in your applications   there is no database server. Complete support for atomic transactions, recovery, and replication help to round out the stability feature set. Of course, they are available on all major operating systems, and APIs are supported for all major programming languages.

This chapter has only touched on the features and functionality available in BDB XML, but hopefully you have a glimpse of the power it offers to index and query XML collections.

CHAPTER 2

■ ■ ■

The Power of an Embedded XML Database

Sleepycats Berkeley DB XML (BDB XML) is an embedded database used to store and index XML documents. Immediately, two core philosophies require some exploration: embedded storage and XML itself. The exploration is riddled   surprisingly to some, old news to others   with biases on all sides. This chapter clarifies the issues and explains the cases where and the reasons why you might want to use BDB XML. My central points are the following:

1. Embedded databases are preferable to dedicated database daemons in *most* common applications.

2. XML and its related technologies (XPath, XQuery, and so on) make for easy and useful data storage and access in *most* common applications.

3. BDB XML simplifies architecture and accelerates development (for *most* common applications).

This chapter is not essential to using BDB XML. However, my experience is that many developers do not reap the benefits of either embedded databases or XML because they lack an understanding of how either can simplify and improve their development, integration, and subsequent support of a software system. Some background on architectural issues is useful for answering this question: "Why would I want to use BDB XML in the first place?"

Database Servers vs. Embedded Databases

The term *embedded* is a loaded one, with various implications in both software and hardware development. Fortunately, it has a relatively simple meaning as applied to a database. Here, "embedded" describes the libraries used to access and manipulate the database files themselves, having been embedded in the application itself.

Consider the popular relational databases (RDBs): Oracle, Sybase, MySQL, and so on. Typical deployments of these products are referred to as *database servers* because each runs a daemon process (or multiple processes) to accept requests and deliver the results of queries. The code that opens, reads, and writes to the actual database files is contained within this server processes. To get data, you connect to the database server, issue an SQL query, and get back results. This provides isolation for the data itself, and ease of controlling access based on permissions. It also allows for simple network access: clients can access the database from the local machine or from across the network or Internet, and permissions controls can accommodate such variables.

In this way, a database server is not unlike a web server, with SQL in place of URLs, raw data streams in place of HTML, and indexes in place of a filesystem. Both take requests over the network and respond with the data requested. In other words, both are servers in the client-server model (see Figure 2-1).

Figure 2-1. *Client-server database design*

Where a web server takes requests from a web browser (the client), the database takes requests from a database client. The client might be a desktop application or, as is often the case, itself a web server.

By contrast, "embedding a database" means that the product does not run a daemon of its own. If you imagine the libraries used by mysqld, for example and import them directly into your own program, you have an embedded database. Rather than connecting over the network to a port and issuing an SQL query, you call a function to open the physical data file, pass your SQL to another function to issue the query, and get back your results. The only difference in this scenario is that there is one process running   your program   rather than two (or more). Most of the more popular RDB products now have embedded variants: MySQL has embedded MySQL, Oracles 10*g* product provides licensing to allow embedding, as does Sybase ASE. Figure 2-2 has moved the database libraries into the application.

Figure 2-2. *Embedded database design*

The effect of embedding the database libraries in the application is that the server is removed from the design completely or that the application itself becomes the server.

Embedding has many advantages over daemons, including application portability and the relative ease of deployment. By embedding the database libraries in a program (and meeting any licensing requirements), developers can produce and sell an application that manages its own data as a powerful database, or even an application that itself acts as a specialized database daemon, without the overhead and complexity of installing, configuring, and running a database server alongside their application. Embedding also has architectural implications for traditional web applications, which I will examine momentarily. By their nature, embedded databases tend to be more developer-focused than their server counterparts. Whereas in some environments a relational database server can be configured to allow nondevelopers to issue simple queries and perform other operations, embedded databases often limit access to the application, over which a nonprogrammer has no control. Unless a developer has provided users a way to issue queries, only the application that embeds the database libraries typically performs queries against it.

Architecture Example

Calling a database server over the network entails a protocol that is usually proprietary to the database, which is why a database "driver" is necessary to communicate with the server. Even SQL statements sent to the DB server are typically delivered in a nontext format, and only the library or driver can understand the response from the server.

Having a server daemon can be beneficial when many users on a network are calling the database directly. Consider a multiplayer game, in which each game client connects directly to the database server. The advantages of a server in this case include the storage of permissions so that only certain users can access certain parts of the database. An example is shown in Figure 2-3.

Figure 2-3. *A basic server-client architecture for a networked game*

Of course, this architecture would not be sufficient for most games. To chat with other players, another server would be required to route and deliver messages in real time. Some program would need to know how to manage battles between players and enforce rules of game play. Figure 2-4 shows the addition of just such a multiuser server.

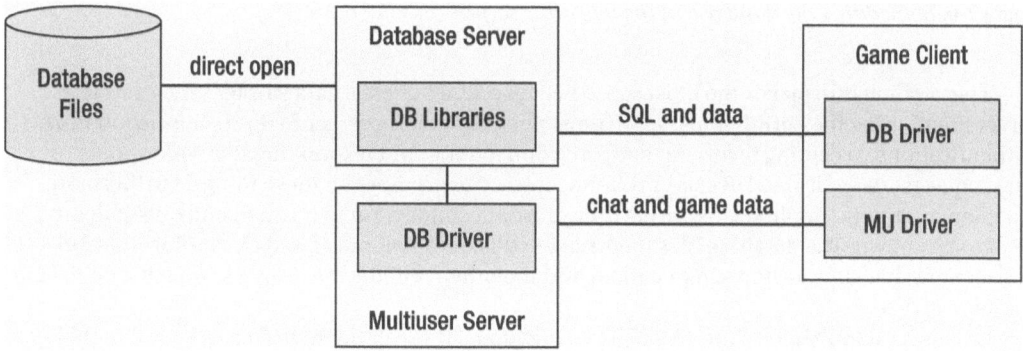

Figure 2-4. *Adding a real-time server to the architecture*

This design incurs some complexity because the game client now needs to maintain network connections with two different servers. The program needs to include libraries for each protocol because they are unlikely to be different. To enforce the game rules, the multiuser server probably needs to query the database to know, for example, whether a given object is in a given area. And we probably want users to have to authenticate to the multiuser server to begin with, meaning it will already be querying the database assuming that's where we keep authentication data. So the next step in our architectural train-of-thought is to have the client go through the multiuser server for everything (shown in Figure 2-5), acting as a single gateway for all the game clients. (Note that this setup can be duplicated in order to scale, and multiple gateways can exist. By *single gateway*, I mean that game clients have one point of contact to the system.)

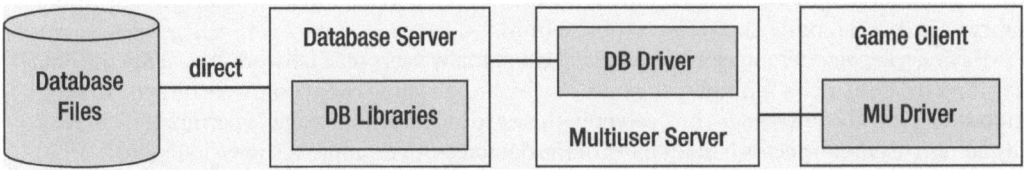

Figure 2-5. *Routing all data through the real-time server, the client is simplified.*

This is the state first described in this chapter and it is where most application server designs find themselves. An RDB server does not meet the functionality required by the server, so a tier is introduced into the server side of the architecture. In this model, the DB server acts simply as a data store. There isn't a good reason to not complete the train-of-thought and move the data access into the multiuser server, embedding the database, as shown in Figure 2-6.

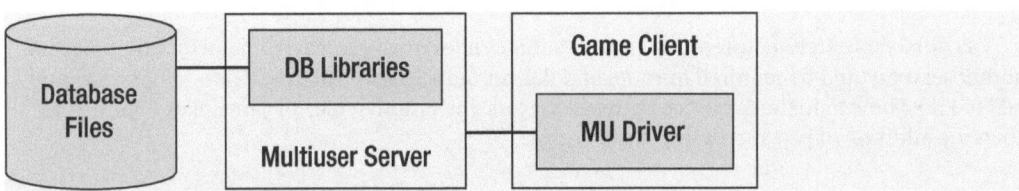

Figure 2-6. *Embedding the database in the real-time server*

This architecture makes the most sense because all we need is data storage. The multiuser server is enforcing the permissions, so we don't need a database server to do so. It is negotiating authentications, accepting incoming network connections, and responding to a wide variety of data requests   a dedicated DB server is not necessary to accomplish these things. Furthermore, our client is greatly simplified, requiring only one data connection to be open and one data protocol to be known. The database files themselves still contain our data and can be subjected to transactions, backups, restores, replication, and the other benefits the design had with a dedicated database server.

Of course, there will be cases in which a dedicated DB server might make sense. But in this architecture, and in many like it, a DB daemon simply incurs more complexity and overhead than is necessary for the design.

Embedded Databases You Might Know

A major example of the embedded philosophy at work is BDB itself, upon which BDB XML is built. Long a staple of Unix distributions, BDB claims more than 200 million installations. Core Internet services and applications use BDB to store data because of the ease of quickly reading and writing organized data from an application. Many major technology companies   including Microsoft, Yahoo!, Google, Sony, Sun, Apple, AOL, Cisco, eBay, HP, and Motorola   use BDB in one form or another.

SQLite

The Open Source database SQLite (http://www.sqlite.org) illustrates the embedded database model well, retaining most features you would expect from an RDB server. It was introduced by D. Richard Hipp in 2000, but gained a large user base in 2005 with the introduction of new features and an award from Google and O•Reilly. SQLite is a library, written in C, which implements most traditional RDB features including transactions and recovery, with APIs available for nearly all popular programming languages. Consider this shell session after installing SQLite:

```
> sqlite everything.db
SQLite version 3.1.3
Enter ".help" for instructions
sqlite> create table people (name varchar(50), birthyear integer);
sqlite> insert into people values ('Charlie Chaplin', 1889);
sqlite> insert into people values ('Martin Luther King', 1929);
sqlite> select * from people
Charlie Chaplin|1889
Martin Luther King|1929
sqlite>
```

This session creates a database called everything.db with a table people. You•ve seen similar tasks performed with database server shell tools. In this case, the sqlite command-line program is writing directly to the database file instead of connecting over the network (regardless of whether the database is local) to the server, and issuing a request. Similarly, accessing this database from within a program (whether in C, Python, Perl, or other) directly reads and manipulates the file. Note, too, that SQLite is a zero-configuration engine, meaning that what you see above is all you need to work with this particular embedded database, after installing. To many, this sounds a bit too lightweight to do much good: "A zero-setup, zero-configuration database with no daemon? Well I *never!*" Nonetheless, SQLite has atomic transactions, supports databases up to two terabytes, has bindings for most languages, and already implements the bulk of SQL92. This from a well-commented, well-tested open source installation with less than a 150 KB optimized code footprint. And SQLite doesn•t have any external code dependencies, making it ideal for embedded devices.

The ease of embedding a database should be obvious to anyone who has dealt with the complexities of installing, configuring, running, and monitoring a dedicated database server (not to mention the millions who have seen the "Driver Error: Could not connect to database server" text in response to a submitted web form).

Wordnet

Almost any homegrown indexing solution can qualify as an embedded database. The Cognitive Science department at Princeton University maintains a freely downloadable lexicon of the English language called Wordnet (http://wordnet.princeton.edu). Wordnet is unique in that it maps relationships between concepts: it can tell you, for example, that a "car" is a kind of "motor vehicle", which is a kind of "vehicle", which is a kind of "transport", which is a kind of "artifact", which is a kind of "object", and so on, up to the most abstract ("primitive") concepts. Wordnet can also tell you what things are a "part of" other things and other "psycholinguistic" attributes. All this information is recorded using pointers from concept to concept. If you•re familiar with the product called Visual Thesaurus, you•ve seen Wordnet at work because it uses Wordnet as its data source. To provide some context to the benefits of more flexible embedded database solutions, as well as give some background on examples in Appendix A, "XML Essentials" and Chapter 7, "XQuery with BDB XML" on queries, I will examine Wordnet in moderate detail.

The database files for Wordnet are simple text files generated by the lexicographer tools used by the department. For each word group (noun, verb, adjective, adverb), there is a space-delimited data file that lists the words along with "pointers" to other words, and an index that lists the words with the "offsets" identifying the byte positions in which those words occur in the data files. Storing byte offsets rather than line numbers makes for faster lookups because the location can be addresses without reading the whole file up to that line number, something it would have to do in order to count newlines. Thus, an index entry will look like Figure 2-7.

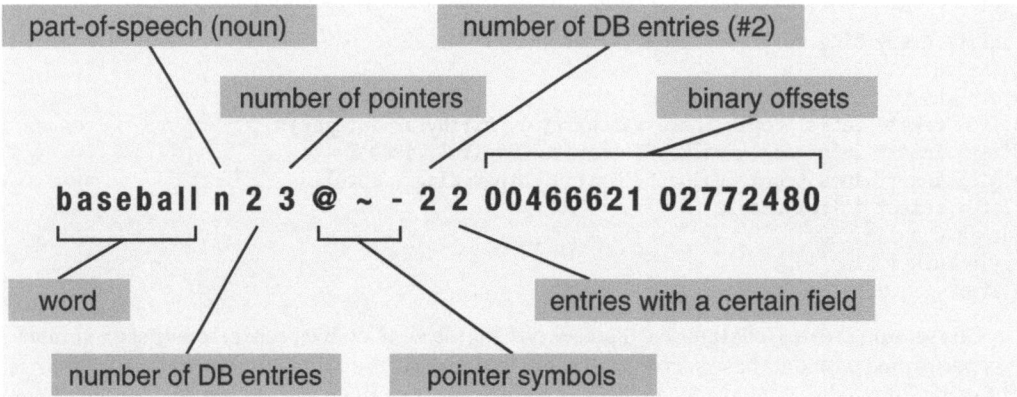

Figure 2-7. *Wordnet index format*

The entries are in alphabetical order. I won't delve into the details, other than to observe that the index entry duplicates information that is also found in the records themselves. The data in the index is space-delimited (requiring spaces in the word itself to be replaced with underscores). The offset numbers at the end identify the location of the records in the data file. There are two records for "baseball": one is the sport; the other, the ball. The "part-of-speech" is "n" for "noun". Notice that the "2", indicating the number of records, is duplicated in the index   in this case, for legacy compatibility. The "3" identifies how many "pointer" symbols follow it, so the index parser can count forward that many characters. In other words, counting from the first element does not tell you the meaning of a given element; the elements themselves determine how many of something will follow. Yes, this is a self-deterministic data format.

In Figure 2-7, the last two numbers are these offsets. Each one identifies an entry in the accompanying data files; Wordnet refers to these entries as *synsets*, meaning a *set of synonyms*. The index for the noun "baseball" identifies two senses: "baseball" the ball (which was illustrated in Figure 2-7) and "baseball" the sport. Opening the data file and seeking to the second offset (using the standard Unix C function) places us at this next line, shown in Figure 2-8, which is the data entry for the sport sense of the word (slightly abbreviated):

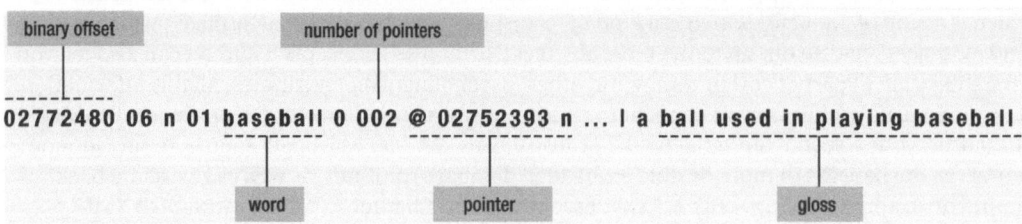

Figure 2-8. *Wordnet data format.*

Remember, this is the entry for baseball "the ball," not the sport. The format is not dissimilar from the index, and I haven't labeled everything. Notice that this record includes much of the same information as the index, albeit with more detail. This time, the pointers themselves are listed. The at sign (@) is Wordnet's symbol for a *hypernym* pointer, denoting a parent IS-A relationship. It shouldn't surprise us that the offset after the @ (02752393) is the offset for the noun "ball" because a baseball is a kind of ball. The other pointer for baseball (note that there are two, indicated by the "number of pointers" digits), here omitted, is also a hypernym, pointing to the "baseball equipment" synset. If we here looked at the data record for "ball", we would see that it has a hypernym pointer to "game equipment". This chain of IS-A pointers continues all the way up to abstract concepts such as "artifact" and "physical entity", just as the baseball "the game" synset (refer to Figure 2-7) had hypernym pointers up to "activity" and "entity".

Similarly, the "ball" synset record has what is called a "hyponym" pointer aimed back to the "baseball" record; this pointer is indicated with a tilde (~). A hyponym is the opposite of a hypernym, indicating a *child* IS-A relationship.

Here is the complete "ball" data record, with the hyponym pointers highlighted.

```
02752393 06 n 01 ball 1 031 @ 03377643 n 0000 ~ 02772480 n 0000 ~ 02775835 n 0000
~ 02812045 n 0000 ~ 02833311 n 0000 ~ 02853649 n 0000 ~ 02854404 n 0000 ...
~ 03102695 n 0000 ~ 03297969 n 0000 ~ 03343022 n 0000 ~ 03409124 n 0000 ...
~ 03550091 n 0000 ~ 03591893 n 0000 ~ 03679835 n 0000 ~ 03700610 n 0000 ...
~ 03898560 n 0000 ~ 03933730 n 0000 ~ 03937405 n 0000 ~ 03978641 n 0000 ...
~ 04067463 n 0000 ~ 04072629 n 0000 ~ 04204317 n 0000 ~ 04206528 n 0000 ...
~ 04357453 n 0000 ~ 04485605 n 0000 ~ 04529397 n 0000 | round object that is hit ..
```

Note that this is the entry for *only* the sense of ball as a "game object" (as opposed to an abstract "globe/ball", "Lucille Ball", a pitch that misses the strike zone, and the cruder plural use of the word). Each of the previously listed hyponyms are IS-A children of "ball", including "basketball", "bowling ball", "racquetball", and so on.

Note Wordnet's hypernym and hyponym pointers are examples of duplicate bidirectional pointers: every hypernym in the database has a corresponding hyponym. The effect is that a given record contains all information about pointers both to and from it. Pointer-heavy databases such as Wordnet often use redundant pointers to provide the most common lookups the fastest access (a list of "kinds of *X*" then requires only one read of the data file). More complex queries such as "all kinds of kinds of *X*" imply inheritance and require recursion so that each record is read in turn.

Wordnet is an example of a relatively fast embedded database that uses plain text as its storage format. The inclusion of data in the index itself (such as the pointer symbols) enables an application reading this index to know certain things about the records without actually accessing them. For example, the index entry tells an application that the database contains two definitions for "baseball", and that it has three pointers for it. A graphical user interface (GUI) displaying search results can thus display this information without opening the data file at all.

The use of normal text for the indexes and data files makes the information useable by many tools, including command-line utilities. Writing a parser for this data is fairly trivial because we can split the string on white space and, knowing the data format, can identify each element. I do so in Appendix A.

The same design decisions that make Wordnet compact and fast also make it essentially a read-only database. Bidirectional pointers require that any pointer change be made in the records as well as the index entries at both ends of the pointer. And because most any change to a record will offset the byte addresses of data, a complete reindexing and rewriting of both data files and indexes is made necessary by nearly every write. Finally, this data format is interpretable only by a processor that knows to use spaces as separators, in order to determine element order dynamically based on the number of fields, and to properly read offsets and perform file seeks.

Note that Wordnet takes advantage of completely inflexible indexing and storage to provide speedy lookups and a compact distribution. Wordnet can afford to do this because it is *intended* as a read-only database. This is not a weakness for the publisher because the Princeton researchers desire to retain control of all modifications. This stiff implementation does result in some fragility, however. Being space-delimited, the meaning of text in any given field of both the index files and data files is entirely dependent on the field order, resulting here in data duplication to retain legacy compatibility. In some cases, the interpretation of a piece of text depends on a value before it, as with the "number of pointers" field. And clearly, being read-only *is* inconvenient for a user who does want to extend or otherwise modify the database.

Embedded Databases on the Desktop

Many desktop applications use embedded databases. Most email clients, for example, index your mail messages to make them easily searchable. Filesystem search utilities often store indexes to speed up the process of finding files. Newer operating systems make indexes of file contents as well, essentially turning the desktop into a database. Apple OS X's Spotlight and Google Desktop on Windows are examples. They illustrate well the purest use of a database for finding information. Because they are required to pull data from disparate sources and varying formats, and are not an authoritative source of information themselves, they cannot enforce specific schemas or information organization on their data sources (email, web bookmarks, address books, and so on). As you'll soon see, XML fits well into this model of a database as a *tool* for indexing and searching, without the generally expected need to cajole the data into a limiting table schema.

XML for Data Exchange

XML has gained mainstream usage primarily as a format for sharing data. HTML is the most obvious example. Long before XHTML came along, many of us (not least of all, search engine companies) were writing spiders to fetch, parse, and make sense of the web. Early versions of HTML did not require balanced tags, and even today many sites do not enforce well-formed XHTML. This places a burden on web browsers as well as crawlers, which must make assumptions about the errors in markup. Of course, many content providers do not intend for their HTML to be parsed and indexed. In many cases, the author of a website wants to exclude this possibility to protect content.

■**Note** Appendix A is a tutorial for those not familiar with XML.

For persons or companies that do want to share their content, HTML makes little sense. Because its purpose is the formatting of text for attractive display, its tags consist of stylistic and organizational elements. Any site "consuming" the content of another will want to put that content within the context and style of its own site, making already-present style information data that must be removed. Imagine that I run a news aggregator and that a news outlet supplied me with the following HTML for display on my own site:

```
<html>
    <body bgcolor="#cccccc">
        <p><font size="+2" face="Arial">Area Man Keeps Promise to Locals</font></p>
        <p><font face="Arial">2:20pm, October 12, 2006</font></p>
        <p><font face="Courier">Rob Stanson, County Correspondent</font></p>
```

```
        <p><font face="Arial">John Yates is not generally considered a man of his
                word. Just ask his wife ...</font></p>
        <p><font face="Arial">We caught up with John and family last week at the
                fair ...</font></p>
    </body>
</html>
```

Clearly I'll want this article to show up on my site looking more like the rest of my site. But I might want to do other things with it, too. It would be nice to be clear about which text is the headline, so that I can show just that title in a listing of articles. I'd probably like to expire the article after a duration of my choosing, requiring me to know the date it was published. I might want to split the article content across several pages to match my site's layout or to maximize advertisers' exposure. Grouping articles by their author could be useful to my readers, too.

Given the preceding HTML, the only way I could accomplish any of these goals would be to either pull out each piece manually or write a program that matches each tag and extracts the information. This would happen with the hope that the format didn't change in the future. Moreover, I'd have to write a parser to convert the date to a format intelligible to my program to allow sorting and expiration of articles.

Because the person giving me the article wants it shown on my aggregator, it is likely to be much easier. Instead of giving me this HTML, imagine that a format existed whereby the provider could provide me with the following:

```
<entry>
    <title>Area Man Keeps Promise to Locals</title>
    <published>2006-10-12T14:20:30Z</published>
    <author><name>Rob Stanson, County Correspondent</name></author>
    <content>John Yates is not generally considered a man of his word. Just ask
            his wife  ... We caught up with John and family last week at
            the fair ...</content>
</entry>
```

With the provider's assurance that this format won't change without prior notification, I can write code to parse it pretty easily. I even have the date in a standard format I can use (datetime).

Of course, after I realize that this text is XML, I won't have to write code to parse it at all. I can use any old XML parser from any programming language I want and simply pull out each piece of data with a path (XPath). I can use XSLT documents to display the source XML on my website, too.

Later, I will be told that this format is an XML standard called *Atom* (okay, technically it's just an excerpt). Not only do I not need to write code to parse it but I also don't need to use an XML parser or template language at all. The content management software I use to run my aggregator already supports Atom (and yes, Really Simple Syndication [RSS]). I can just stick the URL to this news feed into my CMS settings, and my work here is finished. Yes, you'd think I would have known that, seeing as how I run a news aggregator.

One sign of the success of standardized XML formats is that people (users, not necessarily developers) stop thinking about them. RSS used to be a buzzword; now it's an assumed feature of every website, delivering syndication and even business-critical data between people and companies. Nonetheless, it took something as simple (and well-hyped) as XML to make it work.

RSS and Atom are relatively lightweight examples of an XML standard for sharing information. Standards such as XML-RPC and Simple Object Access Protocol (SOAP), also dialects of XML, are used every day to exchange data and request services. They also enjoy a high degree of development ease and fast integration with systems that support them.

This is how XML has helped to make the sharing of information   you'll forgive the term   a *no-brainer*.

XML for Data Storage

Even though XML is used universally for the transfer of organized data, it is only starting to gain strength as a preferred format for data storage. Websites that deliver HTML pages and RSS feeds still pull that data out of a relational database before formatting it in the respective XML dialect and delivering it to the requestor. Given the near-ubiquity of XML as a format for the exchange of data, the obvious question is this: "Why aren't we just storing XML to begin with?"

When you stick data into a relational database, that database saves a record, delimiting the pieces of data internally, using a binary data format. This format is optimized for the recovery of data, but is readable only by the database itself (or libraries that understand the format). SQL is used to retrieve and modify the data, requiring an SQL processor to translate instructions into library-level operations. However, the data files themselves are completely database-dependent. This is the case for an embedded database as well.

Why Are We Using a Database Again?

The advantage of storing data in a binary database file primarily concerns index and search speed. This is an important concept: *the primary purpose of a database is to efficiently index and find information.* If finding information quickly is not a priority, there's really no reason to be using a database. In fact, storing data in a database is usually a *bad* idea if it needn't be indexed. The reason that RDBs provide utilities for "dumping" a database to a text file is twofold. First, the text dump is the only portable format for moving data between databases; second, the text is intelligible to people. If a binary file is corrupted, restoring lost data is difficult and database-specific.

Of course, there are other reasons to use databases. Those that support transactions provide atomicity (grouping operations to either complete fully or not affect data at all) and logging to enable rollbacks and recovery of data in spite of changes. Where data is too large to fit in memory, databases make possible the ease of querying portions. Features such as replication of data in and of themselves make databases attractive. Nonetheless, indexing remains the typical primary purpose of databases, and other means   albeit disparate ones   exist to achieve these benefits (think change control a la CVS, data access via mmap, and rsync for replication) when data is not binary.

Thus, binary storage could be described as a "necessary evil" to effectively index data. To maintain indexes, the data itself must also be stored in a way to effectively let the database know when to update an index, which is the main reason why databases contain the data in addition to the index. Otherwise, you would have to update the indexes manually each time a piece of data changes. This often leads to the database being the only source of the data it contains, although this is not necessarily ideal. The fact that a database query returns the data itself is technically a side effect of the fact that it's stored there: a convenience.

Imagine that you had a database containing contact information, with one record/row per person, but the database didn't store the strings themselves (only the indexes). The result of a query would be the matching row or record, and you would have to then look up the data itself, perhaps in an address file for that person. This may sound overly difficult if you're looking for a phone number. The point is that this is not the purpose of a database: if you need a phone number, you know the person whose number you need so there is no reason to search. You can simply look at the record for that person and read the phone number. By contrast, imagine that you needed to know all the people in your address book who lived in Iowa. The database would return a list of all people who matched the query, which is what you wanted in the first place. The lack of each address book element within the database isn't a problem. The best example of the purpose of a database is a web search engine: the Internet is the data source; Google is an index of the data source. It's true that search engines cache content for convenience and reindexing, but you only view the cached copy of a web page in the event that it is missing or no longer contains the data you need. For practical purposes, a search engine index tells you what matches your query and refers you to the source. It's your job to go there.

This might all sound academic, but it touches on why a database has come to occupy the "center" of an application design: it's not just the index to find data; it *is* the data. Because we use databases to not just find but also to store and organize our data, entire applications start with database schema design: how many columns, what data types, how much data to allow, what columns to index, and so on. Data structure in an RDB is forced by necessity: how could the database index data that had no structure to begin with? Where data already has some structure as is the case with a title element in an HTML document or meta-information from a Word doc a developer will often pull them out and use them as indexed fields. But in most cases, the data, if there is any, exists in an inconsistent and disorganized format. The RDB is intended to enforce a format, and work is needed to adapt existing data to that format. Database schema design is a science with its own graduate degrees because of the difficulties of designing database schemas that are both efficient and flexible, for both existing and expected data.

Prestructured Data

My point in going to such lengths with this explanation is that XML is *already structured*. In fact, an entire database could be dumped as a single XML file with <row/> elements for each row and named values for each key or field. Being already structured, XML does not need a database to organize it. XML schema exists if you want to enforce a common format across a collection of XML files. XML even has its own query language, XPath, which is capable of evaluating against documents and specific node lists. An XML database exists instead for the same main reason that an RDB exists: to effectively index and find information in this case, across a collection of documents.

As with an RDB, XML databases tend to store the data itself to allow autonomous index updates. XML files don't need to exist before they get put into the database; they can be created on the fly as with a RDB row. But more often than with RDBs, an XML database is queried to find document matches and then the file itself is used to pull out the desired data. This is easy given the fact that the same query language can be used on individual files and collections of files. Moreover, technologies such as XSLT are most often used with complete XML files to drive transformations, meaning that having the whole file is useful.

Having your data in XML to begin with means that you are not reliant on a database for its organization or the tools associated with that database to edit it. In fact, many relational databases provide tools to load and dump XML directly from the database for this very reason: XML is standard, well supported, and completely portable. Why rely on an interface that connects to a database to edit the data or (worse yet) have to write your own editors, when you can use nearly any editor of your choice? Consider, too, how often applications translate data from an RDB to XML to deliver it to an accessor in a format it can understand. Wouldn't it have been easier to just hand over the file itself, incurring no more overhead than an HTTP GET request?

The primary benefit of XML over many binary and text data formats is its human-readability and self-contained context. Whether you encounter an XML file from a website, in a log, in an email, or in a database, you won't need to know where it came from to have some clue about where it belongs or what it contains. You won't need to buy or install special software to read it, invent a special protocol to exchange it, or learn a particular programming language to process it. Text data is simple, easy, and given markup semantically rich.

You will soon wonder how to go about indexing it, however. If you're already wondering, read on. If not, start wondering now, and the book will follow right along.

BUT WAIT, MY DATA ISN'T HIERARCHICAL!

Much ado is made over *hierarchical* data and the fact that XML is a hierarchical data format. This observation is not necessarily useful to deciding whether to use XML or understanding XML as a data format.

All data is hierarchical. Even the flattest file records data that in some context belongs to a hierarchy. A user-name and password belong to a user; a user belongs to a system; and so on. When the adjective *hierarchical* is used to describe data, it usually describes the *desired* format, and whether or not some application or person wants the data "flat" or as a tree. But the things being described by the data are always hierarchical, I guess depending on your particular ontological worldview. (In truth, not even a "flat" file is really flat. After all, a file has a filename and exists somewhere in a directory structure. This in and of itself gives the file's contents some context, even if the file contains a single sentence.)

The real objection to putting data into a hierarchical data *format* is usually the difficulty of use. This is a pretty hollow gripe because the tools to write and process XML are everywhere. More often than not, people that try to express data without a hierarchy end up inventing a hierarchy anyway to record metadata (dates, authors, subjects of a document) and do so in a proprietary format. Any such element is a *child* element of the document and a *sibling* of the rest of the stuff in the file. A hierarchy is born, just like that! The data would have been better served to be hierarchical to begin with, able to take advantage of XML standards and tools.

Indexing XML

Long before BDB XML was around, many of us had a need to index XML documents. For example, I wanted to maintain my own copy of the aforementioned Wordnet database in a way that would permit writes without reindexing the collection each time. I've been fascinated with the lexicon for some time and have used it for lots of natural language processing work. In addition to the serious stuff, I wanted to play games such as "20 Questions," in which a program would choose a random concept and I'd have to ask questions to narrow it down. And vice versa (the program would ask the questions). This would require me to add data to the lexicon and pointer types, too. For example, given the concept of "oven," I wanted the lexicon to understand that it was an appliance, it was electrical, and that it was used to cook. An oven was already a kind of an appliance, and the appliance entry implied electrical. So by adding a noun attribute pointer from "appliance" to "electrical," a noun function pointer from "oven" to "prepare/cook" and also to "bake," the user could get correct answers to the following questions: "Are you a thing?" "Are you electrical?" "Are you used to cook?"

A Homegrown Database

I first went about this by using BDB files with the offset numbers for the synset keys and the contents of the synset as values, delimited with double-pipes (||). A second database file contains indexes with all words in the lexicon as keys and the synsets as values. This at least allowed the contents to be changed, synsets to be added, and indexes to be queried and maintained, although queries remained very inflexible. The major drawback to this solution (aside from the madness of custom delimiters) was the inability to edit the data with the tool of my choice. Because the synset contents (pointers, gloss, and so on) had to be packed into the database value after each update, the only decent method was to write the record programmatically, calling my custom API each time. I had created a solution to the "read-only" constraint of Wordnet, but had shackled both my users and myself to a custom data format, proprietary code, and API in a specific programming language. And nobody likes to be shackled.

As soon as XML started gaining mainstream momentum, I decided it was the proper format for editable Wordnet files. In Appendix A I demonstrate the creation of a large XML collection like this one (this very one, as it happens). Here is an example of a resulting XML file; some of this should already be familiar:

```
<Synset fileVersion="1.0" pos="n">
    <Id>14861</Id>
    <WnOffset version="2.1" pos="n">02772480</WnOffset>
    <LexFileNum>06</LexFileNum>
    <SsType>n</SsType>
    <Word lexId="0">baseball</Word>
    <Pointers>
        <Hypernym>14746</Hypernym>
        <Hypernym>14866</Hypernym>
    </Pointers>
    <Gloss>a ball used in playing baseball</Gloss>
</Synset>
```

Notice here that offset numbers aren't used for the pointers. They have been replaced with IDs sequentially assigned to each file, with this file named 14861.xml. 120,000 similar files comprise a fully editable collection, but not one that is very easy to navigate. For example, to find entries for the word "baseball", I'd have to grep 120,000 files. To provide a means of quickly looking up files, I wrote a quick Perl script using libxml2 and Berkeley DB Perl modules (see Listing 2-1).

Listing 2-1. *Poor-Man's XML Indexing*

```
#!/usr/bin/perl -w
use strict;
use XML::LibXML;
use DB_File;
$DB_BTREE->{'flags'} = R_DUP ;

my $datadir = "./xml-src/";
my $indexdir = "./index/";
my $parser = new XML::LibXML;
my %btree;
tie %btree, 'DB_File', "$indexdir/words.index", O_RDWR|O_CREAT, 0666, $DB_BTREE,
        or die "Cannot open $indexdir/words.index: $!\n";
opendir my $dir, $datadir;
while (my $file = readdir($dir)) {
    next if ($file =~ /^\./);
    my $dom = $parser->parse_file("$datadir/$file");
    foreach my $node ($dom->findnodes("/Synset/Word")) {
        my ($textnode) = $node->findnodes("text()");
        my $lcname = lc($textnode->getData);
        if ($textnode) { $btree{$lcname} = $file; }
    }
}
```

This script used a simple XPath query, which it then executed against all 120,000 files (see bold section), writing to a simple database file the result of each query as a key and the filename for that result as the value. So, with an XPath /Synset/Word, each word would be extracted from the synset file and written as a key to the database with the filename as the value. This index file could then be used to look up "baseball" as a key, which would return the values of the two matching synset files.

I hope the constraints of this solution are obvious. Every time a synset is added, deleted, or changed, somebody needs to be sure that entry is modified in the indexes it affects. Certainly there is little query power available unless I feel like writing code to perform set intersections and unions using my various indexes, which, to begin with, are based on XPath that the query engine knows nothing about.

My home-grown indexing had features I don't demonstrate here. I could in fact perform joins on queries and had the ability to monitor file updates to synchronize indexes. I waited and watched the emerging XML databases and then tried each new arrival   hoping for one that matched the features I needed for several large and looming projects. Berkeley DB XML 1 came close. BDB XML 2 nailed it.

High-Performance XML Databases

My own personal criteria for a production-ready XML database included the following.

Open Source, Active Community

"Community" in the software world provides security: security in support, software security, and so on. Developers that share the common interest of developing stable software provide support and help to one another. It's interesting to me that most of the support that developers and users receive for commercial closed source software still comes from user communities via mailing lists and message boards. Having the source code available to the user base makes community support all the more effective, and enhancements are available to anyone willing to put in the time. I wanted an open source XML database for which I could create language bindings if they didn't already exist and integrate with existing open source projects as well as licensed software that form a large part of my development environment. I also looked for an active user mailing list with heavy participation from the software's authors. A willingness by core developers to answer even beginners' questions is a sign of a quality project. A database is a complex piece of software, and I hoped to find a project that built off of existing and stable projects, rather than building something as daunting as an XML database from scratch.

OS and Language Compatibility

As I've said, a major point of XML is complete technology agnosticism. It doesn't make much sense to be using XML but to have to use a specific operating system or programming language to process it.

XQuery Interface and Multiple Data Sources

XPath 1.0 is great, but XQuery and XPath 2.0 make searching XML a joy. I wanted an XML database that enabled me to use the XQuery standard to request and reshape XML with custom functions and multiple data source. I could then do intersections between databases, among other things.

Embedded

I wanted an XML database that would not introduce a lot of operational and environmental complexity.

Transactions, Recovery, Replication

My applications require production-ready deployment. Race conditions, irrecoverable corruption, and the inability to copy data were not acceptable constraints.

Flexible Indexing

The power of any database lies in its indexing options. My applications had to be able to search on a long list of criteria, much unknown at development time. I needed indexing for nodes, elements, attributes, and metadata to support the project. I also needed to not be constrained by a hard-to-mutate schema or table because my data was subject to frequent format changes.

Easy Learning Curve

I was not an expert with XQuery or XML databases when I began the search for a database, and I needed a system that was not overly daunting. I needed code examples, a well-designed API, and an environment I could make sense of to succeed with the project.

I found that these needs were met with BDB XML. Having already long used XML for data storage, I needed a database solid and flexible enough to be used in many environments, with many programming languages, and with constantly changing data. Version 2 of BDB XML is fast, scalable, and best of all easy to use with a modicum of XML knowledge.

BDB XML for Quality Architecture

This chapter has had two themes: embedding databases and using XML for data storage. The two are not entirely dissimilar. The basic goal of XML is to make data more intelligent and intelligible, and embedded databases have the goal to put the data closer to where it gets used. Together, they provide for greatly simplified and more intelligent architectures. The following application examples illustrate cases of moving from a database server architecture to an embedded database architecture. Each is unique in how it uses a database, but in all cases the application gains architectural and operational simplicity.

Websites

Easily the most populous of applications, websites large and small implement a design not unlike the one at the start of the chapter (see Figure 2-9).

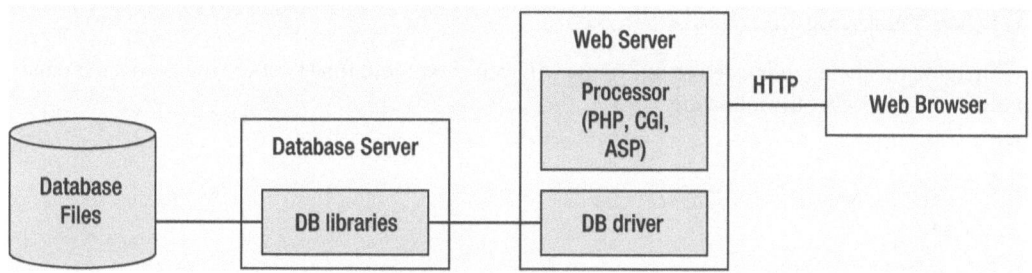

Figure 2-9. *A typical website architecture with database*

The web server takes HTTP requests and then processes a template or script to handle the request, which in turn uses a database driver to query a database server, formatting the results per the template, and outputting HTML back to the web browser. The server architecture has two process tiers. Typically the database contains web content documents and their associated metadata: document titles, dates, subjects, and so on.

Consider the architectural change shown in Figure 2-10.

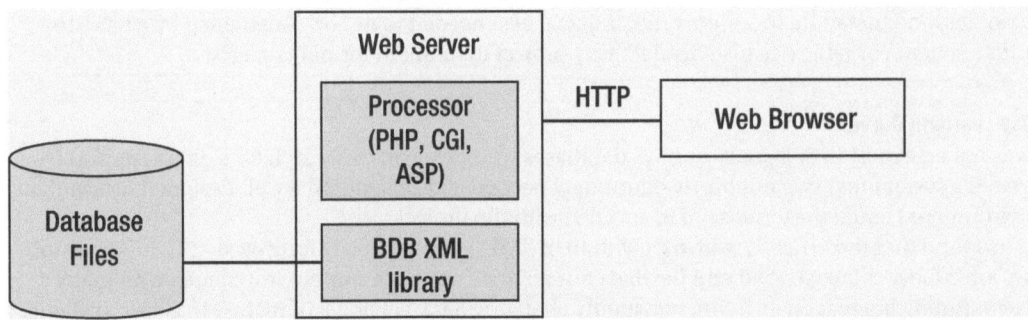

Figure 2-10. *A single-tier website architecture with BDB XML*

Obviously, this is a simpler model, but the benefits go beyond the number of lines in a diagram. The database still contains web content documents and their associated metadata. However, assume that these documents include HTML as well as XML. An HTML document already has embedded metadata, so why duplicate it with extra columns in your database table when you can query it directly with BDB XML?

Moreover, by using XSLT in the document processor, you can quite compactly convert XML from the database into HTML of your liking. You could actually use the BDB XML library as the document processor if you wanted to use XQuery as your templating language! (No, XQuery was not designed for this, but it does let you easily "reshape" XML, making it a simple matter to write templates in XQuery.)

Newcomers to XML are quick to observe that XPath looks a lot like a file path or URL. That's not surprising, given that URLs are intended to address hierarchical data, and both file structures and XML are basically a series of embedded directories. Wikis have become a popular model for websites because of their editability and simple design. A typical wiki URL uses a single parameter to name the file being requested, such as the following:

```
http://www.brians.org/wiki?About+the+Company
```

Imagine this being requested to our BDB XML web server and the HTML of the requested page (in the database) being the following:

```
<html>
    <head>
        <title>About the Company</title>
    </head>
    ...
</html>
```

Rather than naming all the files according to their wiki title, we could allow this simple URL interface by using the parameter in this XPath statement:

```
[/html/head/title = $param]
```

Obviously, this can lend itself to more practical uses of XPath with URLs. There might be times when you want to allow direct database queries via the URL (and other times when you don't). If you were willing to pass the queries along to BDB XML (within predicates, explained in Appendix A), you could grab documents by a certain author:

```
http://www.brians.org/html/head/meta[@name='author' and @content='Danny Brian']
```

Or with certain keywords:

```
http://www.brians.org/html/head/meta[@name='keywords' and contains
    (@content, 'music')]
```

No, I'm not suggesting that you implement an open URL database query server. I mean to illustrate that BDB XML is intended specifically to hold documents, and that the kinds of queries you might want to use look right at home on a URL. The vast majority of documents already have metadata and organized content—an XML document especially so—and BDB XML provides a complete solution to storing, indexing, reading, and manipulating your documents.

Desktop Apps

A native desktop application fits closely with most people's idea of "embedded," particularly if the program is compiled and packaged with an installer. Looking around at the preferences and configuration files for your favorite applications, you'll notice that many or most have moved to XML to store settings. Others now use XML to store all text data documents, whether word processors, spreadsheets, or even slide presentations. All applications need a way to store data to disk, and BDB XML provides an ideal solution for those that deal with lots of XML (see Figure 2-11).

Figure 2-11. *Using BDB XML for embedded data storage*

Features and implementations may evolve, but BDB XML will not constrain you. "Legacy data formats" really aren't an issue; if your XML formats change, you can reshape documents into a new format with only XQuery. Adding new "fields" (elements), moving data around, even storing non-XML data—BDB XML gives you the flexibility to treat user data however you want, and transactions and recovery logs make it a safe system—even when Ctrl+Alt+Delete is used liberally by certain users.

Of course, any of the documents in a BDB XML database can be written to disk, sent over the network, or otherwise treated as simple XML data. Other applications can access the database concurrently. In fact, there's no reason a desktop app couldn't be built expressly for managing a content database that is simultaneously being read by a web server.

Conclusion

BDB XML addresses much of the complexity and rigidity that plague many data stores with an embedded access library. The architectural impact of an embedded database is that you can put it where you want, run it the way you want, access it how you want, and introduce very little system complexity in the process.

Too often, applications get designed around a notion of how their data will look before proceeding to enforce that preconception on the data to keep it compatible and manageable.

Unfortunately (or fortunately, for those of us seeking higher incomes), it is the nature of data to change, and not just the field values but also the entirety of how data is organized. The best applications are those that can evolve to include new features and adapt to bugs and requests. Data is no different! Because data hopefully changes more often than code, data needs a lot of flexibility.

Rigid data solutions are frustrating on many levels. No group or person should have to spend hours or weeks testing the impact of adding a table column for "Country" to a user database because the designer did not anticipate selling internationally. *Agile* is the latest buzzword to describe the speed and ease of change in processes, and it holds true for software design. *The best design is not the one that will never require modification, but the one that will best accommodate modification without unreasonable delay or hassle.* This shouldnt be confused with the danger of "premature optimization:" it is easier to build for change than it is to preempt or prevent change.

In this context, BDB XML is a key piece of the agile software puzzle. You can index collections almost any way you want. You can insert documents that dont comply with a particular schema, or you can enforce a strict schema for the entire collection. You can reshape query results to look however you want. You can read the database directly from your desktop application, or you can stick it on a web server and read it remotely through a web server or service. You can run it on almost any operating system, access it with any major programming language, and use industry-standard tools of your choosing. Using BDB XML as the data layer for any application will ease changes to any part of the application.

CHAPTER 3

■ ■ ■

Installation and Configuration

This chapter covers the installation process with an overview of the dependencies (all included with the distribution) before providing more platform-specific instructions. Note that Berkeley DB XML (BDB XML) requires no site configuration. Aside from the options used to compile BDB XML (installation path, library debugging, compiler and interpreter versions), all database configuration is performed at the database and database environment level. This is convenient for moving databases between environments and even system installations.

BDB XML Packages and Layout

The BDB XML distribution, which is available for download from `http://sleepycat.com`, includes the package dependencies and some build utilities. The source distribution has the following directory layout:

```
dbxml-2.x/
    install/
    db-4.x/
    pathan/
    xerces-c-src/
    xquery-1.x/
```

The Unix BDB XML build places the resulting files (libraries, binaries, and so on) in the `install` directory. The rest contain the individual packages.

Berkeley DB

This is the Berkeley database, atop which BDB XML is built. Even though you might already have a version of BDB installed, this version is included for linking with BDB XML and will ensure compatibility. You needn't uninstall or overwrite your existing BDB installation.

BDB XML uses BDB version 4 to inherit its features, including scalability, caching, flexibility of storage and access, and transactions. This also means that BDB XML databases can store non-XML data in a separate table, as with a traditional BDB database, by using the same database environment.

Xerces C++

Xerces is the Apache project's open source XML parser in C++ and Java (with Perl and COM bindings). It features namespace support, validation using XML Schemas, a complete DOM implementation compliant through Level 2 (and some of Level 3), SAX 1.0 and 2.0, and decent encoding support and performance.

As the parser, Xerces provides BDB XML with its internal parsing and DOM functionality. Note that the version included with BDB XML is the pure Xerces-C source distribution and is included for build convenience.

Pathan

Pathan is an open source XPath processor developed jointly by DecisionSoft, Sleepycat, Data Direct, and Parthenon Computing. Pathan essentially adds XPath functionality to the Xerces DOM. Although Pathan 2.0 (adding XPath 2 conformance) is labeled "beta," it has been stable for some time and was developed primarily for inclusion in other software, including BDB XML. The version of Pathan included in the BDB XML distribution is different from the older official version, which cannot be used.

XQuery

The XQuery package is part of BDB XML, but modularized so it can be used externally. It adds XQuery functionality to the Xerces DOM, using Pathan for its XPath processor. Being an external library has many benefits, not the least of which are the tools that the package includes. XQuery is a powerful language that I•ll explore in its own chapter, making use of this package and its tools.

Berkeley DB XML

The BDB XML library links the rest of the libraries and provides the architecture for containers, documents, and indexes, as well as all underlying query optimization and processing features. Of course, it also provides the APIs for the system. You won•t often need to use any of the APIs from the other packages to work with BDB XML because it has all the classes and methods to accomplish most common operations. The exception is work with the underlying Berkeley DB libraries because they are required to create and manage database environments.

Installation

Installing BDB XML on various operating systems is straightforward, but I•ve included some tips here. The BDB XML source includes all the files for building on any supported platform and the bindings for any supported language; there are not separate distributions for different operating systems or languages.

Windows

Binary and source distributions are available for Win32. Both are described in the following sections.

Binary Install

The best option to install BDB XML on Windows is to use the binary installer (.msi) available for download from Sleepycat. It places the entire compiled distribution   including .dlls, executables, documentation, and sample code   in a directory titled `Program Files/Sleepycat Software/ Berkeley DB XML 2.x` and a prefetch (.pf) file in your system directory (to let programs know where to find the .dlls). The binary Windows install includes precompiled bindings for Python (BDB XML 2.2 and later) and Java, but not for Perl or PHP.

Source Install

Each package subdirectory of the source distribution contains a build_win32 directory, which is used for compiling. This directory in turn has project, workspace, and solution files for MS Visual Studio versions 6 and 7.1 (Visual Studio .NET 2003), the main files in dbxml/build_win32. Sleepycat provides several different versions to meet varying needs, all functional for Windows XP, 2000, NT, and 98 (see Table 3-1).

Table 3-1. *Windows Build File Explanations*

File	MSV* Version	File Type	Description
BDBXML_all.sln	7.1	Solution	All projects for third-party packages and BDB XML examples
BDBXML_all.dsw	6.0	Workspace	Third-party packages and BDB XML examples
Berkeley_DB_XML.sln	7.1	Solution	Projects for Berkeley DB XML libraries only, no examples
Berkeley_DB_XML.dsw	6.0	Workspace	Projects for Berkeley DB XML libraries only, no examples
dbxml_gettingStarted.sln	7.1	Solution	Projects for Berkeley DB XML examples only
dbxml_gettingStarted.sln	6.0	Workspace	Projects for Berkeley DB XML examples only
*.vcproj	7.1	Project	
*.dsp	6.0	Project	

BDB XML can be built from MSVS .NET using the BDBXML_all.sln file, choosing a project configuration from the toolbar (options are Debug, Release, Debug Static, and Release Static), and selecting Build Solution from the Build menu. This will build all third-party libraries, BDB XML, and BDB XML examples. Library files are placed in dbxml-2.x/lib, and executables and DLLs are placed in dbxml-2.x/bin. When using the debug project configuration, executables and DLLs are placed in the subdirectory dbxml-2.x/bin/debug.

Trying the Examples

Before running the example executables, be sure that your PATH includes the location of the BDB XML and third-party libraries. For example:

```
PATH=%PATH%;C:\Program Files\Sleepycat Software\Berkeley DB XML 2.x\bin\
```

Most of the example programs require an example container. These are loaded by changing your directory to dbxml/examples/cxx/gettingStarted, creating a new directory for the database environment, and then running the script dbxml_example_loadExamplesData.cmd with that new directory name and the current directory:

```
dbxml_example_loadExamplesData.cmd exampleDbEnv .
```

The first argument tells the script where to find the environment; the second tells where to find the XML data directory ../../xmlData relative to the current directory. Run from gettingStarted/, this is the current working directory. After loading the database, you can run the other examples to demonstrate BDB XML functionality. Most take an -h command-line option to specify the environment path.

Unix

The BDB XML distribution includes in its top directory a script buildall.sh. This is the primary configuration and build tool, and it greatly simplifies the build on various Unix variants.

■**Note** BDB XML is fairly modern technology so it works best with the latest stable versions of the programs you intend it to work with (gcc, Perl, Python, and so on). I recommend that you install the latest stable versions of such languages and utilities before compiling BDB XML.

The build script accepts arguments for setting prefixes and to build debug libraries, and options to build the third-party language bindings. All options are displayed with this command:

```
$ sh buildall.sh --help
```

Running buildall.sh with no options attempts to configure and build all libraries with default settings, placing them in the directory dbxml-2.x/install, and the C++ examples in dbxml-2.x/dbxml/build_unix. Only the C++ libraries and binaries are built by default, without the other language bindings. The options to buildall.sh include those shown in Table 3-2.

Table 3-2. *Command-Line Options for* buildall.sh

Option	Explanation
--enable-debug	Build the debug libraries
--prefix=*path*	Specify an installation path (default is ./install)
--enable-java	Build the Java API
--enable-perl	Build the Perl interface
--build-one=*library*	Build (or clean) a single library, berkeleydb, xerces, pathan, and so on
--clean	Clean (make clean) the build tree
--distclean	Clean (make distclean) the entire build and reset configuration

Individual language libraries can be built by themselves, as explained in a later section. In many cases, the language bindings can be easier to build alone instead of using the buildall.sh utility. Some language bindings as well as operating systems have build quirks that are addressed in the following sections. Each version of BDB XML improves the build on each platform, so check the installation notes and mailing list for the most up-to-date information.

If you want to install the BDB XML libraries or binaries in a location other than the dbxml-2.x/install directory, you can specify that location to the buillall.sh utility. Be aware that in most configurations the paths used by the dynamic linker must include the location of the libraries for the binaries to execute. This is accomplished on most Unix variants by having the path in your LD_LIBRARY_PATH environment variable or by adding the paths to the ldconfig hints file, usually at /etc/ld.config.

Building the Java API with the `buildall.sh` script requires that you have a working `javac` in your path and a Java version of 1.3 or later. After the build runs `make`, the Java library for BDB XML (`dbxml.jar`) will be located in your build directory (`install/lib`). To use the Java API in your programs, set the environment variable `CLASSPATH` to include the paths to both this and the `db.jar` files, and set the `LD_LIBRARY_PATH` environment variable to include the `.libs/` directory in the installation directory (`install/`).

Note that many of the language bindings, including Perl and Python, have installation scripts that attempt to copy the completed libraries to their production locations (`/usr/local/...`). If you run the `buildall.sh` script with parameters to build language bindings without permissions to install in those locations, the copy will fail. Because the language bindings are compiled after the BDB XML libraries, you can usually just change the directory to the bindings source and do a `make install` or equivalent as root or a user with proper permissions.

Finally, BDB XML requires the specific version of Berkeley DB included with the distribution. Occasionally a source build finds an earlier installed version of BDB and attempts to use it instead. Be certain to either remove the previous installation or modify your paths to use the proper BDB version.

Building and Using Individual Packages

The `buildall.sh` script provides the best means of compiling the individual BDB XML packages. If you need to build them individually, this section details the means. With some exceptions, you should still use the versions included with the BDB XML distribution because several packages have changes or patches not available in the official versions.

Berkeley DB

BDB XML requires Berkeley DB 4.3.28 or newer. This must be configured with the `--enable-cxx` configuration option to build the C++ API and the `--enable-java` option to build the Java API.

```
$ cd dbxml-2.x/db-4.x/build_unix
$ ../dist/configure --enable-cxx
$ make
$ make install
```

This installs BDB in a default location at `/usr/local/BerkeleyDB.4.x`; a different installation directory can be specified with the `--prefix` option. When building BDB XML using this installation, you can use the `--with-berkeleydb` option to tell `buildall.sh` where to find it.

Xerces

All of the BDB XML libraries other than Berkeley DB require the Xerces libraries and source from the Xerces release version 2.7 or newer; releases before BDB XML 2.2 use Xerces 2.6. The `XERCESCROOT` environment variable is used to find the source. An example build for Linux follows:

```
$ cd dbxml-2.x/xerces-c-src2_x
$ export XERCESCROOT=`pwd`
$ cd src/xercesc
$ ./runConfigure -plinux -d -cgcc -xg++ -minmem -nsocket -tnative -rnone
$ make
$ make install
```

This build places the Xerces installation under `/usr/local`; use the `-P` option to specify a different path and use the `buildall.sh` option `--with-xerces` to tell BDB XML where to find it.

Pathan

You must use the version of Pathan included with BDB XML. Pathan can be built alone, as shown in the following example:

```
$ cd dbxml-2.x/pathan
$ ./configure --with-xerces=../xerces-c-src2_x
$ make
$ make install
```

By default, Pathan is installed in /usr/local. Use the --prefix option to change the installation path and use the --with-pathan option to buildall.sh for BDB XML to locate it.

XQuery

The XQuery package included with BDB XML must be used:

```
$ cd dbxml-2.x/xquery-1.x/build_unix
$ ../dist/configure
$ make
$ make install
```

XQuery will be installed under /usr/local/BerkeleyDB.XQuery.1.x by default. You can change the installation directory with the --prefix option to configure, as well as the location for the compiler to find Pathan and Xerces, by using --with-pathan and --with-xerces, respectively. If you change the installation target, you need to supply the --with-xquery argument to buildall.sh when you configure BDB XML.

Unix Variants

This section offers tips for specific operating systems.

Linux

BDB XML builds cleanly "out of the box" on Linux 2.4, 2.5, and 2.6 distributions with gcc 3.2 and later, with no options necessary to buildall.sh. This is also true for the Perl, Python, and Java (1.3 or later) bindings. See the section on building bindings for more information on specific languages.

Mac OS X

BDB XML builds cleanly on Mac OS X 10.4 and later with Apple's Xcode tools version 2.1 and later (available from Apple's Developer Connection at connect.apple.com). This version includes gcc 4.0. Xcode includes ported versions of gcc, javac, and third-party languages.

If you encounter an error when running tests or executables along the lines of Library Not Found, you might need to use OS X's otool and install_name_tool utilities to specify the proper library identifier to the linker. In earlier versions of BDB XML 2.x, the resulting libraries did not always have the proper Xerces identifier specified. If this is the case, you might need to do the same thing for Perl and Python libraries. Run otool on the .so, .bundle, or .dylib files to determine whether the compiler included the correct Xerces identifier. This problem has been corrected in BDB XML 2.2 and later.

Some versions of OS X had dynamic loading problems with conflicting namespaces, resulting in Multiple Definition errors. These problems can be fixed by setting the environment variable MACOSX_DEPLYMENT_TARGET to 10.3 (or current OS X version) and reconfiguring/rebuilding BDB XML. Refer to the ld(1) and dyld(1) man pages for more information on symbol namespaces on OS X.

FreeBSD

The ideal FreeBSD installation requires version 5.3 or later, with gcc/g++ 4.1 or later. The latter can be installed simply from ports, if available:

```
$ cd /usr/ports/lang/gcc41; make install; make clean
```

You then need to specify the proper utilities to the buildall.sh script, being certain to have those programs in your path:

```
$ buildall.sh -m gmake -c gcc41 -x g++41
```

In versions of BDB XML before 2.2, it was easier to compile language bindings separate from the base installation, but it is now fairly easy to install them with buildall.sh using the parameters listed previously.

Some FreeBSD 5.4 users have reported the error:

```
Fatal error 'Spinlock called when not threaded.' at line 87 in file
/usr/src/lib/libpthread/thread/thr_spinlock.c (errno = 0)
```

This problem can be remedied by creating a file /etc/libmap.conf to map libc_r to libpthread. See the libmap.conf man page for more information.

Building Bindings

The easiest way to build language bindings is to use the buildall.sh utility. If you have the need to build individual language bindings separately, refer to the following section. The source directories for each binding are at dbxml/src/*language* within your BDB XML distribution.

Most of the language bindings include examples that require you to populate a sample database, similar to the C++ examples earlier in this chapter. Refer to the README with each source directory for more information on using the examples.

Perl

Paul Marquess, the author of many popular Perl modules, maintains the Perl bindings. They are at dbxml/src/perl within the BDB XML distribution and use an installation familiar to Perl users.

The main Perl package is Sleepycat::DbXml. Each Perl package or class has accompanying POD documentation for reading with perldoc:

```
$ perldoc Sleepycat::XmlContainer
```

(Note that the individual packages are not hierarchical to Sleepycat::DbXml.) The best resource for learning the Perl interface is the test suite (in DbXml/t) and the example scripts in examples/ gettingStarted, which duplicate the functionality of the examples already shown. Each takes command-line arguments; run them without arguments to see the proper syntax:

```
$ perl queryWithContext.pl
This program illustrates how to query for documents that require namespace
usage in the query.  You should pre-load the container using
loadExamplesData.[sh|cmd] before running this example.  You are only required
to pass this command the path location of the database environment that you
specified when you pre-loaded the examples data:

    -h <dbenv directory>
```

Unix

You must have a working `perl` binary in your path of version 5.6.1 or greater. It is strongly recommended that you compile both BDB XML and the Perl bindings using the same compiler that you used to create the `perl` binary. If this is not the case, consider building a new binary using the more recent stable compiler.

Edit the config file to specify the location of the BDB XML libraries and your desired installation location. You can then proceed with the build and install:

```
$ perl Makefile.PL
$ make
$ make test
$ make install
```

This will place the Perl API in the location determined by the Perl binary as appropriate.

Windows

Visual Studio includes a file `vcvars32.bat` to set up your environment to include the `nmake.exe` and `cl.exe` executables in your `PATH`. After running this script, verify your configuration in the config.win32 file before proceeding with the build: perl Makefile.PL -config config.win32.

```
$ nmake
$ cd Db
$ nmake test
$ cd ..\DbXml
$ nmake test
$ nmake install
```

Python

The Python bindings require Python 2.3 or newer. As with Perl, use the same compiler to build both Python and BDB XML. You also need the bsddb3 Python module installed; it is included in the Python core in newer versions; however, this module must be compiled against the same version of Berkeley DB that you are using for BDB XML. Python does include Berkeley DB, but not a version compatible with BDB XML. To install the included bsddb3 package use the following:

```
$ cd dbxml-2.x/dbxml/src/python/bsddb3-4.x
$ python setup.dbxml.py build
$ python setup.dbxml.py install
```

You can then build and install the dbxml module:

```
$ cd ..
$ python setup.py build
$ python setup.py install
```

Python examples are at `dbxml-2.x/dbxml/examples/python`.

PHP

The source for the PHP bindings is at `dbxml-2.x/dbxml/src/php`; the Berkeley DB extension `php_db4` must be already installed. As with other language bindings, the PHP API requires that both BDB XML libraries and the PHP extension be linked with the version of Berkeley DB 4 included with BDB XML. You need to rebuild the `php_db4` extension if one is already installed using a different version of BDB. The source for the extension is included with the BDB XML distribution at `dbxml-2.x/db-4.x/php_db4`; installing this version will ensure compatibility.

Installation of the `dbxml` extension is straightforward from within this directory:

```
$ phpize
$ ./configure --with-dbxml=path
$ make
$ make install
```

The `configure` script also provides options for specifying the location of BDB and other libraries; then adding to your `php.ini` file:

```
extension=db4.so
extension=dbxml.so
```

See the README file in the PHP source directory for additional caveats concerning Linux and Mac OS X installs.

PHP examples are included in the `examples/` directory within the PHP source tree.

Conclusion

Berkeley DB XML has a simple installation procedure for many operating systems and language interfaces. This same ease carries over to using the product, as you‑ll see in the following chapters.

If you have problems building and installing BDB XML, consult the BDB XML mailing list: xml@sleepycat.com. There is a good list archive at http://www.nabble.com/Berkeley-DB-Xml-f730.html, with many installation questions already answered. Otherwise, subscribe to the list (see http://dev.sleepycat.com/community/discussion.html), ask your question, and helpful individuals will point you in the right direction.

CHAPTER 4

■ ■ ■

Getting Started

With a working Berkeley DB XML installation, you're ready to jump into the concepts behind an embedded XML database. Sleepycat has made this easy with a simple database shell, dbxml, which I'll use to illustrate the basics of creating database files, inserting and deleting XML documents, creating indexes, and of course, querying the collection. The lessons here translate to all language bindings, making them a convenient introduction to the system. Consider this chapter a quick tour of BDB XML.

Core Concepts

As you saw in Chapter 3, "Installation and Configuration," BDB XML applications can be written in various programming languages. Each uses the BDB XML libraries directly from the application: no database server will be queried over the network. The program you write opens and closes the database files file permissions at the level of your operating system behave as expected (insofar as the expectations are accurate), and database files can be treated as you do any BDB file.

The architecture of your specific application will depend on the language and your environment. You can write command-line programs, not unlike the examples included with BDB XML, for users to perform queries on databases. You can use BDB XML databases as part of a website using PHP or Perl scripts (or mod_perl modules), which enables visitors to browse and manipulate your database. Multiple applications can access the same database files, from various programming languages, including the BDB XML shell, which I will describe in the next section.

BDB XML documents are stored in files called *containers*. A container is identical to a database for our purposes, holding all records XML files as well as document metadata and indexes. XML files can be stored in different formats, depending on your needs.

Containers are stored in *environments*. An environment is simply a file directory that BDB XML uses to store containers as well as logs when logging is enabled for use in transactions and recovery. Environments are the "operating space" for your databases. You don't need to explicitly use them, and you can have many environments with a BDB XML installation.

The Shell

The BDB XML build places an aptly named binary dbxml in the directory dbxml-2.x/install/bin. (The Windows binary install adds this right to your Start menu, whereas the source install places the file in your dbxml-2.x/bin directory.) This program gives you access to the bulk of BDB XML's functionality without having to write any code of your own, making it useful for testing, maintenance, and of course, learning. Because database containers are self-contained and require zero configuration, experimenting with the shell in a file directory gives you a good opportunity to

learn with no risk to your environment (we're assuming here that you don't do so in your root or
system directories).

Shell Options

The dbxml shell gives you several command-line options (see Table 4-1), none of which we'll be
using immediately. They can be listed with the -h option.

Table 4-1. *Abbreviated List of Shell Command-Line Options*

Option	Description
-h *directory*	Specifies a directory to be used as the database environment; default is the current working directory (.)
-c	Creates a new environment in the directory specified by -h
-s *script*	Runs a file script in a noninteractive mode
-t	Specifies transaction mode, requiring transactions for database writes
-V	Outputs BDB XML version
-P *password*	Specifies a password for the database

Running the shell gives you a database command prompt:

dbxml>

From here, typing **help** (ending with a line feed) will list the available commands; help followed
by one of the listed commands will give you a description and usage syntax:

dbxml> **help openContainer**

```
openContainer -- Opens a container, and uses it as the default container

Usage: openContainer <container> [[no]validate]
This command uses the XmlManager::openContainer() method. It also sets
the default collection, using the XmlQueryContext::setDefaultCollection()
method.
```

Note that the usage text includes the class method used by the command. This makes for a
useful reference because you can experiment with method functionality from within the shell and
refer to the class documentation for it.

Creating Containers

Let's create a container in the current directory using the createContainer command. I'll continue
using the Wordnet XML described in the previous chapters and name the database accordingly:

dbxml> createContainer synsets.dbxml

```
Creating document storage container with nodes indexed
```

The database name and extension here are arbitrary. A file has just been created, synsets.dbxml, and opened by the shell, ready to query. These are binary files, understood only by the BDB XML libraries, and as such should not be edited directly.

We won't delve in to indexes just yet, but note that all containers have a default index created, which is a metadata index for document names. We will provide unique names to the database as we insert documents (of course, the filenames), and these will be automatically indexed.

Tip If you use the BDB XML shell (or any similar command-line program) a lot on Unix, a wrapper like rlwrap can add input history and command completion to dbxml. When demonstrating functionality, I invoke the shell with the following command (in a shell script):

```
/usr/local/bin/rlwrap -c -H .rlhistory -f .rlhistory -l log.txt -r /usr/bin/dbxml
```

This lets me page through my shell history with the up arrow key, and complete filenames with the Tab key, retaining history between shell sessions.

Adding and Deleting Documents

With our new database open, we can insert an XML document using the putDocument command. I'll start with the now-familiar baseball lexicon example. Like many programs, the dbxml shell enables commands to span many lines when each line is terminated with a backslash (\). When placing an XML document into the shell as text, we can enclose it in single-quotes:

```
dbxml> putDocument 14861 '
<Synset fileVersion="1.0" pos="n">
  <Id>14861</Id>
  <WnOffset version="2.1" pos="n">02772480</WnOffset>
  <LexFileNum>06</LexFileNum>
  <SsType>n</SsType>
  <Word lexId="0">baseball</Word>
  <Pointers>
    <Hypernym>14746</Hypernym>
    <Hypernym>14866</Hypernym>
  </Pointers>
  <Gloss>a ball used in playing baseball</Gloss>
</Synset>
' s
```

```
Document added, name = 14861
```

The first argument for putDocument is 14861, which is the document name. The s after the XML string tells the shell that the string is serialized XML. The shell enables documents to be inserted as strings, files, or XQuery expressions. The file syntax is as follows:

```
dbxml> putDocument 14861 '../wordnet/14861.xml' f
```

```
putDocument failed, Error: Document exists: 14861
```

Of course, attempting to place another document with the same name into the container results in a Document Exists error. The default index enforces uniqueness on this piece of metadata; I will discuss this at length in Chapter 6, "Indexes."

■Note Notice in the example that a record's Id value and pointers to other records don't use the full filename (with .xml), so it will be more convenient (and avoid a lot of concat() XPath calls) to simply use the number as the filename going forward.

We can delete the file from the container using its name:

```
dbxml> removeDocument 14861
```

```
Document deleted, name = 14861
```

To demonstrate a bit more shell functionality, lets assume that I have a large collection of XML files in the directory ../wordnet/ (relative to my current working directory). I will add three of those files to my container as follows:

```
dbxml> putDocument 14861 '../wordnet/14861.xml' f
```

```
Document added, name = 14861
```

```
dbxml> putDocument 14862 '../wordnet/14862.xml' f
```

```
Document added, name = 14862
```

```
dbxml> putDocument 14863 '../wordnet/14863.xml' f
```

```
Document added, name = 14863
```

■Tip For the impatient, the dbxml shell permits shortcuts for its commands, using the smallest starting substring, with the commands in alphabetical order. That is, the commands create and even cr are recognized as createDocument, but c alone is short for commit. The BDB XML distribution also supplies a command, dbxml_load_container, which shortcuts the addition of many documents to a container.

Querying Containers

The query command takes as argument a block of XQuery code, which for now we'll limit to XPath with a collection() test at the front:

```
dbxml> query 'collection("synsets.dbxml")/Synset/Word[contains(., "baseball")]'
```

```
3 objects returned for eager expression
'collection("synsets.dbxml")/Synset/Word[contains(., "baseball")]'
```

We can then print out the results with `print`:

```
dbxml> print
```

```
<Word lexId="0">baseball</Word>
<Word lexId="0">baseball bat</Word>
<Word lexId="0">baseball cap</Word>
```

Notice that we're getting back element nodes from the query. Had we appended a `text()` to our query, we would get only the text nodes:

```
dbxml> query 'collection("synsets.dbxml")/Synset/Word[contains(., "baseball")]/string()'
```

```
3 objects returned for eager expression
'collection("synsets.dbxml")/Synset/Word[contains(., "baseball")]/string()
```

```
dbxml> print
```

```
baseball
baseball bat
baseball cap
```

Similarly, had we wanted to get back entire documents, we could have put everything after `/Synset` in a predicate, causing the query to select the root elements:

```
dbxml> query 'collection("synsets.dbxml")/Synset[contains(Word, "baseball")]'
```

```
3 objects returned for eager expression
'collection("synsets.dbxml")/Synset[contains(Word, "baseball")]'
```

```
dbxml> print
```

```
<Synset fileVersion="1.0" pos="n">
  <Id>14861</Id>
  <WnOffset version="2.1" pos="n">02772480</WnOffset>
  <LexFileNum>06</LexFileNum>
  <SsType>n</SsType>
  <Word lexId="0">baseball</Word>
  <Pointers>
    <Hypernym>14746</Hypernym>
    <Hypernym>14866</Hypernym>
  </Pointers>
  <Gloss>a ball used in playing baseball  </Gloss>
</Synset>
...
```

Note that we aren't requiring any structure on our documents at this point (this will be demonstrated in Chapter 5, "Environments, Containers, and Documents"). For now, consider that the lack of constraints on our container makes it very flexible. We can use the document structure to find differences between documents. For example, to find records that have *holonym* pointers, which indicate objects that are "part of" the object for that record, we can query for the existence of an element:

```
dbxml> query 'collection("synsets.dbxml")/Synset/Pointers/Holonym'
```

```
2 objects returned for eager expression
'collection("synsets.dbxml")/Synset/Pointers/Holonym'
```

```
dbxml> print
```

```
<Holonym type="component">18925</Holonym>
<Holonym type="component">15116</Holonym>
```

If we looked at the files for these two numbers, we'd find the first to be "grip" or "handle" (part of the baseball bat) and the second "bill" or "visor" (part of the baseball cap). Of course, after we have added them to the database, we can get all this information with a single query.

Indexing Containers

As we add more documents to the container, we'll start to notice a slow response from the queries because BDB XML has to process each document. Indexes created on a container can significantly reduce the time required for queries to return results. Whenever an index exists for the elements used in a query, the index is used rather than the document itself, making lookups very fast.

We can see the container's indexes with the listIndexes command:

```
dbxml> listIndexes
```

```
Index: unique-node-metadata-equality-string for node
{http://www.sleepycat.com/2002/dbxml}:name
1 indexes found.
```

As mentioned, this metadata name index is added by default when a container is created; it contains the document names used as the first argument to putDocument when a document is added.

I will examine indexes in depth in Chapter 6. For now, we'll add an index for our Word element:

```
dbxml> addIndex "" Word node-element-equality-string
```

```
Adding index type: node-element-equality-string to node: {}:Word
```

The first argument to addIndex is a namespace Uniform Resource Identifier (URI), which we aren't using; the second is the node name; and the third is an index identifier. This string has four parts that determine the indexing strategy. In this example, we created a node index (meaning it will index any nodes Word regardless of where they occur in a document) on an element (as opposed to an attribute or metadata), optimized for equality tests (as opposed to presence or substring queries), with a string index syntax. A fifth part, not used in this example, can be added to force uniqueness for certain data between records within a container.

■Note An index's syntax type does not limit the type of values allowed for the indexed data. Rather, it determines the strategy for the underlying index format.

Now, any query that entails a string equality test on the Word element will use this index. Obviously, the choice of indexing strategies is important when searching large collections of documents because any query that has to access data not indexed needs to process each document in the database, creating long response times.

Deleting an index requires the same parameters used when it was added. We can see them by listing the indexes:

```
dbxml> listIndex
```

```
Index: node-element-equality-string for node {}:Word
Index: unique-node-metadata-equality-string for node
{http://www.sleepycat.com/2002/dbxml}:name
2 indexes found.
```

And delete the Word index:

```
dbxml> delIndex "" Word node-element-equality-string
```

```
Deleting index type: node-element-equality-string from node: {}:Word
```

Indexing itself is a potentially expensive operation because indexing must process every document in the collection. Overly frequent reindexing is therefore something that is possible but should be avoided, especially on production databases. As with relational databases, an index definition causes BDB XML to update indexes each time a document is added, modified, or deleted. Thus, indexes should be created before any documents are inserted.

The impact of indexes on queries, as well as the indexes touched by various queries, can be examined by raising the shell's verbosity:

```
dbxml> setVerbose 2 2
```

It will cause the shell to output query times as well as the indexes that were used during the query. I will later use this information to illustrate indexing strategies. Additionally, the shell provides a command queryPlan to parse a query string and examine its index usage without performing a search.

Using XQuery

Everything demonstrated in the queries thus far is written in XQuery because XQuery inherits much of its features and syntax from XPath; in fact, XQuery and XPath 2.0 share the same functions and operators. XQuery is a full-featured query language in its own right, enabling the reshaping of results and dynamic query construction with its own miniscripting language, dubbed *FLWOR expressions*, named for its main clauses (for, let, where, order, return).

Consider the case of adding documents. The putDocument shell command has a parameter q (in addition to the s for string and the f for file already demonstrated), identifying the query argument as an XQuery statement. The statement returns a value that gets used as the argument to putDocument. Knowing we have 117,597 XML files (in the Wordnet synset example), we can add all of them at once:

```
dbxml> putDocument "" '
for $i in (1 to 117597)
return doc(concat("file:./wordnet/", $i, ".xml"))
' q
```

Yes, this query will take some time because the processor must open each file, parse it, evaluate it for inclusion in any existing indexes, and then write to the database. Note that when issuing putDocument with an XQuery statement, the first argument to putDocument is empty. When an XQuery statement is being used to generate documents, the document name cannot be specified with the command. Instead, BDB XML generates document names that by default have the syntax dbxml_1cb5e, the last characters being a generated unique hexadecimal number. (You can change this definition from the API.)

For the sample Wordnet collection, we want document names that share numbers with the source filenames, so I will not be using these autogenerated ids. As a preview of the API, note that the following Python script accomplishes the same, using the filename as the document name.

```
from bsddb3.db import *
from dbxml import *
import os

mgr = XmlManager()
uc = mgr.createUpdateContext()
container = mgr.openContainer("synset.dbxml")
dir = "wordnet"
for file in os.listdir(dir):
    content = open("wordnet/" + file).read()
    container.putDocument(file, content, uc)
```

Because XQuery can output XML, it can be used to dynamically create documents for insertion. This example populates the database with 100 documents:

```
dbxml> putDocument "" '
for $i in (0 to 99)
return
  <entry id="{$i}">
    {
      if ($i > 50)
      then <second_half>yes</second_half>
      else ""
    }
    <description>Description of {$i}</description>
  </entry>' q
```

XQuery expressions can also reshape query results, enabling you to perform XML transformations within an expression. Note here that we have indexed the container for Word and Id elements; it would be a slow query otherwise. This example also demonstrates the use of variables within XQuery to hold node sets and then to query them directly.

```
dbxml> query '<baseballs>
        {
        for $baseball in
            (collection("synsets.dbxml")/Synset[Word = "baseball"])
        return
            <gloss>{$baseball/Gloss/string()}</gloss>
        }
    </baseballs>'
```

```
1 objects returned for eager expression '<baseballs> ... '
```

```
dbxml> print
```

```
<baseballs><gloss>a ball used in playing baseball  </gloss><gloss>a ball game played with
a bat and ball between two teams of nine players; teams take turns at bat trying to score
runs; "he played baseball in high school"; "there was a baseball game on every empty
lot"; "there was a desire for National League ball in the area"; "play ball!"
</gloss></baseballs>
```

Much is possible with XQuery. Multiple containers can be queried, making set processing (joins, unions, intersections) possible. Results can be flexibly ordered. User functions can be written, making recursive processing of results fairly trivial. The power of BDB XML is fully realized due to XQuery expressions atop its indexes. I examine XQuery more fully in Chapter 7, "XQuery with BDB XML."

Metadata

Regardless of the operating system, file systems associate metadata with the files. This data includes any information not contained within the file itself: the filename, file permissions, creation or modification dates, and file ownership are all types of metadata. BDB XML enables any metadata of your invention to be attributed to documents and indexed just as with document contents.

I have already demonstrated one type of metadata, document names, which are indexed by BDB XML by default. Metadata is set in the shell using the setMetaData command, which takes the document name; a URI for the metadata; plus a metadata name, type, and value. Suppose I want to attribute a document to a certain person without changing the document's content (by adding a <user/> element, for example). I could do this by setting metadata on the document:

```
dbxml> setMetaData 8872 '' user string dbrian
```

```
MetaData item 'user' added to document 8872
```

Metadata can be indexed and used within queries using by using the dbxml:metadata namespace (implemented as a function) for lookups:

```
dbxml> addIndex '' user node-metadata-equality-string
```

```
Adding index type: node-metadata-equality-string to node: {}:user
```

```
dbxml> query 'collection("synsets.dbxml")/Synset[dbxml:metadata("user")] '
```

```
1 objects returned for eager expression '
collection("synsets.dbxml")/Synset[dbxml:metadata("user")]
'
```

You can see the names of metadata items for a given document using the getMetaData command:

```
dbxml> getMetadata 8872
```

```
Metadata for document: 8872
        http://www.sleepycat.com/2002/dbxml:name
        user
```

I explore metadata at more length in Chapter 5.

Transactions

When dbxml is invoked with the -t option, the shell permits transactions. You•ll notice a log file created in your current working directory, unless otherwise specified with the -h option. A better way to maintain transactional containers is to create a BDB XML environment programmatically, described in a later chapter. The dbxml shell does provide a -c command-line option for creation of an environment, but this doesn•t permit control over the initial environment settings. The point here is that you don•t need a configured BDB XML environment to use transactions.

The shell command transaction signals the beginning of a transaction, commit (or a subsequent transaction) tells the shell to commit the current transaction, and abort cancels the current transaction.

```
dbxml> transaction
```

```
Transaction started
```

```
dbxml> putDocument 189861 '<Synset fileVersion="1.0" pos="n"/>' s
```

```
Document added, name = 189861
```

```
dbxml> commit
```

```
Transaction committed
```

```
dbxml> transaction
```

```
Transaction started
```

```
dbxml> removeDoc 189861
```

```
Document deleted, name = 189861
```

```
dbxml> commit
```

```
Transaction committed
```

Conclusion

BDB XMLs shell utility is just an API interface, exposing nearly all the features offered by the API, making it an excellent tool for experimentation and learning. It offers functionality not discussed here, including the ability to modify documents, get container information, and process multiple containers simultaneously. Keep in mind that any queries you can run programmatically can also be run in the shell. When you need to debug query problems in a larger application, there is no better place to start than with the shell.

CHAPTER 5

■ ■ ■

Environments, Containers, and Documents

The three core components of a BDB XML database are environments, containers, and documents. This chapter examines each from the `dbxml` shell as well as the Python API's `XmlManager` class. Other languages are covered in later chapters, but each API translates fairly easily from the examples provided here. This chapter presents the concepts with an overview of their capability, rather than a complete explanation of their operation. Consider it a look at various pieces of functionality, touching on the physical concepts and many of the programming classes used when working with BDB XML.

Environments

An environment is Berkeley DB's way of managing the database memory cache, locking, and features such as transactions and logging. At its simplest, an environment is simply the location (the directory) at which your database files are stored. Note that environments are not specific to BDB XML but are also used by the underlying DB system. Thus, the information presented here is common to both BDB XML installations, as well as non-XML Berkeley DB applications.

■**Tip** Because BDB XML uses the same underlying DB format as regular Berkeley DB databases, an environment can hold both XML and non-XML containers.

When databases are stored on disk, their location is typically an environment. A single environment can contain zero to many databases, and many environments can exist on a single file system. The accessing program or API sets the configuration for each environment. This is an important difference between networked and embedded databases. Whereas a networked database maintains configuration and data such as access permissions at the database server (and usually using a database for that information), embedded databases require that the program itself maintain most of this data. (DB environments can contain a configuration file, discussed later.) Because the application is directly opening the database files, no layer exists to enforce configuration or access rules. The result is less overhead (with one less layer), but also less at-the-ready functionality.

■**Tip** It's possible to create environments and containers in memory, which never get written to disk (other than being paged there by virtual memory management). In fact, this is the default for environments from the `dbxml` shell.

Creating and Opening Environments

A DB environment can be created implicitly, as with most of the examples thus far. However, only by creating an environment explicitly can you use transactional and other advanced features. The -c option to the dbxml command-line tool will create a database environment in the directory specified by -h:

```
$ dbxml -c -h myenv/
dbxml> quit
$ ls myenv/
```

```
__db.001    __db.002
```

Notice that the directory is populated with database files (we won't go into detail on the function of these files). As demonstrated in Chapter 4, "Getting Started," you can also use the -t option to enable transactions for a given shell session.

Creating an environment using the BDB XML API enables more options. It is done using the DBEnv (or DbEnv) class, which gets imported with the dbxml package.

```
from bsddb3.db import *
from dbxml import *

environment = DBEnv()
environment.open("myenv",
    DB_CREATE|DB_INIT_LOCK|DB_INIT_LOG|DB_INIT_MPOOL|
    DB_INIT_TXN|DB_RECOVER, 0)
environment.close(0)
```

After the environment object is constructed, its open method is called, with the first parameter the environment's directory path, the second a series of flags (these are bitwise or'd together), and the last a Unix file mode, ignored on Windows and with a default of readable and writable by owner and group, specified by 0. The environment is then closed, which can be done explicitly as shown or by letting the XmlManager class do this automatically.

An incomplete list of flags with their meanings is shown in Table 5-1.

Table 5-1. *Abbreviated List of Environment Open Flags*

Flag	Description
DB_CREATE	Creates the environment if it doesn't already exist
DB_INIT_LOCK	Initializes the locking subsystem, used with concurrent reads and writes
DB_INIT_LOG	Initializes the logging subsystem, used for database recovery
DB_INIT_MPOOL	Initializes the memory pool subsystem, providing a cache required for multithreaded applications
DB_INIT_TXN	Initializes the transaction subsystem, permitting recovery in case of an error condition within a transaction
DB_RECOVER	Initializes recovery, ensuring that the database files agree with the database logs

Similar flags are passed to many of BDB XML's methods and constructors to modify their behavior. They are covered fully in the API chapters (Chapters 8 through 12) as well as the API reference in Appendix B, "BDB XML API Reference."

An opened environment object can then be passed to the `XmlManager` constructor:

```
manager = XmlManager(environment, 0)
```

The second argument (0) indicates no flags for the constructed `XmlManager` object. Possible flags include `DBXML_ALLOW_EXTERNAL_ACCESS` to permit XQuery queries to access data sources external to a container (network or disk files), and `DBXML_ALLOW_AUTO_OPEN` to automatically open and close unopened containers when an XQuery requires it. As with the environment `open()` method, these flags are bitwise ord when used as a constructor argument.

■**Note** Some language APIs implement slightly different usages with the flags. For example, the Java API uses configuration objects in place of flags for all options.

Additional Environment Configuration

In addition to those already mentioned, the `DBEnv` class provides methods for configuring and manipulating environments. These methods include `dbremove()` for deleting databases and `dbrename()` for moving them.

The `DBEnv` method `set_flags()` provides a long list of flags for manipulation of the environments behavior, many specific to debugging and fine performance tuning. These flags can also be stored in a configuration file called `DB_CONFIG` within the environment directory. In this case, a single configuration line begins with `set_flags`, followed by a single flag parameter. For example, to cause an environment to automatically remove log files that are no longer needed (not necessarily the best practice), add this line to the `DB_CONFIG` file:

```
set_flags DB_LOG_AUTOREMOVE
```

Flags set in the configuration file will silently overrule application configuration. For this reason, its a good idea to set flags in the configuration file when you want them enforced for the environment because setting flags with the `set_flags()` method typically affects only that environment handle or object instance. Table 5-2 shows an abbreviated list of settable flags.

Table 5-2. *Abbreviated List of Environment Set Flags*

Flag	Description
`DB_CDB_ALLDB`	Forces DB applications to perform environment-wide locking, rather than per-database locking
`DB_DSYNC_LOG`	Flushes writes to the log files before returning from log write calls
`DB_LOG_AUTOREMOVE`	Removes log files that are no longer in use

Other `set_*` methods enable you to change an environments cache size, set error callbacks and error message prefixes, and configure locking timeouts. Lastly, `DBEnv` has some informational methods to get the home directory for the environment, retrieve the flags used to open the environment, and print environment statistics. (Complete lists of these methods and their uses are found in Appendix B.)

BDB XML includes several command-line utilities (in `install/bin` for Unix builds) that take an environment path as their argument. The `-h` option is standard for specifying the environment (or home directory) path to all of these. For example, the `db_archive` utility outputs the filenames of any logs that are no longer in use by the environment:

```
$ db_archive -h myenv/
```

The resulting list of files can then be moved to backup media or deleted without interfering with the operation of the databases in that environment.

■**Caution** Permanently deleting log files not in use (as opposed to moving them to a restorable location) will usually make catastrophic recovery (in which the database itself is lost instead of just corrupted) impossible.

For a full reference of command-line utilities and their uses, see Chapter 13, "Managing Databases."

Containers

A BDB XML database is a container, which is a single file on disk that contains all documents within that database, as well as any indexes or metadata. Containers are created within a database environment (as files are created within directories). In previous chapters, in which containers were created in the absence of an explicit environment, the `XmlManager` object itself created a rudimentary environment for the storage of that container.

Containers do not themselves have or maintain any configuration data that does not correspond to the documents they contain. That is, any database settings that concern rules such as file locking or performance settings such as cache behavior are *not* part of containers, so you shouldn't look for them here. All such options are set at the environment to which a container belongs.

One more relationship between environments and containers warrants mention: stand-alone containers are portable which means that you can copy the file itself to another location and still use it and all its indexes, assuming that you didn't copy it in midwrite but contain no historical or transactional data. Thus, if you have not configured an environment with logging and transactions, recovery in case of database corruption will not be possible. A database's portability is a nice benefit of an embedded database, but keep in mind that the environment supplies everything that is not definable as "live data."

Creating and Opening Containers

Containers are easily created by using the `dbxml` shell, as previously demonstrated:

```
dbxml> createContainer synsets.dbxml
```

```
Creating document storage container with nodes indexed
```

This example creates the container file, `synsets.dbxml`, and opens it for operation. The API is almost identical:

```
manager = XmlManager(environment, 0)
container = manager.createContainer("synsets.dbxml")
```

The `createContainer()` method has multiple optional parameters, including a transaction object and a series of container flags. The following example creates a new container and sets a validation flag, causing XML documents subsequently loaded to be validated if they refer to a DTD or XML Schema:

```
container = manager.createContainer("synsets.dbxml", DBXML_ALLOW_VALIDATION)
```

Other common flags to create containers include `DB_RDONLY` to open a container in read-only mode (in which attempted writes will fail) and `DBXML_TRANSACTIONAL` to enable transaction support for the container.

Existing containers can be opened within the dbxml shell using the `openContainer` command:

```
dbxml> openContainer synsets.dbxml
```

The Python API's `openContainer()` method has the same format as `closeContainer()`:

```
container = manager.openContainer("synsets.dbxml")
```

The flags for `openContainer()` are the same as those for `createContainer()`. In fact, the methods are the same, with `createContainer()` always enforcing the `DB_CREATE` and `DB_EXCL` flags, which create the database if it doesn't exist and throw an error if it does, respectively. Thus, containers can be created using `openContainer()` and these flags. A complete list is found in the API chapters. A third `XmlManager` method, `existsContainer()`, enables you to test for the existence of a container with a single argument: the name of the container.

Container Types

BDB XML supports two types of containers, each entailing a slightly different storage technique. The container type can be set only at the time a container is created because it affects how documents are stored in the container and how its documents are indexed.

Containers of type `Wholedoc` store XML documents exactly as they are given to the storage methods, retaining document white space. By contrast, `Node` containers process the document prior to storage and then store documents as individual nodes, with a single leaf node and all its attributes and attribute values. Thus `Node` containers are generally faster to query, but `Wholedoc` containers retrieve entire documents (as opposed to just nodes or values) more quickly because they don't have to reconstruct the document as with containers of type `Node`.

■**Note** `Wholedoc` containers are necessary when an application requires byte equivalence for its documents, for example, to retain checksums.

A good rule is to always use the `Node` type (the default) unless you expect to often retrieve entire XML documents or if your documents are small enough that the query advantage of `Node` containers is negligible. The `Wholedoc` type is intended to store and retrieve small documents; storing documents that approach or are greater than a megabyte using `Wholedoc` is discouraged, but in practice this will depend on your own application's needs, indexing strategy, and so on.

A container type can be set within the dbxml shell when creating a container using the argument after the container name:

```
dbxml> createContainer synsets.dbxml d
```

```
Creating document storage container
```

The d in this example forces the creation of a Wholedoc container; an n would force node storage and is the default. The same is done programmatically via the API with the createContainer() method with an argument after the flags:

```
container = manager.createContainer("synsets.dbxml", DBXML_ALLOW_VALIDATION,
XmlContainer.WholedocContainer)
```

Using the setDefaultContainerType() method of XmlManager, you can change the default container type and then omit it from the createContainer() call:

```
manager.setDefaultContainerType(XmlContainer.WholedocContainer)
container = manager.createContainer("synsets.dbxml")
```

An additional container flag warrants mention in the context of container types. Normally when using containers of type Node (again, the default and generally recommended), BDB XML indexes documents at the document level. This means that index lookups return a list of documents instead of the individual nodes. You can change this behavior using the DBXML_INDEX_NODES flag at container creation time (but not after). The result will be that index lookups return nodes instead of documents. This can be useful when dealing with large documents and needing to get node values to match a query. DBXML_INDEX_NODES is discussed in more detail in Chapter 6, "Indexes."

Some Container Operations

Most of the common BDB XML operations are performed with or on containers. Both createContainer() and openContainer() return objects of class XmlContainer. This class in turn provides methods for many operations on the container, including adding, updating, and deleting documents; adding and removing indexes; and retrieving documents after a database query. Most of these functions are also available in the dbxml shell.

Adding Documents to a Container

The XmlContainer class supplies the method putDocument() to simply add documents to the container. It is versatile in that documents can be strings, XmlDocuments, or input streams. This example adds a document with the name doc12 to the container by using a string:

```
container = manager.openContainer("test.dbxml")
container.putDocument('doc12', '<document id="12">test</document>',
manager.createUpdateContext())
```

Keep in mind that adding many documents before indexes have been created for a container will mean expensive indexing later. Before populating your container, be sure to read the next chapter and create indexes for your database.

Listing All Documents in a Container

To verify a container's contents, it can sometimes be useful to retrieve all documents in that container. Using the Python API, you can use the XmlManager.getAllDocuments() method. This will give a glimpse at working with query results, although we aren't supplying an actual query. This call returns an XmlResults object, which is BDB XML's interface for efficiently iterating results of a query.

```
container = manager.openContainer("synsets.dbxml")
results = container.getAllDocuments(0)
for value in results:
    document = value.asDocument()
    print document.getName()
```

This will output the name for each document in the container. The value here is of class XmlValue, which has a method asDocument() to retrieve the value as a document, returning an object of class XmlDocument. Alternatively, a value could be retrieved as a string or node if our results were from a query.

Performing Queries and Listing Results

The most common operation on containers is, of course, queries. Queries can be "prepared" as with most SQL implementations, or executed on the fly. Queries are executed by using the XmlManager object instead of a container object because they can include multiple (open) containers. This is why the collection() query prefix is used.

This example issues a query and outputs the number of results:

```
container = manager.openContainer("synsets.dbxml")
results = manager.query("collection('synsets.dbxml')/Synset/Word",
manager.createQueryContext())
print results.size()
```

Note the second argument to the query() method. Queries require a context, which provides data such as namespace mappings and variable bindings to the query processor. In this case, we have supplied a default query context. You can then iterate the results thus:

```
for value in results:
    print value.asString()
```

Alternatively, XmlResults objects have next(), previous(), and peek() methods to more efficiently browse query results one value at a time.

Tip XQuery allows for the notion of a default container, allowing a collection() without argument. This is set using the XmlQueryContext.setDefaultCollection function and is the most recently opened container when using the dbxml shell.

Tip The addAlias API method (or corresponding shell command) can be used to create aliases for your collections. This is useful when you have unwieldy paths to a collection and want to simplify your query expressions.

Documents

A single BDB XML document consists of a name, the content, and any metadata attributes that you associate with the document. Document names are the unique identifier for a record within a container and are indexed by default for all new containers.

BDB XML works with documents using the XmlDocument class. Under the hood, BDB XML uses the Xerces DOM to store and manipulate documents. This makes it possible to integrate with Xerces if you have need for a DOM interface to your documents.

■**Tip**   Many BDB XML applications do not necessarily regard the database as the authoritative location for the documents it contains. This is largely a matter of preference and architecture, but because the documents in the database have often been imported or created separately from the database, the documents are retained elsewhere and possibly accessed there by the applications. In such implementations, the database serves the primary function of indexing and querying—indeed, the purpose of a database. Keeping an external collection of XML documents has other benefits, including the ability to rebuild the database at will (although proper logging should make this an uncommon operation), the ability to allow regular changes to the document collection but batch write operations to the database, and so on.

Adding Documents

As was already demonstrated, documents can be added to containers using the XmlContainer.putDocument() method. When a document object is supplied as argument (as opposed to an XML string), the document creation looks like this:

```
document = manager.createDocument()
document.setName('doc13')
document.setContent("<document id='13'>test</document>")
container.putDocument(document, manager.createUpdateContext())
```

The document objects themselves also provide the means to be attached to data streams (using setContentAsXmlInputStream()) or to use a Xerces DOM object (with setContentAsDOM()). For example, to set a document's content using a file (and using an input stream, rather than just loading the file's contents manually):

```
inputFile = manager.createLocalFileInputStream("files/doc12.xml")
document.setContentAsXmlInputStream(input)
```

The API also provides streaming from memory, standard input, and URLs. The Java API provides an additional input stream to feed data from the application directly. Refer to the language-specific chapters for more information.

Retrieving a Document

As has been demonstrated, the XmlResults object returned from XmlManager.query() can iterate results supplied as XmlDocuments:

```
container = manager.openContainer("synsets.dbxml")
results = manager.query("collection('synsets.dbxml')/Synset/Word",
manager.createQueryContext())
for value in results:
    document = value.asDocument()
    print document.getName()
    print document.getContent()
```

You can also retrieve documents directly using their document name:

```
container = manager.openContainer("synsets.dbxml")
document = container.getDocument("doc12")
print document.getContent()
```

Database queries can access an individual document directly using the doc() query (as opposed to collection()), as with the following:

```
doc("synsets.dbxml/doc12")/Synset/Word
```

Or query for a document within a container by its name:

```
collection('synsets.dbxml')/*[dbxml:metadata('dbxml:name')='doc12']
```

Moreover, queries can be performed on individual documents or sets of documents returned from previous queries using the XmlValue and XmlResults classes. XmlValue encapsulates a primitive node's value (roughly equivalent to a node superclass in DOM implementations) and provides DOM-like methods for navigating a node's attributes and children. Queries are covered fully in Chapter 7, "XQuery with BDB XML," and working with documents after queries and with XmlValue is covered in later chapters.

Replacing Documents

Replacing a document within a container is simply a matter of setting its content with the setContent() method and then updating it in the container with the updateDocument() method:

```
container = manager.openContainer("synsets.dbxml")
document = container.getDocument("doc12")
document.setContent("<document id='12'>test again</document>")
container.updateDocument(document, manager.createUpdateContext())
```

Of course, the document's content can be set in other ways, as was already demonstrated with adding documents. Note that there is no performance advantage to using updateDocument() to replace a document as with this example; you might as well remove it and add a new document. Therefore, updateDocument will most often be used when parts of a document content or metadata are being updated and the rest retained.

Modifying Documents Programmatically

BDB XML provides its own class, XmlModify, for basic document manipulation. This is convenient when you want to modify documents in a container "in place" or reuse a series of modification steps across many documents, but not replace an entire document in the database. This operation uses several parameters, including an XmlQueryExpression (an object to store an XQuery string identifying the portion of the document to be modified), an object type identifier (to indicate the type of information being inserted; node, text, and so on), a name, and content. Then, depending on the XmlModify method called, a different change is affected to the document.

For example, the following will add a node to the previously replaced document:

```
container = manager.openContainer("synsets.dbxml")
modify = manager.createModify()
queryContext = manager.createQueryContext()
updateContext = manager.createUpdateContext()

query = manager.prepare("/document", queryContext)
name = "newchild"
content = "new content"
modify.addAppendStep(query, XmlModify::Element, name, content)
document = container.getDocument("doc12")
docValue = XmlValue(document)
modify.execute(docValue, queryContext, updateContext)
```

Note that multiple steps (including appending, removing, and renaming) could be added to the modify object. The execute() method can take an XmlResults object as argument, enabling you to pass an entire document result set. In this case, the modification steps would be performed against every document resulting from a given query.

Deleting Documents

Deleting a document from a container is straightforward using the XmlContainer deleteDocument() method, which takes either the document object or document name as argument:

```
container = manager.openContainer("synsets.dbxml")
updateContext = manager.createUpdateContext()
document = container.getDocument("doc12")
container.deleteDocument(document, updateContext)
```

The document name can also be used:

```
container.deleteDocument("doc12", updateContext)
```

Transactions

Note that most of the functions being demonstrated (and all of those that change containers) also accept an XmlTransaction object. They are *always* taken as the first argument to the method. Deleting a document within a transaction is as follows:

```
container = manager.openContainer("synsets.dbxml")
updateContext = manager.createUpdateContext()
transaction = manager.createTransaction()
container.deleteDocument(transaction, document, updateContext)
transaction.commit()
```

Of course, transactions are possible only on a container that has transactions enabled, as described in the "Creating and Opening Containers" section.

■**Note** When a container is opened transactionally, all modifications are transacted by BDB XML, even if you don't supply a transaction object.

Validation

If a container has the DBXML_ALLOW_VALIDATION flag set (see the section on creating containers), BDB XML will validate documents that contain a DTD or schema reference when documents are placed in a container. Simply place the declaration or association in the XML document, enable the validation container flag, and use the XmlContainer.putDocument() method with the document file or string.

Note that BDB XML does not continually enforce DTD or schema constraints on a document. That is, documents can be modified using XmlModify in such a way as to violate an associated DTD or schema without an error being reported.

Metadata

BDB XML enables arbitrary metadata to be associated with all documents in a container. The filenames themselves are a kind of metadata, created automatically when documents are inserted. Metadata is typically any information about a document that is not contained within that document. Metadata can be advantageously used with XML documents, because some data — particularly data that changes often, such as timestamps and authors — is cumbersome to update within an XML document, and often is better stored elsewhere. Chapter 4 demonstrated the use of metadata within the dbxml shell.

To add metadata to a document record, you use the XmlDocument.setMetaData() method. It takes as arguments a URI (optional to define a namespace for the field), an attribute name, and an attribute value (as an XmlValue) object. Because this is performed on document objects, it must be done before a document is placed in a container, or the document must be updated (if it was retrieved from the container) after metadata has been set.

This API example sets metadata for an existing document:

```
document = container.getDocument("doc12")
value = XmlValue("doc12")
document.setMetaData("http://www.brians.org/2005/", "author", value)
container.updateDocument(document, manager.createUpdateContext())
```

Metadata can then be indexed and queried as with data in XML documents and demonstrated in later chapters.

Note that XmlValue objects can be of many data types — including strings, dates, and decimals all based on the XQuery specification. Creating a metadata field as, for example, a date can be useful when indexing and querying those fields, allowing queries to recognize ordering of dates. This example shows how to create an XmlValue with a data type of DATE_TIME, which XQuery recognizes and can compare in queries:

```
document = container.getDocument("doc12")
value = XmlValue(XmlValue.DATE_TIME, "2006-01-02T21:24:25")
document.setMetaData("http://www.brians.org/2005/ ", "timestamp", value)
```

Note that the URL can be arbitrary, but is recommended. When issuing queries for metadata, the query context must map the namespace for the query to work:

```
queryContext = manager.createQueryContext()
queryContext.setNamespace("brians", "http://www.brians.org/2005/ ")
query = manager.prepare("/*dbxml:metadata('brians:timestamp')", queryContext)
```

Metadata is a powerful and efficient way to keep track of information about documents without storing that information within the documents. Indexing, querying, and working with metadata in the various language APIs are covered in later chapters.

Conclusion

Although later chapters detail the BDB XML API, much of this chapter dealt with the classes and objects used because they map generally to the physical pieces of the database. Figure 5-1 shows the relationship of the database components discussed.

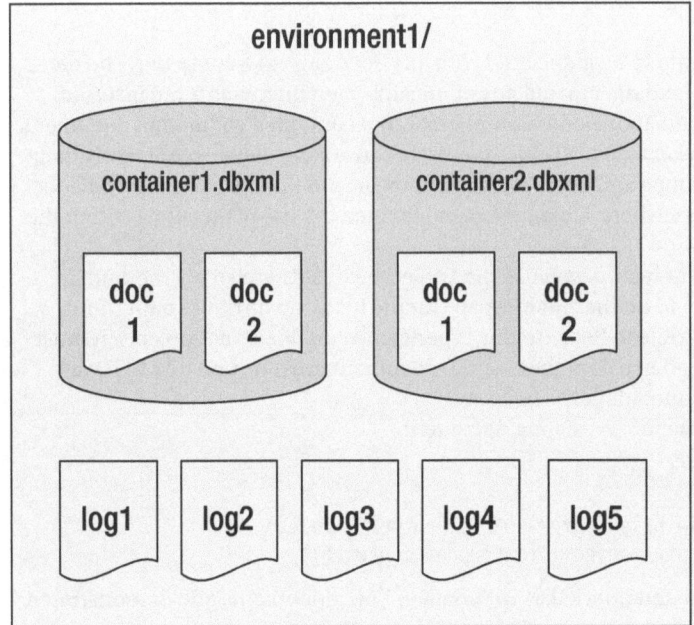

Figure 5-1. *Environments, containers, and documents*

Keep in mind the following key points:

Environments are the outermost piece of a Berkeley database, XML or otherwise (as with non-XML Berkeley DB databases). They are both analogous to and implemented as file directories; in Figure 5-1, environment1/ is a file directory. Although mostly optional, environments are helpful for configuring aspects of the database, and are critical to logging and recovery of data. Environments have their API expression in the DbEnv class, and do not contain functionality or options specific to BDB XML.

Containers are the databases themselves. They exist as files on the file system that are directly opened, read, and manipulated by BDB XMLs libraries. In Figure 5-1, the two listed containers container1.dbxml and container2.dbxml are actual files within the directory environment1/. Containers are managed via the API using the XmlContainer class and are created, opened, and otherwise manipulated with the XmlManager class. Containers are included in a database query, rather than executing queries on the container or container objects themselves. Thus, an XQuery to access container1.dbxml in Figure 5-1 would begin with collection("container1.dbxml")/ after the environment and container had been opened. Finally, a default collection can be set and subsequently excluded from the collection() function.

Documents are well-formed XML documents stored in containers; each can have arbitrary metadata associated with it. Documents can be created programmatically, expressed as a string, or loaded from a file or network stream, prior to placing them in a container. Each of the containers in Figure 5-1 contains two documents, doc1 and doc2, which are XML documents. Documents can be manipulated with regard to their container using the XmlContainer class. Documents have their API implementation in the XmlDocument class   in which name, content, and metadata can be gotten and set   before being written to a container using XmlContainer.putDocument or XmlContainer.updateDocument.

XmlManager is the primary class for working with BDB XML databases and is used to create (as a factory object) from scratch the most common objects for containers, documents, transactions, results, and update and query contexts. It is used to prepare and execute queries on open containers, providing context for those queries. It encapsulates a Berkeley DB environment and the open containers in that environment.

Many API operations   including retrieving query results and changing documents in the database   entail the use of "helper" BDB XML classes, including XmlResults and XmlModify. They do not have a physical correspondence to any part of a BDB XML database.

With an understanding of the basic complements of BDB XML, we next explore more exciting parts of the database: indexes and the queries that use them.

CHAPTER 6

■■■

Indexes

Indexes are a big reason why you use a database in the first place: to find data quickly. BDB XML uses XQuery as its query engine, making it one of the most flexible searches you will ever use. Database performance is only as good as the query expression and the indexes it uses. Of course, indexes are not necessary for queries to happen, but are required for a query to not have to process every document in the database to determine a match.

This chapter examines the options for indexing your XML and strategies for doing so. There is no "ideal index strategy" for all collections of XML documents, or even for a single collection of XML documents. The indexes you should create depend both on the data and the queries you plan to use, as well as the frequency with which they will be used. Understanding how BDB XML indexes your data will prepare you to build a database and maintain its high performance. After an explanation of indexes and methods for their creation, this chapter will cover an indexing strategy for the sample XML data presented earlier in the book.

Creating and Manipulating Indexes

Indexes can be created or deleted on a container at any time, enabling you to change your indexing strategy at will. However, the time to index a container is proportional to the number and size of documents it contains because each document must be processed. Take some time to run some tests using a small container, trying different indexes, before fully populating containers with all the data you intend to use. If you work with actual XML files that you are importing, it is easy because you can quickly repopulate the database.

Note Indexes do not follow external references within XML documents, such as entities or DTDs. Within indexes, such references are removed from character data, and internal entity references are replaced with text. This is important when constructing queries because trying to match such elements will fail. Additionally, CDATA sections are expanded prior to indexing, and where character data is mixed with child data, the character data is concatenated.

Indexes can be created using the dbxml shell or the APIs. Using the API makes the index creation more easily duplicated, of course. After an index is created for a container, that index gets updated each time a document it touches is added, changed, or deleted. This does add overhead to the insertion and change of documents (more indexes means slower writes), but because the process is incremental (as opposed to indexing an already-populated container), it is preferable to not have to change indexes often once a container is populated. When you do perform expensive updates to a container's indexes, keep in mind that read access to those containers will be slow, and write access will be unavailable. For this reason, manipulating indexes is something best performed with offline databases.

■**Note** In my own deployments I do not need immediate writes to live containers. Instead, my "live" containers are read-only copies, and any writes are executed on a separate logging environment. Any index changes are performed there before the container is copied to the live location each night, permitting expensive modifications without container downtime.

Indexes cost disk space, of course. The increase varies greatly depending on the size of a container and the number of documents a given index will "touch."

Indexes are specified on element nodes, attribute nodes, or document metadata. There are different ways of going about this, but you need to decide which parts of your documents you want indexed. Each index has an index type, which determines how the nodes will be indexed, whether they should be unique, the data type they are expected to contain, and the types of operations for which they will be used.

BDB XML also supports default indexes, which enable an index to exist for all nodes of a container's documents that are not otherwise indexed.

Index Nodes

To create an index, BDB XML needs to be told what part of a document to index. This is done using the name of whatever data is being used   an element, an attribute, or metadata. An *edge* where two nodes meet can also be used (as explained in the following section). Either way, the value of each named node or edge of nodes (or metadata) is stored in the resulting index, making the retrieval of the value efficient. Of course, in previous examples we instead retrieved the entire document from the database.

Index Types

Many options are available when creating BDB XML indexes. They are both read and specified with a string of index options. A single index description consists of four and sometimes five pieces of information: uniqueness, a path type, a node type, a key type, and a syntax type. Specified as a string, the options are delimited with a hyphen.

```
[uniqueness]-{path type}-{node type}-{key type}-{syntax type}
```

Here's an example:

```
unique-node-metadata-equality-string
```

This is supplied to the addIndex command in the dbxml shell, or to the XmlContainer.addIndex() method. We'll look at doing this differently using the XmlIndexSpecification class a bit later. First, let's look at the different index options.

■**Note** The order of options in an index string is actually unimportant. The examples in this book stick to the format described for clarity.

Uniqueness

Uniqueness is an optional setting that causes an index to expect unique values for the indexed nodes. If duplicate values are encountered during index creation, an error will be thrown. Also, when a document is changed or inserted that contains a duplicate value for an indexed node, the change will fail. No uniqueness is enforced within indexes (or, of course, documents) by default.

Path Types

When BDB XML indexes documents, either at index creation time or document insertion/change time, it parses the document and looks for a node that matches the supplied node to index. Two types of *paths* are supported to specify this index node. The first is simply the node/attribute/metadata name, which is called the node path type. The second, the edge path type, recognizes the intersection of two nodes, making it more specific.

Recall that more than one `<Word/>` element could exist with our sample XML data because a single record represents synonyms:

```
<Synset fileVersion="1.0" pos="n">
  <Id>2323</Id>
  <WnOffset version="2.1" pos="n">00466621</WnOffset>
  <LexFileNum>04</LexFileNum>
  <SsType>n</SsType>
  <Word lexId="0">baseball</Word>
  <Word lexId="0">baseball game</Word>
  <Gloss>a ball game played with a bat and ball between two teams of nine players...
</Gloss>
  <SearchKeys>
    <Word>ballgame</Word>
  </SearchKeys>
</Synset>
```

By specifying a node index for Word, this file would have three entries in the resulting index: one for baseball, one for baseball game, and yet another for the `<Word/>` element with parent `<SearchKeys/>`, "ballgame". This is the case with an index of either type node or edge; the difference between these types concerns the work needed by the query optimizer to find the intended node. A node index only knows that each of these nodes is called Word and does not keep track of its context. Given a query for /Synset/Word, BDB XML would look up each Word node and then have to examine the parent node of each to satisfy /Synset. If our document had only one Word node, this wouldn't be an issue. But given the fact that we have three, an edge index would help the processing speed for this query. An edge index stores the parent of the target node as part of the index entry. If our /Synset/Word query had the benefit of an edge index on Word, the one index lookup would be enough to tell the query processor which node we are looking for, without having to examine all three.

Path types enable you to tell BDB XML which type of node indexing you prefer. What you prefer depends on the XML being used and the queries you intend to write. The node path type is preferable when you expect no disparate elements of the same name scattered throughout your document. In the previous example, the node path type needed to look up three index entries for that to happen. Where you don't anticipate this overlap, node path types are preferable.

The edge path type enables you to contain more information within the index. It is preferable when you have nodes of the same name in multiple contexts and want the query to benefit from knowing the parent of your indexed node.

Node Types

The next index option, the `node` type, has three possible values: `element`, `attribute`, or `metadata`. As it happens, this specifies the kind of node to be indexed. Elements and attributes correspond here to their XML definitions.

```
<Synset fileVersion="1.0" pos="n">
  <Id>2323</Id>
  <WnOffset version="2.1" pos="n">00466621</WnOffset>
  <Word lexId="0">baseball</Word>
  <Word lexId="0">baseball game</Word>
  ...
</Synset>
```

In our examples, `Word` is an element, and `fileVersion` is an attribute. Note that BDB XML does not index other DOM node types, such as comments. `CDATA` blocks are treated as text within the enclosing element (just as with their output in an XML transformation) and are indexed the same as any other element text.

The third node type, `metadata`, allows indexing of custom document attributes. When creating indexes for metadata, you will supply the URI and name for the metadata field (demonstrated later). Because there are no edges involved with them, only the `node` path type is recognized for use with metadata.

Key Types

An index's key type optimizes the index for a certain type of query test. Different pieces of an XQuery expression can require different information about a given node. Does it exist? Does it have a given value? Does it contain a certain string? The `equality`, `presence`, and `substring` key types enable the index to be tuned for such specific tests.

When queries test a node for equality with a known value   whether string, numeric, or otherwise   the index should have the key type `equality`.

When queries test a node for existence in a document, the `presence` key type is best. Note that the nodes within an XPath or XQuery statement that specify the parents of a target are not equality tests that need indexes. That is, given the following query, the only index that is needed is for node `Hypernym` with a `presence` key type:

```
collection("synsets.dbxml")/Synset/Pointers/Hypernym
```

Indexes are not needed for the query to determine `Synset` or `Pointers` nodes, and they will not aid in response time.

The substring key type benefits queries that match the contents of a value, such as when using the XQuery contains() function. The substring indexes require more disk space than other types and can be relatively expensive. Note, too, that substring indexes are not used with queries that do not use named nodes, such as those that use a current node (.) without context or with wildcards, for example.

The equality, presence, or substring string is supplied as the third (if uniqueness is not used) or fourth (if uniqueness is used) option in the index string.

Syntax Types

The last option for creation of an index is its *syntax type*, which is a data type that indicates to BDB XML the content and format of values to expect from the indexed nodes. Consider that different comparisons and function operations yield different results (and have different implementations) depending on the data type of the query or arguments; a date will be compared to another date with date-specific conversions, a decimal added to a decimal yields a decimal, and so on. Of course, if the key type is presence (as opposed to equality or substring), there is no data type because the values are not stored at all.

A complete list of syntax types is shown in Table 6-1.

Table 6-1. *BDB XML Index Syntax Types*

None	gDay
anyURI	gMonth
base64Binary	gYear
boolean	gYearMonth
date	hexBinary
dateTime	NOTATION
dayTimeDuration	QName
decimal	string
double	time
duration	yearMonthDuration
float	untypedAtomic

Each syntax type is equivalent to an enumerated type within the XmlValue class. The syntax type chosen will, of course, depend on the type of values stored in the indexed nodes.

Managing Indexes

Indexes can be added to or deleted from a container at any time. Again, keep in mind that index changes on large containers can be expensive.

Adding Indexes

Once you have decided on an index type, you can add it via the dbxml shell by using the described index option descriptions or programmatically via the API using either the string descriptions or enumerated types. Within the shell, the addIndex command takes an optional namespace URI (if the node being indexed has a namespace), the node name, and the index description string.

If we want to index the sample synset XMLs <Word/> element (which contains all words for that synonym set), we could do it via the shell, like this:

```
dbxml> addIndex "" Word node-element-equality-string
```

```
Adding index type: node-element-equality-string to node: {}:Word
```

Note that the namespace is blank because our XML is not using namespaces, and our index option string is node-element-equality-string. Word is the name of the element to be indexed. node indicates that we want node path indexing, rather than edges (because the element will only occur in one place within our XML); element that Word is an element (as opposed to attribute or metadata); equality that we anticipate this index to be used for equality queries for Word; string because <Word/> will always contains string data.

The same index could be added programmatically using the same index option string using the API.

```
from bsddb3.db import *
from dbxml import *
mgr = XmlManager()
uc = mgr.createUpdateContext()
container = mgr.createContainer("test.dbxml")
container.addIndex("", "Word", "node-element-equality-string", uc)
```

In this case, the arguments to the addIndex() method are the same as the shell, with the addition of the XmlUpdateContext object. Note that multiple indexes can be created at once within the API by providing multiple index option strings, space delimited:

```
container.addIndex("", "Word", "node-element-equality-string node-element-presence-none", uc)
```

▪Note If you're wondering how the BDB XML API handles exceptions with method calls like those being demonstrated, please refer to the API chapters because each language interface does this differently.

The XmlIndexSpecification class provides an object view of all indexes on a container, for times when making many index changes at once might be preferable to manipulating indexes one at a time.

An XmlIndexSpecification object is returned from the XmlContainer.getIndexSpecification method:

```
indexspec = container.getIndexSpecification()
```

The resulting handle can then be used to specify a series of index changes before updating the specification back to the container. For example, to add two indexes to the container, including the already-applied Word index, use the following:

```
container = manager.openContainer("synsets.dbxml")
uc = manager.createUpdateContext()
indexspec = container.getIndexSpecification()
indexspec.addIndex("", "Word", "node-element-equality-string")
indexspec.addIndex("", "Id", "node-element-equality-string")
container.setIndexSpecification(indexspec, uc)
```

The XmlIndexSpecification class also supplies methods for deleting and replacing existing indexes so a specification can be used to make mass updates to a container. Of course, given the knowledge that creation of a single index on a populated container can be expensive, keep in mind that the same operation performed several times will be more so. However, containers are reindexed only once with a call to setIndexSpecification(), regardless of the number of indexes being changed.

Listing Indexes

Listing a container's existing indexes is a simple matter using the shell's listIndex command, as demonstrated in Chapter 5, "Environments, Containers, and Documents."

```
dbxml> listIndexes
```

```
Index: node-element-equality-string for node {}:Word
Index: unique-node-metadata-equality-string for node
{http://www.sleepycat.com/2002/dbxml}:name
2 indexes found.
```

In this case, the Word node index exists, along with the default document name index. Listing indexes programmatically uses the XmlIndexSpecification class to iterate the indexes.

```
indexspec = container.getIndexSpecification()
for index in container.getIndexSpecification():
    print "%s (%s): %s" % (index.get_name(), index.get_uri(), index.get_index())
```

This outputs the following:

```
Word (): node-element-equality-string
name (http://www.sleepycat.com/2002/dbxml): unique-node-metadata-equality-string
```

Again, different language APIs supply this listing in slightly different ways.

Deleting and Replacing Indexes

Indexes are deleted from containers by using the delIndex command in the shell, by using the XmlContainer.deleteIndex() method, or by manipulating an XmlIndexSpecification object. Each needs a URI, a name, and an index specification. They are needed to identify an index uniquely because multiple indexes can exist for a single node.

From the shell:

```
dbxml> delIndex "" Word node-element-equality-string
```

```
Deleting index type: node-element-equality-string from node: {}:Word
```

With an XmlContainer object using the index option string:

```
container = manager.openContainer("synsets.dbxml")
uc = manager.createUpdateContext()
container.deleteIndex("", "Word", "node-element-equality-string", uc)
```

And finally, using the XmlIndexSpecification, deleting two indexes at once:

```
container = manager.openContainer("synsets.dbxml")
uc = manager.createUpdateContext()
indexspec = container.getIndexSpecification()
indexspec.deleteIndex("", "Word", "node-element-equality-string")
indexspec.deleteIndex("", "Id", "node-element-equality-string")
container.setIndexSpecification(indexspec, uc)
```

Note that the same XmlIndexSpecification object can be used to add, delete, and also replace indexes. This example uses the replaceIndex() method to change the Word node to a substring index:

```
indexspec = container.getIndexSpecification()
indexspec.replaceIndex("", "Word", "node-element-substring-string")
container.setIndexSpecification(indexspec, uc)
```

As with adding and deleting indexes, the XmlContainer class offers a replaceIndex() method for convenience. (All index manipulation convenience methods use the getIndexSpecification() and setIndexSpecification() "under the covers.")

Default Indexes

BDB XML provides for a special index strategy to be supplied for all nodes within a container that are not otherwise indexed. Default indexes can be created for a single node type, element, attribute, and metadata. They can enhance performance for unplanned queries or queries that touch unindexed nodes.

Default indexes for a container are created and deleted by using either the dbxml shell or via the API using the XmlIndexSpecification class or the XmlContainer convenience methods. The addIndex and delIndex shell commands operate on the default indexes when no URI or node name is supplied:

```
dbxml> addIndex node-element-equality-string
```

```
Adding default index type: node-element-equality-string
```

From the API, the XmlContainer.addDefaultIndex() and XmlContainer.deleteDefaultIndex() methods can be used, as well as the XmlIndexSpecification's addDefaultIndex() and deleteDefaultIndex() methods. Here, too, many operations could be performed with an XmlIndexSpecification object, completely replacing both default and individual node indexes for a container.

Index Strategies

An *index strategy* is the index type combined with the syntax type, as indicated by the index option strings. Although Chapter 7, "XQuery with BDB XML," will make clear how indexes will benefit certain types of queries, its worth looking at a complete example set of index strategies. In this example, we will build an index specification using the Python API.

Recall the sample XML data used to populate the synsets.dbxml container. A single (abbreviated) document reads as follows:

```
<Synset fileVersion="1.0" pos="n">
  <Id>2323</Id>
  <WnOffset version="2.1" pos="n">00466621</WnOffset>
  <LexFileNum>04</LexFileNum>
  <SsType>n</SsType>
```

```
<Word lexId="0">baseball</Word>
<Word lexId="0">baseball game</Word>
<Pointers>
  <Hypernym>2322</Hypernym>
  <DomainMember type="category">2322</DomainMember>
  <Hyponym>2324</Hyponym>
  <Hyponym>2325</Hyponym>
  <Hyponym>3655</Hyponym>
  <DomainMember type="category">91752</DomainMember>
</Pointers>
<Gloss>a ball game played with a bat and ball between two teams of nine players
...</Gloss>
</Synset>
```

Each document has an Id, Words, a Gloss entry defining it, and a Pointers section containing various children that in turn refer to other documents• Id value, as well as other miscellaneous information. You already saw indexes created for the Word and Id elements. Because we•ll need to look up the record for a given word, and because no <Word/> element exists elsewhere in our documents, we create the Word as an element node equality index with string syntax. If we anticipated having to do partial text matches on Words, we could create a substring index for Word as well. We don•t anticipate presence tests for Word elements, because every one of our documents contains at least one. For now, the one index will do. Our specification starts as follows:

```
from bsddb3.db import *
from dbxml import *

environment = DBEnv()
environment.open("myenv2", DB_CREATE|DB_INIT_LOCK|DB_INIT_LOG|DB_INIT_MPOOL|DB_INIT_TXN,
0)
manager = XmlManager(environment, 0)
container = manager.openContainer("synsets.dbxml")
indexspec = container.getIndexSpecification()
uc = manager.createUpdateContext()

indexspec = container.getIndexSpecification()
indexspec.addIndex("", "Word", "node-element-equality-string")
```

Next, we•ll add an index for the Id elements. Because the pointers in every document use this ID to reference one another, they will be queried in many contexts, as demonstrated in Chapter 7. They occur in only one place in our document, so we don•t need edge indexes. When creating the XML files, we incremented the assigned IDs for each record and need subsequent IDs to be unique. Additionally, we anticipate only equality lookups, not presence or substring. We don•t require numeric operations on these IDs, so we use a syntax of string.

```
indexspec.addIndex("", "Id", "unique-node-element-equality-string")
```

For Gloss, we do anticipate substring lookups to find keywords within the definition texts. The most common of them are queries that use the XPath contains() function:

```
collection("synsets.dbxml")/Synset[contains(Gloss, "baseball")]/Id
```

Although these Gloss queries might be infrequent, performing such a search without an index would be enormously expensive. We add a substring index to Gloss nodes:

```
indexspec.addIndex("", "Gloss", "node-element-substring-string")
```

Lookups on the various children of the Pointer element are frequent because in this example they indicate relation data including what "kind of thing" baseball is, what records are "kinds of baseball", and so on. For example, knowing that the Id for the "sport, athletics" record is "2582", we could query for the kinds of sports:

```
collection("synsets.dbxml")/Synset[Pointers/Hypernym="2582"]
```

(We could instead just list the hyponyms listed in the document named "2582", but as you'll see later, we don't necessarily retain the bidirectional pointers for our records, making this a safer query.)

We need an equality index for each pointer type. Here, too, these element names occur in only one location:

```
indexspec.addIndex("", "Hypernym", "node-element-equality-string")
indexspec.addIndex("", "Hyponym", "node-element-equality-string")
indexspec.addIndex("", "DomainMember", "node-element-equality-string")
```

In the case of the DomainMember element, an attribute type indicates additional required data. For this and for the pos ("part-of-speech") attribute of the Synset element, we add attribute indexes. In this case, the WnOffset element also has a pos attribute, and although the type attribute does not occur elsewhere, it's a common enough attribute name to warrant an edge index:

```
indexspec.addIndex("", "type", "edge-attribute-equality-string")
indexspec.addIndex("", "pos", "edge-attribute-equality-string")
```

Finally, we create a default index for all nonindexed data to allow unplanned queries and apply the strategies to our container:

```
indexspec.addDefaultIndex("node-element-equality-string")
container.setIndexSpecification(indexspec, uc)
```

Note For the curious, this particular container with no indexes is about 127 MB in size (sizes aren't necessarily consistent across deployments). The listed indexes, minus the Gloss substring index, add approximately 92 MB to the container size. The Gloss substring index alone adds another 85 MB for a container totaling 304 MB.

At this point, if we ran the listIndexes command with the container opened in the dbxml shell, we'd see this:

```
dbxml> listIndexes
Default Index: node-element-equality-string
Index: node-element-equality-string for node {}:DomainMember
Index: edge-attribute-equality-string for node {}:DomainMember/@type
Index: node-element-substring-string for node {}:Gloss
Index: node-element-equality-string for node {}:Hypernym
Index: node-element-equality-string for node {}:Hyponym
Index: unique-node-element-equality-string for node {}:Id
Index: edge-attribute-equality-string for node {}:Synset/@pos
Index: node-element-equality-string for node {}:Word
Index: unique-node-metadata-equality-string for node
{http://www.sleepycat.com/2002/dbxml}:name
10 indexes found.
```

Query Plans

BDB XML provides a convenient tool to determine the effectiveness of index strategies. Each time an XQuery is processed via the shell as well as the API XmlManager.prepare() and XmlManager.query(), a plan is constructed for the tests that any available indexes will satisfy. (In the case of prepare(), the query plan is generated once and can be reused; with query(), the query plan is discarded after the query is performed.) BDB XML allows this plan to be output as an XML document itself, enabling you to determine whether your queries are using the available indexes as intended and then modify strategies accordingly.

■**Caution** The syntax of a query plan as output by the dbxml shell is subject to change and not completely documented anywhere other than in the BDB XML source code.

Query plans are examined using the dbxml shell's queryPlan command. It has the same syntax and argument as the query command, but does not execute the supplied query. It instead outputs the aforementioned XML description of the query plan BDB XML will use to satisfy the search. Continuing with the example from the previous section, imagine that I wanted to execute the following query to find any Synset records with Word element values of the word "hand":

```
collection("synsets.dbxml")/Synset[Word = "hand"]
```

Instead of using the query command, I'll use queryPlan via the shell to output the query processor's plan:

```
dbxml> queryPlan '
collection("synsets.dbxml")/Synset[Word = "hand"]
'
```

This outputs the following:

```
<XQuery>
  <Navigation>
    <QueryPlanFunction result="collection" container="synsets.dbxml">
      <OQPlan>n(V(node-element-equality-string,Word,=,'hand'),P(node-element-equality-
string,prefix,Synset))</OQPlan>
    </QueryPlanFunction>
    <Step axis="child" name="Synset" nodeType="element"/>
    <DbXmlFilter>
      <Navigation>
        <Step axis="child" name="Word" nodeType="element"/>
        <DbXmlCompare name="equal">
          <Sequence>
            <AnyAtomicTypeConstructor value="hand"
typeuri="http://www.w3.org/2001/XMLSchema" typename="string"/>
          </Sequence>
        </DbXmlCompare>
      </Navigation>
    </DbXmlFilter>
  </Navigation>
</XQuery>
```

The full plan XML contains a complete breakdown of the XQuery expression, further described in Chapter 7. Of note here is the <OQPlan/> element, which identifies the index, if any, that is used to satisfy the given part of the query expression. (The element name stands for Optimized Query Plan.) The whole string is included in the parenthesized string n(...), which indicates an intersection, and then two intersecting sets V(...) and P(...), each with indexes. The V indicates a value lookup; the P indicates a presence lookup. Here we can see that the Word index is being used for this value looking in our query expression, as we would expect.

Now suppose we changed our query to be for an Id element, and wrote it thus:

```
collection("synsets.dbxml")/Synset[Id = 2323]
```

Executing this query as shown will be very slow given the current indexes. Its query plan shows this OQPlan element:

```
<OQPlan>n(P(node-element-equality-string,prefix,Synset),P(unique-node-element-equality-string,prefix,Id))</OQPlan>
```

In this case, the query could not use the Id index to satisfy the query because our query's equals (=) comparison was numeric, but the Id index is of syntax string. (This is a basic example of how casting happens "under the hood" of BDB XML.) For this reason, the query plan shows two presence lookups, but no index being used for a value lookup. Our query has to process every document in the previous set and compare the supplied value with each. The proper query would have been this:

```
collection("synsets.dbxml")/Synset[Id = "2323"]
```

It yields a query plan OQPlan of this:

```
<OQPlan>n(V(node-element-equality-string,Id,=,'2323'),P(node-element-equality-string,prefix,Synset))</OQPlan>
```

Here we can see that the Id index is being used in a V set for a value lookup. Our query will also be very fast, a good indicator that the indexes are satisfying the query in the way we intend.

Examining query plans can be useful for understanding how BDB XML translates a query into index lookups and helps to make your index selection and query construction more effective. Chapter 7 will examine XQuery and include more details on examining and optimizing indexing strategies.

Conclusion

I demonstrated a rudimentary and entirely inflexible XML indexing solution in Chapter 2, "The Power of an Embedded XML Database." In this chapter, you saw a robust and comprehensive indexer for XML. It's important to keep in mind that XML is the reason why such a powerful indexing solution is possible: being already-organized data, the database can concern itself purely with indexing and querying instead of the minutiae of rows and columns, and data organization enforced by the database itself. Being XML, the same query language works for both documents and collections of documents. The BDB XML index options make for flexibility in how you query collections to allow for optimal performance.

In Chapter 7, we'll exploit these indexes to build powerful queries that involve multiple databases, identify relationships between many documents, and even output results to look any way we want them to.

CHAPTER 7

■ ■ ■

XQuery with BDB XML

XQuery is a unique query language, providing all the XML referencing power of XPath with a complete miniature scripting language. It allows modular coding and importing, mathematical operations, function definitions, results post-processing, and even reshaping and outputting of new XML. Applied to BDB XML, a single XQuery expression can query many containers (or documents) simultaneously, performing set operations on multiple data sources. With the BDB XML indexes powering the query processor, XQuery makes possible some impressive searches with huge collections of XML data.

Simply put, XQuery 1.0 is to XML what SQL is to relational database (RDB) tables: it is used to get information out of XML-formatted data. The language represents something of a coming of age for XML, with support in all major database engines (IBM, Oracle, Microsoft) and a mature W3C recommendation on its way to becoming a standard. XQuery is built on existing XML technologies, including XPath and XML Schema, making it immediately familiar to most XML users, with additional features making it sophisticated enough for complex query processing.

Appendix A, "XML Essentials," looks at XPath 1.0 and explains the fundamentals of paths, predicates, and functions. XPath 2.0 and XQuery share these basics and are supersets of the functionality thus far described. This chapter will explain XQuery basics, presuming XML and XPath knowledge on the part of the reader. XQuery is a topic on which entire books could be (and have been) written, and its details are out of the scope of this one. Nonetheless, this chapter will provide a thorough look at its core functionality. More information is available from the resources listed at the end of the chapter, and Appendix C, "XQuery Reference," contains a reference for the language's operators and functions.

Trying XQuery

All good development software enables quick experimentation, as with the BDB XML `dbxml` shell utility. The tool provides an -s option that allows a file containing a script to be provided as argument. This script needs to provide the same commands and syntax as the shell in interactive mode, meaning a query will take this form:

```
query 'expression'
```

The `print` command is then necessary to see the query's result.

The XQuery distribution used by and included with BDB XML 2.2.x also provides a command-line tool `eval` found in the directory `xquery-1.x/examples/eval/` of the distribution. This tool permits execution of XQuery queries stored in files on disk, making it an excellent way to debug and experiment with XQuery. It takes an XQuery file as argument, along with a number of optional parameters. BDB XML 2.3 will see the XQuery implementation moved to a new project, XQilla, in which this tool is called xqilla. Many of the command-line options are the same; the options for both are shown in Table 7-1, with options added by xqilla identified with an asterisk (*).

Table 7-1. *Options for the* eval/xqilla *XQuery Utility*

Option	Description
-q	Quiet mode, suppresses output
-n	Runs the query a provided number of times
-i	Loads the provided XML file and binds it as the context item for the query
-b	Sets the base Uniform Resource Identifier (URI) for the context
-o	Writes the result to the specified file
-d	Enables remote debugging on the specified host:port
-p	Parses in XPath 2 mode, as opposed to the default XQuery*
-P	Parses in XPath 1.0 compatibility mode, as opposed to the default XQuery*
-t	Outputs an XML representation of the syntax tree*

All the XQuery examples in this section can be loaded as shown into an XQuery file or executed using the dbxml shell (provided as a query argument). Of course, where collection() is used within queries to refer to a BDB XML container, only the dbxml shell will yield the expected results.

Two Integrated Device Electronics (IDEs) are worth mentioning in the context of BDB XML and XQuery. First, Stylus Studio is a visual editor for XML, XSL, XQuery, and XML Schema that includes integration for several databases, including BDB XML. This allows a BDB XML collection to be queried using XQuery written and debugged within the editor.

Another offering, <oXygen/>, provides a similar editor environment with support for XML diffs and merges, schemas, XSLT 1.0 and 2.0, and so on. It permits execution against BDB XML containers, environment configuration from within the IDE, as well as monitoring of debugging messages to view query plans.

Depending on your preference, there are many options to learning and using XQuery with BDB XML. After queries (and your XQuery knowledge) are refined, you'll likely either copy them into your own BDB XML application or save them as XQuery files that your application (or another query) can then load and process.

Sample Data

Throughout this chapter, the XQuery examples shown apply to a file or a collection of files similar to the <person/> data used in Appendix A, and the Wordnet data used in Chapter 2, "The Power of an Embedded XML Database," Chapter 4, "Getting Started," and Chapter 6, "Indexes." An example of our person data for a container people.dbxml is shown in Listing 7-1.

Listing 7-1. *Sample XML Data for the Container* people.dbxml

```
<person id="6641">
    <name>
        <last>Brown</last>
        <first>Jim</first>
        <middle>Austin</middle>
        <nick>Big</nick>
    </name>
```

```
        <age>24</age>
        <phone>
            <office>612-555-0091</office>
            <home/>
        </phone>
        <street> Attn: Jim Brown
                 Pleax Systems, Inc.
                 18520 25ᵗʰ Ave
        </street>
        <city>Minneapolis</city>
        <state>MN</state>
        <sex>male</sex>
        <hobby>boats</hobby>
        <hobby>carpentry</hobby>
</person>
```

Listing 7-2 contains an example of the Wordnet synset data; they are basically dictionary entries with numeric pointers to other entries for relationships such as " this is a kind of X" and "Y is a part of this". Further knowledge on this format is not necessary for understanding the examples in this chapter.

Listing 7-2. *Sample XML Data for the* synsets.dbxml *Container*

```
<Synset fileVersion="1.0" pos="n">
    <Id>14861</Id>
    <WnOffset version="2.1" pos="n">02772480</WnOffset>
    <LexFileNum>06</LexFileNum>
    <SsType>n</SsType>
    <Word lexId="0">baseball</Word>
    <Pointers>
        <Hypernym>14746</Hypernym>
        <Hypernym>14866</Hypernym>
    </Pointers>
    <Gloss>a ball used in playing baseball</Gloss>
</Synset>
```

We•ll be basing the example queries in this chapter on these two samples, so feel free to refer to them often.

XPath

The first thing to know about XQuery is that virtually all XPath 1.0 expressions are valid XQuery expressions, depending slightly on the implementation. The same path syntax and usage (step selections, predicates, operators, functions) are available within XQuery.

Thus, the following XPath expression will execute without trouble, assuming that the processor knows what the context node is. (Context nodes here are what the query processor sees as the "current" node within the document, making queries relative to that node.)

```
/person[@id="6641"]/name/first
```

Other programs have different ways to bind the context node. Within the dbxml shell, you can make the query "absolute" by using the doc() function:

```
doc('file:./person.xml')/person[@id='6641']/name/first
```

> **■Tip** You can also use the `contextQuery` command within the `dbxml` shell to set the context to a query's results.

Within XQuery, the same path selection syntax is used when addressing particular nodes and constructing predicates for their selection. The major difference between XPath 1.0 and 2.0 is the addition of new functions, including `doc()` and `collection()`, a complete set of data types based on XML Schema, sequence expressions, and some of the functional clauses explained later. As an example, the following XPath 2.0 expression evaluated against our `<person/>` XML will output each child element of `<name/>` using the `for` and `return` clauses:

```
for $name in (doc("file:./person.xml")/person[@id="6641"]/name/*)
return $name
```

This is equivalent to the following, which is more straightforward:

```
doc("file:./person.xml")/person[@id="6641"]/name/*
```

The use of the `for` clause to iterate the results of the path selection makes it easy to expand the query to include conditionals, additional iteration, and more advanced functionality, as you•ll see.

Expressions

Every piece of an XQuery expression evaluates to a value, including the path expressions just discussed. Thus, the following is valid XQuery:

```
2+2
```

```
4
```

To see this, type `q '2+2'` right into the `dbxml` shell, followed by `print`. Individual function calls are legal as well.

```
upper-case("test string")
```

```
TEST STRING
```

Nearly all expressions can be nested in XQuery, as with this predicate:

```
doc("file:./person.xml")/person[@id="6641"]/name/*[2+2]
```

This makes for simplified debugging and testing of larger examples because they can often be broken down and evaluated in smaller parts. There are many types of expressions in XQuery, from this simple arithmetic to complex sequence comparisons and logic computations.

> **■Note** As with other XML technologies such as XPath and XSLT, XQuery is a "zero-side-effect" language, although this may change with a future version. At the present time, XQuery does not provide a means of changing XML or otherwise updating its data sources unless user-created functions are called within XQuery to accomplish the same. XQuery is a declarative language.

Knowing the value of a given expression is helpful for understanding how it affects its context within XQuery because expressions as simple as comparisons can yield different results depending on the values and their data types. BDB XML does not use XML Schema type information associated with given XML within queries; nonetheless, types defined for data and casted values within queries can yield varying results when used in comparisons and other processing. For example, an XQuery comparison such as equality (eq) will yield a true result when equal values of the same data type are compared or when equal untyped values are compared, and will yield false with the same conditions when the values are not equal. An error results when two values of incompatible types are compared, however. A section later in this chapter discusses data types at more length, but note that evaluating small expressions within the dbxml shell will quickly give you an idea of what you can expect to result from such expressions.

Expressions in XQuery can and usually do span multiple lines, as we've seen. They might themselves contain XML. This expression evaluates to true:

```
string(<test>Hello</test>) eq "Hello"
```

Seeing XML inside XQuery is a bit "trippy" for newcomers used to the compact syntax of XPath. As you can imagine, it plays a bit part in allowing XQuery to reshape results by itself returning XML, as seen in Listing 7-3.

Listing 7-3. *Reshaping Results*

```
for $name in (doc("file:./person.xml")/person[@id="6641"]/name/*)
return <name>{$name/string()}</name>
```

```
<name>Brown</name>
<name>Jim</name>
<name>Austin</name>
<name>Big</name>
```

Of course, this is BDB XML, and working within a single XML document is a constraint we don't have. So to accomplish something similar, we'll use collection() in our expression in Listing 7-4.

Listing 7-4. *Querying Document Collections*

```
for $name in (collection("people.dbxml")/person[@id="6641"]/name/*)
return <name>{$name/string()}</name>
```

We'll delve deeper into XQuery's main clauses later.

Sequences

Those familiar with XPath 1.0 will take note of the variable assignment in the previous section as storing a node set. In XQuery, what was a node set is now a *sequence*, which is much more powerful. Sequences within XQuery are constructed with parentheses:

```
(1, 2, "B", <test/>)
```

Formally speaking, a sequence is an ordered sequence of one or more items, where items are usually (but not necessarily) values. A sequence can contain values of any data type including nodes, and expressions and functions may accept and return sequences themselves. Sequences are never nested; a sequence within a sequence is seen by XQuery as a flattened list. This permits otherwise cumbersome operations to be made quite simple; for example, a general comparison of sequences:

```
(1, 4, 8) < (1, 4, 7)
```

This general less-than (<) comparison determines whether any values in the left sequence are less than any value in the right sequence, evaluating to true in this case.

In truth, every XQuery expression evaluates to a sequence, even though that sequence often contains a single item. Sequences are especially useful when it comes time to perform set operations. You•ll see some examples later in this chapter.

A Complete Example

Listing 7-5 contains a complete XQuery example that demonstrates many of the language•s core features, which I will dissect it into its component parts.

Listing 7-5. *A Complete XQuery Example*

```
declare namespace people = "urn:something";
declare variable $name as xs:string external;
declare function people:age-ok($age) {
    if (21 < $age and $age < 100)
        then true()
        else false()
};
(: Here is a comment. :)
<people>
    {
    for $person in collection("people.dbxml")/person
    where people:age-ok($person/age/number()) and $person/name/*/string() = $name
    order by $person/name/last
    return
    <person>
        <name>{$person/name/*}</name>
        <age>{$person/age/string()}</age>
    </person>
    }
</people>
```

This example queries for every <person/> in our people.dbxml container with an age value between 21 and 100 that has at least one name equal to the value of $name, has an external variable supplied by the processor (set in the dbxml shell using the setVariable command), and returns the results as an XML document with document node <people/>. Of course, such a query could be written many ways, but here we want to look at the various parts of such an example. The result of this query follows:

```
<people>
    <person>
        <name>
            <last>Brown</last>
            <first>Jim</first>
            <middle>Austin</middle>
            <nick>Big</nick>
```

```
        </name>
        <age>24</age>
    </person>
</people>
```

Everything prior to the comment (surrounded by a parenthesis and colon) in this example is the XQuery *prolog*. The prolog is optional, and is used to declare global and external variables, declare namespaces, import external modules, and declare modules. The rest of the example comprises the query *body*, which is evaluated to produce the query result.

The expressions within the body will ring some bells for SQL users, given the presence of the where clause, establishing query criteria for what functions like an SQL SELECT statement. Of course, the entire path selection on people.dbxml could have been written using a predicate expression:

```
...
for $person in collection("people.dbxml")/person[people:age-ok(age/number() and name/* eq
    $name]
...
```

Breaking it up as in Listing 7-5 makes the expression more readable and maintainable because additional logic could be added to for example make parts of our query criteria conditional. Suppose that we expected $name to be given a value by our application prior to evaluating the query, but want to accommodate cases in which no such parameter exists. Because XQuery expressions might be nested, even a where clause can be made conditional. As you'd expect, the where expression evaluates to true and false for the criteria it precedes. This makes putting an if conditional after where a simple matter:

```
...
for $person in collection("people.dbxml")/person
    where if (empty($name)) then true() else $person/name/*/string() = $name
...
```

Of course, we want this query to select records that both match $name and meet the age range requirement:

```
...
for $person in collection("people.dbxml")/person
    where if (empty($name)) then true() else $person/name/*/string() = $name
    and people:age-ok($person/age/number())
...
```

And that's not even doing sorting! We'll get to that shortly. Don't worry if this real world example is confusing; we'll back up momentarily and break things apart a bit more in the following sections. But first let's consider a more complex query example this time using the <Synset/> files stored in synsets.dbxml. Recall that each record has a word or words, and also a short definition for the record stored in <Gloss/>. Imagine that we wanted to get the <Id/> of every record that has a pointer of any kind to any other record named "baseball"; perhaps we're hoping that the result set will be a good smattering of all things baseball. (SQL programmers will recognize this as a join operation.) We'd need the <Id/> of each baseball record first and then use it in the predicate of the pointer query. We do this in Listing 7-6 using a straight path expression.

Listing 7-6. *Performing a "Join" with a Pure Path Expression*

```
collection("synsets.dbxml")/Synset[Pointers/Hypernym =
    collection("synsets.dbxml")/Synset[Word="baseball"]/Id/string()]/Id
```

But that will only take us so far, particularly when we start performing set operations on these results. Listing 7-7 shows the more intelligible XQuery version.

Listing 7-7. *A "Join" with XQuery*

```
for $baseball in collection("synsets.dbxml")/Synset[Word="baseball"]/Id,
    $synset in collection("synsets.dbxml")/Synset
where $synset/Pointers/Hypernym = $baseball/Id
return $synset/Id
```

There are other ways this query could be written, but not all will take adequate advantage of BDB XML's indexes. In Listing 7-7, the query processor is required to retrieve all matches to both path expressions in our for clause before performing the comparisons. We'd be better off depending on our indexing strategy to store our "baseball IDs" in a sequence using XQuery's let clause before using it in a where clause to perform our select, as evidenced in Listing 7-8.

Listing 7-8. *Storing and Reusing a Sequence*

```
let $baseballs := collection("synsets.dbxml")/Synset[Word="baseball"]/Id
for $synset in collection("synsets.dbxml")/Synset
    where $synset/Pointers/Hypernym = $baseballs
return $synset/Id
```

Later in this chapter we'll discuss tips for building queries to use indexing strategies and for building queries to best use indexing strategies. We'll now look more closely at these clauses themselves.

FLWOR Expressions

FLWOR (pronounced "flower") stands for the five main clauses in XQuery: for, let, where, order by, and return. These clauses make many expressions simpler, but their main purpose is to construct sequences that require processing beyond path expressions, such as joins, as well as to reorder items.

A FLWOR expression consists of one or more for clauses, one or more let clauses (for and let may occur in any order), optional where and order by clauses (in that order), and a return clause. Each of them is described in the following subsections.

for

The for clause brings in to scope one or more variables. In this way it is not unlike let, but acts iteratively, with the variable value changing for each item in a sequence. In this way it is analogous to the start of a code "block" in traditional programming languages and the keyword for is appropriate for this reason. Its syntax follows this pattern:

```
for $var in expression at $position, $var2 in expression2, ...
```

We already demonstrated the introduction of multiple variables in previous examples; the keyword at is used to add a position variable. This variable is then updated with each iteration, storing the respective variable's value location in the sequence. Variables brought into scope by for remain in scope the life of the query's evaluation; they only pass out of scope with the query itself, at which point, well, there really isn't any scope.

You can have many `for` clauses in a query, which is useful when a lot of iteration is needed to perform joins.

let

The `let` clause functions like `for` to introduce variables into scope, assigning to them values, but does so without iteration. The common use is to store values that are used repeatedly, such as the "baseball IDs" expression shown earlier. XQuery variables cannot be updated repeatedly within a single scope. The syntax is the following:

```
let $var := expression, $var2 := expression2, ...
```

Keep in mind that XQuery variables can store any XQuery data type, making them useful for storing results from expression, as well as user-supplied sequences with items of any data types. Variables introduced by `let` are available to all other expressions within the query; there is no "block scope" as with traditional programming languages.

Tip XQuery is smart about the identity of nodes. When an item in a sequence is a node, variables retain the absolute identity of that node. In other words, two variables both assigned a node of the same name and string value will not equate upon comparison because they are not the same node. Two variables each assigned the exact same node (in the same external document, at the same document location, and so on) equate as expected: `true`.

---

where

The `where` clause supplies a condition expression for the query. This expression is like any other in XQuery, except that rather than evaluating to a sequence, it is converted to a boolean value capable of use as a conditional. This makes possible conditional conditionals, in which `where` may be following with an `if` clause. Again, as a language with nested expressions, its easy to try individual parts of larger expressions in the `dbxml` shell to be certain of their result value.

The syntax for `where` is simply this:

```
where condition
```

Multiple conditions may be supplied by simply stringing multiple expressions together with `and`, and placing them after `where`. The functions `true()` and `false()` can be used where a condition expression needs to explicitly name the boolean. The `where` clause is nearly identical in function to a path predicate, acting as a filter for results.

order by

It wouldnt be a good query language without a versatile means of reordering results. The `order by` clause takes the query results (after being filtered with the `where` clause) and applies sorting using a supplied value and order. The syntax for `order by` is as follows:

```
order by key modifier, key2 modifier2, ...
```

The sort key is a variable or expression to be used for the sorting, and the modifier specifies a sort direction, `ascending` or `descending`. Several other modifiers are available (but not described here) to determine string sort orders and where empty values should occur in the sort. The keys with their modifiers are used in the order listed, of course.

return

This last clause of FLWOR builds the actual result returned from a query, after results are filtered and sorted. Keep in mind that `return` occurs only as the final clause in a query; as with the other FLWOR clauses, it is not allowed within expressions or even functions. The syntax is simply this:

```
return expression
```

You already saw examples of `return` that included XML to reshape results. Here again, remember that expressions themselves might contain XML, and the one provided to `return` is no different. The `return` expression can contain its own path selection, function calls, and comparisons.

■**Tip** XQuery processors maintain what is commonly referred to as a *tuple space* while processing expressions. This is essentially a matrix containing values and sequences each time a variable is introduced with `for` and `let`, filtered with the `where` clause, and sorted with `order by`. Understanding the tuple space is not critical to using XQuery, but it does provide insight into how XQuery processors compute sequence operations through the life of a query expression using FLWOR. Refer to the XQuery specification or other online XQuery resources for more information.

Data Types

We've talked a little about XQuery's data types being derived from XML Schema. We'll fill this out a bit more in this section, but please refer to XQuery and XML Schema documentation for a full explanation of types in XQuery. You can skip this discussion and still use XQuery with BDB XML to near full capacity, and then return to it when you begin having trouble with your data types.

■**Note** XML documents you add to BDB XML containers that have associated XML Schemas are validated only when the document is inserted into a container—and only then if validation is explicitly enabled. BDB XML does not retain this information and does not enforce the types thereafter. Within your XQuerys, you can make the schema's type declarations available using the `import schema` expression from a query's prolog.

Data types in XQuery belong to a type hierarchy. This inheritance tree determines in large part how operations see different values and what the results from operations will be. Every value in XQuery is a sequence of zero or more `items`, and `item` is the primitive XQuery data type (because sequence is not a data type). Because all values are a sequence, a single `item` is equivalent to a sequence containing that one item (singleton). The rest of XQuery's data types derive from `item`, but `item` is not a creatable data type (abstract). Figure 7-1 contains a tree of the common XQuery data types in their relationship to `item`. Note that all types are either types of nodes or atomic types because all descend from either `node` or `xdt:anyAtomicType`, which are also abstract.

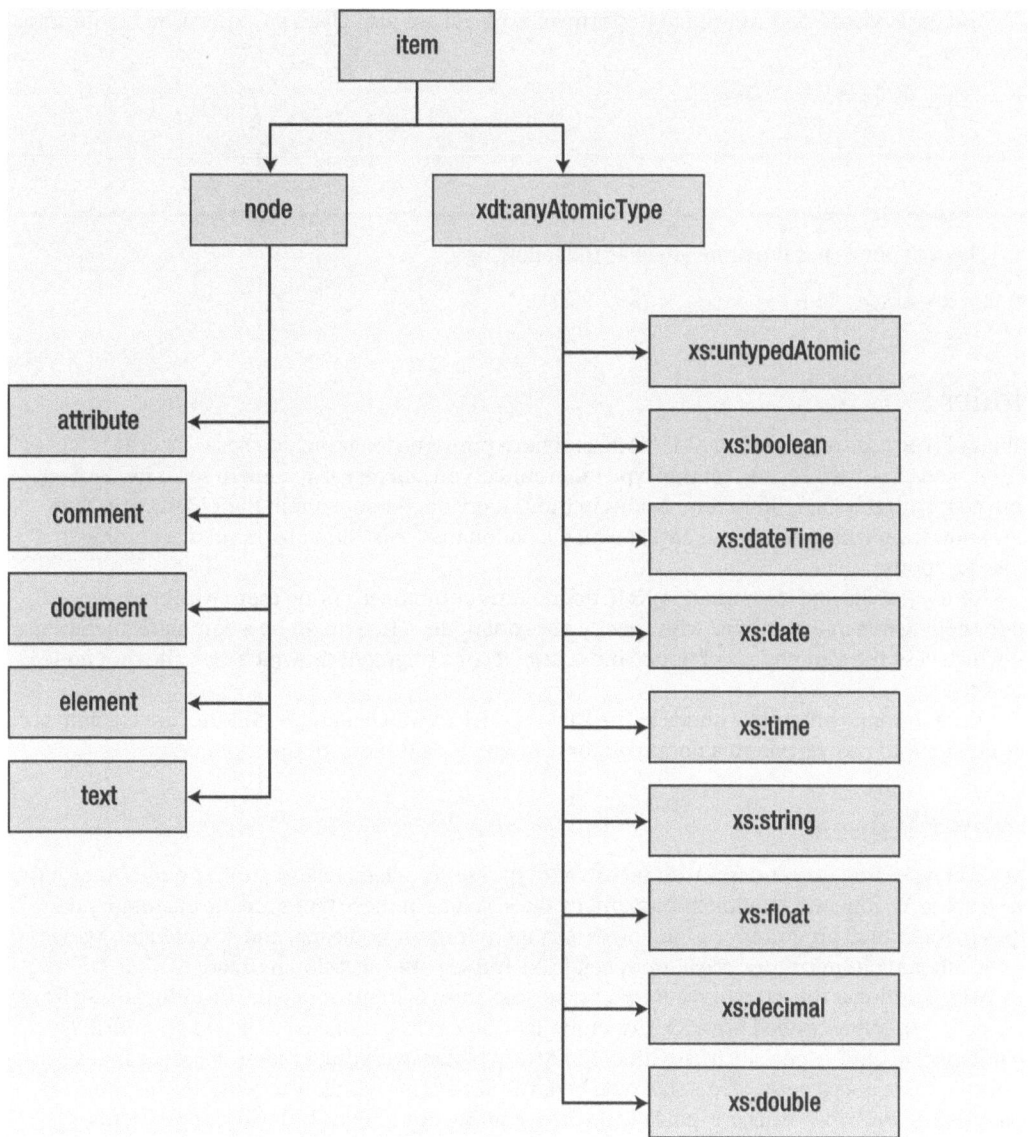

Figure 7-1. *Abbreviated XQuery data type tree*

XQuery data types can be cast into other data types using the function of the same name as the type. Thus, a document value can be cast as a string using string() and so on. Within a path expression (and when called with no arguments), these functions match the data type they represent (as with text() at the end of a path expression), or convert the paths value to the given data type (as string() at the end of a path expression). When necessary, the XQuery keyword castable as can be used to test an expression for "castability," given an expression before and a type after:

```
"person" castable as xs:integer
```

```
false
```

And the keyword `cast` as used to perform an explicit cast, also given an expression before and a type after:

```
<b>person</b> cast as xs:string
```

```
person
```

This, of course, has the same effect as the following:

```
string(<b>person</b>)
```

Nodes

Values of type `node` represent an XML node and have properties that include `node-name`, `attributes`, `parent`, and `children`. Because of this type inheritance, you can test any value to see if it's derived from `node` with the `node()` function. Nodes in the XQuery data model retain their identity in that they know from which document and at which location they exist, and are ordered according to those locations.

Nodes are selected from existing XML documents or by constructing them within a query. All nodes belong to a tree, each tree with exactly one root node. A tree might be a complete document (in which case the root node is of node kind `document`) or a fragment (in which case the root node is not a `document`).

Nodes operate not unlike nodes in the DOM model, in which a node's children are elements, comments, and text; its parent a document or element node (unless it's the root node).

Atomic Values

Values of types that descend from `xdt:anyAtomicType` are so called because, unlike nodes, they have no structure or inherent relationship to other values. Values of these types are the customary data types in traditional programming languages: strings, numbers, booleans, and so on. In all, XQuery has 50 different atomic types; most are specialized and see only occasional usage.

Worth noting is the `xdt:untypedAtomic` type, for values with no data type, including those from untyped XML. Values pulled from XML documents   unless a `node` or cast as a `string`   are likely to be untyped. (This is especially true with BDB XML, in which everything that isn't cast or indexed as a specific value is `untypedAtomic`.) This type behaves like `string` with few exceptions, resulting in behavior you probably expect (especially if you're coming from XPath 1.0) without problems.

Boolean values are expressed with the `true()` and `false()` functions, as has been demonstrated.

Navigation

Appendix A describes XPath 1.0 path expressions at length; they remain compatible in XQuery, and I won't expound much on what is there. In XQuery, as with XPath 1.0, a path consists of steps similar to a file directory expression. Each step depends on the previous step for its context, and defines an axis or direction. The `@` is a shortcut for the `attribute` axis, `..` for `parent`, `.` for `self`, and empty for the most-common `child` axis.

The only substantial differences with path expressions in XQuery (aside from the XQuery expressions allowed in predicates [ ]) are as follows:

Unlike XPath 1.0, namespaces and variables in XQuery are often defined within the query, as opposed to outside of it.

XQuery expressions can declare user functions and call them inside path expressions.

XQuery provides many navigation functions, including `collection()` and `doc()`, which occur regularly in path expressions.

XQuery adds several ways to establish context for a path; for example XPath 1.0 had `position()` and `last()`, XQuery adds `current-date()` and `base-uri()` to the list.

See Appendix C for a list of navigation functions and context functions in XQuery.

Tip Because XQuery allows grouping of expressions using parentheses, predicates can be applied to larger queries to apply predicates to a nested expression:

```
(collection("synsets.dbxml")/Synset[Word="baseball"])[1]
```

Comparisons

XQuery has a wide range of operators and functions, many providing similar functionality for different data types. For example, XQuery provides XPath 1.0's comparison operators (<, >, =, and so on), but calls them *general comparison operators*. The earlier section on sequences showed how these operators behave with multi-item sequences, in which any item in the sequences on each side of the operator can satisfy the test. This can have the unexpected result of the following expression evaluating to `true`:

```
(2, 5) = (2, 3)
```

Because the left sequence has an item (2) equal to an item in the right sequence (2), the expression is true.

As with XQuery's many data types, several other comparisons are necessary to achieve the desired result. *Value comparisons* use the letter notations (`lt`, `gt`, `eq`, and so on) to perform straight value tests, as with the following that evaluates to `false`:

```
5 lt 3
```

These comparisons work for strings and other types as you'd expect, but do not work for sequences of more than one item (nonsingleton sequences).

Note String comparisons in XQuery are implementation-specific and use an XQuery "collation" that can be modified. This is typically the Unicode code point collation, as is the case with BDB XML.

Several other comparisons are available in XQuery, including the `is` operator to compare nodes. This example evaluates to `true`:

```
let $team := doc("file:./person.xml")
return $team is doc("file:./person.xml")
```

Recall the discussion about nodes retaining their identity? The following expression is `false`:

```
<person/> is <person/>
```

This is because XQuery constructs the node on each side of the operator, making them different nodes by definition. The is comparison operator returns true only when the same node, in the same file, at the same location, is being compared to itself. For this reason, it can be useful for locating a point at which two sequences "intersect," as demonstrated in Listing 7-9.

Listing 7-9. *Navigating to a Node via Two Expressions*

```
for $person in collection("people.dbxml")//person[name/first = "Jim"]
for $known in collection("people.dbxml")//person[name/last = "Brown"]
where $person is $known
return $person
```

■**Tip** Although not an operator, XQuery's deep-equal() function allows for the comparison of entire sequences as well as XML trees.

User Functions

User-defined functions are declared in a query's prolog or imported as part of a separate module. They use the following syntax:

```
declare function funcname ( parameters ) { expression };
```

Functions can also be defined to cast the function's result and to declare a function as "external" and supplied by the implementation. The parameter definition contains both typed and untyped variables that are made available to the scope of the function. They are typed using the as keyword, and the list is separated with a comma. Functions can include a namespace (BDB XML requires one). They cannot override built-in functions, and they cannot declare optional parameters or accept a variable number of parameters (overloaded). A simple example of a user-defined function is given in Listing 7-10.

Listing 7-10. *A Simple User-Defined Function*

```
declare namespace my = "http://brians.org/temperature";
declare function my:celsius-to-fahrenheit ($celsius as xs:decimal) as xs:decimal {
    ($celsius + 32) * (9 div 5)
};
my:celsius-to-fahrenheit(15)
```

84.6

User-defined functions can be anything allowed in a standard query body (including FLWOR expressions) as long as the declarations are proper. The evaluated value of a function given parameters is the result value for a function call, making it a convenient way to organize, test, and debug code.

Modules

User-defined functions would be more useful if they could be imported as modules, as is the case. In truth, the query expressions we have examined thus far comprise a *main module* as the XQuery engine sees things; additional modules that are loaded are *library modules*. They get loaded via the import module expression; most imports follow this form:

```
import module namespace at location;
```

The module itself has a module declaration of the following form:

```
module namespace namespace = uri;
```

As an example, if I had saved the example from the previous section into a file temperature.xqm, I would have the code contained in Listing 7-11.

Listing 7-11. *A Simple Library Module*

```
module namespace temp = "http://brians.org/temperature";
declare function temp:celsius-to-fahrenheit ($celsius as xs:decimal) {
    ($celsius + 32) * (9 div 5)
};
```

I could import it into the main module and call it as shown in Listing 7-12.

Listing 7-12. *Importing a Library Module and Calling One of Its Functions*

```
import module namespace temp = "http://brians.org/temperature" at "temperature.xqm";
temp:celsius-to-fahrenheit(10)
```

75.6

Some XQuery Tricks

The word *tricks* implies techniques that are obscure, which these are not. However, for a newcomer to XQuery (especially one familiar with SQL, XPath, or XSLT), the ease and power of many operations with XQuery is refreshing. No, it isn't *always* the case that an XQuery implementation is simpler than its SQL counterpart, but this is XML we're working with. The following are some useful examples for getting results with XQuery.

Iteration vs. Filtering

XQuery makes easy many queries that are not possible with path expressions, even though the operation seems a simple one. Consider the case in which we want to select from our people.dbxml record all persons with phone numbers in the 612 area code. We're tempted to use this query:

```
collection("people.dbxml")/person[starts-with(phone, "612")]
```

However, this query will fail unless the path expression before our predicate yields only one result, which it clearly does not. This is because the starts-with() function (as well as contains() and matches())accepts only singleton arguments, not sequences of more than one item. Note that this is true of many operators and functions in XQuery. In such a case, FLWOR provides the solution (see Listing 7-13).

Listing 7-13. *Supplying a* where *Clause to Filter Results*

```
for $person in collection("people.dbxml")/person
where starts-with($person/phone, "612")
return $person
```

Not so fast. Of course, starts-with() again gets a first argument of a multi-item sequence because our people.dbxml records tend to have multiple phone numbers. One more iteration could do the trick, as evidenced in Listing 7-14.

Listing 7-14. *Two Iterations*

```
for $person in collection("people.dbxml")/person
for $phone in $person/phone
where starts-with($phone, "612")
return $person
```

We have thus created a "join" operation. Of course, this type of iteration is not always desirable because this returns the <person/> document each time it finds a match, which in this case is twice when both phone numbers start with "612".

The key to this query lays in the XQuery every and some condition keywords, which both begin a quantifier expression that evaluates to true. They are often placed after the FLWOR where clause to qualify filtered results beyond a single expression. The some quantifier takes this form:

```
some $variable in expression1 satisfies expression2
```

The variable (or variables) in the statement functions as introduced for the scope of both expressions, the first providing its value or iteration values (as with for ... in); the second expression determining whether the expression will evaluate to true or false. The some operator causes the conditional to be true of any iterations of the variable that satisfy the condition expression; every evaluates to true only if all iterations satisfy the expression. Listing 7-15 gives us the proper query.

Listing 7-15. *Using a* some ... in ... satisfies *Conditional*

```
for $person in collection("people.dbxml")/person
where some $phone in $person/phone satisfies (starts-with($phone, "612"))
return $person
```

Regular Expressions

In the previous section, the starts-with() function was used to match an area code in a string. Although this function is retained in XQuery for compatibility with XPath 1.0, XQuery's matches() function is the desired replacement and offers the power of regular expression matching to the language. The equivalent example using matches() retains the variable as the first argument, with the second the "612" string matched to the start of the string with the ^ anchor, as seen in Listing 7-16.

■**Note** BDB XML does not currently optimize matches(), meaning you should only use it on small queries that do not need the benefit of indexes. The contains() function is optimized to use substring indexes, however.

Listing 7-16. *Using Regular Expressions to Match an Area Code*

```
for $person in collection("people.dbxml")/person
where some $phone in $person/phone satisfies (matches($phone, "^612"))
return $person
```

Of course, more-sophisticated queries using regular expressions could also include a determination of whether a phone number actually has an area code (versus "612" being the prefix of a seven-digit number):

```
matches("612-3321", "^612-\\d{3}-\\d{4}$")
```

```
false
```

Regular expression can permit several different delineating characters besides the hyphen.

```
matches("612.423.1124", "^612[-\\.]\d{3}[-\\.]\\d{4}$")
```

```
true
```

Tip For many queries to run in the dbxml shell, characters need escaping for the query processor to see them. This includes the backslashes in the pattern matching quotes, which need to be written as double backslashes (\\) because of the layers of interpolation before the expression is interpreted.

And variables can be inserted into a query; remember that the variables content is here used as part of the regular expression. An example is given in Listing 7-17.

Listing 7-17. *Using a Dynamic Regular Expression to Match an Area Code and Phone Number*

```
let $areacode := "612"
let $match := concat("^", $areacode, "[-\\.]\\d{3}[-\\.]\\d{4}$")
return matches("612.423.1124", $match)
```

```
true
```

Querying for Metadata

BDB XML exposes document metadata attributes via the dbxml:metadata() function, making it easy to include metadata queries in your expressions. This function takes the metadata attribute name as argument, allowing comparisons as shown in Listing 7-18, retrieving by document name.

Listing 7-18. *Query Using a Document's Name as BDB XML Metadata*

```
for $document in collection("people.dbxml")/*
where $document[dbxml:metadata("dbxml:name") = "person1"]
return $document
```

Because BDB XML enables metadata attributes of any supported type, these comparisons can include anything from `dateTime` timestamps to price `decimal` data, allowing some complex range time and price queries, respectively.

Querying Multiple Data Sources

Comparing RDBs to XML data sources can be difficult, especially when dealing with BDB XML containers or multiple containers. Operations such as joins can happen within a single XML file, in which we could compare certain elements, groups of elements, and even XML fragments to RDB tables. But BDB XML containers are not properly analogous to tables; if a parallel is to be drawn, it would be to an RDB in its entirety. Thus, the equivalent of querying and processing data from multiple containers and documents could be performing set operations across many RDBs at once. Luckily, we won't be doing that.

Querying multiple containers or documents in a single XQuery expression is as simple as placing the input functions in our path expressions wherever we want them. Listing 7-19 shows an example of this.

Listing 7-19. *Querying Multiple Data Sources as a Join*

```
for $x in collection("people.dbxml")/person/name/first
for $y in collection("synsets.dbxml")/Synset/Word
where contains($y, $x)
return (string($x), "=>", string($y))
```

XQuery has a unary (|) or set union operator for computing the union between sets. Among its uses within expressions is to allow the same path expression to be tested against different containers.

```
(collection("people.dbxml") | collection("synsets.dbxml"))/person[name/first = "Jim"]
```

Because everything in XQuery is an expression, containers as well as stand-alone documents both on disk and on the network can be involved in queries using both techniques.

Recursion

Recursion is the capability of a function to call itself. With hierarchical data, recursion is a common means to repeatedly call a method to drill down with each invocation. Those familiar with XSLT are typically (and sometimes grossly) versed in the art of recursion because XSLT does not allow variables to be assigned values more than once. This prevents a variable from being used to cumulatively update a value toward the end of a total. Recursion is equally useful in XQuery because variables are assigned values only once.

Recall the `synset.dbxml` container? It holds XML documents representing synsets—similar to dictionary entries—from the Wordnet database. This data is interesting primarily because each record contains "pointers" a la foreign keys to other records, effectively telling us what things are "kinds" of other things. (A "banana" is a "fruit" is a "plant," and so on.) A recursive function is ideal for stepping up this kind of hierarchy. We're going to do this using the "banana" record, in fact, which is shown in Listing 7-20.

Listing 7-20. *The synset XML file for "banana". Stand.*

```
<Synset fileVersion="1.0" pos="n">
    <Id>41886</Id>
    <WnOffset version="2.1" pos="n">07647890</WnOffset>
```

```
<LexFileNum>13</LexFileNum>
<SsType>n</SsType>
<Word lexId="0">banana</Word>
<Pointers>
    <Hypernym>41581</Hypernym>
    <Meronym type="component">65855</Meronym>
    <Meronym type="component">65852</Meronym>
</Pointers>
<Gloss>elongated crescent-shaped yellow fruit with soft sweet flesh</Gloss>
</Synset>
```

More of this data can be ignored for our purposes; we'll focus on the /Synset/Pointers/Hypernym value, which is a "kind of" pointer to the record /Synset[Id = 41581]. That document will in turn have a <Hypernym/> element, pointing to another document, and so on until the top of this lexicon is reached. We want a function that will take the document itself as argument and give us a nicely printed list of this entry's "hypernym tree." We'll call the function hypernyms (it is defined in Listing 7-21).

Listing 7-21. *Recursively Processing Pointers Between Records*

```
declare namespace my = "http://brians.org/synsets";
declare function my:hypernyms ($synset) {
    let $hyp := $synset/Pointers/Hypernym[1]/string()
    return
        if (empty($hyp))
        then ($synset/Word)[1]/string()
        else
            let $next := my:hypernyms(collection("synsets.dbxml")/Synset[Id = $hyp])
            return concat($next, " => ", $synset/Word[1])
};
my:hypernyms((collection("synsets.dbxml")/Synset[Word="banana"])[1])
```

```
entity => physical entity => substance => solid => food => produce => edible fruit => banana
```

Notice the liberal use of the numeric predicates ([1]) throughout this example; they are to avoid errors during comparisons and functions in which a singleton is required. If we filled this example out a bit more, we'd iterate the values in those expressions to end up with more interesting output. But for this example, using only the first value in each sequence sufficed.

This next (academic?) example uses a recursive function to convert a decimal value into a string representation of its binary equivalent. Listing 7-22 shows an example of this.

Listing 7-22. *Converting Decimal to Binary Using a Recursive Function*

```
declare namespace my = "http://brians.org/temperature";
declare function my:binary ($dec as xs:decimal) {
    if ($dec eq 0 or $dec eq 1)
    then $dec
    else
        let $m := xs:integer($dec div 2)
        let $j := $dec mod 2
        let $D := my:binary($m)
        return concat(string($D), string($j))
};
```

```
my:binary(46)
```

```
101110
```

Well, you never know.

Reshaping Results

You've already seen how XQuery lets you output XML. You can do this with inline XML elements or you can use XQuery's constructors to build individual node types in XQuery variables. In Listing 7-23, we'll modify the example from Listing 7-21 to use the node constructors element and attribute to build XML containing the actual hierarchy represented in the record pointers.

Listing 7-23. *Building XML to Mirror a Conceptual Hierarchy*

```
declare namespace my = "http://brians.org/synsets";
declare function my:steps ($synset) as element() {
    let $hyp := $synset/Pointers/Hypernym[1]/string()
    return
        if (empty($hyp))
        then element step { attribute name {($synset/Word)[1]} }
        else
            let $next := my:steps(collection("synsets.dbxml")/Synset[Id = $hyp])
            return element step {
                attribute name { $synset/Word[1] },
                $next
            }
};
my:steps((collection("synsets.dbxml")/Synset[Word="banana"])[1])
```

```
<step name="banana">
    <step name="edible fruit">
        <step name="produce">
            <step name="food">
                <step name="solid">
                    <step name="substance">
                        <step name="physical entity">
                            <step name="entity"/>
                        </step>
                    </step>
                </step>
            </step>
        </step>
    </step>
</step>
```

We have results, but they aren't quite the results we're after. In fact, they're the inverse of what we want, where the <step/> element would have an attribute name with value entity as the root element of our fragment. We need to turn this XML inside out.

We don't have too many options for reversing things because we have to crawl "up" the hierarchy, and there's no good way to append to existing nodes. This could be done most easily by having
two recursive functions: one to build our step list as a sequence (similar to what Listing 7-21 generated), and another that takes that sequence and outputs the XML to represent it. In Listing 7-24,
our hypernyms function will return a sequence of Id strings. Note that we're reversing our sequence
(using the reverse() function) to build the XML in inverted order and using the remove() function
to remove the first item in the sequence with each function iteration. This time, the XML includes
the IDs in preparation for the example in the next section.

Listing 7-24. *Building XML to Reflect a Conceptual Hierarchy: Take Two*

```
declare namespace my = "http://brians.org/synsets";
declare function my:hypernyms ($synset) {
    let $hyp := $synset/Pointers/Hypernym[1]/string()
    return
        if (empty($hyp))
        then $synset/Id/string()
        else
            let $next := my:hypernyms(collection("synsets.dbxml")/Synset[Id = $hyp])
            return ($synset/Id/string(), $next)
};
declare function my:tree ($idlist) {
    if (empty($idlist))
    then ()
    else
        element step {
            attribute id {$idlist[1]},
            attribute name {collection("synsets.dbxml")/Synset[Id = $idlist[1]]/Word[1]},
            my:tree(remove($idlist, 1))
        }
};
let $list := my:hypernyms((collection("synsets.dbxml")/Synset[Word="flan"])[1])
return my:tree(reverse($list))
```

```
<step id="1" name="entity">
    <step id="2" name="physical entity">
        <step id="23" name="substance">
            <step id="80020" name="solid">
                <step id="40564" name="food">
                    <step id="41580" name="produce">
                        <step id="41581" name="edible fruit">
                            <step id="41886" name="banana"/>
                        </step>
                    </step>
                </step>
            </step>
        </step>
    </step>
</step>
```

Now we have an XML hierarchy that reflects the actual hierarchy being represented.

Utilizing Hierarchy

If you're like me, there will be cases in which you'll want to use XQuery not only to pull information out of existing XML but also to use its computing power for its own sake. Where you can define the XML yourself—as we did in the previous section—the effect can be not unlike relational key tables, in which a single table is used only to store keys for mappings between tables and use them to perform complex joins.

Some readers, knowing that the synsets.dbxml data I've been working with is a flat hierarchy, will wonder why this hierarchy doesn't match up to an XML hierarchy. After all, isn't storing this information in XML files with hierarchy "pointers" to other files basically equivalent to using an RDB for the same task? The answer is, absolutely, and we've just seen how we could instead reflect a real conceptual hierarchy in our data hierarchy. A container full of such documents would provide for useful lookups, effectively functioning as a pure index data source.

The dbxml shell lets you supply a query such as this to the putDocument command, enabling an entire container to be populated with XQuery-generated documents. Having created a container steps.dbxml and added equality indexes for id and name attributes, we can issue the putDocument with the query and the q parameter. BDB XML autogenerates document names with this usage, which is fine for our purposes. I abbreviated the function definitions from Listing 7-25.

Listing 7-25. *Populating a Container with XQuery via the* dbxml *Shell*

```
dbxml> open steps.dbxml
dbxml> preload synsets.dbxml
dbxml> putDocument "" '
...
for $id in (1 to 1000)
let $strid := $id cast as xs:string
let $list := my:hypernyms(collection("synsets.dbxml")/Synset[Id = $strid])
return my:tree(reverse($list))
' q
```

```
Document added, name = dbxml_2, content = <step id="1" name="entity"/>
Document added, name = dbxml_3, content = <step id="1" name="entity"><step id="2"
name="physical entity"/></step>
Document added, name = dbxml_4, content = <step id="1" name="entity"><step id="3"
name="abstract entity"/></step>
...
```

Granted, this is a fairly large database container with a lot of duplicate information. (In all, the container holds 117,598 documents—some small; others large.) But the effect is that we can now query our hierarchy as if it were contained in a single XML file, with our path expressions matching the conceptual hierarchy itself. Listing 7-26 queries for all presidents (ID value 56161) in the database.

Listing 7-26. *Querying* steps.dbxml *for Every President of the United States*

```
collection("steps.dbxml")//*[@id = "56161"]//*
```

```
<step id="58176" name="Adams"/>
<step id="58177" name="Adams"/>
<step id="58266" name="Arthur"/>
<step id="58509" name="Buchanan"/>
```

```
<step id="58539" name="Bush"/>
<step id="58541" name="Bush"/>
<step id="58589" name="Carter"/>
<step id="58677" name="Cleveland"/>
<step id="58680" name="Clinton"/>
...
```

We would use these IDs to retrieve the full records from synsets.dbxml.

Note The steps.dbxml examples in this section don't reflect the fact that records in Wordnet can have multiple hypernyms ("kind of" pointers), or that words can exist in many synsets. Nor are they taking into account the other pointer types in Wordnet. The examples here are simplified to demonstrate functionality.

Its easy to imagine the hierarchy being used for a game of "20 Questions", in which an application first executes the query in Listing 7-27 to get a random word. Random number generation in any functional language is a fairly inelegant ordeal; rather than demonstrate a poor example, our function will rely on an externally generated random decimal between 0 and 1.

Listing 7-27. *A "Random" Record Selector*

```
declare namespace my = "http://brians.org/synsets";
declare variable $rand as xs:decimal external;
declare function my:random-synset () {
    let $count := 250000    (: the number of records for our set :)
    let $synset := (collection("steps.dbxml")//*[@id="9"]//*)[($count * $rand) cast as
        xs:integer]
    return ($synset/@id/string(), $synset/@name/string())
};
my:random-synset()
```

```
56056
policeman
```

When the user supplies a guess as a question of the form ("Are you a[n] *X*?"), the application parses the word, looks up its ID, and calls the guess() function in Listing 7-28, supplying the answer and the guess. We could imagine the user asking, "Are you a person?" and "Are you a cook?" (shown in the code at the end of the listing).

Listing 7-28. *A Question Function for "20 Questions"*

```
declare namespace my = "http://brians.org/synsets";
declare function my:guess($answerId as xs:decimal, $guessId as xs:decimal) {
    if (collection("steps.dbxml")//*[@id = $guessId]//*[@id = $answerId])
    then true()
    else false()
};
my:guess(56056, 19),    (: policeman, person :)
my:guess(56056, 53188)   (: policeman, cook :)
```

```
true, false
```

The example in Listing 7-29 queries for every record that descends from "food" (ID value 24) and has a name ending with the letters "an".

Listing 7-29. *Searching for All Foods that End with the Letters "an"*

```
for $step in collection("steps.dbxml")//*[@id = "24"]//*
    where matches($step/@name, "an$")
    return $step/@name/string()
```

```
bran
jelly bean
marzipan
flan
veal parmesan
broad bean
vanilla bean
Parmesan
moo goo gai pan
White Russian
manhattan
```

And finally a query for any words that describe both a person (ID value "19") and some kind of man-made thing (ID value "23") is shown in Listing 7-30.

Listing 7-30. *Searching for All Words that Describe Both People and Things*

```
for $person in collection("steps.dbxml")//*[@id = "19"]//*/@name
for $artifact in collection("steps.dbxml")//*[@id = "23"]//*/@name
    where $person = $artifact
    return $person/string()
```

```
precursor
ace
bishop
conductor
batter
bomber
builder
cookie
cracker
joker
suit
stud
...
```

Ranges

Range queries are useful for many data types, including timestamps (finding all values within a certain time span) and decimal values such as prices (finding all products within a certain price range). XQuery's regular expressions even allow you to test and match characters in given Unicode ranges.

Zip codes and area codes are often used to compute approximate proximity; for example, the distance of a store to a customer's location, with the information typically served by a website. Less often, exact latitude and longitude (and altitude) are used, but are becoming more common as geographic data becomes more readily available. Several XML dialects have emerged to express geographic coordinates and other data, but none are quite as striking as Google Earth's use of the KML format. Thousands of these files are available online to establish *placemarks* within the Google Earth application, and loading them into a BDB XML container gives us a chance to use them in searches. A typical (but shortened) placemark file is shown in Listing 7-31.

Listing 7-31. *Typical KML Placemark File*

```
<kml xmlns="http://earth.google.com/kml/2.0">
    <Placemark id="property_1">
        <name>Four Seasons Cairo at Nile Plaza</name>
        <description><![CDATA[<p>1089 Corniche El Nile<br/>Cairo, Egypt </p>
        <p><strong>Score: <span style="color:red;">86.09</span></strong></p>
        <p>30-story hotel near Garden City on the east bank of the river. </p>
            ...
        &#169; 2006 <em>Travel + Leisure</em></p>]]></description>
        <Point>
            <altitudeMode>relativeToGround</altitudeMode>
            <coordinates>31.229338,30.03595,0</coordinates>
        </Point>
    </Placemark>
</kml>
```

Notice that the <coordinates/> element combined the latitude, longitude, and altitude in a single string value, separated by commas. (The KML format does allow for individual longitude and latitude elements, but not all have them.) This will make the individual values difficult to query and impossible to index properly. If we were insistent on maintaining the original files, one option would be to store each individual value as a metadata attribute for the document; unfortunately, many placemarks can be stored in a single document, so this is not an option. Instead, writing new documents (to the same or a new container) will let us break these values up; we do this using the tokenize() function, which splits a string into a sequence of strings, provided a string on which to split. We have already added decimal equality indexes for both latitude and longitude. An example follows in Listing 7-32.

Listing 7-32. *Populating a Container with Reshaped XML*

```
dbxml> openContainer coord.dbxml
dbxml> preload kml-files.dbxml
dbxml> putDocument '' '
declare namespace google = "http://earth.google.com/kml/2.0";
for $place in collection("kml-files.dbxml")//google:Placemark
let $coord := tokenize($place/google:Point[1]/google:coordinates, ",")
return <place>
            <name>{$place/google:name/string()}</name>
            <longitude>{$coord[1]}</longitude>
            <latitude>{$coord[2]}</latitude>
        </place>' q
```

Range queries are also now fairly straightforward, given some coordinates of our own. Making the search a function that accepts a longitude value, a latitude value, and a range lets us reuse it.

Ranges here are in degrees, in which a degree is about 69.2 miles (1/360th of the earth's circumference). Listing 7-33 shows an example of this.

Listing 7-33. *Function for Range Queries*

```
declare namespace my = "http://brians.org/range";
declare function my:in-range ($myLon as xs:decimal, $myLat as xs:decimal, $range as
    xs:decimal) {
    for $place in collection("coord.dbxml")/place
        where ($place/latitude > ($myLat - $range) and $place/latitude < ($myLat +
            $range))
            and ($place/longitude > ($myLon - $range) and $place/longitude < ($myLon +
                $range))
        return $place/name/text()
};
my:in-range (-111.651862515931, 40.00652821419428, 2)
```

Stein Eriksen Lodge

Note that our range function returns text nodes instead of strings. This is intentional because nodes are required for the set operations, retaining their context identity.

■**Note** If the reader is looking for an interesting XQuery challenge, I suggest writing a function to find the record with the shortest coordinate distance from a given coordinate, without a provided range.

Unions, Intersections, and Differences

Set operations are easy with XQuery, a fact owed in large part to sequences as the underlying data list format. All the examples in this section operate only on sequences of node values.

A union — returning all nodes from two sets with duplicates removed — can be computed simply by using the union operator, which works on node sequences. The example query in Listing 7-34 demonstrates a union computation. In this case, the union is performed on the sequences of places "close" to two locations, generating a list of both without duplicates. This example is using the in-range() function from Listing 7-33.

Listing 7-34. *Union Computation On a Sequence of Nodes*

```
declare namespace my = "http://brians.org/range";
declare function my:in-range ($myLon as xs:decimal, $myLat as xs:decimal, $range as
    xs:decimal) {
    for $place in collection("coord.dbxml")/place
        where ($place/latitude > ($myLat - $range) and $place/latitude < ($myLat +
            $range))
            and ($place/longitude > ($myLon - $range) and $place/longitude < ($myLon +
                $range))
        return $place/name/text()
};

let $placesCloseToHome := my:in-range (-111.651862515931, 40.00652821419428, 12)
let $placesCloseToJim := my:in-range (-93.49764084020113, 45.01312134030998, 12)
```

```
return $placesCloseToHome union $placesCloseToJim
```

```
Little Nell
St. Regis Resort, Aspen
Grand Hotel, Minneapolis
...
```

An intersection returning all nodes from two sets that exist in both sequences is similarly straightforward. This example omits the declarations (as do the rest of the examples in this section) that are the same as Listing 7-34. Here, we use the intersect operator between the sequences. This could be used to tell us, for example, which luxury hotels are within a certain range from two locations.

```
...
let $placesCloseToHome := my:in-range (-111.651862515931, 40.00652821419428, 12)
let $placesCloseToJim := my:in-range (-93.51860234945821, 45.0018515180072, 12)
return $placesCloseToHome intersect $placesCloseToJim
```

```
The Broadmoor
```

The set difference identifies all nodes in one set, but not in the other. This, too, is a simple operation, using XQuery's difference operator, except, which returns all nodes from the first set that are not in the second set.

```
...
return $placesCloseToHome except $placesCloseToJim
```

Finally, the symmetric difference is the list of nodes that are only in one of the sequences, and not both. This is computed with a union between the difference of each set.

```
...
return ($placesCloseToHome except $placesCloseToJim)
       union ($placesCloseToJim except $placesCloseToHome)
```

It's important to remember that they set operations for node values only. XQuery does provide the distinct-values() function for computing the union of untyped value sequences, but does not have built-in functions for arbitrary value intersection or difference. These operations require iteration, which I'll leave as an exercise to the reader.

Indexes and Queries

When determining an indexing strategy, as described in Chapter 6, it's important to consider the types of queries you intend to execute. The opposite is true as well, in that queries within BDB XML must be written with an awareness of the existing indexing strategy. This section considers some of the previous examples with respect to BDB XML indexing, including some potential pitfalls to be avoided.

Query Plans

We won't delve much more into query plans than we already did in the previous chapter, but do not be hesitant to examine query plans for any given query to better understand how it utilizes indexes and areas in which room for improvement can be found. The dbxml shell's queryPlan command functions just like the query command, but instead outputs the processor's "action plan" in the form of a syntax tree for your query. Pay particular attention to the Plan elements; each starts with a key character, followed by the index description for the index that will be used to satisfy that step in the query operation. A description for each query plan element name is shown in Table 7-2 and a legend for the key characters is shown in Table 7-3. They are valid for BDB XML version 2.2 and are subject to change.

Table 7-2. *Query Plan Element Descriptions*

Element	Description
<RQPlan/>	Raw Query Plan; identifies query steps prior to any optimizations. The content will describe the plan before variable lookups and before pertinent indexes are determined.
<POQPlan/>	Partially Optimized Query Plan; includes incomplete optimizations.
<OQPlan/>	Optimized Query Plan; describes a query step after optimization. It names the index used to look up the query step's result.

Table 7-3. *Query Plan Key Legend*

Key	Description
P	Presence lookup; the named index is used to determine the presence of a node, as opposed to node value for equality or substring tests.
V	Value lookup; the index is used to look up the value of a node to satisfy an equality or substring test.
R	Range lookup; the index is used to satisfy a range query.
D	Document name lookup; the index is used to get a document's name as metadata.
U	Universal set; all documents in the container are used to satisfy the query step.
E	Empty set; no documents in the container are used to satisfy the query step.
n	Intersection; sets are being intersected to satisfy the query step.
u	Union; a set union operation is being performed to satisfy the query step.

Primarily the <OQPlan/> elements can help you understand the query results and their lookup speed. Within the dbxml shell, turning up verbosity (with the setVerbose command) will yield additional information upon query execution, including query processing times.

It's worth noting that node and edge indexes can be used to satisfy presence tests, making presence indexes the "lowest common denominator" as far as indexes are concerned. In other words, you don't need presence indexes where you have value indexes. This shortcut has a downside in that some queries will result in query plans with a P (presence) step where you expect to see a V (value) lookup. This happens when BDB XML cannot determine the correct type for a lookup from the query and tests for presence instead of value. In such cases, the query should use some explicit casting; it isn't always enough to use the data type functions (string(), number(), and so on) to convert values. In such cases, don't be afraid to declare additional variables, coping the value of another using the cast as expression and using the new variable in your expression.

Node Names and Wildcards

BDB XML indexes nodes using their name, not their path within an XML document. The query optimizer needs to know a node's name to effectively determine the index to use to satisfy the query. This means that any query that does not know the name of nodes for which it must test cannot take full advantage of indexes. Consider our `people.dbxml` container, with XML containing a `<phone/>` element with children `<home/>` and `<office/>`:

```
<person id="6645">
    ...
    <phone>
        <office>612-555-0133</office>
        <home>612-555-9901</home>
    </phone>
</person>
```

We may want to query for any phone number that matches 612-555-9901 and use a query something like this:

```
collection("people.dbxml")/person[phone/*/string() = "612-555-9901"]
```

Unfortunately, this query does not give the query processor enough information to utilize indexes that exist for the `<office/>` and `<home/>` nodes. Going about this with iteration (see Listing 7-35) doesn't solve the problem because the `<office/>` and `<home/>` indexes are still not being used for the lookup, as a glance at the query plan will show.

Listing 7-35. *A Wildcard Misses the Mark*

```
for $person in collection("people.dbxml")/person
    for $phone in $person/phone/*/string()
    where $phone = "612-555-9901"
    return $person
```

For this query to work with speed, we'd need to include both node names in the query:

```
collection("people.dbxml")/person[phone/office eq "612-555-9901" or phone/home eq "612-
555-9901"]
```

Or we need to use a more "XQuery style," shown in Listing 7-36.

Listing 7-36. *Iterating for Individual Element Tests*

```
for $person in collection("people.dbxml")/person
    for $office in $person/phone/office
    for $home in $person/phone/home
    where $office = "612-555-9901" or $home = "612-555-9901"
    return $person
```

It's true that XQuery is probably overkill for this example, but if instead we wanted to get the phone number itself from a record before a cross-lookup that uses it ... you get the idea.

Note that in cases in which you control or create the XML itself, indexing limitations can be effectively bypassed. Imagine that our `people.dbxml` files follow this format:

```
<person id="6645">
    ...
    <phone loc="office">612-555-0133</phone>
    <phone loc="home">612-555-9901</phone>
</person>
```

And we have an index for the <phone/> elements. Because we plan to perform lookups using its value, it makes more sense to organize our data in this way. Grabbing the @loc attribute value is a simple matter after we have the matching node, and if we did want to use the @loc in our query, it would just mean another index and an appended query. If we make the phone number external, we have the example in Listing 7-37.

Listing 7-37. *Better Queries When You Have Control Over the XML*

```
declare variable $phone xs:string external;
for $person in collection("people.dbxml")/person
    where $person/phone eq $phone
    return concat($person/name/first, "'s ", $person/phone[string() = $phone]/@loc,
            " phone is: ", $phone)
```

```
Julie's home phone is: 612-555-9901
```

You can see why understanding how BDB XML indexes documents is useful for writing effective queries and why understanding how queries use an indexing strategy is useful for creating that indexing strategy. But where possible, creating XML that makes it easy to key name-value pairs within your queries will result in easier queries *and* simpler indexing strategies.

Queries Against Results

BDB XML permits queries to be executed against the results from a previous query stored in an XmlResults API object. However, unless these queries use the collection() or doc() functions, they do not utilize BDB XML indexes. This typically isn't an issue because the results set is small to begin with, but keep in mind that if your results sets are potentially large, you won't have indexes to speed up queries when issuing subqueries against them. It's better to get as narrow a results set as you intend to use with the initial query than to depend on subsequent queries against results to get needed information.

Conclusion

BDB XML's query strength lies in XQuery, which combined with BDB XML's flexible indexing, enables some powerful processing of large document collections. This chapter has presented a cross-section of XQuery functionality; more information is available from resources dedicated to the subject, including the following web locations:

W3C XQuery 1.0 recommendation: http://www.w3.org/TR/xquery/

W3C XQuery tutorials: http://www.w3schools.com/xquery/default.asp

XQuery 1.0 and XPath 2.0 data model: http://www.w3.org/TR/xpath-datamodel/

CHAPTER 8

■ ■ ■

BDB XML with C++

Although their usage tends to vary with each languages idiosyncrasies, all of the BDB XML included APIs share similar if not identical class and function names. Because all APIs derive their interface from the C++ API and in fact are built atop the C++ libraries an understanding of the C++ API is beneficial alongside any other language. Although not essential, familiarity with the C++ interfaces is particularly useful for understanding the reason for behaviors that might seem confusing as used by the other language interfaces.

This chapter comprises both an overview of using the BDB XML C++ API and a general reference for all applicable classes. The examples are platform-agnostic. Please refer to Chapter 3, "Installation and Configuration," for instructions on building the C++ libraries and compiling the applications that use them. All the code listings in this chapter are complete in that you should be able to copy them as shown and compile without trouble, assuming that your environment is properly configured. However, for the sake of readability, unnecessary (but strongly recommended) features such as exception handling are often omitted.

Compiling Applications

Building programs that use the C++ API requires that Berkeley DB XML and all its required libraries (refer to Chapter 3) be installed. Compiling on Unix is straightforward, passing the include and library paths to the compiler. Assuming that you are using g++ and that the distributions postbuild install/ directory has been copied to /usr/local/dbxml/, a BDB XML application called test.cpp can be built as follows. First, compile the object:

```
$ g++ -I/usr/local/dbxml/install/include/ -I/usr/local/dbxml/install/include/dbxml/
-c test.cpp
```

Then link as follows:

```
$ g++ -o test test.o -L/usr/local/dbxml/install/lib/ -lpathan -lxquery -lxerces-c -ldbxml-
2.2 -ldb_cxx-4.3
```

The library names might differ depending on your version of BDB XML, but for version 2.2 they include libpathan, libxquery, libxerces-c, libdbxml, and libdb_cxx (in BDB XML 2.3, xquery and pathan are replaced with a single library, xqilla). Also note that the BDB XML apps do not link to libdb because they use the C++ libraries instead (libdb_cxx).

Compiling a program on Windows requires the same libraries and that the include files for each be available. Each dynamic link library (DLL) must be found in a directory in your PATH, either by copying them there or adding the installation directories to PATH. Remember that DLLs are installed by the BDB XML build in the `bin/` directory within the distribution. For BDB 2.2, the necessary DLL files are the following:

```
libdbxml2x.dll
libdb4x.dll
xerces-x_2.dll
libxquery12.dll
Pathan.dll (VC6)
Pathan_7.1.dll (VC7)
```

The first pathan DLL is required for Visual Studio/C++ 6, and the second is required for Visual Studio .NET. Note that version numbers might differ from your installation, depending on the distribution version.

Assuming that you have installed either a binary distribution or have built BDB XML successfully, only the `include/` distribution directory is needed for includes, and `lib/` is needed for all linking libraries. If you find the main `include/` to be insufficient for satisfying your programs includes, an extended list should include the following:

```
include/
dbxml/include/
db-4.x/build_win32/
```

The library files to note when building your application (depending on your version of BDB XML) are as follows:

```
libdbxml2x.lib
libdb43.lib
xerces-c_x.lib
```

Note that version numbers might not correspond to your distribution. Here, too, the Xerces library is needed only when your application makes direct use of the Xerces API. Finally, the `lib/` directory contains two versions of these libraries: one for production and another for debug builds, indicated by the addition of a "d" in the library name.

It is recommended that you refer to (or even copy and use as program templates) the BDB XML examples, described in Chapter 3 and found in the `dbxml/build_win32` directory, to ensure that your build finds the necessary include, library, and DLL files.

Class Organization

All C++ classes exist in the `DbXml` namespace, and the header file `DbXml.hpp` is included at the head of applications. All examples in this chapter thus begin as follows:

```
#include "DbXml.hpp"

using namespace DbXml;
```

The C++ API consists of 19 classes. With few exceptions, BDB XML classes exhibit no virtual behavior and are not designed to be extended. The major classes are listed in Table 8-1 in their construction (not inheritance) hierarchy, indicating which class objects provide methods to construct other objects. (In many cases numerous classes provide methods that return or use objects of a given class, as with the `XmlValue` class, which is used to store values of different data types. The indents of class names in Table 8-1 merely indicate where constructors exist, not necessarily all classes that return objects of a given class.) Omitted are minor classes, but they are covered later in the chapter.

Table 8-1. *Major DBD XML C++ Classes*

Class Name	Description
DbXml	A small class to adjust logging settings and define global variables.
XmlManager	The main application class, used to create, open, and maintain containers; execute queries; and create other BDB XML objects.
XmlContainer	A container handle, with methods for managing documents, manipulating indexes, and so on.
XmlIndexSpecification	An interface to programmatically manage the indexes for a container.
XmlDocument	A document within a container, with methods for getting and managing content.
XmlResults	Encapsulates the results of a query or lookup operation as a sequence of XmlValue objects.
XmlModify	A programmatic interface to modify documents using stepped changes.
XmlQueryContext	Encapsulates the namespaces, variable bindings, and flags for use with container queries.
XmlUpdateContext	Encapsulates the context for updates to a container; all C++ methods that modify containers take an update context object as a required parameter.
XmlQueryExpression	A parsed/prepared XQuery expression.
XmlException	The BDB XML exception class, thrown during and representing error conditions.
XmlTransaction	The BDB XML transaction object.
XmlValue	Used to store XML node values when retrieving and storing data, and to encapsulate typed atomic values (strings, decimals, dates).
DbEnv	A Berkeley DB class for managing a DB environment.

Errors and Exception Handling

BDB XML C++ operations throw exceptions when errors are encountered. They are thrown as XmlException objects. Therefore, all methods should be executed in try blocks. These objects are derived from std::exception from the standard library, so that XmlException can be caught for BDB XML errors, whereas std::exception can still be caught for other application errors.

Listing 8-1 demonstrates exception handling with the C++ API.

Listing 8-1. *Exception Handling*

```
#include "DbXml.hpp"

using namespace DbXml;
int main(void)
{
    // Create an XmlManager
    XmlManager myManager;
    try {
        // Open a container
```

```
        XmlContainer myContainer =
            myManager.openContainer("container.dbxml");
    } catch (XmlException &xe) {
        printf ("%s\n", xe.what());
    } catch (std::exception &e) {
        // Other error handling goes here
    }
}
```

Compiled and run in a directory without a `container.dbxml`, this program will output this:

```
Error: No such file or directory
```

This message is the result of the XmlException::what() method, which returns a string description of the error. The XmlException class also provides methods for retrieval of an error code as well
as a Berkeley DB error number for use when the exception code is DATABASE_ERROR.

Exceptions are often not sufficient to debug problems with your application. In such cases, the
Berkeley DB class DbEnv provides an error stream that can be set to a C++ stream, demonstrated in
Listing 8-2.

Listing 8-2. *Setting an Error Stream*

```
#include "DbXml.hpp"

using namespace DbXml;
int main(void)
{
    // Create an XmlManager
    XmlManager myManager;
    myManager.getDbEnv()->set_error_stream(&std::cerr);
}
```

Using error streams is useful for general debugging as well because the DbXml class allows for
the logging level to be varied. The methods setLogCategory() and setLogLevel() allow for changes
to the granularity of log messages. Listing 8-3 demonstrates activating full debugging categories and
levels. Categories describe the BDB XML subsystem to be logged and include indexer messages,
query messages, and container messages. Levels include debugging, informational messages, and
warnings. A full list of categories and log levels is found in the reference at the end of the chapter.

Listing 8-3. *Setting the Log Level*

```
#include "DbXml.hpp"

using namespace DbXml;
int main(void)
{
    // Create an XmlManager
    XmlManager myManager;
    // Set the errors stream to standard out
    myManager.getDbEnv()->set_error_stream(&std::cerr);
    try {
        XmlContainer myContainer = myManager.openContainer("container.dbxml");
        DbXml::setLogLevel(DbXml::LEVEL_ALL, true);
        DbXml::setLogCategory(DbXml::CATEGORY_ALL, true);
```

```
    } catch (XmlException &xe) {
        // Error handling here
    }
}
```

Opening Environments

As has been discussed, environments are the BDB XML mechanism to provide logging, locking, and transaction support. Chapter 5, "Environments, Containers, and Documents," described the creation of DB environments using the Python API. With C++, an environment needs to exist either explicitly or implicitly   for an XmlManager object to operate with it. (Note that in previous code listings in this chapter, environments have been opened automatically by XmlManager.) Environments are not specific to BDB XML, which is why there is no "XML" in the class used to manage them; DbEnv is used by both Berkeley DB and, by association, Berkeley DB XML applications.

The DbEnv class provides many methods for configuration of a database environment. Here I discuss instantiation as well as opening and closing environments. An abbreviated reference for DbEnv is provided in Appendix B, "BDB XML API Reference."

The DbEnv::open() method takes a directory path, a bitwise OR'd set of environment flags, and a Unix file mode (ignored on Windows) as arguments. This object will later be passed to the XmlManager constructor. Listing 8-4 demonstrates the opening of a database environment with a standard set of flags and exception handling.

Listing 8-4. *Opening a Database Environment*

```
#include "DbXml.hpp"

using namespace DbXml;
u_int32_t env_flags = DB_CREATE |   // Create if environment doesn't exist
    DB_INIT_LOCK |                   // Initialize the locking subsystem
    DB_INIT_LOG |                    // Initialize the logging subsystem
    DB_INIT_MPOOL |                  // Initialize the cache
    DB_INIT_TXN;                     // Initialize transactions for this environment
std::string envPath("/myEnv");

int main(void)
{
    DbEnv *myEnv = new DbEnv(0);
    try {
        myEnv->open(envPath.c_str(), env_flags, 0);
    } catch(DbException &e) {
        std::cerr << "Error opening database environment: "
                  << envPath << std::endl;
        std::cerr << e.what() << std::endl;
    } catch(std::exception &e) {
        std::cerr << "Error opening database environment: "
                  << envPath << std::endl;
        std::cerr << e.what() << std::endl;
    }
}
```

An environment is closed automatically when it passes out of scope or can be closed using the DbEnv::close() method. When doing so, be certain that containers in that environment are closed, and similar exception handling should be used.

XmlManager Class

XmlManager is the primary class for working with containers and for managing the other objects used within the BDB XML API. It is used to create, open, rename, and delete containers; create document and context objects; and prepare and execute XQuery queries, to name a few.

Instantiating XmlManager Objects

XmlManager objects are created with their constructor and are destroyed using their destructor and passing them out of scope. If you provide a DbEnv object to the constructor, XmlManager will automatically close and destroy that DbEnv object for you if you set the DBXML_ADOPT_DBENV flag at instantiation time. If you do not provide a DbEnv object to XmlManager's constructor, it will automatically create an environment for you. This latter option carries some constraints with it because you do not have the ability to configure subsystems and you must tell XmlManager where to create and open your containers. It is generally preferable to create your own DbEnv object and pass it to the XmlManager constructor. Listing 8-5 shows the creation of an XmlManager object using an opened DbEnv.

Listing 8-5. *Instantiating an XmlManager*

```
#include "DbXml.hpp"

using namespace DbXml;
int main(void)
{
    u_int32_t env_flags = DB_CREATE |   // Create environment if it doesn't exist
        DB_INIT_LOCK |                   // Initialize locking
        DB_INIT_LOG |                    // Initialize logging
        DB_INIT_MPOOL |                  // Initialize the cache
        DB_INIT_TXN;                     // Initialize transactions

    std::string envPath("/myEnv");
    DbEnv *myEnv = new DbEnv(0);
    XmlManager *myManager = NULL;

    try {
        myEnv->open(envPath.c_str(), env_flags, 0);
        myManager = new XmlManager(myEnv, DBXML_ADOPT_DBENV);
    } catch(DbException &e) {
        std::cerr << "Error opening database environment: "
                  << envPath << std::endl;
        std::cerr << e.what() << std::endl;
    } catch (XmlException &xe) {
        std::cerr << "Error opening database environment: "
                  << envPath
                  << " or opening XmlManager." << std::endl;
        std::cerr << xe.what() << std::endl;
    }
}
```

Subsequently deleting the myManager object will force a close and destroy on myEnv as well.

Managing Containers

Container creating, opening, renaming, and deleting are performed with the XmlManager object. Open and create operations share a list of container flags, detailed in the reference at the end of this chapter. A container is opened using the XmlManager::openContainer() method, and a single container might be opened multiple times within your application. The createContainer() method creates and subsequently opens a container. Containers are closed by allowing the container handle to go out of scope.

Listing 8-6 demonstrates a simple container creation. This and subsequent code examples tend to omit the environment instantiation for the sake of brevity, although normally DbEnv would be used.

Listing 8-6. *Creating a Container*

```
#include "DbXml.hpp"

using namespace DbXml;
int main(void)
{
    XmlManager myManager;
    XmlContainer myContainer =
        myManager.createContainer("/path/to/myContainer.bdbxml");
    return(0);
}
```

Listing 8-7 shows the creation of a container using more arguments to createContainer(), including flags to enable transactions for the container and perform validation, a container type, and a Unix file mode.

Listing 8-7. *Creating a Container with a Transaction, Flags, and Container Type*

```
#include "DbXml.hpp"

using namespace DbXml;
int main(void)
{
    XmlManager myManager;
    XmlContainer myContainer = myManager.createContainer(
        "/path/to/myContainer.bdbxml",
        DBXML_ALLOW_VALIDATION,
        XmlContainer::NodeContainer, 766 );
    return(0);
}
```

Opening an already-created container uses an identical syntax with the XmlManager::openContainer() method. The same set of arguments and flags are accepted as createContainer(), but some have no use unless the DB_CREATE flag is used with the call to openContainer(). For example, a container type cannot be set on an already-created container, and DB_EXCL (to throw an error if a container exists) is relevant only when creating a new container.

Listing 8-8 demonstrates the opening of a container twice, in which case two object references are created. Remember that a container is automatically closed when its references pass out of scope.

Listing 8-8. *Opening a Container*

```
#include "DbXml.hpp"

using namespace DbXml;
int main(void)
{
```

```
    XmlManager myManager;
    XmlContainer myContainer = myManager.openContainer("/path/to/myContainer.bdbxml");
    return(0);
    // Container will be closed at the end of main()
}
```

Renaming and deleting containers is performed using the `XmlManager::renameContainer()` and `XmlManager::removeContainer()` methods, and both succeed only on unopened containers. The first takes two string arguments: the current name of the container, and the new name. The second simply takes the name of the container to remove. Both take an options transaction object as the first argument. Listing 8-9 demonstrates both.

Listing 8-9. *Renaming and Deleting Containers*

```
#include "DbXml.hpp"

using namespace DbXml;
int main(void)
{
    XmlManager myManager;
    myManager.renameContainer("/path/to/myContainer.bdbxml",
        "/new/path/to/myNewContainer.bdbxml");
    myManager.removeContainer("/path/to/myContainer2.bdbxml");
    return(0);
}
```

Loading Documents

Documents are most typically loaded into a container directly using `XmlManager` to create an input stream, which allows files to be loaded as a string object, from a file on disk, from a network URL, from a memory buffer, or from standard input. Note that no validation is performed on input streams by BDB XML. Only when a document is put into a container does the system read from the stream, parse the content, and validate it. No errors are thrown when an input stream is created using an invalid location, filename, or so on, until the put operation is performed.

`XmlManager` provides several methods for creation of these input streams, as listed in Table 8-2. All these methods return an object of class `XmlInputStream`, which is then used to load the document into the container (or into a document object, as will be shown).

Table 8-2. *XmlManager's Input Stream Creation Methods*

Method	Description
`XmlManager::createLocalFileInputStream()`	Takes as its argument a filename
`XmlManager::createURLInputStream()`	Takes as arguments three URL IDs
`XmlManager::createMemBufInputStream()`	Takes as arguments memory address and byte counts
`XmlManager::createStdInInputStream()`	Takes no argument

The `XmlInputStream` object resulting from any of these methods is then used in one of two ways. Most often, it is passed to the `XmlContainer::putDocument()` method, which loads the data using the input stream, parses the document and performs necessary validation, and then stores the document in the container, immediacy depending on whether or not a transaction is used.

Tip XmlInputStream is one of the few BDB XML classes that is virtual and permits user implementation. This allows applications to supply XML data from within the program or other source.

Listing 8-10 shows the loading of a document into a container using a local file input stream.

Listing 8-10. *Adding a Document to a Container from a Local File*

```
include "DbXml.hpp"

using namespace DbXml;
int main(void)
{
    std::string docFilename = "file176.xml"; // the filename

    XmlManager myManager;
    XmlContainer myContainer = myManager.openContainer("container.bdbxml");

    // The update context is needed to add the document.
    XmlUpdateContext theContext = myManager.createUpdateContext();

    // Create the file input stream
    XmlInputStream *myStream = myManager.createLocalFileInputStream(docFilename);

    // Put the document in the container
    myContainer.putDocument(docFilename, myStream, theContext, 0);

    return(0);
}
```

In this example, the filename as stored in docFilename is used both as the argument to create the input stream (which would work only if the file was in the current working directory) and the argument to putDocument() specifying the document name. This isn't necessarily always or even usually the case, especially when the document file is outside the current working directory. Note again that the omission of exception handling from this example (as well as the absence of a DbEnv and perhaps an XmlTransaction) is for brevity. It is recommended that you do not omit exception handling from your own code.

Tip The XmlContainer::putDocument method also provides a convenience syntax, taking a std::string as the content argument. Given well-formed XML, the content will be parsed and added to the container.

Alternatively, the XmlInputStream is used as the argument to the XmlDocument::setContentAsXmlInputStream() method, directly setting the content of the in-memory document object. The XmlDocument object in question could have been created afresh via a call to XmlManager::createDocument(), in which case it does not yet exist in the container or having been retrieved from a container with XmlContainer::getDocument().

Finally, an XmlDocument object can be retrieved after a query using the methods of the XmlResults class. Each technique is demonstrated elsewhere. Refer to the later sections on managing documents for more details and examples of using the described input streams. The next section discusses the XmlContainer class in more depth.

Preparing and Executing Queries

XQuery queries are performed on containers using the XmlManager objects prepare() and query() methods. Because queries can span multiple containers, they are not centric to any one container, making this the logical class for queries to take place.

The XmlManager::prepare() method takes an XQuery expression string and a query context object as arguments (and an optional transaction object), returning an XmlQueryExpression object. This object encapsulates the parsed and optimized XQuery expression for repeated use in multiple operations. Calling its execute() method evaluates the expression against the containers (or documents) referred to by the query.

The XmlQueryContext object indicates to the query engine the context within which to perform a query. This context includes the namespace mappings, variable bindings, and flags to indicate how a query is to be performed and its results returned   everything the query engine needs to do its job, given the query string.

Listing 8-11 shows the creation of an XmlQueryContext object, using it to set a default collection (enabling us to omit the argument to collection() from our query) and then preparing and executing a query.

Listing 8-11. *Using XmlQueryContext*

```
#include "DbXml.hpp"

using namespace DbXml;
int main(void) {
    XmlManager myManager;
    XmlContainer myContainer = myManager.openContainer("myContainter.dbxml");
    XmlQueryContext myContext = myManager.createQueryContext();
    myContext.setDefaultCollection("myContainer.dbxml");
    std::string myQuery = "collection()/person[name='Bob']";
    XmlQueryExpression qe = myManager.prepare(myQuery, myContext);
    XmlResults results = qe.execute(myContext);
}
```

If our XML collection made use of namespaces, we would use the XmlQueryContext object to define those. Imagine that instead of <person/>, our top-level document elements looked like this:

```
<people:person xmlns:wordnet="http://brians.org/people">
```

We could now use the namespace in our query. In Listing 8-12 we declare this namespace mapping, and also set a variable for use in the XQuery query.

Listing 8-12. *Declaring Namespaces and Variables*

```
#include "DbXml.hpp"

using namespace DbXml;
int main(void) {
    XmlManager myManager;
    XmlContainer myContainer = myManager.openContainer("myContainer.dbxml");
    XmlQueryContext myContext = myManager.createQueryContext();
    myContext.setNamespace("people", "http://brians.org/people");
    myContext.setVariableValue("name", "Bob");
    std::string myQuery =
            "collection('myContainer.dbxml')/people:person[name=$name]";
    XmlQueryExpression qe = myManager.prepare(myQuery, myContext);
    XmlResults results = qe.execute(myContext);
    // Change the variable, and requery without recompiling query.
```

```
    myContext.setVariableValue("name", "Julie");
    results = qe.execute(myContext);
}
```

Because the `XmlQueryContext` object is passed to `execute()` for a prepared query expression, the context can be manipulated without having to recompile the query expression. Note that in Listing 8-12 the query variable $name was changed and the query reissued, without recompiling the prepared query expression.

BDB XML also allows for queries to be executed in a "one-off" fashion, without query preparation. This is helpful when you know queries will not be used repeatedly. Listing 8-13 demonstrates the use of the `XmlManager::query()` method to execute a query once.

Listing 8-13. *Performing a One-Off Query*

```
#include "DbXml.hpp"

using namespace DbXml;
int main(void) {
    XmlManager myManager;
    XmlContainer myContainer = myManager.openContainer("myContainer.dbxml");
    XmlQueryContext myContext = myManager.createQueryContext();
    std::string myQuery = "collection('myContainer.dbxml')/person[name='Bob']";
    XmlResuts results = myManager.query(myQuery, myContext);
}
```

In addition to namespaces and variables, `XmlQueryContext` can determine how queries are executed and the values they return. The `setEvaluationType()` method allows for one of two evaluation types: eager and lazy.

Table 8-3. *Query Evaluation Types*

Type	Description
`XmlQueryContext::Eager`	The query is executed, with resulting values determined and stored in memory before the query returns. This is the default.
`XmlQueryContext::Lazy`	The query is executed, but the resulting values are not determined or stored in memory until the API refers to them by iterating the result set. This means a query uses less overall memory and makes retrieval of the first result faster.

Listing 8-14 demonstrates setting the evaluation type to lazy using the `setEvaluationType()` method; this type might also be provided to the `XmlQueryContext` constructor.

Listing 8-14. *Querying with Lazy Evaluation*

```
#include "DbXml.hpp"

using namespace DbXml;
int main(void) {
    XmlManager myManager;
    XmlContainer myContainer = myManager.openContainer("myContainer.dbxml");
    XmlQueryContext myContext = myManager.createQueryContext();
    myContext.setEvaluationType(XmlQueryContext::Lazy);
    std::string myQuery = "collection('myContainer.dbxml')/person[name='Bob']";
    XmlResults results = myManager.query(myQuery, myContext);
}
```

Because the example does not iterate the query results, no values are actually retrieved, having set the evaluation type to lazy.

Using Query Results

The XmlQueryExpression::execute() and XmlManager::query() methods both return objects of class XmlResults, used to iterate the result set. The object is a sequence of XmlValue objects, which in turn represent any of the BDB XML supported data types. The XmlResults uses an iteration interface with next() and previous() methods to navigate results. Each takes as argument an XmlValue object (or an XmlDocument object), into which it stores the next or previous result.

Listing 8-15 demonstrates outputting the results of a query to the console. It also uses the XmlResults::size() method to retrieve the size of the results set.

■**Note** With a lazily evaluated query, XmlResults acts as an "on-demand" iterator, retrieving results with each next() method call. Note that previous() and size() are not available for lazy evaluations, being that the results are not in memory for reverse iteration, and the size of the result set is not known.

Listing 8-15. *Retrieving Query Results*

```
#include "DbXml.hpp"

using namespace DbXml;
int main(void) {
    XmlManager myManager;
    XmlContainer myContainer = myManager.openContainer("myContainer.dbxml");
    XmlQueryContext myContext = myManager.createQueryContext();
    std::string myQuery = "collection('myContainer.dbxml')/person[name='Bob']";
    XmlResults results = myManager.query(myQuery, myContext);
    printf("%i results from query.\n", results.size());
    XmlValue value;
    while (results.next(value)) {
        XmlDocument myDoc = value.asDocument();
        std::string docContent = value.asString();
        std::string docName = myDoc.getName();
        std::cout << "Document " << docName << ":" << std::endl;
        std::cout << docContent << std::endl;
    }
}
```

Note here the use of several new methods, including XmlValue::asString() and XmlDocument.getName(). Certain pieces of document information, including its name within the container, are available only by querying directly or retrieving the result as a document. When your queries require the node values themselves, as opposed to the documents matching a query, asString() is all that is needed.

The XmlValue class also provides a DOM-like interface to not only retrieve values (as with the asString() and asDocument() methods) but also to navigate the nodes it represents. Its methods include getNextSibling(), getAttributes(), and getFirstChild(), making it useful for any post-query processing that you might need to do on query results.

The BDB XML query engine is capable of evaluating XQuery queries on documents and even individual query results, in addition to database containers. Listing 8-16 does exactly this by executing several queries using the XmlValue object. Because our document query will repeat for each result, it makes sense to prepare this using an XmlQueryExpression object.

Listing 8-16. *Querying Results*

```
#include "DbXml.hpp"

using namespace DbXml;
int main(void) {
    XmlManager myManager;
    XmlContainer myContainer = myManager.openContainer("myContainer.dbxml");
    XmlQueryContext myContext = myManager.createQueryContext();
    XmlResults results = myManager.query(
        "collection('myContainer.dbxml')/person[name='Bob']", myContext);
    printf("%i results from query.\n", results.size());
    XmlQueryExpression phoneQuery =
        myManager.prepare("/person/phone/string()", myContext);
    XmlValue value;
    while (results.next(value)) {
        XmlQueryContext phoneContext = myManager.createQueryContext();
        XmlResults phoneResults = phoneQuery.execute(value, phoneContext);
        XmlDocument myDoc = value.asDocument();
        std::string docName = myDoc.getName();
        std::cout << "Document " << docName << ":" << std::endl;
        XmlValue phoneValue;
        while (phoneResults.next(phoneValue)) {
            std::cout << "  Phone: " << phoneValue.asString() << std::endl;
        }
    }
}
```

The exact same thing can be done with the XmlDocument object resulting from a call to XmlValue::asDocument(), passing that object as argument to XmlQueryExpression::execute(). Of course, if we anticipate only one <phone/> element in this example, we can instead just call XmlResults::next() instead of creating a while block. Our second query in this example can be relative to the result node, using the current node (.) instead:

```
./phone/string()
```

This same technique of querying results and documents can be useful for pulling data out of large documents, enabling us to work within the context of previous result sets.

We'll look more closely at the use of XmlDocument in a later section to demonstrate the retrieval of metadata.

Creating Other Objects

The bulk of XmlManager's remaining methods serve to simply construct objects of other DbXml subclasses. Many of them have already been demonstrated, as with the XmlManager::createTransaction() method, which instantiates an XmlTransaction object. All such method names begin with create, and most default to no-default arguments, serving as basic constructors. They include createDocument() to instantiate an XmlDocument object, createIndexLookup() to instantiate an XmlIndexLookup object, createModify() to instantiate an XmlModify object, createQueryContext() to instantiate an XmlQueryContext object, and createResults() to create an empty XmlResults object. These methods are examined in the following sections, in which their returned objects are demonstrated.

Using XmlContainer

The XmlContainer class provides most of the functionality that concerns a container and its contents, including the adding, replacing, updating and deleting of documents; direct retrieval of documents (using the getDocument() method); and management of indexes for the container. If it reads and writes to the database, its probably part of XmlContainer.

As has been shown, an XmlContainer object is created using the XmlManager::createContainer() and XmlManager::openContainer() methods. With it, documents can be added using the putDocument() method, taking as argument either an XmlDocument or XmlInputStream. The previous section demonstrated this while supplying a document name and input stream or document container. The method will also accept an XML string and will generate document names itself if one is not provided and if the call includes the DBXML_GEN_NAME flag. Listing 8-17 uses putDocument() without providing a document name.

Listing 8-17. *Letting BDB XML Generate Document Names*

```
#include "DbXml.hpp"

using namespace DbXml;
int main(void)
{
    std::string fileName = "/export/testdoc1.xml";
    XmlManager myManager;
    XmlContainer myContainer = myManager.openContainer("container.bdbxml");
    XmlUpdateContext myContext = myManager.createUpdateContext();
    std::string docContent = "<person><name>Bob</name></person>";
    myContainer.putDocument("",                    // The name prefix
                docContent,                        // The document's content as string
                myContext,                         // The update context
                DBXML_GEN_NAME);                   // Autogenerate document name
}
```

If a name is provided along with the DBXML_GEN_NAME flag, it is used as a prefix for the generated name. With this usage, BDB XML guarantees the uniqueness of document names, incrementing them with each call to putDocument().

Documents are deleting from a container using the XmlContainer::deleteDocument() method, which accepts with the document name or document object as its argument. The latter is useful when you want to iterate over a result set, deleting each document it contains, without having to retrieve the document name. This is demonstrated in Listing 8-18.

Listing 8-18. *Deleting Documents*

```
#include "DbXml.hpp"

using namespace DbXml;
int main(void) {
    XmlManager myManager;
    XmlContainer myContainer = myManager.openContainer("myContainer.dbxml");
    XmlQueryContext myContext = myManager.createQueryContext();
    XmlUpdateContext myUpdateContext = myManager.createUpdateContext();
    XmlResults results = myManager.query(
        "collection('myContainer.dbxml')/person[name='Bob']", myContext);
    printf("Deleting %i documents matching query.\n", results.size());
    XmlDocument docToDelete;
```

```
    while (results.next(docToDelete)) {
        myContainer.deleteDocument(docToDelete, myUpdateContext);
    }
}
```

Note that an XmlDocument object is passed to each call of XmlResults::next(), which is smart enough to know to store the result there as a complete document.

When we want to replace a document in a container (instead of modifying it in place), we can use the XmlContainer::updateDocument() method. In fact, this operation works with any XmlDocument object, setting its name to be identical to the document to be replaced, and handing it to the updateDocument() method. Normally, we retrieve the document from the database, set new content using the XmlDocument::setContent() method (or setContentAsDOM() or setContentAsXmlInputStream()), and save it back to the container. Listing 8-19 retrieves a document from the container using the XmlContainer::getDocument() method, before replacing its content and saving it back to the container.

Listing 8-19. *Replacing a Document*

```
#include "DbXml.hpp"

using namespace DbXml;
int main(void) {
    XmlManager myManager;
    XmlContainer myContainer = myManager.openContainer("myContainer.dbxml");
    XmlQueryContext myContext = myManager.createQueryContext();
    XmlUpdateContext myUpdateContext = myManager.createUpdateContext();
    XmlDocument myDoc = myContainer.getDocument("114.xml");
    myDoc.setContent("<person><name>Charles</name></person>");
    myContainer.updateDocument(myDoc, myUpdateContext);
}
```

The BDB XML API provides two ways to partially modify a document in a container instead of replacing its contents outright. The first is with the Xerces DOM (which is not examined here), using the XmlDocument::getContentAsDOM() and XmlDocument::setContentAsDOM() methods. The second is to use the XmlModify class, which allows a description of changes to be built before applying them to one or many documents in a container. This process is demonstrated in the following section.

A final major function of the XmlContainer class is the management of container indexes. Chapter 6, "Indexes," described the specifics of indexing strategies; here we will examine the adding, deleting, and examining of indexes from the API.

Indexes can be added using an index description string, as demonstrated in Listing 8-20.

Listing 8-20. *Adding an Index to a Container with an Index Description String*

```
#include "DbXml.hpp"

using namespace DbXml;
int main(void) {
    XmlManager myManager;
    XmlContainer myContainer = myManager.openContainer("myContainer.dbxml");
    XmlUpdateContext myUpdateContext = myManager.createUpdateContext();
    myContainer.addIndex("", "person", "node-element-equality-string", myUpdateContext);
}
```

The XmlContainer::getIndexSpecification() method returns an index specification for the container, encapsulating a description of all current indexes. It provides the addIndex() and deleteIndex() methods to manipulate the index description before applying it back to the container. The example in Listing 8-21 deletes one index and adds another using an XmlIndexSpecification object.

Listing 8-21. *Manipulating a Container's Index Specification*

```
#include "DbXml.hpp"

using namespace DbXml;
int main(void) {
    XmlManager myManager;
    XmlContainer myContainer = myManager.openContainer("myContainer.dbxml");
    XmlUpdateContext myUpdateContext = myManager.createUpdateContext();
    XmlIndexSpecification myIndexSpec = myContainer.getIndexSpecification();
    myIndexSpec.deleteIndex("", "person", "node-element-equality-string");
    myIndexSpec.addIndex("", "name", "node-element-equality-string");
    myContainer.setIndexSpecification(myIndexSpec, myUpdateContext);
}
```

The XmlIndexSpecification object also provides methods for replacing an index, manipulating the default indexes, and iterating through the indexes within the specification.

One more class bears mentioning in the context of containers and indexes: XmlIndexLookup. Objects of this class are instantiated by XmlManager::createIndexLookup() and enable the retrieval of all nodes or documents that have keys in any given index. An example is shown in Listing 8-22.

Listing 8-22. *Listing All Documents Referenced by an Index*

```
#include "DbXml.hpp"

using namespace DbXml;
int main(void) {
    XmlManager myManager;
    XmlContainer myContainer = myManager.openContainer("myContainer.dbxml");
    XmlQueryContext myQueryContext = myManager.createQueryContext();

    XmlIndexLookup myLookup = myManager.createIndexLookup(myContainer,
            "", "firstName", "node-element-equality-string");
    XmlResults myResults = myLookup.execute(myQueryContext);
    XmlDocument myDoc;
    while (myResults.next(myDoc)) {
        std::string dummyString;
        std::cout << myDoc.getName() << ": " << myDoc.getContent(dummyString)
                << std::endl;
    }
}
```

When a container is of type WholedocContainer, the XmlIndexLookup::execute() operation always returns entire documents. This is also true for containers of type NodeContainer unless the DBXML_INDEX_NODES flag was specified at container creation time. In that case, the lookup returns the individual nodes referred to in the index's keys.

The XmlIndexLookup class provides further access to an index's internal workings with methods to set bounds for ranged lookups and the capability to set a parent node for indexes that use edge paths rather than node paths. Listing 8-23 shows a direct index lookup for values greater than or equal to 16, and less than 35, sorted in reverse of the index order.

Listing 8-23. *Ranged Index Lookup with Reverse-Sorted Results*

```
#include "DbXml.hpp"

using namespace DbXml;
int main(void) {
    XmlManager myManager;
    XmlContainer myContainer = myManager.openContainer("myContainer.dbxml");
    XmlQueryContext myQueryContext = myManager.createQueryContext();
    XmlIndexLookup myLookup = myManager.createIndexLookup(myContainer, "", "age",
        "node-element-equality-decimal",
        XmlValue(XmlValue::DECIMAL, 16),
    XmlIndexLookup::GTE);
    myLookup.setHighBound(XmlValue(XmlValue::DECIMAL, 35), XmlIndexLookup::LT);
    XmlResults myResults = myLookup.execute(myQueryContext, DBXML_REVERSE_ORDER);
    XmlDocument myDoc;
    while (myResults.next(myDoc)) {
        std::string dummyString;
        std::cout << myDoc.getName() << ": " << myDoc.getContent(dummyString)
                << std::endl;
    }
}
```

XmlIndexLookup can also perform equality and inequality lookups, making it a powerful tool when you want to deal directly with BDB XML indexes.

Using XmlDocument

The XmlDocument class is used throughout the API primarily as a document handle, passed to and from methods of other classes. It also provides methods for getting and setting document content as already demonstrated, getting and setting document metadata, and setting the document's name. This section also looks at the use of the XmlModify class to modify documents.

A document's metadata is set with the XmlDocument::setMetaData() method. Document metadata entails an attribute name, value, and an optional URI. This is demonstrated in Listing 8-24.

Listing 8-24. *Adding Metadata to a Document*

```
#include "DbXml.hpp"

using namespace DbXml;
int main(void)
{
    XmlManager myManager;
    std::string URI = "http://brians.org/metadata";
    std::string metadataName = "createdOn";
    XmlValue metadataValue(XmlValue::DATE_TIME, "2006-02-05T05:23:14");
    XmlContainer myContainer = myManager.openContainer("myContainer.dbxml");
    XmlUpdateContext myUpdateContext = myManager.createUpdateContext();
    XmlDocument myDoc = myContainer.getDocument("114.xml");
    myDoc.setMetaData(URI, metadataName, metadataValue);
    myContainer.updateDocument(myDoc, myUpdateContext);
}
```

Metadata can be retrieved from an XmlDocument using the getMetaData() method, shown in Listing 8-25.

Listing 8-25. *Reading Metadata from a Document*

```
#include "DbXml.hpp"

using namespace DbXml;
int main(void)
{
    XmlManager myManager;
    XmlContainer myContainer = myManager.openContainer("myContainer.dbxml");
    XmlDocument myDoc = myContainer.getDocument("114.xml");
    XmlValue metadataValue;
    myDoc.getMetaData("http://brians.org/metadata", "createdOn", metadataValue);
    std::cout << "Document 114.xml, created on " << metadataValue.asString()
              << std::endl;
}
```

Using XmlModify

Documents can be modified within a container by using the XmlModify class without the need to replace the document or copy it to memory. This class enables us to construct a series of steps for manipulating the contents of a document and then apply it to one or many documents within a container. It thus becomes a simple matter to perform container-wide document changes.

The XmlModify object is instantiated with a call to XmlManager::createModify(). A series of methods are exposed to provide for appending content, inserting and replacing content, and renaming and removing nodes. Assume that our database was filled with documents having the following structure:

```
<person>
    <name>Samuel</name>
    <age>51</age>
</person>
```

We want to create a new attribute node called "type" under the <name/> element, with the value "given". (Assume that the need to add surnames to the database has been discovered.) This procedure involves an append changes to our document, appending to the <name/> element. Calling the XmlModify::addAppendStep() method with the target node, the node type we are appending, and the attribute name and value, we get the example shown in Listing 8-26.

Listing 8-26. *Modifying a Document*

```
#include "DbXml.hpp"

using namespace DbXml;
int main(void)
{
    XmlManager myManager;
    XmlContainer myContainer = myManager.openContainer("myContainer.dbxml");
    XmlQueryContext myQueryContext = myManager.createQueryContext();
    XmlUpdateContext myUpdateContext = myManager.createUpdateContext();
    XmlModify myModify = myManager.createModify();
    XmlQueryExpression myQuery = myManager.prepare("/person/name", myQueryContext);
    myModify.addAppendStep(myQuery, XmlModify::Attribute, "type", "given");
    XmlDocument myDoc = myContainer.getDocument("114.xml");
    XmlValue docValue(myDoc);
    myModify.execute(docValue, myQueryContext, myUpdateContext);
}
```

Any series of XmlModify steps can be included. Note that XmlModify is executed on an XmlValue instead of an XmlDocument. The execute() method also accepts an XmlResults object, enabling us to apply the XmlModify object to all documents in a query result. Listing 8-27 performs a query for all documents that have a /person/name element and adds the @type="given" attribute to each.

Listing 8-27. *Modifying All Documents In a Result Set*

```cpp
#include "DbXml.hpp"

using namespace DbXml;
int main(void)
{
    XmlManager myManager;
    XmlContainer myContainer = myManager.openContainer("myContainer.dbxml");
    XmlQueryContext myQueryContext = myManager.createQueryContext();
    XmlUpdateContext myUpdateContext = myManager.createUpdateContext();
    XmlModify myModify = myManager.createModify();
    XmlQueryExpression myQuery = myManager.prepare("/person/name", myQueryContext);
    myModify.addAppendStep(myQuery, XmlModify::Attribute, "type", "given");
    XmlResults myResults = myManager.query(
        "collection('myContainer.dbxml')/person/name", myQueryContext);
    myModify.execute(myResults, myQueryContext, myUpdateContext);
}
```

This process changes all documents matching the query according to the XmlModify object. Keep in mind that it can be an expensive operation, but less so than retrieving and replacing each pertinent document in the container. The API reference at the end of this chapter contains a description of the XmlModify methods.

Using XmlTransaction

Basic transaction handling was demonstrated early in this chapter, but most code listings have omitted transactions for the sake of clarity. This section will summarize the functionality of the BDB XML transactional subsystem and its usage from C++.

■**Note** Transactional processing is a large topic that cannot be fully covered here. Please refer to the Berkeley DB documentation for a more in-depth treatment of the subject.

Berkeley DB XML inherits the Berkeley DB transactions, enabling option transactional processing for all operations. Transactions require that certain parameters be set for the environment and containers within it. Four Berkeley DB subsystems must be enabled for an environment to perform transactions: locking, logging, the cache, and transactions. With a transactional environment, containers must be created and opened with the DBXML_TRANSACTIONAL flag. Listing 8-28 shows the opening of an environment with these flags set and creating a transactional container.

Listing 8-28. *Opening an Environment and Container for Transactional Processing*

```cpp
#include "DbXml.hpp"

using namespace DbXml;
int main(void)
{
```

```
    u_int32_t env_flags = DB_CREATE |  // Create environment if it doesn't exist
        DB_INIT_LOCK |                  // Initialize locking
        DB_INIT_LOG |                   // Initialize logging
        DB_INIT_MPOOL |                 // Initialize the cache
        DB_INIT_TXN;                    // Initialize transactions

    DbEnv myEnv(0);
    myEnv.open("/path/to/environment", env_flags, 0);
    XmlManager myManager = new XmlManager(myEnv, DBXML_ADOPT_DBENV);
    XmlContainer myContainer = myManager.openContainer(
            "myContainer.dbxml", DB_CREATE | DBXML_TRANSACTIONAL);
}
```

With transactions enabled for the environment and container, transaction objects of class XmlTransaction are instantiated with XmlManager::createTransaction(). The object should be passed as the first argument to every read and write operation you want to include in the transaction. Note that the transaction object is not container- or database-specific; the same object can be used for all operations within a given environment. When all operations for the transaction have been created, XmlTransaction::commit() is called, and the write operations are carried out. This invalidates the XmlTransaction object, so another must be created for further transactional operations. If in the course of constructing the transaction an exception is encountered, you should call XmlTransaction::abort() to terminate the transaction and discard its operations.

■**Caution** Whenever a container is opened transactionally, BDB XML automatically protects individual writes for you if you do not use a transaction object. This convenience requires that when you *do* use transaction objects, they must be provided to all calls to a modifying operation. Because BDB XML creates another transaction in cases where an open transaction is missing from the parameter list, self-deadlocking can occur—with each transaction waiting for the other.

Listing 8-29 contains a complete example of transactional processing, including exception handling. We would normally use a try/catch block for the environment and container opens, but have omitted them for brevity.

Listing 8-29. *Transactional Processing*

```
#include "DbXml.hpp"

using namespace DbXml;
int main(void)
{
    u_int32_t env_flags = DB_CREATE |          // Create environment if it doesn't exist
                    DB_INIT_LOCK |             // Initialize locking
                    DB_INIT_LOG |             // Initialize logging
                    DB_INIT_MPOOL |          // Initialize the cache
                    DB_INIT_TXN;             // Initialize transactions
    XmlManager *myManager = NULL;
    XmlTransaction myTxn;
    try {
        DbEnv *myEnv = new DbEnv(0);
        myEnv->open("/myEnv", env_flags, 0);
        myManager = new XmlManager(myEnv, DBXML_ADOPT_DBENV);
        XmlContainer myContainer = myManager->openContainer(
            "myContainer.dbxml", DB_CREATE | DBXML_TRANSACTIONAL);
```

```
    myTxn = myManager->createTransaction();

    XmlUpdateContext myUpdateContext = myManager->createUpdateContext();
    XmlInputStream *theStream =
        myManager->createLocalFileInputStream("myfile12.xml");
    myContainer.putDocument(myTxn,             // the transaction object
                "myfile12",                    // the document's name
                theStream,                     // the document
                myUpdateContext,               // The update context
                0);                            // Put flags.
    myTxn.commit();
} catch(XmlException &error) {
    std::cerr << "Error in transaction: "
                << error.what() << "\n"
                << "Aborting." << std::endl;
    myTxn.abort();
    }
}
```

As a rule, transactions incur overhead in exchange for database integrity. Overhead can be minimized by keeping transactions alive for as short a time as possible, lessening the size of data written on commit (and the duration that containers must be write-locked), and performing fewer operations within a given transaction.

BDB XML Event API

Berkeley DB XML 2.3 adds an event API to its XML input and output options. At the time of writing, this interface is not yet released. The event API allows applications to bypass BDB XML's XML parsing and serialization, enabling developers to utilize BDB XML databases using their own or third-party XML parsers and serializers. The event API will also make integration with other XML technologies an easy task.

The event API adds two classes to those already discussed: XmlEventReader and XmlEventWriter. Listing 8-30 contains an example of XmlEventReader to read a document using events. XmlDocument:: getContentAsEventReader() creates the reader object, which is then used to generate node events not unlike a Simple API for XML (SAX) parser.

Listing 8-30. *Example of* XmlEventReader *to Read a Document*

```
XmlDocument doc = container.getDocument("doc12");
XmlEventReader &reader = doc.getContentAsEventReader();
while (reader.hasNext()) {
    XmlEventType type = reader.next();
    if (type == StartElement) {
        cout << "Event is StartElement for node: " <<
            reader.getLocalName();
    }
    reader.close(); // release resources
}
```

The corresponding writer class allows the reverse, with methods such as writeElement() and writeAttribute() to feed raw XML to an XmlContainer object.

Please consult the BDB XML (>= 2.3) documentation and website for more details on the event API.

Conclusion

The BDB XML C++ API is the core used by the other language APIs, providing a straightforward implementation of all BDB XML functionality. Therefore, understanding its workings is useful, regardless of the API you choose for your applications.

The following resources are the best locations for complete and up-to-date documentation on the C++ API.

Sleepycat's C++ tutorials and complete C++ API reference, hyperlinked for all classes and methods: http://www.sleepycat.com/xmldocs/.

The Berkeley DB product FAQs, documentation, and mailing lists: http://dev.sleepycat.com/.

CHAPTER 9

■ ■ ■

BDB XML with Python

The Python API included with BDB XML exposes all the classes and methods of the C++ API. Because of Python's popularity and compatibility across many platforms, it is a popular BDB XML interface. BDB XML's Python API is nearly identical to the C++ API, but the interface still feels very "Python-esque" in usage.

This chapter is both an overview of using BDB XML's Python API, as well as a general reference for all applicable classes. As in Chapter 8, "BDB XML with C++," the code examples are platform-agnostic. (Refer to Chapter 3, "Installation and Configuration," for instructions on building the Python libraries and compiling applications that use them.) All the code listings in this chapter are complete, in that you should be able to copy them as shown and execute without trouble, assuming that your environment is properly configured. However, for the sake of readability, unnecessary (but strongly recommended) features such as exception handling are often omitted.

Running Applications

If your BDB XML libraries are properly compiled, and the Python bindings are successfully built and installed, executing a Python script that uses the API is simply a matter of importing both the bsddb3 and dbxml modules:

```
from bsddb3.db import *
from dbxml import *
```

Note that Python 2.3 and later include a build-in Berkeley DB module: bsddb. The bsddb3 module is included with BDB XML and should work in circumstances in which the standard Python library does not.

The examples included with the BDB XML distribution are located in the directory dbxml/examples/python/, and demonstrate much of the Python API's functionality.

■Tip The proper reference for the Python Berkeley DB module is the pybsddb project at http://pybsddb.sourceforge.net.

Class Organization

The Python API follows the same class organization as the C++ API, but does not require that any namespace declaration be present.

The major API classes are described in Table 9-1. Omitted are minor classes (they are covered later in the chapter).

Table 9-1. *Major BDB XML Python Classes*

Class Name	Description
XmlManager	The main application class used to create, open, and maintain containers; execute queries; and so on.
XmlContainer	A container handle with methods for managing documents, manipulating indexes, and so on.
XmlIndexSpecification	An interface to programmatically manage the indexes for a container.
XmlDocument	A document within a container with methods for getting and managing content.
XmlResults	Encapsulates the results of a query or lookup operation.
XmlModify	A programmatic interface to modifying documents using stepped changes.
XmlQueryContext	Encapsulates the namespaces, variable bindings, and flags for use with container queries.
XmlUpdateContext	Encapsulates the context for updates to a container.
XmlQueryExpression	A parsed/prepared XQuery expression.
XmlTransaction	The BDB XML transaction object.
XmlValue	Used to store XML node values when retrieving and storing data.
DBEnv	A Berkeley DB class for managing a DB environment.

Errors and Exception Handling

The BDB XML Python API does not support Python's native exception classes because the Python interpreter is halted when the underlying BDB XML libraries throw exceptions. However, surrounding database operations in try / except / finally will enable you to catch any RuntimeError thrown by BDB XML when problems are encountered.

Exceptions are often not sufficient to debug problems with your application. Some additional granularity is available from the bsddb module in the form of low-level exceptions. Refer to the bsddb documentation for exception codes and handling.

Environments

Environments provide logging, locking, and transaction support for database containers. Chapter 5, "Environments, Containers, and Documents," demonstrated the creation of DB environments using the Python API; it requires XmlManager object, which has managed the environments automatically in most examples thus far. Environments are not specific to BDB XML, which is why there is no "XML" in the class used to manage them; DBEnv is used by both Berkeley DB and, by association, Berkeley DB XML applications.

The DBEnv class provides many methods for configuration of a database environment. Here I will discuss only instantiation as well as opening and closing environments.

The DBEnv.open() method takes a directory path, a bitwise ORd set of environment flags, and a Unix file mode (ignored on Windows) as arguments. This object is then passed to the XmlManager constructor. Listing 9-1 demonstrates the opening of a database environment with a standard set of flags and the instantiation of an XmlManager object.

Listing 9-1. *Opening a Database Environment*

```
from bsddb3.db import *
from dbxml import *

myenv = DBEnv()
myenv.open("myenv/",
    DB_CREATE|DB_INIT_LOCK|DB_INIT_LOG|DB_INIT_MPOOL|DB_INIT_TXN, 0)
mgr = XmlManager(myenv, 0)
```

An environment is closed automatically when its object passes out of scope or can be closed explicitly using the DBEnv.close() method.

XmlManager

XmlManager is the primary class for working with containers and for managing the other objects used within the BDB XML API. It is used to create, open, rename, and delete containers; create document and context objects; and prepare and execute XQuery queries, to name a few.

Instantiating XmlManager Objects

XmlManager objects are created with their constructor and are destroyed using their destructor or passing them out of scope. If you do not provide a DBEnv object to XmlManager's constructor, it will automatically create an environment for you. This option carries some constraints with it because you do not have the ability to configure subsystems and must tell XmlManager where to create and open your containers. Generally, it is preferable to create your own DBEnv object and pass it to the XmlManager constructor. Listing 9-1 shows the creation of an XmlManager object using an opened DBEnv. Note that the scope of a DBEnv object must be "larger" than an XmlManager that uses it.

Managing Containers

Container creating, opening, renaming, and deleting are performed with the XmlManager object. Open and create operations share a list of container flags, which are detailed in the reference at the end of this chapter. A container is opened using the XmlManager.openContainer() method, and a single container can be opened multiple times within your application. The createContainer() method creates and subsequently opens a container. Containers are closed by allowing the container handle to go out of scope or by explicitly deleting them.

Listing 9-2 demonstrates a simple container creation. This example and subsequent code examples tend to omit the environment instantiation for the sake of brevity, although normally DBEnv would be used.

Listing 9-2. *Creating a Container*

```
from bsddb3.db import *
from dbxml import *

mymgr = XmlManager()
mycontainer = mymgr.createContainer("test.dbxml")
```

Listing 9-3 shows the creation of a container using some of the possible arguments to createContainer(), including flags to enable transactions for the container and perform validation and a container type.

Listing 9-3. *Creating a Container with Flags and Container Type*

```
from bsddb3.db import *
from dbxml import *

myenv = DBEnv()
myenv.open("myenv", DB_CREATE|DB_INIT_LOCK|DB_INIT_LOG|DB_INIT_MPOOL|DB_INIT_TXN, 0)
mymgr = XmlManager(myenv, 0)

mycontainer = mymgr.createContainer("test.dbxml",
    DBXML_TRANSACTIONAL|DBXML_ALLOW_VALIDATION,
    XmlContainer.NodeContainer )
del mycontainer
```

■**Caution** Open containers must be explicitly closed using the Python API to avoid a segmentation fault.

Opening an already-created container uses an identical syntax with the `XmlManager.`
`openContainer()` method. The same set of arguments and flags are accepted as `createContainer()`,
but some have no use unless the `DB_CREATE` flag is used with the call to `openContainer()`. For example, a container type cannot be set on an already-created container, and `DB_EXCL` (to throw an error
if a container exists) is only relevant when creating a new container.

Renaming and deleting containers are performed using the `XmlManager.renameContainer()` and
`XmlManager.removeContainer()` methods. Both will succeed only on unopened containers. The first
takes two string arguments: the current name of the container and the new name. The second simply takes the name of the container to remove. Both take an optional transaction object as the first
argument. Listing 9-4 demonstrates both.

Listing 9-4. *Renaming and Deleting Containers*

```
from bsddb3.db import *
from dbxml import *

mymgr = XmlManager()

mymgr.renameContainer("test.dbxml", "newtest.dbxml")
mymgr.removeContainer("newtest.dbxml")
```

Loading Documents

Documents are most typically loaded into a container directly by using `XmlManager` to create an
input stream. This allows files to be loaded as a string object, from a file on disk, from a network
URL, from a memory buffer, or from standard input. Note that no validation is performed on input
streams by BDB XML. Only when a document is put into a container does the system read from the
stream, parse the content, and validate it. No errors are thrown when an input stream is created
using an invalid location, filename, or so on until the put operation is performed.

`XmlManager` provides several methods for creation of these input streams, as listed in Table 9-2.
All these methods return an object of class `XmlInputStream`, which is then used to load the document
into the container (or into a document object, as will be shown).

Table 9-2. *XmlManager's Input Stream Creation Methods*

Method	Description
XmlManager.createLocalFileInputStream()	Takes as its argument a filename
XmlManager.createURLInputStream()	Takes as arguments three URL IDs
XmlManager.createMemBufInputStream()	Takes as arguments memory address and byte counts

The XmlInputStream object resulting from any of these methods is then used in one of two ways. Most often, it is passed to the XmlContainer. putDocument() method, which loads the data using the input stream, parses the document and performs any necessary validation, and then stores the document in the container. Of course, putDocument() will also accept an XML document in the form of a string, but the BDB XML input stream can save the overhead in memory of loading the text via Python as well. Listing 9-5 shows the loading of a document into a container using a local file input stream.

Listing 9-5. *Adding a Document to a Container from a Local File*

```
from bsddb3.db import *
from dbxml import *

mymgr = XmlManager()

mycontainer = mymgr.openContainer("test.dbxml")
xmlucontext = mymgr.createUpdateContext()
xmlinput = mymgr.createLocalFileInputStream("file14.xml")
mycontainer.putDocument("file14", xmlinput, xmlucontext)
del mycontainer
```

Note that the filename as specified for the input stream is different from the document name supplied to putDocument(). They could be the same, of course.

An alternative to passing the XmlInputStream object to putDocument() is to supply it as an argument to the XmlDocument.setContentAsXmlInputStream() method, directly setting the content of the in-memory document object. The XmlDocument object in question could have been created afresh via a call to XmlManager.createDocument(), in which case it does not yet exist in the container, or having been retrieved from a container with XmlContainer.getDocument(). Finally, an XmlDocument object can be retrieved after a query using the methods of the XmlResults class. Each technique is demonstrated elsewhere. Refer to the later sections on managing documents for more details and examples of using the described input streams. The next section discusses the XmlContainer class in more depth.

Preparing and Executing Queries

XQuery queries are performed on containers using the XmlManager objects prepare() and query() methods. Because queries can span multiple containers, they are not centric to any one container, making this the logical class for queries to take place.

The XmlManager.prepare() method takes an XQuery expression string and a query context object as arguments (as well as the optional transaction object) and then returns an XmlQueryExpression object. This object encapsulates the parsed and optimized XQuery expression for repeated use in multiple operations. Calling its execute() method evaluates the expression against the containers (or documents) referred to by the query.

The XmlQueryContext object indicates to the query engine the context within which to perform a query. This context includes the namespace mappings, variable bindings, and flags to indicate how a query is to be performed and its results returned   everything the query engine needs to do its job, given the query string.

Listing 9-6 shows the creation of an XmlQueryContext object, using it to set a default collection (enabling you to omit collection() from your query), and then preparing and executing a query.

Listing 9-6. *Using XmlQueryContext*

```
from bsddb3.db import *
from dbxml import *

mymgr = XmlManager()
myquery = r"collection()/person[name='Bob']"

mycontainer = mymgr.openContainer("test.dbxml")
xmlqcontext = mymgr.createQueryContext()

qcontext.setDefaultCollection("test.dbxml")
queryexp = mymgr.prepare(myquery, qcontext)
results = queryexp.execute(qcontext)

del mycontainer
```

If the XML collection made use of namespaces, you would use the XmlQueryContext object to define them. Imagine that instead of <person/>, your top-level document elements looked like this:

```
<people:person xmlns:wordnet="http://brians.org/people">
```

You could now use the namespace in your query. In Listing 9-7, you•ll declare this namespace and also set a variable for use in the XQuery query.

Listing 9-7. *Declaring Namespaces and Variables*

```
from bsddb3.db import *
from dbxml import *

mymgr = XmlManager()
myquery = r"collection('test.dbxml')/people:person[name=$name]"
mycontainer = mymgr.openContainer("test.dbxml")
qcontext = mymgr.createQueryContext()

qcontext.setNamespace("people", "http://brians.org/people")
qcontext.setVariableValue("name", XmlValue("Bob"))
queryexp = mymgr.prepare(myquery, qcontext)
results = queryexp.execute(qcontext)
qcontext.setVariableValue("name", XmlValue("Jane"))
results = queryexp.execute(qcontext)

del mycontainer
```

Because the XmlQueryContext object is passed to execute() for a prepared query expression, the context can be manipulated without having to recompile the query expression. Note that in Listing 9-7, the query variable $name was changed and the query reissued without recompiling the prepared query expression.

BDB XML also allows for queries to be executed in a "one-off" fashion, without query preparation. This is helpful when you know that queries will not be used repeatedly or when you need to save the memory used by an XmlQueryExpression object. Listing 9-8 demonstrates the use of XmlManager's query() method to execute a query once.

Listing 9-8. *Performing a One-Off Query*

```
from bsddb3.db import *
from dbxml import *

mymgr = XmlManager()
myquery = r"collection('test.dbxml')/person[name='Jim']"

mycontainer = mymgr.openContainer("test.dbxml")
qcontext = mymgr.createQueryContext()
results = mymgr.query(myquery, qcontext)

del mycontainer
```

In addition to namespaces and variables, XmlQueryContext can determine how queries are executed and the values they return. The setEvaluationType() method allows for one of two evaluation types: eager and lazy, defined in Table 9-3.

Table 9-3. *Query Evaluation Types*

Type	Description
XmlQueryContext.Eager	The query is executed, with resulting values determined and stored in memory before the query returns. This is the default.
XmlQueryContext.Lazy	The query is executed, but the resulting values are not determined or stored in memory until the API refers to them by iterating the result set. This means that a query uses less overall memory and makes retrieval of the first result faster.

Listing 9-9 demonstrates setting the evaluation type to lazy.

Listing 9-9. *Querying with Lazy Evaluation*

```
from bsddb3.db import *
from dbxml import *

mymgr = XmlManager()
myquery = r"collection('test.dbxml')/person[name='Jim']"

mycontainer = mymgr.openContainer("test.dbxml")
qcontext = mymgr.createQueryContext()
qcontext.setEvaluationType(XmlQueryContext.Lazy)
results = mymgr.query(myquery, qcontext)

del mycontainer
```

Because the example does not iterate the query results, no values are actually retrieved, having set the evaluation type to lazy.

Using Query Results

The XmlQueryExpression.execute() and XmlManager.query() methods both return objects of class XmlResults, used to iterate the result set. The object is essentially a collection of XmlValue objects, which in turn represent any of BDB XMLs supported data types. The XmlResults uses an iteration interface with next() and previous() methods to navigate results. Each takes as argument an XmlValue object (or an XmlDocument object), into which it stores the next or previous result. The Python API makes this process more idiomatic (although you are free to use next() and previous() if you choose) by allowing for iteration over XmlResults, resulting in a single XmlValue object per iteration. Listing 9-10 demonstrates outputting the results of a query to standard out.

Listing 9-10. *Retrieving Query Results*

```
from bsddb3.db import *
from dbxml import *

mymgr = XmlManager()
myquery = r"collection('test.dbxml')/person[name='Fred']"

mycontainer = mymgr.openContainer("test.dbxml")
qcontext = mymgr.createQueryContext()

results = mymgr.query(myquery, qcontext)
for value in results:
    document = value.asDocument()
    name     = document.getName()
    content  = value.asString()
    print name, ": ", content

del mycontainer
```

Note here the use of several new methods, including XmlValue.asString() and XmlDocument.getName(). Certain pieces of document information, including its name within the container, are available only by querying directly or retrieving the result as a document. When your queries require the node values themselves, as opposed to the documents matching a query, asString() is all that is needed.

The XmlValue class also provides a DOM-like interface to not only retrieve values (as with the asString() and asDocument() methods) but also to navigate the nodes that the class represents. Its methods include getNextSibling(), getAttributes(), and getFirstChild(), making it useful for any postquery processing that you might need to do on query results.

The BDB XML query engine is capable of evaluating XQuery queries on documents and even individual query results, in addition to database containers. Listing 9-11 does exactly this by executing several queries using the XmlValue object. Because the document query will repeat for each result, it makes sense to prepare it by using an XmlQueryExpression object.

Listing 9-11. *Querying Results*

```
from bsddb3.db import *
from dbxml import *

mymgr = XmlManager()

mycontainer = mymgr.openContainer("test.dbxml")
qcontext = mymgr.createQueryContext()

results = mymgr.query("collection('test.dbxml')/person[name='Fred']", qcontext)
phonequery = mymgr.prepare("/person/phone", qcontext);
```

```
for value in results:
    phoneresults = phonequery.execute(value, qcontext)
    for phones in phoneresults:
        print "   phone: ", phoneresults.asString(), "\n"
```

```
del mycontainer
```

The exact same thing can be done with the XmlDocument object resulting from a call to XmlValue.asDocument(), passing that object as argument to XmlQueryExpression.execute(). Of course, if you anticipated only one <phone/> element in this example, you could instead just call XmlResults.next() instead of creating a for block. Note that the same XmlQueryContext object was used for both the container query and then the result query. The query object retains context information for query results, keeping track of a node's location in the larger document. Because of this, the second query in this example could have been relative to the result node, using the current node (.) instead:

```
./phone/text()
```

This same technique of querying results and documents can be useful for pulling data out of large documents, enabling you to work within the context of previous result sets.

You'll look more closely at the use of XmlDocument in a later section to demonstrate the retrieval of metadata.

Creating Other Objects

The bulk of XmlManager's remaining methods serve to simply construct objects of other subclasses. Many of them have already been demonstrated, as with the XmlManager.createTransaction() method, which instantiates an XmlTransaction object. All such method names begin with create, and most take no arguments, serving as basic constructors. They are createDocument() to instantiate an XmlDocument object, createIndexLookup() to instantiate an XmlIndexLookup object, createModify() to instantiate an XmlModify object, createQueryContext() to instantiate an XmlQueryContext object, and createResults() to create an empty XmlResults object. They are examined in the following sections, in which their returned objects are demonstrated.

Using XmlContainer

The XmlContainer class provides most of the functionality that concerns a container and its contents, including adding, replacing, updating and deleting documents; directly retrieving documents (using the getDocument() method); and managing indexes for the container.

As has been shown, an XmlContainer object is created using the XmlManager.createContainer() and XmlManager.openContainer() methods. With it, documents can be added using the putDocument() method, taking as argument either an XmlDocument or XmlInputStream. The previous section demonstrated this while supplying a document name and input stream or document container. The method will also accept an XML string, and will generate document names itself if one is not provided and if the call includes the DBXML_GEN_NAME flag. Listing 9-12 uses putDocument() without providing a document name.

Listing 9-12. *Letting BDB XML Generate Document Names*

```
from bsddb3.db import *
from dbxml import *

mymgr = XmlManager()
```

```
mycontainer = mymgr.openContainer("test.dbxml")
ucontext = mymgr.createUpdateContext()

content = r"<person><name>Bob</name></person>"
mycontainer.putDocument("", content, ucontext, DBXML_GEN_NAME)
del mycontainer
```

If a name is provided along with the DBXML_GEN_NAME flag, it is used as a prefix for the generated name. With this usage, BDB XML will guarantee the uniqueness of document names, incrementing them with each put document.

Documents are deleted from a container using the XmlContainer.deleteDocument() method, which accepts the document name or document object as its argument. The latter is useful when you want to iterate over a result set, deleting each document it contains, without having to retrieve the document name. This is demonstrated in Listing 9-13.

Listing 9-13. *Deleting Documents*

```
from bsddb3.db import *
from dbxml import *

mymgr = XmlManager()

mycontainer = mymgr.openContainer("test.dbxml")
qcontext = mymgr.createQueryContext()
ucontext = mymgr.createUpdateContext()

results = mymgr.query("collection('test.dbxml')/person[name='Bob']", qcontext)
for result in results:
    document = result.asDocument()
    print "Deleting document: ", document.getName(), "\n"
    mycontainer.deleteDocument(document, ucontext)

del mycontainer
```

When you want to replace a document in a container (as opposed to programmatically modifying it), you can use the XmlContainer.updateDocument() method. In fact, this operation works with any XmlDocument object, setting its name to be identical to the document to be replaced and handing it to the updateDocument() method. Normally, you will retrieve the document from the database, set new content using the XmlDocument.setContent() method (or setContentAsDOM() or setContentAsXmlInputStream()), and save it back to the container. Listing 9-14 retrieves a document from the container using the XmlContainer.getDocument() method, before replacing its content and saving it back to the container.

Listing 9-14. *Replacing a Document*

```
from bsddb3.db import *
from dbxml import *

mymgr = XmlManager()

mycontainer = mymgr.openContainer("test.dbxml")
qcontext = mymgr.createQueryContext()
ucontext = mymgr.createUpdateContext()

document = mycontainer.getDocument("12.xml")
document.setContent("<person><name>Bob</name></person>")
```

```
mycontainer.updateDocument(document, ucontext)
```

```
del mycontainer
```

The BDB XML API provides a more programmatic interface to partially modifying documents using the XmlModify class, which allows a description of changes to be built before applying them to one or many documents in a container. This is demonstrated in the following section.

A final major function of the XmlContainer class is the management of container indexes. Chapter 6, "Indexes," described the specifics of indexing strategies; this chapter examines adding, deleting, and examining indexes from the API.

Indexes can be added by using an index description string, as demonstrated in Listing 9-15.

Listing 9-15. *Adding an Index to a Container with an Index Description String*

```
from bsddb3.db import *
from dbxml import *

mymgr = XmlManager()

mycontainer = mymgr.openContainer("test.dbxml")
ucontext = mymgr.createUpdateContext()
```

```
mycontainer.addIndex("", "person", "node-element-equality-string", ucontext)
```

```
del mycontainer
```

The XmlContainer.getIndexSpecification() method returns an index specification for the container, encapsulating a description of all current indexes. It provides the addIndex() and deleteIndex() methods to manipulate the index description before applying it back to the container. The example in Listing 9-16 deletes one index and adds another by using an XmlIndexSpecification object.

Listing 9-16. *Manipulating a Container's Index Specification*

```
from bsddb3.db import *
from dbxml import *

mymgr = XmlManager()

mycontainer = mymgr.openContainer("test.dbxml")
ucontext = mymgr.createUpdateContext()
```

```
indexspec = mycontainer.getIndexSpecification()
indexspec.deleteIndex("", "person", "node-element-equality-string")
indexspec.addIndex("", "person", "node-attribute-equality-string")
mycontainer.setIndexSpecification(indexspec, ucontext)
```

```
del mycontainer
```

The XmlIndexSpecification object also provides methods for replacing an index, manipulating the default indexes, and iterating through the indexes within the specification.

One more class bears mentioning in the context of containers and indexes: XmlIndexLookup. Objects of this class are instantiated by the XmlManager.createIndexLookup() and enable you to retrieve all nodes or documents that have keys in any given index, as well as perform direct equality and range lookups. Listing 9-17 shows the listing of all documents for an index.

Listing 9-17. *Listing All Documents Referenced by an Index*

```
from bsddb3.db import *
from dbxml import *

mymgr = XmlManager()
mycontainer = mymgr.openContainer("test.dbxml")
qcontext = mymgr.createQueryContext()

indexlookup = mymgr.createIndexLookup(mycontainer, "", "name", "node-element-equality-
string")
results = indexlookup.execute(qcontext)
for result in results:
    document = result.asDocument()
    print document.getName(), ": ", document.getContent()

del mycontainer
```

The `XmlIndexLookup.execute()` operation returns entire documents unless the `DBXML_INDEX_NODES` flag was specified at container creation time, in which case the lookup returns the individual nodes referred to in the index keys.

The `XmlIndexLookup` class provides further access to an index's internal workings with methods to set bounds for ranged lookups, as well as the ability to set a parent node for indexes that use edge paths rather than node paths.

Using XmlDocument and XmlModify

The `XmlDocument` class is used throughout the API primarily as a document handle, passed to and from methods of other classes. It also provides methods for getting and setting document content (as already demonstrated), getting and setting document metadata, and setting the document's name.

A document's metadata is set with the `XmlDocument.setMetaData()` method. Document metadata entails an attribute name, a value, and an optional URI, demonstrated in Listing 9-18.

Listing 9-18. *Adding Metadata to a Document*

```
from bsddb3.db import *
from dbxml import *

mymgr = XmlManager()
mycontainer = mymgr.openContainer("test.dbxml")
ucontext = mymgr.createUpdateContext()

uri = "http://brians.org/metadata"
metaname = "createdOn"
metavalue = XmlValue(XmlValue.DATE_TIME, "2006-02-05T05:23:14")
document = mycontainer.getDocument("114.xml")
document.setMetaData(uri, metaname, metavalue)
mycontainer.updateDocument(document, ucontext, DBXML_LAZY_DOCS)

del mycontainer
```

Metadata can be retrieved from an `XmlDocument` using the `getMetaData()` method. This is an example of a method that doesn't have a particularly idiomatic usage (in Python), but instead uses the C++ library calls. Listing 9-19 demonstrates the reading of metadata using the `getMetaData()` method.

Listing 9-19. *Reading Metadata from a Document*

```
from bsddb3.db import *
from dbxml import *

mymgr = XmlManager()
mycontainer = mymgr.openContainer("test.dbxml")

uri = "http://brians.org/metadata"
metaname = "createdOn"
document = mycontainer.getDocument("114.xml")
metavalue = XmlValue()
document.getMetaData(uri, metaname, metavalue)
print "114.xml, created on ", metavalue.asString(), "\n"

del mycontainer
```

Note that the metavalue variable had to be instantiated and passed as an argument to the getMetaData() method, which in turn set its value. Because getMetaData() returns a boolean, it is the required usage.

Tip Three BDB XML classes implement Python iterators: XmlResults, XmlMetaDataIterator, and XmlIndexSpecification. They allow idiomatic retrieval of query results, metadata attributes, and index specifications, respectively.

This section will also look at the use of the XmlModify class to modify documents. Documents can be modified within a container using the XmlModify class without the need to replace the document or copy it to memory. This class enables you to construct a series of steps for manipulating the contents of a document and then apply it to one or many documents within a container. It thus becomes a simple matter to perform container-wide document changes.

The XmlModify object is instantiated with a call to XmlManager.createModify(). A series of methods is exposed to provide for appending content, inserting and replacing content, and renaming and removing nodes. Assume that your database was filled with documents having the following structure:

```
<person>
    <name>Samuel</name>
    <age>51</age>
</person>
```

You want to create a new attribute node called "type" under the <name/> element and with the value "given". (You can assume that the need to add surnames to the database has been discovered.) This involves an append change to your document, appending to the <name/> element. If you call the XmlModify.addAppendStep() method with the target node, the node type you are appending, and the attribute name and value, you get the example in Listing 9-20.

Listing 9-20. *Modifying a Document*

```
from bsddb3.db import *
from dbxml import *

mymgr = XmlManager()
mycontainer = mymgr.openContainer("test.dbxml")
qcontext = mymgr.createQueryContext()
ucontext = mymgr.createUpdateContext()
```

```
mymodify = mymgr.createModify()
queryexp = mymgr.prepare("/person/name", qcontext)
mymodify.addAppendStep(queryexp, XmlModify.Attribute, "type", "given")
document = mycontainer.getDocument("61.xml")
docvalue = XmlValue(document)
mymodify.execute(docvalue, qcontext, ucontext)
```

```
del mycontainer
```

Any series of XmlModify steps could be included. Note that XmlModify is executed on an XmlValue instead of on an XmlDocument. The execute() method will also accept an XmlResults object, enabling you to apply the XmlModify object to all documents in a query result. Listing 9-21 performs a query for all documents that have a /person/name element and adds the @type="given" attribute to each.

Listing 9-21. *Modifying All Documents in a Result Set*

```
from bsddb3.db import *
from dbxml import *

mymgr = XmlManager()
mycontainer = mymgr.openContainer("test.dbxml")
qcontext = mymgr.createQueryContext()
ucontext = mymgr.createUpdateContext()

mymodify = mymgr.createModify()
queryexp = mymgr.prepare("/person/name", qcontext)
mymodify.addAppendStep(queryexp, XmlModify.Attribute, "type", "given")

results = mymgr.query("collection('test.dbxml')/person[name='Bill']", qcontext)
mymodify.execute(results, qcontext, ucontext)
```

```
del mycontainer
```

This changes all documents matching the query according to the XmlModify object. Keep in mind that this can be an expensive operation, but less so than retrieving and replacing each pertinent document in the container. The API reference at the end of this chapter contains a description of the all XmlModify methods.

Transactions

Berkeley DB XML inherits Berkeley DB's transactions, enabling optional transactional processing for all operations. Transactions require that certain parameters be set for your environment and the containers within it. Four Berkeley DB subsystems must be enabled for an environment to perform transactions: locking, logging, the cache, and transactions. With a transactional environment, containers must be created and opened with the DBXML_TRANSACTIONAL flag.

■**Caution** Whenever a container is opened transactionally, BDB XML will automatically protect individual writes for you if you do not use a transaction object. This convenience requires that when you *do* use transaction objects, they must be provided to all calls to a modifying operation. Because BDB XML will create another transaction in cases in which an open transaction is missing from the parameter list, it can result in self-deadlocking, with each transaction waiting for the other.

The XmlManager.createTransaction() method is used after a container is opened to begin a transaction, and the resulting XmlTransaction objects commit() method to complete it (or abort() to cancel it). Listing 9-22 shows opening of an environment with the appropriate flags set, creating a transactional container, and adding a document using a transaction object.

Listing 9-22. *Creating a Transactional Container and Inserting a Document Transactionally*

```
from bsddb3.db import *
from dbxml import *

environment = DBEnv()
environment.open("myEnv",
    DB_CREATE|DB_INIT_LOCK|DB_INIT_LOG|DB_INIT_MPOOL|DB_INIT_TXN, 0)
mymgr = XmlManager(environment, 0)
uc = mymgr.createUpdateContext()
container = mymgr.createContainer("test.dbxml", DBXML_TRANSACTIONAL)
txn = mymgr.createTransaction()
container.putDocument(txn, "doc12", "<person>Bill</person>", uc)
txn.commit()
```

Conclusion

Python developers should feel right at home with the BDB XML Python API. Its simple interface makes for compact access to a powerful set of XML database manipulation, index, and query processing options.

At the time of writing, an official tutorial or reference for the Python BDB XML API doesn't exist. Please refer to Appendix B, "BDB XML API Reference," for a class and function reference for all APIs, including Python. Note also that the BDB XML distribution includes Python examples that can serve as templates for your own applications.

CHAPTER 10

■ ■ ■

BDB XML with Java

The Java API included with BDB XML exposes all classes and methods of the C++ API. Because of the API design and the similarity of the languages, the Java API is nearly identical to the C++ interface, including its exception handling. The primary difference is that manager, container, and document configurations are handled with configuration classes instead of bitwise OR'd method parameters.

This chapter is both an overview of using the BDB XML Java API and a general reference for applicable classes. As in Chapter 9, "BDB XML with Python," the code examples are platform-agnostic. Please refer to Chapter 3, "Installation and Configuration," for instructions on building Java libraries and compiling the applications that use them. All the code listings in this chapter are complete, so you should be able to copy them as shown and compile without trouble assuming that your environment is properly configured. However, for the sake of readability, unnecessary (but strongly recommended) features such as exception handling are often omitted.

Running Applications

If your BDB XML libraries are properly compiled and the Java interface is successfully built and installed, compiling a Java file that uses the API to bytecode is simply a matter of importing the necessary classes. Unlike some bindings, in Java they are imported individually:

```
import com.sleepycat.dbxml.XmlContainer;
import com.sleepycat.dbxml.XmlException;
import com.sleepycat.dbxml.XmlManager;
```

Or they are imported by using a wildcard:

```
import com.sleepycat.dbxml.*;
```

All classes necessary to compile BDB XML applications are contained in the dbxml.jar and db.jar class libraries, installed on Unix by default in the install/lib/ directory of the BDB XML distribution and in jar/ on Windows. They must be referenced with a CLASSPATH environment variable or via command-line arguments. Similarly, the dynamic libraries must be found in an LD_LIBRARY_PATH environment variable or equivalent. The following compiles a class using the Java API on Unix, given proper class paths:

```
$ javac -classpath "/path/to/dbxml-x/install/lib/dbxml.jar:/path/to
    /dbxml-x/install/lib/db.jar" myDbXml.java
```

The resulting .class file can then be executed (assuming that it contains a main() method). In this case, it assumes a class name of myDbXmlTest:

```
$ java myDbXmlTest
```

The examples included with the BDB XML distribution are located in the dbxml/examples/java/ directory and demonstrate much of the Java API functionality.

Class Organization

The major API classes are listed in Table 10-1 in their construction (not inheritance) hierarchy, indicating which class objects provide methods to construct other objects. The class names in Table 10-1 indicate where constructors exist, not necessarily all classes that return objects of a given class. Omitted are minor classes, but they are covered later in the chapter.

Table 10-1. *Major BDB XML Java Classes*

Class Name	Description
XmlManager	The main application class used to create, open, and maintain containers; execute queries; and so on
XmlContainer	A container handle with methods for managing documents, manipulating indexes, and so on
XmlIndexSpecification	An interface to programmatically manage the indexes for a container
XmlDocument	A document within a container with methods for getting and managing content
XmlResults	Encapsulates the results of a query or lookup operation
XmlModify	A programmatic interface to modifying documents using stepped changes
XmlQueryContext	Encapsulates the namespaces, variable bindings, and flags for use with container queries
XmlUpdateContext	Encapsulates the context for updates to a container
XmlQueryExpression	A parsed/prepared XQuery expression
XmlException	A BDB XML exception class, thrown during and representing error conditions
XmlTransaction	A BDB XML transaction object
XmlValue	Used to store XML node values when retrieving and storing data
Environment	A Berkeley DB class for managing a DB environment

Errors and Exception Handling

BDB XML Java operations throw exceptions when errors are encountered. They are thrown as XmlException objects, inherited from the Berkeley DB DbException class and derived from the standard Java Exception class. This process enables you to catch BDB XML exceptions separate from those of other classes.

Listing 10-1 demonstrates exception handling with the Java API.

Listing 10-1. *Exception Handling*

```
import com.sleepycat.dbxml.XmlContainer;
import com.sleepycat.dbxml.XmlException;
import com.sleepycat.dbxml.XmlManager;
```

```
class myDbXml {
    public static void main(String args[]) throws Throwable
    {
        // Create an XmlManager
        XmlManager myManager = null;
        try {
            // Open a container
            XmlContainer myContainer = myManager.openContainer("container.dbxml");
            myContainer.delete();
        } catch (XmlException e) {
            // Error handling goes here
        } catch (Exception e) {
            // Error handling goes here
        }
    }
}
```

Exceptions are often not sufficient to debug problems with your application. In such cases, the Berkeley DB Environment class provides an error stream that can be set to System.err. The Java API provides an EnvironmentConfig class for managing settings specific to database environments. Listing 10-2 demonstrates setting an error stream.

Listing 10-2. *Setting an Error Stream*

```
import com.sleepycat.dbxml.*;
import com.sleepycat.db.Environment;
import com.sleepycat.db.EnvironmentConfig;
import java.io.File;

class myDbXml {
    public static void main(String args[]) throws Throwable
    {
        File myDir = new File("myEnv/");

        // Open environment
        EnvironmentConfig myEnvConf = new EnvironmentConfig();
        myEnvConf.setErrorStream(System.err);
        Environment myEnv = new Environment(myDir, myEnvConf);

        // Create an XmlManager
        XmlManagerConfig myManagerConf = new XmlManagerConfig();
        XmlManager myManager = new XmlManager(myEnv, myManagerConf);
    }
}
```

Error streams are also useful for general debugging because the XmlManager class enables the logging level to be varied. The methods setLogCategory() and setLogLevel() allow for changes to the granularity of log messages. Listing 10-3 demonstrates the activation of full debugging categories and levels. Categories describe the BDB XML subsystem to be logged and also include indexer messages, query messages, and container messages. Levels include debugging, informational messages, and warnings. See Appendix B, "BDB XML API Reference," for a full list of categories and log levels.

Listing 10-3. *Setting the Log Level*

```
import com.sleepycat.dbxml.*;
import com.sleepycat.db.*;
import java.io.*;
```

```java
class myDbXml {
    public static void main(String args[]) throws Throwable
    {
        File myDir = new File("myEnv/");

        // Open environment
        EnvironmentConfig myEnvConf = new EnvironmentConfig();
        myEnvConf.setErrorStream(System.err);
        Environment myEnv = new Environment(myDir, myEnvConf);

        // Create an XmlManager
        XmlManagerConfig myManagerConf = new XmlManagerConfig();
        XmlManager myManager = new XmlManager(myEnv, myManagerConf);
        myManager.setLogLevel(XmlManager.LEVEL_ALL, true);
        myManager.setLogCategory(XmlManager.CATEGORY_ALL, true);
    }
}
```

Environments

Environments provide logging, locking, and transaction support for database containers. Creating and opening environments require the XmlManager object, which has managed the environments automatically in most examples thus far. Environments are not specific to BDB XML, which is why there is no *XML* in the class used to manage them; Environment and EnvironmentConfig are used by Berkeley DB and, by association, Berkeley DB XML applications.

The EnvironmentConfig class provides many methods for configuring a database environment. This section discusses instantiation (as well as opening and closing environments).

The Environment constructor takes a directory path (as a File object), an EnvironmentConfig object, and a Unix file mode (ignored on Windows) as arguments, automatically opening the environment. The object is then passed to the XmlManager constructor. Listing 10-4 demonstrates opening a database environment with some typical settings and the instantiation of an XmlManager object.

Listing 10-4. *Opening a Database Environment*

```java
import com.sleepycat.dbxml.*;
import com.sleepycat.db.*;
import java.io.*;

class myDbXml {
    public static void main(String args[]) throws Throwable
    {
        File myDir = new File("myEnv/");

        // Open environment
        EnvironmentConfig myEnvConf = new EnvironmentConfig();
        myEnvConf.setErrorStream(System.err);
        myEnvConf.setAllowCreate(true);        // create if it doesn't exist
        myEnvConf.setInitializeCache(true);    // turn on shared memory
        myEnvConf.setTransactional(true);      // transactions on
        myEnvConf.setInitializeLocking(true); // locking on
        myEnvConf.setInitializeLogging(true); // logging on
        Environment myEnv = new Environment(myDir, myEnvConf);
```

```
        // Create an XmlManager
        XmlManagerConfig myManagerConf = new XmlManagerConfig();
        XmlManagerConfig.setAdoptEnvironment(true);
        XmlManager myManager = new XmlManager(myEnv, myManagerConf);
        myManager.setLogLevel(XmlManager.LEVEL_ALL, true);
        myManager.setLogCategory(XmlManager.CATEGORY_ALL, true);
    }
}
```

XmlManager

XmlManager is the primary class for working with containers and for managing the other objects used within the BDB XML API. It is used to create, open, rename, and delete containers; create document and context objects; and prepare and execute XQuery queries.

Instantiating XmlManager Objects

XmlManager objects are created with their constructor and destroyed using their delete() method. If you provide an Environment object to the constructor (along with the XmlManagerConfig object having called setAdoptEnvironment(true)), XmlManager automatically closes that Environment object. If you do not provide an Environment object to the XmlManager constructor, it automatically creates an environment for you. This latter option carries some constraints because you do not have the ability to configure subsystems and you must tell XmlManager where to create and open your containers. It is generally preferable to create your own Environment object and pass it to the XmlManager constructor. Listing 10-4 demonstrated the creation of an XmlManager object using an opened Environment object.

■**Caution** Because Java garbage collects objects (instead of destroying them when they leave scope), problems arise for libraries such as BDB XML that require an explicit release of resources. All objects should therefore be deleted explicitly (they include a delete() method for this purpose).

Managing Containers

You can create, open, rename, and delete containers with the XmlManager object. Open and create operations share a list of container flags (see Appendix B for more information). A container is opened by using the XmlManager.openContainer() method, and a single container can be opened multiple times within your application. The createContainer() method creates and subsequently opens a container. Containers are closed with the objects delete() method.

■**Caution** Take care to always close open containers to avoid stale locks.

Listing 10-5 demonstrates a simple container creation. This example and subsequent code examples tend to omit the environment instantiation for the sake of brevity (although Environment would normally be used). The XmlContainerConfig class is used to set options for an opened or created container. In this case, the container is created to allow XML validation and to be a node container. Unlike the other language APIs, which take bitwise ORd flags as arguments, the Java API enables most configuration options to be set by using these configuration classes.

Listing 10-5. *Creating a Container*

```
import com.sleepycat.dbxml.*;
import com.sleepycat.db.*;

class myDbXml {
    public static void main(String args[]) throws Throwable
    {
        // Create an XmlManager
        XmlManagerConfig myManagerConf = new XmlManagerConfig();
        XmlManager myManager = new XmlManager(myManagerConf);

        XmlContainerConfig myContainerConf = new XmlContainerConfig();
        myContainerConf.setAllowValidation(true);
        myContainerConf.setNodeContainer(true);

        XmlContainer myContainer = myManager.createContainer
            ( "myContainer.bdbxml", myContainerConf );
        myContainer.delete();
        myManager.delete();
    }
}
```

Opening an already-created container uses an identical syntax with the XmlManager.openContainer() method. The same set of arguments is accepted as createContainer(), but some arguments have no use unless the XmlContainerConfig.setAllowCreate() flag is set to true before the call to openContainer(). For example, a container type cannot be set on an already-created container, and XmlContainerConfig.setExclusiveCreate() is relevant only when creating a new container (it throws an error if a container exists).

Renaming and deleting containers is performed by using the XmlManager.renameContainer() and XmlManager.removeContainer() methods. Both succeed only on unopened containers. The first takes two string arguments: the current name of the container and the new name. The second simply takes the name of the container to remove. Both take an optional transaction object as the first argument. Listing 10-6 demonstrates both methods.

Listing 10-6. *Renaming and Deleting Containers*

```
import com.sleepycat.dbxml.*;
import com.sleepycat.db.*;

class myDbXml {
    public static void main(String args[]) throws Throwable
    {
        // Create an XmlManager
        XmlManager myManager = new XmlManager();
        myManager.removeContainer("newtest.dbxml");
        myManager.renameContainer("test.dbxml", "newtest.dbxml");
        myManager.delete();
    }
}
```

Loading Documents

Documents are most efficiently loaded into a container directly by using XmlManager to create an input stream, which enables files to be loaded as string objects, from a file on disk, from a network URL, from a memory buffer, or from standard input. Note that no validation is performed on input streams by BDB XML. Only when a document is put into a container does the system read from the stream, parse the content, and validate it (not necessarily schema-validated or Data Type Definition [DTD].validated). No errors are thrown when an input stream is created using an invalid location, filename, and so on until the operation is performed.

XmlManager provides several ways to create these input streams, as listed in Table 10-2. All these methods return an object of class XmlInputStream, which is then used to load the document into the container (or into a document object, as will be shown).

Table 10-2. *XmlManager Input Stream-Creation Methods*

Method	Description
XmlManager.createLocalFileInputStream()	Takes as its argument a filename
XmlManager.createURLInputStream()	Takes as arguments three URL IDs
XmlManager.createMemBufInputStream()	Takes as arguments memory address and byte counts
XmlManager.createInputStream()	Creates an XmlInputStream from a javaio. InputStream, taking the latter as argument

The XmlInputStream object resulting from any of these methods is then used in several ways. Most often, it is passed to the XmlContainer.putDocument() method, which loads the data using the input stream, parses the document, performs any necessary validation, and then stores the document in the container (the immediacy depends on whether a transaction is used). Of course, putDocument() also accepts an XML document in the form of a string, but the BDB XML input stream can save the overhead of loading the text. Listing 10-7 loads a document into a container using a local file input stream.

Listing 10-7. *Adding a Document to a Container from a Local File*

```
import com.sleepycat.dbxml.*;

class myDbXml {
    public static void main(String args[]) throws Throwable
    {
        XmlManager myManager = new XmlManager();
        XmlContainer myContainer = myManager.openContainer("container.bdbxml");

        // The update context is needed to add the document.
        XmlUpdateContext theContext = myManager.createUpdateContext();

        // Create the file input stream
        XmlInputStream myStream =
            myManager.createLocalFileInputStream("./file176.xml");

        // Put the document in the container
        myContainer.putDocument("176", myStream, theContext);
```

```
        // ... clean up
        myUpdateContext.delete();
        myContainer.delete();
        myManager.delete();
    }
}
```

Note that the filename specified for the input stream is different from the document name supplied to putDocument(). (They could have the same filename, of course.)

An alternative to passing the XmlInputStream object to putDocument() is to supply it as an argument to the XmlDocument.setContentAsXmlInputStream() method, directly setting the content of the in-memory document object. The XmlDocument object in question can be created anew via a call to XmlManager.createDocument() or be retrieved from a container with XmlContainer.getDocument(). Finally, an XmlDocument object can be retrieved after a query using the methods of the XmlResults class. See the sections on managing documents for more details and examples of using the described input streams. The next section discusses the XmlContainer class in more depth.

Preparing and Executing Queries

XQuery queries are performed on containers by using the XmlManager object prepare() and query() methods. Because queries can span multiple containers, they are not centric to any one container, so XmlManager is the logical class for queries.

The XmlManager.prepare() method takes an XQuery expression string and a query context object as arguments (as well as the optional transaction object) and returns an XmlQueryExpression object. This object encapsulates the parsed and optimized XQuery expression for repeated use in multiple operations. Calling the execute() method evaluates the expression against the containers (or documents) referred to by the query.

The XmlQueryContext object indicates to the query engine the context within which to perform a query. This context includes the namespace mappings, variable bindings, and flags to indicate how a query is to be performed and its results returned   everything the query engine needs to do its job given the query string.

Listing 10-8 demonstrates creating an XmlQueryContext object, using it to set a default collection (enabling you to omit the argument to collection() from the query), and then preparing and executing a query.

Listing 10-8. *Using the XmlQueryContext Object*

```
import com.sleepycat.dbxml.*;
class myDbXml {
    public static void main(String args[]) throws Throwable {
        XmlManager myManager = new XmlManager();
        XmlContainer myContainer = myManager.openContainer("myContainer.dbxml");

        XmlQueryContext myContext = myManager.createQueryContext();
        myContext.setDefaultCollection("myContainer.dbxml");
        String myQuery = "collection()/Synset[Word='wisdom']";
        XmlQueryExpression qe = myManager.prepare(myQuery, myContext);
        XmlResults results = qe.execute(myContext);

        // ...
        results.delete();
        qe.delete();
        myContext.delete();
```

```
        myContainer.delete();
        myManager.delete();
    }
}
```

■**Note** Java applications typically put object cleanup in a `finally` block.

If the XML collection made use of namespaces, you could use the `XmlQueryContext` object to define them. Imagine that instead of `<person/>`, your top-level document elements look like this:

`<people:person xmlns:wordnet="http://brians.org/people">`

You can now use the namespace in the query. Listing 10-9 declares this namespace and sets a variable for use in the XQuery expression.

Listing 10-9. *Declaring Namespaces and Variables*

```
import com.sleepycat.dbxml.*;

class myDbXml {
    public static void main(String args[]) throws Throwable {
        XmlManager myManager = new XmlManager();
        XmlContainer myContainer = myManager.openContainer("myContainer.dbxml");

        XmlQueryContext myContext = myManager.createQueryContext();
        myContext.setNamespace("people", "http://brians.org/people");
        myContext.setVariableValue("name", new XmlValue("Bob"));
        String myQuery = "collection('myContainer.dbxml')/people:person[name=$name]";

        XmlQueryExpression qe = myManager.prepare(myQuery, myContext);

        XmlResults results = qe.execute(myContext);

        // ...
        results.delete()
        qe.delete();
        myContext.delete();
        myContainer.delete();
        myManager.delete();
    }
}
```

Because the `XmlQueryContext` object is passed to `execute()` for a prepared query expression, the context can be manipulated without having to recompile the query expression. In Listing 10-9 the query variable `$name` was changed, and the query was reissued without recompiling the prepared query expression.

BDB XML also enables queries to be executed in a one-off fashion without query preparation. This process is helpful when you know that the queries will not be used repeatedly or when you need to save the memory used by an `XmlQueryExpression` object. Listing 10-10 demonstrates using the `XmlManager` `query()` method to execute a query just once.

Listing 10-10. *Performing a One-Off Query*

```
import com.sleepycat.dbxml.*;

class myDbXml {
    public static void main(String args[]) throws Throwable {
        XmlManager myManager = new XmlManager();
        XmlContainer myContainer = myManager.openContainer("myContainer.dbxml");

        XmlQueryContext myContext = myManager.createQueryContext();
        String myQuery = "collection('myContainer.dbxml')/person[name='Jim']";
        XmlResults myResults = myManager.query(myQuery, myContext);

        // ...
        myResults.delete();
        myContext.delete();
        myContainer.delete();
        myManager.delete();
    }
}
```

The XmlQueryContext object can also determine how queries are executed and the values they return. The setEvaluationType() method allows for two evaluation types: *eager* and *lazy* (see Table 10-3).

Table 10-3. *Query Evaluation Types*

Type	Description
XmlQueryContext.Eager	The query is executed with the resulting values determined and stored in memory before the query returns. This is the default.
XmlQueryContext.Lazy	The query is executed, but the resulting values are not determined or stored in memory until the API refers to them by iterating the result set. The query uses less overall memory and enables a quicker retrieval of the first result.

Listing 10-11 demonstrates setting the evaluation type to lazy.

Listing 10-11. *Querying with Lazy Evaluation*

```
import com.sleepycat.dbxml.*;

class myDbXml {
    public static void main(String args[]) throws Throwable {
        XmlManager myManager = new XmlManager();
        XmlContainer myContainer = myManager.openContainer("myContainer.dbxml");

        XmlQueryContext myContext = myManager.createQueryContext();
        myContext.setEvaluationType(XmlQueryContext.Lazy);
        String myQuery = "collection('myContainer.dbxml')/person[name='Jim']";
        XmlResults myResults = myManager.query(myQuery, myContext);

        myContainer.close();
        myManager.delete();
    }
}
```

Because the example does not iterate the query results, no values are actually retrieved (with the evaluation type set to lazy).

Using Query Results

The XmlQueryExpression.execute() and XmlManager.query() methods return objects of class XmlResults, which are used to iterate the result set. The object is essentially a collection of XmlValue objects, which in turn represent any of the BDB XML supported data types. The XmlResults class uses an iteration interface with the next() and previous() methods to navigate results. Each takes as argument an XmlValue object (or an XmlDocument object), into which it stores the next or previous result. Listing 10-12 demonstrates outputting the results of a query to standard output.

Listing 10-12. *Retrieving Query Results*

```
import com.sleepycat.dbxml.*;

class myDbXml {
    public static void main(String args[]) throws Throwable {
        XmlManager myManager = new XmlManager();
        XmlContainer myContainer = myManager.openContainer("myContainer.dbxml");

        XmlQueryContext myContext = myManager.createQueryContext();
        String myQuery = "collection('myContainer.dbxml')/person[name='Jim']";

        XmlResults myResults = myManager.query(myQuery, myContext);
        XmlValue myValue = myResults.next();
        while (myValue != null) {
            XmlDocument myDocument = myValue.asDocument();
            String name = myDocument.getName();
            String content = myValue.asString();
            System.out.print("Document " + name + ":\n");
            System.out.print(content);
            myValue = myResults.next();
        }

        myValue.delete();
        myResults.delete();
        myQuery.delete();
        myContext.delete();
        myContainer.delete();
        myManager.delete();
    }
}
```

Note the use of several new methods, including XmlValue.asString() and XmlDocument.getName(). Certain pieces of document information, including the name within the container, are available only by querying directly or retrieving the result as a document. When your queries require the node values instead of the documents matching a query, asString() is all you need.

The XmlValue class provides a Document Object Model (DOM)-like interface to not only retrieve values (as with the asString() and asDocument() methods) but also to navigate the nodes it represents. Because its methods include getNextSibling(), getAttributes(), and getFirstChild(), the XmlValue class is useful for any post-query processing on query results.

The BDB XML query engine is capable of evaluating XQuery queries on documents and individual query results in addition to database containers. Listing 10-13 does exactly this by executing several queries using the XmlValue object. Because the document query repeats for each result, it makes sense to prepare it by using an XmlQueryExpression object.

Listing 10-13. *Querying Results*

```java
import com.sleepycat.dbxml.*;

class myDbXml {
    public static void main(String args[]) throws Throwable {
        XmlManager myManager = new XmlManager();
        XmlContainer myContainer = myManager.openContainer("myContainer.dbxml");
        XmlQueryContext myContext = myManager.createQueryContext();

        XmlQueryExpression mySubquery =
                myManager.prepare("/person/phone", myContext);
        XmlResults myResults =
                myManager.query("collection('myContainer.dbxml')/person[name='Jim']",
                myContext);
        XmlValue myValue = myResults.next();
        while (myValue != null) {
            XmlResults subResults = mySubquery.execute(myValue, myContext);
            XmlValue subValue = subResults.next();
            while (subValue != null) {
                XmlDocument myDocument = subValue.asDocument();
                String name = myDocument.getName();
                String content = subValue.asString();
                System.out.print("Document " + name + ":\n");
                System.out.print(content);
                subValue = subResults.next();
            }
            myValue = myResults.next();
            subValue.delete();
            subResults.delete();
        }

        myValue.delete();
        myResults.delete();
        mySubquery.delete();
        myContext.delete();
        myContainer.delete();
        myManager.delete();
    }
}
```

Of course, if you anticipate only one <phone/> element in this example, you can just call the XmlResults.next() method instead of creating a for block.

The second query in this example can be made relative to the result node by using the current node (.) instead:

```
./phone/string()
```

This same technique of querying results and documents can be useful for pulling data out of large documents, enabling you to work within the context of previous result sets.

You will learn more about the use of XmlDocument to demonstrate the retrieval of metadata later in this chapter.

Creating Other Objects

The bulk of the remaining XmlManager methods serve to construct objects of other BDB XML subclasses. Many of them have already been demonstrated, as with the XmlManager.createTransaction() method, which instantiates an XmlTransaction object. All such method names begin with create and most take no arguments, serving as basic constructors. These methods include createDocument() to instantiate an XmlDocument object, createIndexLookup() to instantiate an XmlIndexLookup object, createModify() to instantiate an XmlModify object, createQueryContext() to instantiate an XmlQueryContext object, and createResults() to create an empty XmlResults object. These methods are examined in the following sections, in which their returned objects are demonstrated.

Using XmlContainer

The XmlContainer class provides most of the functionality that concerns a container and its contents, including adding, replacing, updating and deleting documents; directly retrieving documents (using the getDocument() method); and managing indexes for the container.

An XmlContainer object is created with the XmlManager.createContainer() and XmlManager.openContainer() methods. Documents can be added by using the putDocument() method, taking as argument either XmlDocument or XmlInputStream. The previous section demonstrated this while supplying a document name and input stream or document container. The method also accepts an XML string; it generates document names if one is not provided and if the call includes the XmlDocumentConfig.setGenerateName() setting. Listing 10-14 uses putDocument() without providing a document name.

Listing 10-14. *Letting BDB XML Generate Document Names*

```
import com.sleepycat.dbxml.*;

class myDbXml {
    public static void main(String args[]) throws Throwable
    {
        XmlManager myManager = new XmlManager();
        XmlContainer myContainer = myManager.openContainer("myContainer.dbxml");
        XmlUpdateContext theContext = myManager.createUpdateContext();
        XmlDocumentConfig docConfig = new XmlDocumentConfig();

        docConfig.setGenerateName(true);
        String content = "<person><name>Bob</name></person>";
        myContainer.putDocument("", content, theContext, docConfig);
        myContainer.delete();
        myManager.delete();
    }
}
```

With this usage, BDB XML guarantees the uniqueness of document names, incrementing them with each document.

Documents are deleted from a container by using the XmlContainer.deleteDocument() method, which accepts with the document name or document object as its argument. The latter is useful when you want to iterate over a result set, deleting each document it contains, without having to retrieve the document name. Deleting is demonstrated in Listing 10-15.

Listing 10-15. *Deleting Documents*

```
import com.sleepycat.dbxml.*;

class myDbXml {
    public static void main(String args[]) throws Throwable {
        XmlManager myManager = new XmlManager();
        XmlContainer myContainer = myManager.openContainer("myContainer.dbxml");
        XmlQueryContext qContext = myManager.createQueryContext();
        XmlUpdateContext uContext = myManager.createUpdateContext();
        String myQuery = "collection('myContainer.dbxml')/person[name='Steve']";

        XmlResults myResults = myManager.query(myQuery, qContext);
        XmlValue myValue = myResults.next();
        while (myValue != null) {
            XmlDocument myDocument = myValue.asDocument();
            String name = myDocument.getName();
            System.out.print("Deleting " + name + "\n");
            myContainer.deleteDocument(myDocument, uContext);
            myValue = myResults.next();
        }
        myContainer.close();
    }
}
```

When you want to update a document in a container (instead of partially modifying it), you can use the XmlContainer.updateDocument() method. This operation works with any XmlDocument object, setting its name to be identical to the document to be replaced and handing it to the updateDocument() method. You normally retrieve the document from the database, set new content using the XmlDocument.setContent() method (or setContentAsDOM() or setContentAsXmlInputStream()), and save it back to the container. Listing 10-16 retrieves a document from the container using the XmlContainer.getDocument() method before replacing its content and saving it back to the container.

Listing 10-16. *Replacing a Document*

```
import com.sleepycat.dbxml.*;

class myDbXml {
    public static void main(String args[]) throws Throwable
    {
        XmlManager myManager = new XmlManager();
        XmlContainer myContainer = myManager.openContainer("myContainer.dbxml");
        XmlUpdateContext uContext = myManager.createUpdateContext();

        XmlDocument myDocument = myContainer.getDocument("12.xml");
        myDocument.setContent("<person><name>Bob</name></person>");
        myContainer.updateDocument(myDocument, uContext);

        myContainer.delete();
        myManager.delete();
    }
}
```

The BDB XML API provides a more programmatic interface to partially modifying documents using the XmlModify class, which enables a description of changes to be built before applying them to one or many documents in a container. This process is demonstrated in the following section.

A final major function of the XmlContainer class is to manage container indexes. Chapter 6, "Indexes," described the specifics of indexing strategies; this chapter examines adding, deleting, and examining indexes from the API.

Indexes can be added by using an index description string, as shown in Listing 10-17.

Listing 10-17. *Adding an Index to a Container with an Index Description String*

```java
import com.sleepycat.dbxml.*;

class myDbXml {
    public static void main(String args[]) throws Throwable
    {
        XmlManager myManager = new XmlManager();
        XmlContainer myContainer = myManager.openContainer("myContainer.dbxml");
        XmlUpdateContext uContext = myManager.createUpdateContext();

        myContainer.addIndex("", "person", "node-element-equality-string", uContext);

        myContainer.delete();
        myManager.delete();
    }
}
```

The XmlContainer.getIndexSpecification() method returns an index specification for the container, encapsulating a description of all current indexes. It provides the addIndex() and deleteIndex() methods to manipulate the index description before applying it back to the container. The example in Listing 10-18 uses an XmlIndexSpecification object to delete one index and add another.

Listing 10-18. *Manipulating a Container's Index Specification*

```java
import com.sleepycat.dbxml.*;

class myDbXml {
    public static void main(String args[]) throws Throwable
    {
        XmlManager myManager = new XmlManager();
        XmlContainer myContainer = myManager.openContainer("myContainer.dbxml");
        XmlUpdateContext uContext = myManager.createUpdateContext();

        XmlIndexSpecification myIndexSpec = myContainer.getIndexSpecification();
        myIndexSpec.deleteIndex("", "person", "node-element-equality-string");
        myIndexSpec.addIndex("", "person", "node-attribute-equality-string");
        myContainer.setIndexSpecification(myIndexSpec, uContext);

        myContainer.delete();
        myManager.delete();
    }
}
```

The XmlIndexSpecification object also provides methods for replacing an index, manipulating the default indexes, and iterating through the indexes within the specification.

One more class bears mentioning in the context of containers and indexes: XmlIndexLookup. Objects of this class are instantiated by the XmlManager.createIndexLookup() method and enable you to retrieve all nodes or documents that have keys in any given index. Listing 10-19 demonstrates such a lookup operation.

Listing 10-19. *Listing All Documents Referenced by an Index*

```
import com.sleepycat.dbxml.*;

class myDbXml {
    public static void main(String args[]) throws Throwable {
        XmlManager myManager = new XmlManager();
        XmlContainer myContainer = myManager.openContainer("myContainer.dbxml");
        XmlQueryContext qContext = myManager.createQueryContext();
        XmlIndexLookup myLookup = myManager.createIndexLookup(myContainer, "", "name",
            "node-element-equality-string");

        XmlResults myResults = myLookup.execute(qContext);
        XmlValue myValue = myResults.next();
        while (myValue != null) {
            XmlDocument myDocument = myValue.asDocument();
            String name = myDocument.getName();
            System.out.print("Index touches " + name + "\n");
            myValue = myResults.next();
        }
        myContainer.delete();
        myManager.delete();
    }
}
```

When a container is of type WholedocContainer, the XmlIndexLookup.execute() operation always returns entire documents. This is also true for containers of type NodeContainer unless the DBXML_INDEX_NODES flag was specified at container-creating time, in which case the lookup returns the individual nodes referred to in the index's keys.

The XmlIndexLookup class provides further access to an index's internal workings with methods to set bounds for ranged lookups and the capability to set a parent node for indexes that use edge paths instead of node paths.

Using XmlDocument and XmlModify

The XmlDocument class is primarily used throughout the API as a document handle that is passed to and from methods of other classes. It also provides methods for getting and setting document content, getting and setting document metadata, and setting the document's name. This section will also look at the use of the XmlModify class to modify documents.

A document's metadata is set with the XmlDocument.setMetaData() method. Document metadata involves an attribute name, value, and an optional Uniform Resource Identifier (URI), as shown in Listing 10-20.

Listing 10-20. *Adding Metadata to a Document*

```
import com.sleepycat.dbxml.*;
import java.io.*;
```

```
class myDbXml {
    public static void main(String args[]) throws Throwable
    {
        XmlManager myManager = new XmlManager();
        XmlContainer myContainer = myManager.openContainer("myContainer.dbxml");
        XmlUpdateContext uContext = myManager.createUpdateContext();

        XmlDocument myDocument = myContainer.getDocument("114.xml");
        myDocument.setMetaData("http://brians.org/metadata", "createdOn",
                new XmlValue(XmlValue.DATE_TIME, "2006-02-05T05:23:14"));
        myContainer.updateDocument(myDocument, uContext);

        myContainer.delete();
        myManager.delete();
    }
}
```

■**Caution** To avoid retrieving the document when performing nonread operations such as modifying metadata, use an XmlDocumentConfig object with setLazyDocs() set to true when calling the getDocument() method.

Metadata can be retrieved from an XmlDocument by using the getMetaData() method, as shown in Listing 10-21.

Listing 10-21. *Reading Metadata from a Document*

```
import com.sleepycat.dbxml.*;

class myDbXml {
    public static void main(String args[]) throws Throwable
    {
        XmlManager myManager = new XmlManager();
        XmlContainer myContainer = myManager.openContainer("myContainer.dbxml");
        XmlUpdateContext uContext = myManager.createUpdateContext();

        XmlDocument myDocument = myContainer.getDocument("114.xml");

        XmlValue metaValue = new XmlValue();
        myDocument.getMetaData("http://brians.org/metadata", "createdOn", metaValue);
        System.out.print("114.xml created on " + metaValue.asString() + "\n");

        myContainer.delete();
        myManager.delete();
    }
}
```

The metavalue variable had to be instantiated and passed as an argument to the getMetaData() method, which in turn set its value. Because getMetaData() returns a boolean, it is the required usage.

Documents can be modified within a container by using the XmlModify class without having to replace the document or copy it to memory. This class enables you to construct a series of steps for manipulating the contents of a document and then apply it to one or many documents within a container. It is thus a simple matter to perform container-wide document changes.

The XmlModify object is instantiated with a call to XmlManager.createModify(). A series of methods is exposed to provide for appending content, inserting and replacing content, and renaming and removing nodes. Assume that the database was filled with documents having the following structure:

```
<person>
    <name>Samuel</name>
    <age>51</age>
</person>
```

You want to create a new attribute node called type under the <name/> element with the value "given" (assume that the need to add surnames to the database has been discovered). Doing this involves an append change to the document   appending to the <name/> element. Calling the XmlModify.addAppendStep() method with the target node, the node type you are appending, and the attribute name and value, you get the code shown in Listing 10-22.

Listing 10-22. *Modifying a Document*

```java
import com.sleepycat.dbxml.*;

class myDbXml {
    public static void main(String args[]) throws Throwable
    {
        XmlManager myManager = new XmlManager();
        XmlContainer myContainer = myManager.openContainer("myContainer.dbxml");
        XmlQueryContext qContext = myManager.createQueryContext();
        XmlUpdateContext uContext = myManager.createUpdateContext();

        XmlModify myModify = myManager.createModify();
        XmlQueryExpression myQuery = myManager.prepare("/person/name", qContext);
        myModify.addAppendStep(myQuery, XmlModify.Attribute, "type", "given");
        XmlDocument myDocument = myContainer.getDocument("114.xml");
        XmlValue docValue = new XmlValue(myDocument);
        myModify.execute(docValue, qContext, uContext);

        myContainer.delete();
        myManager.delete();
    }
}
```

Any series of XmlModify steps can be included. Note that XmlModify is executed on an XmlValue or XmlResults object instead of on XmlDocument. The execute() method also accepts an XmlResults object, enabling you to apply the XmlModify object to all documents in a query result. Listing 10-23 performs a query for all documents that have a /person/name element and adds the @type="given" attribute to each.

Listing 10-23. *Modifying All Documents in a Result Set*

```java
import com.sleepycat.dbxml.*;

class myDbXml {
    public static void main(String args[]) throws Throwable
    {
        XmlManager myManager = new XmlManager();
        XmlContainer myContainer = myManager.openContainer("myContainer.dbxml");
        XmlQueryContext qContext = myManager.createQueryContext();
        XmlUpdateContext uContext = myManager.createUpdateContext();
```

```
        XmlModify myModify = myManager.createModify();
        XmlQueryExpression myQuery = myManager.prepare("/person/name", qContext);
        myModify.addAppendStep(myQuery, XmlModify.Attribute, "type", "given");
        XmlResults myResults = myManager.query
            ("collection('myContainer.dbxml')/person[name='Bill']", qContext);
        myModify.execute(myResults, qContext, uContext);

        myContainer.delete();
        myManager.delete();
    }
}
```

This listing changes all documents matching the query according to the XmlModify object. Keep in mind that this can be an expensive operation, but it is cheaper than retrieving and replacing each pertinent document in the container.

Conclusion

The BDB XML Java API follows its C++ counterpart closely (except for configuration interfaces). This chapter provided a brief tutorial of its basic functionality, but Appendix B contains a complete API reference for Java and other languages. Please refer to the C++ API for additional information on usage and behavior of the various API classes and methods.

More information about the BDB XML API is available from the Javadoc pages that accompany the distribution and at the following links:

Berkeley DB XML website at http://www.sleepycat.com

Sleepycat BDB XML mailing list at xml@sleepycat.com (details at http://dev.sleepycat.com/ community/discussion.html)

■ ■ ■

## CHAPTER 11

BDB XML with Perl

The BDB XML package includes a comprehensive Perl API, Sleepycat::DbXml, which was written by Paul Marquess (the author of many popular Perl modules).

The official API exposes most of the classes and methods of the C++ API. Note the following when using the Perl API:

The XmlResolver class is not supported by the Perl API.

Perl scalars are used anywhere the C++ API uses std::string as well as XmlData and Dbt objects (the Perl interface does not need them).

Where a DbXml method takes an XmlValue parameter, either an XmlValue object or a Perl scalar can be used.

Other Perl-specific behavior is noted in the following sections.

Running Applications

Having successfully built the BDB XML libraries and Perl interface, the Perl API can be loaded as follows:

```
use Sleepycat::DbXml;
```

The use pragma also accepts the "simple" parameter, which will make XmlTransaction objects optional to those DbXml methods that support transactions:

```
use Sleepycat::DbXml "simple";
```

It is highly recommended to make this your default usage for the module. The Perl examples included with the BDB XML distribution are located in the directory dbxml/src/perl/examples/ and demonstrate most of the Perl API's functionality.

Class Organization

The Perl API follows the same class organization as the C++ API, but does not require that any namespace declaration be present.

The major API classes are listed in Table 11-1 in their construction (not inheritance) hierarchy, indicating which class objects provide methods to construct other objects. The indents of class names in the table indicate where constructors exist; not necessarily all classes that return objects of a given class. Omitted are minor classes, but they are covered later in the chapter. Note that most

BDB XML classes have no virtual behavior and should not be extended directly. This design helps to keep the various language APIs compatible with the C++ interface with minimal maintenance.

Table 11-1. *Major BDB XML Perl Classes*

Class Name	Description
DbXml	A small class to adjust logging settings and implement some global variables.
XmlManager	The main application class. Used to create, open, and maintain containers; execute queries; and create other BDB XML objects (as factory objects).
XmlContainer	A container handle with methods for managing documents, manipulating indexes, and so on.
XmlIndexSpecification	An interface to programmatically manage the indexes for a container.
XmlDocument	A document within a container, with methods for getting and managing content.
XmlResults	Encapsulates the results of a query or lookup operation; a sequence of XmlValue objects.
XmlModify	A programmatic interface to modify documents using stepped changes.
XmlQueryContext	Encapsulates the namespaces, variable bindings, and flags for use with queries.
XmlUpdateContext	Encapsulates the context for updates to a container; used by all functions that modify a container.
XmlQueryExpression	A parsed/prepared XQuery expression.
XmlException	The BDB XML exception class thrown during error conditions.
XmlTransaction	The BDB XML transaction object.
XmlValue	Used to store XML node values when retrieving and storing data.
DbEnv	A Berkeley DB class for managing a database environment.

Errors and Exception Handling

The C++ BDB XML interface uses exceptions to report errors. Using the Perl API, these exceptions should be caught by enclosing code in an eval block and then using the XmlException class to report errors. They take the following form:

```
eval {
    my $mgr = new XmlManager();
    # operations here
};

if (my $e = catch XmlException) {
    print $e->what();
    # error handling here
}
```

The $e object is of class XmlException, which enables specifics of the error to be retrieved and output. Note the semicolon after the eval { } code; eval is a function, not technically a block identifier.

The examples in this chapter omit exception handling in the interest of brevity. You should enclose all operations in eval blocks and implement exception handling as appropriate for your particular application.

Environments

Environments provide logging, locking, and transaction support for database containers. As with the other interfaces, Perl programs can manage environments by using the XmlManager class. Environments are not specific to BDB XML, which is why there is no "XML" in the class used to manage them; DbEnv is used by Berkeley DB and (by association) Berkeley DB XML applications.

The DbEnv class provides many ways to configure a database environment. This section discusses instantiation as well as opening and closing environments. A reference for DbEnv is provided in Appendix B, "BDB XML API Reference."

The DbEnv::open() method takes a directory path, a bitwise OR'd set of environment flags, and a Unix file mode (ignored on Windows) as arguments. This object is then passed to the XmlManager constructor. Listing 11-1 demonstrates opening a database environment with a standard set of flags and instantiating an XmlManager object.

Listing 11-1. *Opening a Database Environment*

```
use Sleepycat::DbXml 'simple';
use strict;

my $env = new DbEnv;
$env->open("myenv/", Db::DB_CREATE|Db::DB_INIT_LOCK|Db::DB_INIT_LOG|
        Db::DB_INIT_MPOOL|Db::DB_INIT_TXN, 0);

my $mgr = new XmlManager($env, 0);
```

An environment is closed automatically (along with manager objects) when its object passes out of scope. It also can be closed explicitly by using the DbEnv::close() method.

XmlManager

XmlManager is used to create, open, rename, and delete containers; create document and context objects; and prepare and execute XQuery queries.

Instantiating XmlManager Objects

XmlManager objects are created with their constructor and are destroyed by using their destructor or passing them out of scope. If you do not provide a DbEnv object to the XmlManager constructor, it will automatically create an environment for you. This latter option carries some constraints with it because you do not have the ability to configure subsystems and you must tell XmlManager where to create and open your containers. It is usually preferable to create your own DbEnv object and pass it to the XmlManager constructor. Listing 11-1 showed the creation of an XmlManager object using an opened DbEnv object.

Managing Containers

Container creation, opening, renaming, and deletion are all performed with the XmlManager object. Open and create operations share a list of container flags, detailed in Appendix B. A container is opened by using the XmlManager::openContainer() method, and a single container can be opened multiple times within your application. The createContainer() method creates and subsequently opens a container. Containers are closed by enabling the container handle to go out of scope.

Listing 11-2 demonstrates a simple container creation. This example and subsequent code examples tend to omit the environment instantiation for the sake of brevity, although DbEnv would normally be used.

Listing 11-2. *Creating a Container*

```
use Sleepycat::DbXml 'simple';
use strict;

my $mgr = new XmlManager();
$mgr->createContainer("test.dbxml");
```

Listing 11-3 shows how to create a container using some of the possible arguments to createContainer(), including flags to enable transactions for the container, and perform validation (and also a container type).

Listing 11-3. *Creating a Container with Flags and a Container Type*

```
use Sleepycat::DbXml 'simple';
use strict;

my $env = new DbEnv;
$env->open("myenv/",
        Db::DB_CREATE|Db::DB_INIT_LOCK|Db::DB_INIT_LOG|
        Db::DB_INIT_MPOOL|Db::DB_INIT_TXN, 0);
my $mgr = new XmlManager($env, 0);
my $container = $mgr->createContainer("test.dbxml", DbXml::DBXML_TRANSACTIONAL|
        DbXml::DBXML_ALLOW_VALIDATION, XmlContainer::NodeContainer);
```

Opening an already-created, container uses an identical syntax with the XmlManager.openContainer() method. The same arguments and flags as createContainer() are accepted, but some have no use unless the DB_CREATE flag is used with the call to openContainer(). For example, a container type cannot be set on an already-created container, and DB_EXCL (to throw an error if a container exists) is relevant only when creating a new container.

Renaming and deleting containers is performed using the XmlManager::renameContainer() and XmlManager::removeContainer() methods. Both will succeed only on unopened containers. The first takes two string arguments: the current name of the container and the new name. The second simply takes the name of the container to remove. Both take an optional transaction object as the first argument. Listing 11-4 demonstrates both.

Listing 11-4. *Renaming and Deleting Containers*

```
use Sleepycat::DbXml 'simple';
use strict;

my $mgr = new XmlManager();
$mgr->renameContainer("test.dbxml", "old-test.dbxml");
$mgr->removeContainer("backup-test.dbxml");
```

Loading Documents

Documents are most typically loaded into a container directly by using XmlManager to create an input stream. This process enables files to be loaded as a string object, from a file on disk, from a network URL, from a memory buffer, or from standard input. Note that no validation is performed on input streams by BDB XML; only when a document is put into a container does the system read from the stream, parse the content, and validate it. No errors are thrown when an input stream is created using an invalid location or filename until the operation is performed.

XmlManager provides several methods for creating these input streams, as listed in Table 11-2. All these methods return an object of class XmlInputStream, which is then used to load the document into the container (or into a document object, as will be shown).

Table 11-2. *XmlManager's Input Stream–Creation Methods*

Method	Description
XmlManager::createLocalFileInputStream()	Takes as its argument a filename
XmlManager::createURLInputStream()	Takes as arguments three URL IDs
XmlManager::createMemBufInputStream()	Takes as arguments memory address and byte counts

The XmlInputStream object resulting from any of these methods is then used in one of two ways. Most often, it is passed to the XmlContainer::putDocument() method, which loads the data using the input stream, parses the document and performs any necessary validation, and then stores the document in the container. Of course, putDocument() will also accept an XML document in the form of a string, but the BDB XML input stream can save the overhead in memory of loading the text via Perl as well. Listing 11-5 shows loading a document into a container by using a local file input stream.

Listing 11-5. *Adding a Document to a Container from a Local File*

```
use Sleepycat::DbXml 'simple';
use strict;

my $mgr = new XmlManager();
my $container = $mgr->openContainer("test.dbxml");
my $ucontext = $mgr->createUpdateContext();
my $xmlinput = $mgr->createLocalFileInputStream("file14.xml");
$container->putDocument("file14", $xmlinput, $ucontext);
```

Note that the filename specified for the input stream is different from the document name supplied to putDocument(). (They could be the same, of course.)

An alternative to passing the XmlInputStream object to putDocument() is to supply it as an argument to the XmlDocument::setContentAsXmlInputStream() method, directly setting the content of an in-memory document object. The XmlDocument object in question could have instead been created via a call to XmlManager::createDocument() (or with new XmlDocument()). In that case, the document it represents does not yet exist in the container, unlike documents retrieved from a container with XmlContainer::getDocument(). Finally, an XmlDocument object can be retrieved after a query using the methods of the XmlResults class. Each technique is demonstrated elsewhere. Refer to the later sections on managing documents for more details and examples of using the described input streams. The next section discusses the XmlContainer class in more depth.

Preparing and Executing Queries

XQuery queries are performed on containers by using the XmlManager objects prepare() and query() methods. Because queries can span multiple containers, they are not centric to any one container. So XmlManager is the logical class to execute queries.

The XmlManager::prepare() method takes an XQuery expression string and a query context object as arguments and then returns an XmlQueryExpression object. This object encapsulates the parsed and optimized XQuery expression for repeated use in multiple operations. Calling the execute() method evaluates the expression against the containers (or documents) referred to by the query.

The XmlQueryContext object indicates to the query engine the context within which to perform a query. This context includes the namespace mappings, variable bindings, and flags to indicate how a query is to be performed and its results returned   everything the query engine needs to do its job, given the query string.

Listing 11-6 creates an XmlQueryContext object, uses it to set a default collection (enabling you to omit the argument to collection() from your query), and then prepares and executes a query.

Listing 11-6. *Using XmlQueryContext*

```
use Sleepycat::DbXml 'simple';
use strict;

my $mgr = new XmlManager();
my $query = "collection()/person[name='Bob']";

my $container = $mgr->openContainer("test.dbxml");
my $qcontext = $mgr->createQueryContext();
$qcontext->setDefaultCollection("test.dbxml");

my $query_exp = $mgr->prepare($query, $qcontext);
my $results = $query_exp->execute($qcontext);
```

If your XML collection made use of namespaces, you would use the XmlQueryContext object to define them. Imagine that your top-level document elements looked like this instead of <person/>:

```
<people:person xmlns:wordnet="http://brians.org/people">
```

You could now use the namespace in your query. Listing 11-7 maps this namespace to the people prefix and sets a variable for use in the XQuery query.

Listing 11-7. *Declaring Namespaces and Variables*

```
use Sleepycat::DbXml 'simple';
use strict;

my $mgr = new XmlManager();
my $query = "collection('test.dbxml')/people:person[name='\$name']";

my $container = $mgr->openContainer("test.dbxml");
my $qcontext = $mgr->createQueryContext();
$qcontext->setNamespace("people", "http://brians.org/people/");
$qcontext->setVariableValue("name", new XmlValue("Bob"));

my $query_exp = $mgr->prepare($query, $qcontext);
my $results = $query_exp->execute($qcontext);
```

Because the XmlQueryContext object is passed to execute() for a prepared query expression, the context can be manipulated without having to recompile the query expression. In Listing 11-7, the query variable $name (the XQuery variable, not the Perl variable) was changed, and the query was reissued without recompiling the prepared query expression.

BDB XML also enables queries to be executed in a one-off fashion without query preparation, which is helpful when you know that queries will not be used repeatedly. Listing 11-8 demonstrates using the XmlManager query() method to execute a query only once.

Listing 11-8. *Performing a One-Off Query*

```
from bsddb3.db import *
use Sleepycat::DbXml 'simple';
use strict;

my $mgr = new XmlManager();
my $query = "collection('test.dbxml')/person[name='Jim']";
my $container = $mgr->openContainer("test.dbxml");
my $qcontext = $mgr->createQueryContext();
my $results = $mgr->query($query, $qcontext);
```

Besides namespaces and variables, XmlQueryContext can determine how queries are executed and the values they return. The setEvaluationType() method allows for two evaluation types: eager and lazy (see Table 11-3).

Table 11-3. *Query Evaluation Types*

Type	Description
XmlQueryContext::Eager	The query is executed, with resulting values determined and stored in memory before the query returns. This is the default.
XmlQueryContext::Lazy	The query is executed, but the resulting values are not determined or stored in memory until the API refers to them by iterating the result set. This type is useful for queries with large result sets because it consumes less memory and enables the first result to be retrieved more quickly.

Listing 11-9 demonstrates setting the evaluation type to lazy.

Listing 11-9. *Querying with Lazy Evaluation*

```
use Sleepycat::DbXml 'simple';
use strict;

my $mgr = new XmlManager();
my $query = "collection('test.dbxml')/person[name='Jim']";

my $container = $mgr->openContainer("test.dbxml");
my $qcontext = $mgr->createQueryContext();
$qcontext->setEvaluationType(XmlQueryContext::Lazy);

my $results = $mgr->query($query, $qcontext);
```

Because this example does not iterate the query results, no values are actually retrieved   the evaluation type was set to lazy. In the next section, which demonstrates retrieving results, lazy evaluation will return the first result as soon as possible and retrieve subsequent results on demand.

Using Query Results

The XmlQueryExpression::execute() and XmlManager::query() methods return objects of class XmlResults, which are used to iterate the result set. The object is a sequence of XmlValue objects (or an on-demand result iterator for lazy evaluation) that in turn represent any of the BDB XML supported data types. The XmlResults class uses an iteration interface with the next() and previous() methods to navigate results. Each takes as argument an XmlValue object (or an XmlDocument object), into which it stores the next or previous result (although previous() is unavailable with lazily evaluated queries). Passing a storage scalar to the next() method might seen unidiomatic to Perl programmers, but doing so makes for concise iteration. Listing 11-10 demonstrates outputting the results of a query to STDOUT. Here, $value is created as an XmlValue object, but a plain scalar can also be used.

Listing 11-10. *Retrieving Query Results*

```
use Sleepycat::DbXml 'simple';
use strict;

my $mgr = new XmlManager();
my $query = "collection('test.dbxml')//Word";

my $container = $mgr->openContainer("test.dbxml");
my $qcontext = $mgr->createQueryContext();
my $results = $mgr->query($query, $qcontext);

my $value = new XmlValue();
while ($results->next($value)) {
    my $document = $value->asDocument();
    my $name     = $document->getName();
    my $content  = $value->asString();
    print $name . ": " . $content . "\n";
}
```

Note the use of several new methods, including XmlValue::asString() and XmlDocument:: getName(). Certain pieces of document information, including its name within the container, are available only by querying directly or retrieving the result as a document. When your queries require node values instead of the documents matching a query, asString() is all you need.

The XmlValue class also provides a Document Object Model (DOM)-like interface to not only retrieve values (as with the asString() and asDocument() methods) but also to navigate the nodes it represents. Its methods include getNextSibling(), getAttributes(), and getFirstChild(), so it is useful for any post-query processing that you might need to perform on query results.

The BDB XML query engine is capable of evaluating XQuery queries on documents (and even on individual query results) in addition to database containers. Listing 11-11 does exactly this by executing several queries using the XmlValue object. Because the document query will repeat for each result, it makes sense to prepare it by using an XmlQueryExpression object.

Listing 11-11. *Querying Results*

```
use Sleepycat::DbXml 'simple';
use strict;

my $mgr = new XmlManager();
my $query = "collection('test.dbxml')/person[name='Fred']";
my $subquery = "/person/phone";
```

```
my $container = $mgr->openContainer("test.dbxml");
my $qcontext = $mgr->createQueryContext();
my $phoneqcontext = $mgr->createQueryContext();

my $results = $mgr->query($query, $qcontext);
my $phonequery = $mgr->prepare($subquery, $phoneqcontext);

my $value = new XmlValue();
my $phonevalue = new XmlValue();
while ($results->next($value)) {
    my $phoneresults = $phonequery->execute($value, $phoneqcontext);
    while ($phoneresults->next($phonevalue)) {
        print $phonevalue->asString() . "\n";
    }
}
```

The same process can be performed with the XmlDocument object resulting from a call to XmlValue::asDocument(), passing that object as argument to XmlQueryExpression::execute(). Of course, if you anticipate only one <phone/> element in this example, you can just call XmlResults:: next() instead of creating a while block.

You used different XmlQueryContext objects for the query and the subquery in this example. Although you could use the same query context, it might not be a safe operation in all cases (for example, when the main query is lazily evaluated).

The second query in this example could have been relative to the result node by using the current node (.) instead:

```
./phone/string()
```

This same technique of querying results and documents can be useful for pulling data out of large documents, enabling you to work within the context of previous result sets.

A later section looks more closely at the use of XmlDocument to demonstrate metadata retrieval.

Creating Other Objects

Most of the remaining XmlManager methods simply construct objects of other DbXml subclasses. Many of them have already been demonstrated (for example, the XmlManager::createTransaction() method, which instantiates an XmlTransaction object). All such method names begin with create. Most take no default arguments, serving as basic constructors. They include createDocument() to instantiate an XmlDocument object, createIndexLookup() to instantiate an XmlIndexLookup object, createModify() to instantiate an XmlModify object, createQueryContext() to instantiate an XmlQueryContext object, and createResults() to create an empty XmlResults object. These methods are examined in the following sections, in which their returned objects are demonstrated.

Using XmlContainer

The XmlContainer class provides most of the functionality that concerns a container and its contents, including adding, replacing, updating, and deleting documents; directly retrieving documents (using the getDocument() method); and managing indexes for the container.

An XmlContainer object is created by using the XmlManager::createContainer() and XmlManager:: openContainer() methods. Documents can be added by using the putDocument() method, taking as argument either an XmlDocument or XmlInputStream. The previous section demonstrated it while supplying a document name and input stream or document container. The method also accepts an XML string (and generates document names if not provided) if the call supplies the DBXML_GEN_NAME flag. Listing 11-12 uses putDocument() without providing a document name.

Listing 11-12. *Letting BDB XML Generate Document Names*

```perl
use Sleepycat::DbXml 'simple';
use strict;

my $mgr = new XmlManager();
my $container = $mgr->openContainer("test.dbxml");
my $ucontext = $mgr->createUpdateContext();

my $content = "<person><name>Bob</name></person>";
my $docname = $container->putDocument("", $content, $ucontext,
        DbXml::DBXML_GEN_NAME);
```

With this usage, BDB XML guarantees the uniqueness of document names, incrementing them with each put document.

Documents are deleted from a container by using the XmlContainer::deleteDocument() method, which accepts with the document name or document object as its argument. The latter is useful when you want to iterate over a result set, deleting each document it contains, without having to retrieve the document name. Listing 11-13 shows document deletion.

Listing 11-13. *Deleting Documents*

```perl
use Sleepycat::DbXml 'simple';
use strict;

my $mgr = new XmlManager();
my $container = $mgr->openContainer("test.dbxml");
my $ucontext = $mgr->createUpdateContext();
my $qcontext = $mgr->createQueryContext();

my $content = "<person><name>Bob</name></person>";
$container->putDocument("", $content, $ucontext, DbXml::DBXML_GEN_NAME);

my $results = $mgr->query("collection('test.dbxml')/person[name='Bob']", $qcontext);
my $value = new XmlValue();
my $phonevalue = new XmlValue();
while ($results->next($value)) {
    my $document = $value->asDocument();
    print "Deleting document: " . $document->getName() . "\n";
    $container->deleteDocument($document, $ucontext);
}
```

Note that an XmlDocument object is passed to each call of XmlResults::next(), which is "smart" enough to know to store the result there as a complete document.

When you want to replace a document in a container (instead of modifying it in place), you can use the XmlContainer::updateDocument() method. This operation works with any XmlDocument object, setting its name to be identical to the document to be replaced and handing it to the updateDocument() method. You usually retrieve the document from the database, set new content by using the XmlDocument::setContent() method (or setContentAsDOM() or setContentAsXmlInputStream()), and save it back to the container. Listing 11-14 retrieves a document from the container using the XmlContainer::getDocument() method before replacing its content and saving it back to the container.

Listing 11-14. *Replacing a Document*

```
use Sleepycat::DbXml 'simple';
use strict;

my $mgr = new XmlManager();
my $container = $mgr->openContainer("test.dbxml");
my $ucontext = $mgr->createUpdateContext();

my $newcontent = "<person><name>Bob</name></person>";

my $document = $container->getDocument("file12.xml");
$document->setContent("<person><name>Bob2</name></person>");
$container->updateDocument($document, $ucontext);
```

The BDB XML API provides a programmatic interface to partially modifying documents using the XmlModify class, which enables a description of changes to be built before applying them to one or many documents in a container (demonstrated in the following section).

A final major function of the XmlContainer class is managing container indexes. Chapter 6, "Indexes," described the specifics of indexing strategies; this section discusses adding to, deleting from, and examining indexes of the API.

You can add indexes by using an index description string, as demonstrated in Listing 11-15.

Listing 11-15. *Adding an Index to a Container with an Index Description String*

```
use Sleepycat::DbXml 'simple';
use strict;

my $mgr = new XmlManager();
my $container = $mgr->openContainer("test.dbxml");
my $ucontext = $mgr->createUpdateContext();

$container->addIndex("", "person", "node-element-equality-string", $ucontext);
```

The XmlContainer::getIndexSpecification() method returns an index specification for the container, encapsulating a description of all current indexes. It provides the addIndex() and deleteIndex() methods to manipulate the index description before applying it back to the container. The example in Listing 11-16 deletes one index and adds another using an XmlIndexSpecification object.

Listing 11-16. *Manipulating a Container's Index Specification*

```
use Sleepycat::DbXml 'simple';
use strict;

my $mgr = new XmlManager();
my $container = $mgr->openContainer("test.dbxml");
my $ucontext = $mgr->createUpdateContext();

my $indexspec = $container->getIndexSpecification();
$indexspec->deleteIndex("", "person", "node-element-equality-string");
$indexspec->addIndex("", "person", "node-attribute-equality-string");
$container->setIndexSpecification($indexspec, $ucontext);
```

The XmlIndexSpecification object also provides methods for replacing an index, manipulating the default indexes, and iterating through the indexes within the specification.

One more class bears mentioning in the context of containers and indexes: XmlIndexLookup. Objects of this class are instantiated by XmlManager::createIndexLookup(), and you can retrieve all nodes or documents that have keys in any given index (see Listing 11-17).

Listing 11-17. *Listing All Documents Referenced by an Index*

```
use Sleepycat::DbXml 'simple';
use strict;

my $mgr = new XmlManager();
my $container = $mgr->openContainer("test.dbxml");
my $qcontext = $mgr->createQueryContext();

my $indexlookup = $mgr->createIndexLookup($container, "", "person",
        "node-element-equality-string");
my $results = $indexlookup->execute($qcontext);

my $value = new XmlValue();
while ($results->next($value)) {
    my $document = $value->asDocument();
    print $document->getName() . ": " . $document->getContent();
}
```

When a container is of type WholedocContainer, the XmlIndexLookup::execute() operation always returns entire documents. This is also true for containers of type NodeContainer, unless the DBXML_INDEX_NODES flag was specified when the container was created. In that case, the lookup returns the individual nodes referred to in the index's keys.

The XmlIndexLookup class provides further access to an index's internal workings, enabling equality and inequality lookups, methods to set bounds for range lookups, and the ability to set a parent node for indexes that use edge paths rather than node paths.

Using XmlDocument

The XmlDocument class is used throughout the API primarily as a document handle, passed to and from methods of other classes. It also provides methods for getting and setting document content, getting and setting document metadata, and setting a document's name.

A document's metadata is set with the XmlDocument::setMetaData() method. Included in the document metadata are a name, a value, and an optional URI. Listing 11-18 adds metadata to a document.

Listing 11-18. *Adding Metadata to a Document*

```
use Sleepycat::DbXml 'simple';
use strict;

my $mgr = new XmlManager();
my $container = $mgr->openContainer("test.dbxml");
my $ucontext = $mgr->createUpdateContext();

my $uri = "http://brians.org/metadata/";
my $metaname = "createdOn";
my $metavalue = new XmlValue(XmlValue::DATE_TIME, "2006-02-05T05:23:14");
```

```
my $document = $container->getDocument("file14.xml");
$document->setMetaData($uri, $metaname, $metavalue);
$container->updateDocument($document, $ucontext);
```

You can retrieve metadata from an XmlDocument by using the getMetaData() method (see Listing 11-19).

Listing 11-19. *Retrieving Metadata from a Document*

```
use Sleepycat::DbXml 'simple';
use strict;

my $mgr = new XmlManager();
my $container = $mgr->openContainer("test.dbxml");
my $ucontext = $mgr->createUpdateContext();

my $uri = "http://brians.org/metadata/";
my $metaname = "createdOn";
my $metavalue = new XmlValue();

my $document = $container->getDocument("file14.xml");
$document->getMetaData($uri, $metaname, $metavalue);
print "file14.xml, created on " . $metavalue->asString() . "\n";
```

Note that the $metavalue variable had to be instantiated and passed as an argument to the getMetaData() method, which in turn set its value. Because getMetaData() returns a boolean, it is the required usage.

■Tip Metadata can be retrieved just like XML values within queries by using the dbxml:metadata() function. See Chapter 7, "XQuery with BDB XML," for details.

Finally, note that containers can contain metadata-only documents that store only metadata key/value pairs with no XML content.

Using XmlModify

Using the XmlModify class enables you to modify a document within a container without having to replace the document or copy it to memory. You can construct a series of steps to manipulate the contents of a document and then apply these steps to one or many documents within a container. It then becomes a simple matter to perform container-wide document changes.

The XmlModify object is instantiated with a call to XmlManager::createModify(). A series of methods is exposed to provide for appending content, inserting and replacing content, and renaming and removing nodes. Assume that your database is filled with documents having the following structure:

```
<person>
    <name>Samuel</name>
    <age>51</age>
</person>
```

Under the <name/> element, you want to create a new attribute node called "type" with the value "given". (You can assume that the need to add surnames to the database has been discovered.) This involves an append change to the document: appending to the <name/> element. Calling the XmlModify::addAppendStep() method with the target node, the node type you are appending, and the attribute name and value, you get the example shown in Listing 11-20.

Listing 11-20. *Modifying a Document*

```
use Sleepycat::DbXml 'simple';
use strict;

my $mgr = new XmlManager();
my $container = $mgr->openContainer("test.dbxml");
my $qcontext = $mgr->createQueryContext();
my $ucontext = $mgr->createUpdateContext();

my $modify = $mgr->createModify();
my $queryexp = $mgr->prepare("/person/name", $qcontext);

$modify->addAppendStep($queryexp, XmlModify::Attribute, "type", "given");

my $document = $container->getDocument("file14");
my $doc_value = new XmlValue($document);

$modify->execute($doc_value, $qcontext, $ucontext);
```

Any series of XmlModify steps can be included. Note that XmlModify is executed on an XmlValue instead of on an XmlDocument. The execute() method also accepts an XmlResults object, enabling you to apply the XmlModify object to all documents in a query result. Listing 11-21 performs a query for all documents that have a /person/name element and then adds the @type="given" attribute to each.

Listing 11-21. *Modifying All Documents in a Result Set*

```
use Sleepycat::DbXml 'simple';
use strict;

my $mgr = new XmlManager();
my $container = $mgr->openContainer("test.dbxml");
my $qcontext = $mgr->createQueryContext();
my $ucontext = $mgr->createUpdateContext();

my $modify = $mgr->createModify();
my $queryexp = $mgr->prepare("/person/name", $qcontext);

$modify->addAppendStep($queryexp, XmlModify::Attribute, "type", "given");

my $results = $mgr->query("collection('test.dbxml')/person[name='Bill']",
        $qcontext);
$modify->execute($results, $qcontext, $ucontext);
```

This code changes all documents matching the query according to the XmlModify object. Keep in mind that it can be an expensive operation, but it is cheaper than retrieving and replacing each pertinent document in the container. The API reference in Appendix B contains a description of all XmlModify methods.

Conclusion

The BDB XML Perl API is straightforward and comprehensive, and this chapter provided a brief tutorial of its basic functionality. Appendix B contains a complete API reference for Perl and other languages, and the C++ API has additional information on usage and behavior of various API classes and methods.

More information about the BDB XML API is available from the man pages (`perldoc`) that accompany each Perl module and at the following links:

Berkeley DB XML website: `http://www.sleepycat.com`

Sleepycat BDB XML mailing list: `xml@sleepycat.com` (details at `http://dev.sleepycat.com/community/discussion.html`)

## CHAPTER 12

BDB XML with PHP

The BDB XML package includes a comprehensive PHP API, exposing most of the classes and methods of the C++ API. This chapter explains the basic functionality of the API with PHP examples. Please refer to Chapter 8, "BDB XML with C++," and Appendix B, "BDB XML API Reference," for additional details on API functionality. The examples in this chapter omit the surrounding `<?php ... ?>` code tags for brevity.

Running Applications

Having successfully built the BDB XML and PHP interface, the API can be loaded via the `php.ini` file as follows:

```
extension=db4.so
extension=dbxml.so
```

The BDB XML PHP shared object must be linked against the libraries included with the BDB XML distribution, although most PHP installations use the system libraries instead. Refer to the `README` file in the PHP source directory (`dbxml/src/php/`) for details on PHP configuration. The PHP examples included with the BDB XML distribution are located in the directory `dbxml/src/php/examples/` and demonstrate most of the PHP API functionality.

Class Organization

The PHP API follows the same class organization as the C++ API, but does not require that any namespace declaration be present. Loading extensions from the initialization file (`php.ini`) handles class imports under PHP.

The major API classes are listed in Table 12-1 in their construction (not inheritance) hierarchy, indicating which class objects provide methods to construct other objects. Omitted are minor classes.

Table 12-1. *Major BDB XML PHP Classes*

Class Name	Description
XmlManager	The main application class. Used to create, open, and maintain containers, execute queries; and create other BDB XML objects (as factory objects).
XmlContainer	A container handle with methods for managing documents, manipulating indexes, and so on.

Continued

Table 12-1. *Continues*

Class Name	Description
XmlIndexSpecification	An interface to programmatically manage the indexes for a container.
XmlDocument	A document within a container, with methods for getting and managing content.
XmlResults	Encapsulates the results of a query or lookup operation; a sequence of XmlValue objects.
XmlModify	A programmatic interface to modify documents using stepped changes.
XmlQueryContext	Encapsulates the namespaces, variable bindings, and flags for use with container queries.
XmlUpdateContext	Encapsulates the context for updates to a container; used by all functions that modify a container.
XmlQueryExpression	A parsed/prepared XQuery expression.
XmlTransaction	The BDB XML transaction object.
XmlValue	Used to store XML node values when retrieving and storing data.
Db4Env	A Berkeley DB class for managing a database environment.

Environments

Environments provide logging, locking, and transaction support for database containers. As with the other interfaces, PHP documents can manage environments by using the XmlManager class. Environments are not specific to BDB XML, which is why there is no "XML" in the class used to manage them; Db4Env is used by Berkeley DB and (by association) Berkeley DB XML applications.

The Db4Env class provides many ways to configure a database environment. This section discusses instantiation as well as opening and closing environments. A reference for Db4Env is provided in Appendix B.

■**Note** The PHP database environment object does not provide all the methods of the underlying C++ API, including set methods for configuration. Environment configuration using PHP usually requires the use of a DB_CONFIG file, as described in the database documentation.

The Db4Env::open() method takes a directory path, a bitwise ORd set of environment flags, and a Unix file mode (ignored on Windows) as arguments. This object is then passed to the XmlManager constructor. Listing 12-1 demonstrates opening a database environment with a standard set of flags and instantiating an XmlManager object using the environment handle.

Listing 12-1. *Opening a Database Environment*

```
$env = new Db4Env();
$env->open("myenv/", DB_CREATE|DB_INIT_LOCK|DB_INIT_LOG|DB_INIT_MPOOL|DB_INIT_TXN, 0);
$mgr = new XmlManager($env, 0);
```

An environment is closed automatically (along with manager objects) when its object passes out of scope. It can also be closed explicitly using the Db4Env::close() method.

■**Caution** Unlike the other BDB XML APIs, the PHP API defaults to using transactions. In Listing 12-1, if the open() method were called with no flags, the same flags would be used as the default. Explicit flags must be passed using the PHP API to not enable transactions for the session.

XmlManager

XmlManager functions create, open, rename, and delete containers; create document and context objects; and prepare and execute XQuery queries.

Instantiating XmlManager Objects

XmlManager objects are created with their constructor and are destroyed using their destructor or passing them out of scope. If you provide a Db4Env object to the constructor, as just demonstrated, XmlManager automatically closes and destroys that Db4Env object for you if you set the DBXML_ADOPT_DBENV flag at instantiation time. If you do not provide a Db4Env object to the XmlManager constructor, it automatically creates an environment for you. This latter option carries some constraints with it because you do not have the ability to configure subsystems and you must tell XmlManager where to create and open your containers. It is usually preferable to create your own Db4Env object and pass it to the XmlManager constructor. Listing 12-1 showed the creation of an XmlManager object using an opened Db4Env object.

Managing Containers

Container creation, opening, renaming, and deletion are all performed with the XmlManager object. Open and create operations share a list of container flags, detailed in Appendix B. A container is opened using the, XmlManager::openContainer() method, and a single container can be opened multiple times within your application. The createContainer() method creates and subsequently opens a container. Containers are closed by allowing the container handle to go out of scope.

Listing 12-2 demonstrates a simple container creation. This example and subsequent code examples tend to omit the environment instantiation for the sake of brevity, although Db4Env would normally be used.

Listing 12-2. *Creating a Container*

```
$mgr = new XmlManager();
$mgr->createContainer("test.dbxml");
```

Listing 12-3 shows creates a container by using some of the possible arguments to createContainer(), including flags to enable transactions for the container and perform validation (and also a container type).

Listing 12-3. *Creating a Container with Flags and a Container Type*

```
$env = new Db4Env;
$env->open("myenv/",
        DB_CREATE| DB_INIT_LOCK| DB_INIT_LOG|
        DB_INIT_MPOOL| DB_INIT_TXN, 0);
        // default flags, so none could be used instead
```

```
$mgr = new XmlManager($env, 0);
$container = $mgr->createContainer("test.dbxml",
        DBXML_TRANSACTIONAL| DBXML_ALLOW_VALIDATION,
        XmlContainer::NodeContainer);
```

Opening an, already-created container uses an identical syntax with the
XmlManager::openContainer() method. The same arguments and flags as createContainer() are
accepted, but some have no use unless the DB_CREATE flag is used with the call to openContainer().
For example, a container type cannot be set on an already-created container, and DB_EXCL (to throw
an error if a container exists) is relevant only when creating a new container.

■**Caution** It's a good idea to unset() document objects before closing containers—and always before
deleting/renaming them—even if the PHP API tries hard to know when object destruction is needed.

Renaming and deleting containers is performed using the XmlManager::renameContainer() and
XmlManager::removeContainer() methods. Both will succeed only on unopened containers. The first
takes two string arguments: the current name of the container and the new name. The second simply takes the name of the container to remove. Both take an optional transaction object as the first
argument. Listing 12-4 demonstrates both.

Listing 12-4. *Renaming and Deleting Containers*

```
$mgr = new XmlManager();
$mgr->renameContainer("test.dbxml", "old-test.dbxml");
$mgr->removeContainer("backup-test.dbxml");
```

Loading Documents

Documents are usually loaded into a container directly by using XmlManager to create an input
stream. This process enables files to be loaded as a string object, from a file on disk, from a network
URL, from a memory buffer, or from standard input. Note that no validation is performed on input
streams by BDB XML; only when a document is put into a container does the system read from the
stream, parse the content, and validate it. No errors are thrown when an input stream is created
using an invalid location, filename, or so on until the put operation is performed.

XmlManager provides several methods for creating these input streams, as listed in Table 12-2.
All these methods return an object of class XmlInputStream, which is then used to load the document into the container (or into a document object, as will be shown).

Table 12-2. *XmlManager Input Stream-Creation Methods*

Method	Description
XmlManager::createLocalFileInputStream()	Takes as its argument a filename
XmlManager::createURLInputStream()	Takes as arguments three URL IDs
XmlManager::createMemBufInputStream()	Takes as arguments memory address and byte counts

The XmlInputStream object resulting from any of these methods is then used in one of two
ways. Most often, it is passed to the XmlContainer::putDocument() method, which loads the data
using the input stream, parses the document and performs any necessary validation, and then

stores the document in the container. The immediacy depends on whether or not a transaction is used. Of course, putDocument() will also accept an XML document in the form of a string, but the BDB XML input stream can save the overhead in memory of loading the text via PHP as well. Listing 12-5 loads a document into a container using a local file input stream.

Listing 12-5. *Adding a Document to a Container from a Local File*

```
$mgr = new XmlManager();
$container = $mgr->openContainer("test.dbxml");
$xmlinput = $mgr->createLocalFileInputStream("file14.xml");
$container->putDocument("file14", $xmlinput);
```

Note that the filename specified for the input stream is different from the document name supplied to putDocument(). (They could be the same, of course.)

An alternative to passing the XmlInputStream object to putDocument() is to supply it as an argument to the XmlDocument::setContentAsXmlInputStream() method, directly setting the content of an in-memory document object. The XmlDocument object in question could have been created afresh via a call to XmlManager::createDocument() (or with new XmlDocument(), in which case it does not yet exist in the container) or having been retrieved from a container with XmlContainer::getDocument(). Finally, an XmlDocument object can be retrieved after a query by using the methods of the XmlResults class. Each technique is demonstrated elsewhere. See the later sections on managing documents for more details and examples of using the described input streams. The next section discusses the XmlContainer class in more depth.

Preparing and Executing Queries

XQuery queries are performed on containers using the XmlManager objects prepare() and query() methods. Because queries can span multiple containers, they are not centric to any one container. So XmlManager is the logical class for queries to take place.

The XmlManager::prepare() method takes an XQuery expression string and a query context object as arguments and then returns an XmlQueryExpression object. This object encapsulates the parsed and optimized XQuery expression for repeated use in multiple operations. Calling its execute() method evaluates the expression against the containers (or documents) referred to by the query.

The XmlQueryContext object indicates to the query engine the context within which to perform a query. This context includes the namespace mappings, variable bindings, and flags to indicate how a query is to be performed and its results returned   everything the query engine needs to do its job, given the query string.

Listing 12-6 shows the creation of an XmlQueryContext object, using it to set a default collection (enabling you to omit the argument to collection() from the query), and then preparing and executing a query.

Listing 12-6. *Using XmlQueryContext*

```
$mgr = new XmlManager();
$query = "collection()/person[name='Bob']";

$container = $mgr->openContainer("test.dbxml");
$qcontext = $mgr->createQueryContext();
$qcontext->setDefaultCollection("test.dbxml");

$query_exp = $mgr->prepare($query, $qcontext);
$results = $query_exp->execute($qcontext);
```

If your XML collection made use of namespaces, you would use the XmlQueryContext object to define them. Imagine that your top-level document elements looked like this instead of <person/>:

```
<people:person xmlns:wordnet="http://brians.org/people">
```

You could now use the namespace in your query. Listing 12-7 maps this namespace to the people prefix and sets a variable for use in the XQuery query.

Listing 12-7. *Declaring Namespaces and Variables*

```
$mgr = new XmlManager();
$query = "collection('test.dbxml')/people:person[name='\$name']";

$container = $mgr->openContainer("test.dbxml");
$qcontext = $mgr->createQueryContext();
$qcontext->setNamespace("people", "http://brians.org/people/");
$qcontext->setVariableValue("name", new XmlValue("Bob"));

$query_exp = $mgr->prepare($query, $qcontext);
$results = $query_exp->execute($qcontext);
```

Because the XmlQueryContext object is passed to execute() for a prepared query expression, the context can be manipulated without having to recompile the query expression. In Listing 12-7, the query variable $name (the XQuery variable, not the PHP variable) was changed, and the query was reissued without recompiling the prepared query expression.

BDB XML also allows for queries to be executed in a one-off fashion, without query preparation, which is helpful when you know that queries will not be used repeatedly. Listing 12-8 demonstrates using the XmlManager query() method to execute a query only once.

Listing 12-8. *Performing a One-Off Query*

```
$mgr = new XmlManager();
$query = "collection('test.dbxml')/person[name='Jim']";
$container = $mgr->openContainer("test.dbxml");
$results = $mgr->query($query, $qcontext);
```

Besides namespaces and variables, XmlQueryContext can determine how queries are executed and the values they return. The setEvaluationType() method allows for two evaluation types: eager and lazy (see Table 12-3).

Table 12-3. *Query Evaluation Types*

Type	Description
XmlQueryContext_Eager	The query is executed, with resulting values determined and stored in memory before the query returns. This is the default.
XmlQueryContext_Lazy	The query is executed, but the resulting values are not determined or stored in memory until the API refers to them by iterating the result set. This type is useful for queries with large result sets because it consumes less memory and enables the first result to be retrieved more quickly.

Listing 12-9 demonstrates setting the evaluation type to lazy.

Listing 12-9. *Querying with Lazy Evaluation*

```php
$mgr = new XmlManager();
$query = "collection('test.dbxml')/person[name='Jim']";

$container = $mgr->openContainer("test.dbxml");
$qcontext = $mgr->createQueryContext();
$qcontext->setEvaluationType(XmlQueryContext_Lazy);

$results = $mgr->query($query, $qcontext);
```

Because this example does not iterate the query results, no values are actually retrieved because the evaluation type was set to lazy. In the next section, which demonstrates retrieving results, lazy evaluation returns the first result as soon as possible and retrieves subsequent results on demand.

Using Query Results

The XmlQueryExpression::execute() and XmlManager::query() methods return objects of class XmlResults, which are used to iterate the result set. The object is a sequence of XmlValue objects (or an on-demand result iterator in the case of lazy evaluation) that in turn represent any of the BDB XML supported data types. The XmlResults class uses an iteration interface with the next() and previous() methods to navigate results. Each returns an XmlValue containing the next or previous result (although previous() is unavailable with lazily evaluated queries). Listing 12-10 demonstrates outputting the results of a query to STDOUT.

Listing 12-10. *Retrieving Query Results*

```php
$mgr = new XmlManager();
$query = "collection('test.dbxml')//Word";

$container = $mgr->openContainer("test.dbxml");
$qcontext = $mgr->createQueryContext();
$results = $mgr->query($query, $qcontext);

while ($results->hasNext()) {
    $value = $results->next();
    $document = $value->asDocument();
    $name     = $document->getName();
    $content = $value->asString();
    print $name . ": " . $content . "\n";
}
```

Note the use of several new methods, including XmlValue::asString() and XmlDocument::getName(). Certain pieces of document information, including its name within the container, are available only by querying directly or retrieving the result as a document. When your queries require the node values instead of the documents matching a query, asString() is all you need.

The XmlValue class also provides a Document Object Model (DOM)-like interface to not only retrieve values (as with the asString() and asDocument() methods) but also to navigate the nodes it represents. Its methods include getNextSibling(), getAttributes(), and getFirstChild(), making it useful for any post-query processing that you might need to perform on query results.

The BDB XML query engine is capable of evaluating XQuery queries on documents (and even on individual query results) in addition to database containers. Listing 12-11 does exactly this by executing several queries by using the XmlValue object. Because the document query will repeat for each result, it makes sense to prepare it by using an XmlQueryExpression object.

Listing 12-11. *Querying Results*

```
$mgr = new XmlManager();
$query = "collection('test.dbxml')/person[name='Fred']";
$subquery = "/person/phone";

$container = $mgr->openContainer("test.dbxml");
$qcontext = $mgr->createQueryContext();
$phoneqcontext = $mgr->createQueryContext();

$results = $mgr->query($query, $qcontext);
$phonequery = $mgr->prepare($subquery, $phoneqcontext);

while ($results->hasNext()) {
    $value = $results->next();
    $phoneresults = $phonequery->execute($value, $phoneqcontext);
    while ($phoneresults->hasNext()) {
        $phonevalue = $phoneresults->next();
        print $phonevalue->asString() . "\n";
    }
}
```

The same process can be performed with the XmlDocument object resulting from a call to XmlValue::asDocument(), passing that object as argument to XmlQueryExpression::execute(). Of course, if you anticipate only one <phone/> element in this example, you can just call XmlResults:: next() instead of creating a while block.

You used different XmlQueryContext objects for the query and the subquery in this example. Although you could use the same query context, it might not be a safe operation in all cases (for example, when the main query is lazily evaluated).

The second query in this example could be relative to the result node by using the current node (.) instead:

```
./phone/string()
```

This same technique of querying results and documents can be useful for pulling data out of large documents, enabling you to work within the context of previous result sets. A later section looks more closely at the use of XmlDocument to demonstrate the retrieval of metadata.

Creating Other Objects

Most of the remaining XmlManager methods serve to simply construct objects of other DbXml subclasses. Many of them have already been demonstrated (for example, the XmlManager::createTransaction() method, which instantiates an XmlTransaction object). All such method names begin with create and most take no default arguments, serving as basic constructors. They include createDocument() to instantiate an XmlDocument object, createIndexLookup() to instantiate an XmlIndexLookup object, createModify() to instantiate an XmlModify object, createQueryContext() to instantiate an XmlQueryContext object, and createResults() to create an empty XmlResults object. These methods are examined in the following sections, in which their returned objects are demonstrated.

Using XmlContainer

The XmlContainer class provides most of the functionality that concerns a container and its contents, including adding, replacing, updating, and deleting documents; directly retrieving documents (using the getDocument() method); and managing indexes for the container.

An XmlContainer object is created by using the XmlManager::createContainer() and XmlManager:: openContainer() methods. Documents can be added using the putDocument() method, taking as argument either an XmlDocument or XmlInputStream. The previous section demonstrated it while supplying a document name and input stream or document container. The method will also accept an XML string (and will generate document names if not provided) if the call supplies the DBXML_GEN_NAME flag. Listing 12-12 uses putDocument() without providing a document name.

Listing 12-12. *Letting BDB XML Generate Document Names*

```
$mgr = new XmlManager();
$container = $mgr->openContainer("test.dbxml");
$ucontext = $mgr->createUpdateContext();

$content = "<person><name>Bob</name></person>";
$container->putDocument("", $content, $ucontext, DBXML_GEN_NAME);
```

With this usage, BDB XML guarantees the uniqueness of document names, incrementing them with each put document.

Documents are deleted from a container by using the XmlContainer::deleteDocument() method, which accepts with the document name or document object as its argument. The latter is useful when you want to iterate over a result set, deleting each document it contains, without having to retrieve the document name. Deleting documents is demonstrated in Listing 12-13.

Listing 12-13. *Deleting Documents*

```
$mgr = new XmlManager();
$container = $mgr->openContainer("test.dbxml");
$ucontext = $mgr->createUpdateContext();
$qcontext = $mgr->createQueryContext();
$content = "<person><name>Bob</name></person>";
$container->putDocument("", $content, $ucontext, DBXML_GEN_NAME);
$results = $mgr->query("collection('test.dbxml')/person[name='Bob']", $qcontext);
while ($results->hasNext()) {
    $value = $results->next();
    $document = $value->asDocument();
    print "Deleting document: " . $document->getName() . "\n";
    $container->deleteDocument($document, $ucontext);
}
```

Note that here an XmlDocument object is returned from each call to XmlResults::next().

When you want to replace a document in a container (instead of modifying it in place), you can use the XmlContainer::updateDocument() method. This operation will work with any XmlDocument object, setting its name to be identical to the document to be replaced and handing it to the updateDocument() method. You usually retrieve the document from the database, set new content by using the XmlDocument::setContent() method (or setContentAsXmlInputStream()), and save it back to the container. Listing 12-14 retrieves a document from the container using the XmlContainer::getDocument() method before replacing its content and saving it back to the container.

Listing 12-14. *Replacing a Document*

```
$mgr = new XmlManager();
$container = $mgr->openContainer("test.dbxml");
$ucontext = $mgr->createUpdateContext();
$newcontent = "<person><name>Bob</name></person>";
$document = $container->getDocument("file12.xml");
$document->setContent("<person><name>Bob2</name></person>");
$container->updateDocument($document, $ucontext);
```

The BDB XML API provides a programmatic interface to partially modifying documents using the XmlModify class, which enables a description of changes to be built before applying them to one or many documents in a container (this is demonstrated in the following section).

A final major function of the XmlContainer class is managing container indexes. Chapter 6, "Indexes," described the specifics of indexing strategies; this section discusses adding to, deleting from, and examining indexes of the API.

You can add indexes by using an index description string, as shown in Listing 12-15.

Listing 12-15. *Adding an Index to a Container with an Index Description String*

```
$mgr = new XmlManager();
$container = $mgr->openContainer("test.dbxml");
$container->addIndex("", "person", "node-element-equality-string");
```

Unlike most of the BDB XML APIs, the PHP interface does not support adding indexes using enumerated types. Given that the C++ interfaces enumerated types are deprecated, this is not a necessary feature.

■**Note** Supplying update context objects is optional for most PHP API methods that accept them. When not present, BDB XML creates and uses its own default contexts. For XmlQueryContext, the default options include eager query evaluation, no user-defined variables of namespaces, and so on.

The XmlContainer::getIndexSpecification() method returns an index specification for the container, encapsulating a description of all current indexes. It provides the addIndex() and deleteIndex()methods to manipulate the index description before applying it back to the container. The example in Listing 12-16 deletes one index and adds another using an XmlIndexSpecification object.

Listing 12-16. *Manipulating a Container's Index Specification*

```
$mgr = new XmlManager();
$container = $mgr->openContainer("test.dbxml");
$ucontext = $mgr->createUpdateContext();

$indexspec = $container->getIndexSpecification();
$indexspec->deleteIndex("", "person", "node-element-equality-string");
$indexspec->addIndex("", "person", "node-attribute-equality-string");
$container->setIndexSpecification($indexspec, $ucontext);
```

The XmlIndexSpecification object also provides methods for replacing an index, manipulating the default indexes, and iterating through the indexes within the specification.

One more class bears mentioning in the context of containers and indexes: XmlIndexLookup. Objects of this class are instantiated by XmlManager::createIndexLookup(),and you can retrieve all nodes or documents that have keys in any given index (see Listing 12-17).

Listing 12-17. *Listing All Documents Referenced by an Index*

```
$mgr = new XmlManager();
$container = $mgr->openContainer("test.dbxml");
$qcontext = $mgr->createQueryContext();
$indexlookup = $mgr->createIndexLookup($container, "", "person",
        "node-element-equality-string");
$results = $indexlookup->execute($qcontext);

while ($results->hasNext()) {
    $value = $results->next();
    my $document = $value->asDocument();
    print $document->getName() . ": " . $document->getContent();
}
```

When a container is of type WholedocContainer, the XmlIndexLookup::execute() operation always returns entire documents. This is also true for containers of type NodeContainer, unless the DBXML_INDEX_NODES flag was specified at container creation time. In that case, the lookup returns the individual nodes referred to in the index's keys.

The XmlIndexLookup class provides further access to an index's internal workings, enabling equality and inequality lookups, methods to set bounds for range lookups, and the ability to set a parent node for indexes that use edge paths rather than node paths.

Using XmlDocument

The XmlDocument class is used throughout the API primarily as a document handle, passed to and from methods of other classes. It also provides methods for getting and setting document content, getting document metadata, and setting a document's name.

■**Note** The PHP API in BDB XML 2.2.13 is missing the setMetaData() method. A patch is available from the BDB XML mailing list, referenced at the end of the chapter.

A document's metadata is set with the XmlDocument::setMetaData() method. Included in the document metadata are a name, a value, and an optional URI. Listing 12-18 demonstrates adding metadata to a document.

Listing 12-18. *Adding Metadata to a Document*

```
$mgr = new XmlManager();
$container = $mgr->openContainer("test.dbxml");

$uri = "http://brians.org/metadata/";
$metaname = "createdOn";
$metavalue = new XmlValue(XmlValue_DATE_TIME, "2006-02-05T05:23:14");
$document = $container->getDocument("file14.xml");
$document->setMetaData($uri, $metaname, $metavalue);
$container->updateDocument($document);
```

■**Tip** You can create a DATE_TIME index on this metadata attribute to facilitate fast date lookups.

You can retrieve metadata from an XmlDocument by using the getMetaData() method (see Listing 12-19).

Listing 12-19. *Retrieving Metadata from a Document*

```
$mgr = new XmlManager();
$container = $mgr->openContainer("test.dbxml");
$ucontext = $mgr->createUpdateContext();

$uri = "http://brians.org/metadata/";
$metaname = "createdOn";
$metavalue = new XmlValue();

$document = $container->getDocument("file14.xml");
$metavalue = $document->getMetaData($uri, $metaname);
print "file14.xml, created on " . $metavalue->asString() . "\n";
```

Note that containers can contain metadata-only documents that store only metadata key/value pairs with no XML content.

Using XmlModify

Using the XmlModify class enables you to modify a document within a container without having to replace the document or copy it to memory. You can construct a series of steps to manipulate the contents of a document and then apply these steps to one or many documents within a container. It then becomes a simple matter to perform container-wide document changes.

The XmlModify object is instantiated with a call to XmlManager::createModify(). A series of methods is exposed to provide for appending content, inserting and replacing content, and renaming and removing nodes. Assume that your database is filled with documents having the following structure:

```
<person>
    <name>Samuel</name>
    <age>51</age>
</person>
```

Under the <name/> element, you want to create a new attribute node called "type" with the value "given". (You can assume that the need to add surnames to the database has been discovered.) This process involves an append change to the document: appending to the <name/> element. Calling the XmlModify::addAppendStep() method with the target node, the node type you are appending, and the attribute name and value, you get the example in Listing 12-20.

Listing 12-20. *Modifying a Document*

```
$mgr = new XmlManager();
$container = $mgr->openContainer("test.dbxml");
$qcontext = $mgr->createQueryContext();
$ucontext = $mgr->createUpdateContext();
$modify = $mgr->createModify();
$queryexp = $mgr->prepare("/person/name", $qcontext);

$modify->addAppendStep($queryexp, XmlModify_Attribute, "type", "given");
$document = $container->getDocument("file14");
$doc_value = new XmlValue($document);
$modify->execute($doc_value, $qcontext, $ucontext);
```

Any series of XmlModify steps can be included. Note that XmlModify is executed on an XmlValue instead of on an XmlDocument. The execute() method also accepts an XmlResults object, enabling you to apply the XmlModify object to all documents in a query result. Listing 12-21 performs a query for all documents that have a /person/name element and then adds the @type="given" attribute to each.

Listing 12-21. *Modifying All Documents in a Result Set*

```
$mgr = new XmlManager();
$container = $mgr->openContainer("test.dbxml");
$qcontext = $mgr->createQueryContext();
$ucontext = $mgr->createUpdateContext();
$modify = $mgr->createModify();
$queryexp = $mgr->prepare("/person/name", $qcontext);

$modify->addAppendStep($queryexp, XmlModify_Attribute, "type", "given");
$results = $mgr->query("collection('test.dbxml')/person[name='Bill']", $qcontext);
$modify->execute($results, $qcontext, $ucontext);
```

This code changes all documents matching the query according to the XmlModify object. Keep in mind that this can be an expensive operation, but it is cheaper than retrieving and replacing each pertinent document in the container. The API reference in Appendix B contains a description of more XmlModify methods.

Conclusion

The PHP API makes the BDB XML functionality accessible to PHP. This chapter provided a brief tutorial overview of that functionality.

Appendix B contains a reference for the PHP API (as well as other languages), and the C++ API has additional information. The PHP examples included with the BDB XML distribution provide an overview of functionality, and the README file in the PHP source directory summarizes the API usage.

The following links are useful for learning more about BDB XML with PHP:

Berkeley DB XML website; http://www.sleepycat.com

Sleepycat BDB XML mailing list: xml@sleepycat.com (details at http://dev.sleepycat.com/community/discussion.html)

Db4Env PHP documentation: http://www.sleepycat.com/docs/ref/ext/php.html

Slides from George Schlossnagles BDB XML on PHP OSCON presentation: http://www.sleepycat.com/docs/ref/ext/php.html

## CHAPTER 13

Managing Databases

The BDB XML distribution includes several command-line utilities that implement many common database operations. These utilities provide easy interfaces to many tasks that can also be implemented via the BDB XML API, making them useful as an API reference as well. After building the distribution, the utilities are located in the install/bin/ directory for Unix installations and the bin/ directory under Win32. They are described here with their options.

■**Note** The topic of Berkeley DB database management is a complex one; users should refer to the Sleepycat docs on this subject (see the references at the end of this chapter) for a thorough treatment of backing up and restoring databases.

Populating Containers

Previous examples demonstrated populating containers by using the API. Because it is an operation that is not often repeated, a ready-made utility, dbxml_load_container, is provided for this purpose. It takes a file list as arguments and optionally creates the specified container. Keep in mind that you should create indexes for a container before populating it with many documents, so initial container creation might be best left to your own program or the dbxml shell.

■**Caution** The dbxml_load_container utility is intended only for off-line use because it cannot share environments with other processes. Be certain that there are no processes (including the dbxml shell) with open handles to the container. Also, because dbxml_load_container does not write transactionally, if you want the logs to restore the container upon data loss, dump the container after loading to ensure recoverability.

The following command-line example creates the node-type container people.dbxml in the environment located at ./project-db/ and populates it with the *.xml files in the current working directory.

```
$ dbxml_load_container -h ./project-db/ -c people.dbxml -s node *.xml
```

```
adding: 12.xml
adding: 13.xml
...
adding: 52.xml
```

Options for the dbxml_load_container utility are listed in Table 13-1.

Table 13-1. *Abbreviated Options for the* dbxml_load_container *Utility*

Option	Description
-h	Specifies the environment directory; the current working directory is the default. The directory must exist.
-c	Specifies the container name. If the named file doesn't exist, it will be created.
-s	Specifies the type for the container: node (the default and preferred type) or wholedoc. See Chapter 5, "Environments, Containers, and Documents," for details on container types.
-f	Specifies a file containing a list of XML files to load into the container. This option is useful when a list already exists or is preferred to a file list on the command line.
-p	When the -f option is provided, this option specifies a path prefix to prepend to the file list.

Dumping Containers

BDB XML provides two command-line utilities for dumping the contents of a container as text: db_dump and dbxml_dump. Both utilities output to standard output (or a file when specified) portable flat-text data (*not* XML), which restore a container when supplied to db_load or dbxml_load, respectively. The dumped output of db_dump includes container indexes; the dbxml_dump output does not, making the resulting file much smaller. The output of the two dump utilities is not mutually compatible; db_dump provides lower-level options and can be used with both standard Berkeley DB databases and BDB XML containers, whereas dbxml_load provides the necessary options to work specifically with BDB XML containers. Because BDB XML uses Berkeley DB databases in ways not necessarily exposed to the user, some of the db_dump functions   such as listing databases in a database file and dumping individual records by number   are not particularly useful to BDB XML containers.

■**Caution** To avoid corrupt output, this utility should be used only when other processes are not modifying the containers being dumped. It should also always be allowed to exit gracefully to detach from the container being dumped. Sending an interrupt signal (SIGINT) causes a clean exit to occur.

This example dumps the container we just created to file dump-1:

```
$ dbxml_dump -h project-db/ -f dump1 people.dbxml
```

The resulting file can be used with dbxml_load to restore a container to the state at which it was dumped.

The options for dbxml_dump are provided in Table 13-2. Refer to the Berkeley DB documentation if you require the lower-level functions of db_dump.

Table 13-2. *Abbreviated Options for the* dbxml_dump *Utility*

Option	Description
-h	Specifies the environment directory; the current working directory is the default. The directory must exist.
-f	Specifies the file to write the dump. Otherwise, the database will be dumped to standard output.
-r	Causes the utility to salvage data from a possibly corrupt file.
-R	Operates as -r, but aggressively salvages data all possible data from the file is returned, including deleted data. The resulting dump will probably not be loadable without editing.

Loading Containers

The dbxml_load utility reads the format output by dbxml_dump and loads it into a specified container. When loading to an existing container, it will output keys that already exist in the container, not overwrite them, and the process will exit with a status of 1. It is strongly recommended that you not use dbxml_load with existing containers; delete a container prior to performing a load. The following example loads the file dumped in the previous example:

```
$ dbxml_load -h project-db/ -f dump1 people.dbxml
```

The options for dbxml_load are listed in Table 13-3.

Table 13-3. *Abbreviated Options for the* dbxml_load *Utility*

Option	Description
-h	Specifies the environment directory; the current working directory is the default. The directory must exist.
-f	Specifies the file from which to load. Otherwise, data will be read from standard input.

Managing Logs

For environments and containers with logging and transactions enabled, BDB XML provides utilities to read logs and determine when to remove them. The db_printlog program prints log information in a human-readable format that can be used to identify all operations belonging to a particular transaction.

■**Note** An in-depth discussion of db_printlog is out of the scope of this book; please refer to the Berkeley DB documentation for details.

Many log files will accumulate for environments that use transactions. The db_archive utility tells you which are no longer in use (that is, no longer involved in active transactions). These log files can be deleted to save disk space, but recovery of an environment in the case of catastrophic failure is not possible without all logs for the life of the environment. Therefore, it is recommended that you back up old log files if complete recovery is potentially necessary.

The following example lists "old" log files for our environment:

```
$ db_archive -h project-db/
```

The options for db_archive are listed in Table 13-4.

Table 13-4. *Abbreviated Options for the* db_archive *Utility*

Option	Description
-h	Specifies the environment directory; the current working directory is the default.
-a	Causes the utility to output absolute pathnames.
-d	Removes the inactive log files automatically.
-l	Prints pathnames of all log files, regardless of whether they are involved in active transactions.
-v	Verbose mode; lists the checkpoints in the log files as they are reviewed.
-s	Prints pathnames of all database files that need to be archived to guarantee recovery resulting from catastrophic failure.

Detecting Deadlocks

A *deadlock* occurs when concurrent threads or processes compete for the same resource, as well as when multiple locks are requested within a single-threaded BDB XML application (called a *self-deadlock*). The latter is an application bug (or, less often, a BDB XML bug), for which the only symptom is a hanging process.

BDB XML provides the db_deadlock utility to be run either as a daemon process or called regularly by another process when multiple threads or processes access and modify a database. The utility aborts lock requests when it detects a deadlock.

■**Note** Like other utilities, db_deadlock uses underlying Berkeley DB and BDB XML APIs; in this case, it uses DB_ENV->lock_detect(). Applications should plan to perform their own lock detection and take appropriate action.

The options for db_deadlock are listed in Table 13-5.

Table 13-5. *Abbreviated Options for the* db_deadlock *Utility*

Option	Description
-h	Specifies the environment directory; the current working directory is the default.
-a	Specifies the action to take when a deadlock is detected. For example, an m value will abort the locker with the most locks, o will abort the locker with the oldest lock, and e will abort any lock request that has timed out.
-L	Logs the utility output to the specified file in the following format: db_deadlock: [process ID] [date].
-t	Causes an environment to check every specified number of seconds/microseconds; a review is forced when a process has been forced to wait for a lock.

Option	Description
-v	Verbose mode; messages are printed when the detector runs.
-s	Prints pathnames of all database files that need to be archived to guarantee recovery resulting from catastrophic failure.

Checkpointing Transactions

Another (optional) daemon utility, db_checkpoint, monitors database logs and performs automatic checkpointing. (It also uses the underlying API, DB_ENV->txn_checkpoint(), as your own BDB XML applications do.) Checkpointing flushes the databases memory pool, writes a checkpoint record to the log, and flushes the log. The following example checkpoints the logs for the environment once and then exits:

```
$ db_checkpoint -h ./project-db/ -1
```

Table 13-6 contains some of the options for db_checkpoint.

Table 13-6. *Abbreviated Options for the* db_checkpoint *Utility*

Option	Description
-h	Specifies the environment directory; the current working directory is the default.
-1	Checkpoints the log once and then exits.
-L	Logs the utility output to the specified file in this format: db_checkpoint: [process ID] [date].
-k	Checkpoints the database when the specified number of kilobytes of log file are written.
-v	Verbose mode; messages are printed when the detector runs.
-p	Checkpoints the database at least as often as the specified number of minutes.

Recovery

Whenever an unexpected event   system failure, application crash, and so on   leaves a database in an unknown state, the db_recover utility should be run to bring the database to a known (stable) state. Any transactions committed before the event are guaranteed to be consistent, and uncommitted transactions are undone. Recovery is possible only if log files exist for the given database.

The options for db_recover are shown in Table 13-7.

Table 13-7. *Abbreviated Options for the* db_recover *Utility*

Option	Description
-h	Specifies the environment directory; the current working directory is the default.
-c	Performs a catastrophic recovery instead of a normal recovery.
-t	Recovers to a time (instead of the current date) specified in the form [CC[YY]]MMDDhhmm[.SS].
-v	Verbose mode.

Debugging Databases

Status and statistics checks can be performed on databases by using the db_verify and db_stat utilities.

The db_verify command (and its corresponding DB->verify() API method) opens a database file and verifies the integrity of its contents, including sort ordering. It also takes the -h option and a list of one or more database files.

The db_stat utility (which uses the API methods DB->stat(), DB_ENV->lock_stat(), DB_ENV->log_stat(), and DB_ENV->txn_stat()) outputs useful statistics for an environment, including locking statistics, subsystem configuration for the environment, and cache statistics. For example, use the following to see log statistics for the environment:

```
$ db_stat -h ./project-db/ -l
```

```
10      Log version number
32KB    Log record cache size
0660    Log file mode
10Mb    Current log file size
...
1       Current log file number
7295    Current log file offset
1       On-disk log file number
7295    On-disk log file offset
0       Maximum commits in a log flush
0       Minimum commits in a log flush
96KB    Log region size
0       The number of region locks that required waiting (0%)
```

The options for db_stat are listed in Table 13-8.

Table 13-8. *Abbreviated Options for the* db_stat *Utility*

Option	Description
-h	Specifies the environment directory; the current working directory is the default.
-c	Displays locking subsystem statistics.
-d	Displays database statistics for the specified file.
-e	Displays database environment information, including configured subsystems.
-l	Displays logging subsystem statistics.
-t	Displays transaction subsystem statistics.
-m	Displays cache statistics.
-z	Resets the statistics after reporting them.

Backup and Restore

This section provides a brief and relatively safe overview of backing up and restoring BDB XML databases. Refer to the Berkeley DB documentation for more details.

A *standard backup* requires that database writes be discontinued during a backup (reads can continue). A *hot backup* enables database reads and writes to continue, but generates more data.

It is a *duration snapshot*; it covers the space of time required to make the backup and is not a true *point in time* snapshot of the database, as with standard backups. A standard backup entails the following steps:

1. Commit (or abort) all open transactions and stop writes (all filesystem operations) to the database. Reads can continue.

2. Perform an environment checkpoint using the `db_checkpoint` utility (described previously) or its corresponding `DB_ENV->txn_checkpoint()` API method.

3. Copy all data files to a backup device. This is the output of `db_archive -s`.

4. Copy the last log file to a backup device. This is the highest-numbered log output by `db_archive -l`.

A hot backup has many of the same steps, but instead enables writes to continue and does not require an environment checkpoint. The major difference is that the database data files must be copied sensitive to database pages, and all log files (those in use) must be archived after the data files. Refer to the Berkeley DB documentation for details on hot backups, page atomicity, and database recoverability. Note, too, that the Berkeley DB distribution (but not the BDB XML distribution) includes an example utility: `db_hotbackup`.

When an environment snapshot is sufficient for database recovery, simply removing the existing environment directory and re-creating it with the backed-up data and log files is usually sufficient. When data recovery is required because of a failure, the `db_recover` utility should be used.

Conclusion

Berkeley DB XML provides many tools via its APIs and command-line utilities to manage your databases. Please refer to the following documentation for more details on database maintenance:

The Berkeley DB reference guide, with manuals on deadlocking, transactional granularity and logging, and recovery procedures, as well as the related APIs: `http://www.sleepycat.com/docs/ref/toc.html`.

Manuals for the BDB XML command-line utilities: `http://www.sleepycat.com/xmldocs/utility/index.html`.

XML Essentials

Most XML tutorials focus on the XML itself—its syntax and rules. These subjects will be covered here, of course, but beginners can best understand XML with a focus on the data. This chapter will not only explain the "why" and "how" of XML (assuming that you have no previous XML experience) but also provide sufficient information for you to begin working with BDB XML.

It's About the Data

A common misunderstanding about XML is that it is a markup language. Although this is a true statement, the classification implies that XML is similar to HTML or is somehow an outgrowth of it. Although XML can be used like HTML to mark up documents, indicate formatting rules, and so on, these usages are just a few of many. The real purpose of XML is to *describe data*. In this way, it isn't so different from other data formats. Consider the case of the typical comma-delimited list (they are often called *comma separated values [CSV]*):

```
Brown, Jim, 24, 612-323-0091, Minneapolis, MN, male
Thompson, Sarah, 51,,,, female
Jackson, Jeremy, 31,, Salt Lake City, UT, male
Jones, Sue, 19, 313-555-1123, San Jose, CA, female
Carter, Frank,, 800-555-1123,,, male
```

Other examples include tab-delimited and space-delimited data (for instance, the Wordnet example in Chapter 2, "The Power of an Embedded XML Database"). Data formats such as these are usually used when dumping data from actual databases. With read-only databases such as Wordnet, however, they are sometimes used in production.

Note XHTML—the strict specification for HTML—is a dialect of XML. XML can express blocks and styles of text as well as define its own organization.

Humans can gather the meaning of fields from their contents: the first field is most likely a surname; the second is probably a given name; following fields might contain age, phone number, city, state, and gender. Of course, any program that has to interpret this data needs identifiers for each field, which can sometimes occur at the top of the file in the field of table field names:

```
Last name, First name, Age, Phone, City, State, Sex
```

A script or application can now parse this file, understand what each field means, and then do something with the data. Blank values are left empty, indicating that the information is not available.

If you have used a comma- or tab-delimited format extensively, you know that certain text must be *escaped*. Values with commas break the formatting, which can lead to conditions that require special rules. Values with commas are required to be contained in double quotes. Picture a field that lists hobbies, like so:

```
Brown, Jim, 24, 612-323-0091, Minneapolis, MN, male, "sports, boats, carpentry"
```

One solution is to create a field for each hobby; you embedded a CSV row into a value instead. What if one of the values contains double quotes? You have to replace the quotes in the value with two consecutive double quotes and include the value itself in double quotes:

```
Brown, """Big"" Jim", 24, 612-323-0091, Minneapolis, MN, male, "sports, boats, carpentry"
```

And because your CSV file uses line breaks to separate the records themselves, adding a field for a street address and a value with a line break also requires double quotes:

```
Brown, """Big"" Jim", 24, 612-323-0091, "Attn: Jim Brown
Pleax Systems, Inc.
18520 25th Ave
",Minneapolis, MN, male, "sports, boats, carpentry"
```

Its easy to see how such a format can grow unwieldy, but the rules are necessary to keep the format machine-interpretable.

Going back to the original CSV example, a novice translation of this data to an XML format might look something like this (abbreviated to only the first record):

```
<list>
    <entry>
        <field>
            <name>Last name</name>
            <value>Brown</value>
        </field>
        <field>
            <name>First name</name>
            <value>Jim</value>
        </field>
        <field>
            <name>Age</name>
            <value>24</value>
        </field>
        <field>
            <name>Phone</name>
            <value>612-323-0091</value>
        </field>
        <field>
            <name>City</name>
            <value>Minneapolis</value>
        </field>
        <field>
            <name>State</name>
            <value>MN</value>
        </field>
        <field>
            <name>Sex</name>
            <value>male</value>
        </field>
    </entry>
</list>
```

XML documents typically have the extension .xml, so this document can be called list.xml. In the example, a person has attempted to describe the CSV data in XML. The bold text indicates XML *values*. A novice might look at this example and comment on how long or redundant the XML is when compared with the CSV: "What a waste of space!" Of course, there is a better way to use XML.

The phrase *semantically rich* is frequently used in connection with XML. XML is a self-defining markup language, so you are essentially free to invent your own format. The best *tags* the names in the brackets (< >) are those that describe the data itself.

Recall that the novice document example was given the name list.xml. This seems a poor choice for a filename because a person seeing the file would have no idea about the nature of its contents; a better name might be people.xml.

This problem also occurs with the tag names. Consider the tags to take the place of the field names at the top of the CSV document. This would give you an XML translation closer to the following (note that the XML values are still bold):

```
<people>
    <person>
        <lastname>Brown</lastname>
        <firstname>Jim</firstname>
        <age>24</age>
        <phone>612-323-0091</phone>
        <city>Minneapolis</city>
        <state>MN</state>
        <sex>male</sex>
    </person>
</people>
```

The field names have moved into tags. The outermost tag is called people because this document supposedly contains a list of people. You can tell what any given value means, even if the value itself is ambiguous, without looking at the top of the file for field names or counting commas in a CSV file. Tag names, called *elements* in XML, are similar in this example to relational database (RDB) field names in tables. XML is a semantically rich data format because each value has complete identification its meaning is clear without reference to tables or remote sources. Editing this record manually is simply a matter of editing a file and then replacing or adding the elements and values that you want. Semantically rich formats provide readability for humans, editability for humans and programs, and self-contained meaning throughout the document. Although this format requires a longer file than others (the CSV example, for instance), it brings a dramatic increase in usability. The extra bytes are a small price to pay for context: with XML, data has "inline meaning."

A single XML file can contain an entire database, or individual records can be stored in many XML files. (This is where BDB XML will come into play.) What might be considered a single record or row in an RDB can be treated as a single file. Individual records can contain hierarchical data all their own. Suppose that you want to add a list of hobbies to your record, permit multiple phone numbers, and enable the addition of a middle name or name prefix. You could change the XML to read as follows:

```
<person>
    <name>
        <last>Brown</last>
        <first>Jim</first>
        <middle>Austin</middle>
    </name>
    <age>24</age>
    <phone>
        <office>612-323-0091</office>
        <home/>
    </phone>
```

```
    <city>Minneapolis</city>
    <state>MN</state>
    <sex>male</sex>
    <hobby>sports</hobby>
    <hobby>boats</hobby>
    <hobby>carpentry</hobby>
</person>
```

Notice that the outermost element is now called person because this file contains only one. New elements have been added to the <name/> tag: <last/>, <first/>, and <middle/>.

▌Note In referring to the elements, I am using their empty counterparts, although they are not empty in the document. In the context of describing them, however, they have no content. Chalk it up to excessive logic.

The new elements make sense conceptually because the full name comprises a first, middle, and last name. Options for multiple phone numbers are also available under the <phone/> tag. In this example, there is no home phone, so its element is empty. It is a shortcut for (but carries the same meaning as) the following:

```
<home></home>
```

There is now a <hobby/> tag for each of the hobbies. (You could instead add a tag named <hobbies/> and then add three <hobby/> tags inside of it.)

Finally, add the quoted nickname and street address containing line breaks:

```
<person>
    <name>
        <last>Brown</last>
        <first>"Big" Jim</first>
        <middle>Austin</middle>
        <nick>Big</nick>
    </name>
    <age>24</age>
    <phone>
        <office>612-323-0091</office>
        <home/>
    </phone>
    <street> Attn: Jim Brown
             Pleax Systems, Inc.
             18520 25th Ave
    </street>
    <city>Minneapolis</city>
    <state>MN</state>
    <sex>male</sex>
    <hobby>sports</hobby>
    <hobby>boats</hobby>
    <hobby>carpentry</hobby>
</person>
```

For illustration, I added the nickname to both the <first/> tag and a new <nick/> tag. This would be a matter of personal preference. For the new <street> tag, notice that because XML is not based on line breaks for record delimitation, no escaping is needed with this value. Of course, you might guess that greater-than and less-than brackets in values break the XML format. You'll learn about that soon enough.

Note that we invented the markup shown here: `<person/>`, `<name/>`, `<age/>`. All the tags used here have no meaning outside of the document. This is what makes XML flexible: you can make up your own formats, use them in files and applications, and retain compatibility with any XML tools or applications. Of course, there are many standardized XML formats   they include address book formats (vCard), content syndication formats (Really Simple Syndication [RSS] and Atom), and HTML itself (XHTML, specifically).

XML can be used for markup as with HTML. It does not tend to make XML easier to learn for beginners, so I will continue to describe XML in the pure context of data. We will return to this topic at the end of the chapter.

XML Building Blocks

XML consists primarily of two basic pieces: elements and attributes.

Elements

An *element* is what people commonly describe as a *tag*:

`<city>Minneapolis</city>`

This tag has a name and a value. Its name is `city` and its value is `Minneapolis`. An XML document always has one or more elements. All but one of these elements are required to be inside other elements, and the outermost element is referred to as the *root* element. In this example, `<city/>` is the root element because it is the only element.

Element names can contain letters, numbers, and other characters (including non-English and non-ASCII characters), but they must start with a letter. Nonetheless, it's a good idea to avoid using characters that might cause confusion or look out of place. For example, a reader   or software might interpret a dash to be a minus sign or interpret a period to be an object method. The software you use (or write) to process XML usually imposes restrictions on the characters you use before XML does. Element names cannot contain spaces or start with the letters *xml*. They should be short and concise. Most XML dialects stick to lowercase letters (names are case-sensitive), but this is a matter of preference.

Element values can include other elements, text (`Minneapolis`, in this case), or a combination of the two. The content of an XML element is everything from its opening tag to its closing tag, including white space. Elements can be empty, as shown earlier.

Attributes

The second main piece of an XML document (and a reason why element names cannot contain spaces) is the *attribute*. An attribute is a name/value pair just like an element, but with stricter usage rules. The attribute occurs inside of the element tag, with a name, equal sign, and a value in quotes. Here, two are added:

`<city latitude="44°57'N" longitude="93°16'W">Minneapolis</city>`

Attributes are usually used to "qualify" the element. More than one attribute in the same tag cannot use the same name. The naming restrictions are the same as elements, and attribute values are typically of the short variety.

Well-Formedness

Well-formedness describes the compliance of a format to its rules. For XML, these rules are rather straightforward. An element can contain other elements and each element can contain one or many attributes.

Tag names are case-sensitive, so opening and closing tag names must be spelled identically. Elements must always have an opening and a closing tag unless they're empty (in that case, the `<tag/>` format can be used). Elements must never *cross* elements must be closed at the same level in which they are opened. The following is not legal:

```
<person>
    <name>
        <first>Mike</first>
        <last>Stevens</name>
    </last>
</person>
```

It's helpful to imagine XML elements as file directories that can contain other directories: you can't jump up to a parent directory and remain inside of the subdirectory. Following this analogy, the files within a directory would be an element's text content, and the directory name and permissions could be considered attributes.

Unquoted attribute values are illegal:

```
<city latitude=44°57'N>
```

The proper syntax is as follows:

```
<city latitude="44°57'N">
```

You will notice that most XML documents especially those created by a program start with an XML *declaration*. This provides the XML version and character encoding of the document, which is discussed later.

```
<?xml version="1.0" encoding="UTF-8"?>
```

For now, note that most of the examples in this book omit this declaration and most XML parsers do not enforce it.

White space in the content of elements is preserved with XML unless you specify a different behavior to your XML parser. This is unlike HTML, which consolidates consecutive white space (spaces, tabs, and so on) to a single space. Also note that a new line is always stored as line feed (LF) in XML documents. Windows applications usually store a new line as a pair of characters (a carriage return plus an LF); in Macintosh Classic applications, a carriage return (CR) is typically used. But XML applications on all platforms (should) know to read and store lines in an XML file terminated with a single LF.

Because the greater-than and less-than signs are used for tags, when they occur in the content of an element they must be replaced with an equivalent *entity*, which is already familiar to HTML users. Assume that the text is the following:

```
$x > $y
```

This text can be placed into an element as follows:

```
<statement>$x &gt; $y</statement
```

You can define your own entities to be used (discussed later); the default XML entities are those characters used in the tags (see Table A-1).

Table A-1. *Default XML Entities*

Entity	Meaning	Character
lt	Less-than sign	<
gt	Greater-than sign	>
amp	Ampersand	&
apos	Single quote	'
quote	Double quote	"

Finally, XML files can contain comments in the following form:

```
<! comment -->
```

Tip XML editors check for compliance with the syntax rules as you type. Alternatively, shell tools such as the libxml2 xmllint utility (http://www.xmlsoft.org) can be used to check syntax:

```
$ xmllint --noout people.xml
```

This code outputs contextual errors in the file or outputs nothing if the file is well-formed XML.

CDATA

An XML parser parses the text content inside elements; it must do this to determine where the closing tag occurs. This is why illegal characters   such as the greater-than and less-than characters   must be escaped (expressed as entities).

XML does provide for the storage of data without using entities. For example, you might want to store a math equation or a script in the content of an XML element (this will be familiar to JavaScript users), and escaping every greater-than and less-than symbol could be excessive. To force the XML parser to ignore the content of an element, you can use a CDATA section. It begins with the text `<![CDATA[` and ends with `]]>`, as shown in this example:

```
<script>
<![CDATA[
    function decide(x,y) {
        if  (x > y && y > 0) then {
            return x;
        }
    }
]]>
</script>
```

The only string the CDATA section cannot contain is `]]>`, making nested CDATA sections impossible.

You should use CDATA sparingly; it is not intended as means of "getting around" strict XML formatting. XML Stylesheet Language Transformations (XSLT) beginners sometimes put HTML fragments in these sections to recombine them later. This practice usually leads to unintended results and lessens the benefits of using XML and/or XSLT in the first place. When using CDATA, keep in mind that to the XML processor, the following are equivalent:

```
<example><![CDATA[ x > y ]]></example>

<example>x &gt; y</example>
```

The effect of CDATA sections is to have the processor treat element content that is not escaped as if it were. After these examples have been parsed, they are essentially the same to the program.

That's really all there is to the syntax rules of XML. There are a few more content types, but we'll get to those later. You can probably tell that XML itself has little to do with its usefulness as applied to real-world formats.

Relationships

Many XML technologies use the relationship between elements and attributes to process the XML. The outermost element is the root element, and elements inside of it are child elements. All elements in an XML document have one (and only one) parent element   with the exception of the root element. In this example, the <name/> element has a parent and children.

```
<person>
    <name>
        <last>Brown</last>
        <first>"Big" Jim</first>
        <middle>Austin</middle>
    </name>
    <age>24</age>
</person>
```

For element <name/>, its parent is <person/>; its children are <last/>, <first/>, and <middle/>. The element <age/> has no child elements; its parent is also <person/>. Because elements <name/> and <age/> share the same parent, they are *siblings*.

All elements that occur inside of another are *descendants* of that element. The descendants of <person/> are <name/>, <last/>, <first/>, <middle/>, and <age/> (every element in the document other than itself). Similarly, all elements that occur as a parent or parents-of-parents are *ancestors*. In this example, <middle/> has the ancestors <name/> and <person/>.

Attributes that occur within an element tag are technically children of that element and have the same relationships just described.

Namespaces

Whether on the web, in programming languages, or elsewhere, a *namespace* qualifies some piece of data to make it unique. The HTTP path index.html depends on the URL before it to be located and differentiated from all other index.html paths. XML also provides namespaces to make element names unique. Take the case of this XML document:

```
<img>
    <path>/images/stephan.jpg</path>
    <size>122K</size>
</img>
```

The <img/> element, which is reminiscent of the HTML image element, could lead to conflicts by processors or people. By using namespaces, element and attribute names can be qualified with a prefix:

```
<myapp:img>
    <path>/images/stephan.jpg</path>
    <size>122K</size>
</myapp:img>
```

■**Note** You might wonder why we would want to use a namespace if a document contains only one kind of
<img/> element, and any application that uses this document is unlikely to know about the HTML version. In practice, most XML documents do not need to use namespaces. If you intend your XML to be used by several people or multiple applications, it's probably a good idea to use them. It can also save headaches if you later decide to distribute your XML or use it in different environments, but it is by no means required.

XML namespaces are still local to the file in which they occur. To be unique outside of your file, the prefix gets associated with a unique Uniform Resource Identifier (URI). Here again is the previous example:

```
<myapp:img xmlns:myapp="http://www.apress.com/myapp">
    <myapp:path>/images/stephan.jpg</myapp:path>
    <myapp:size>122K</myapp:size>
</myapp:img>
```

The xmlns attribute prefix is special; it tells the reading application to associate the namespace prefix myapp with the specified URI. Thus, the element namespace myapp is arbitrary: the XML parser relies on the URI to determine uniqueness. Putting this declaration in the <myapp:img/> element causes all child elements with the same namespace (notice that these were added) to also be associated with that URI. The parser sees this URI (in this case, a URL) as simply a string, used to give the namespace a unique name. The URI is not accessed or used by the parser.

To avoid repeating a namespace for every child or an element, a default namespace can be declared:

```
<img xmlns="http://www.apress.com/myapp">
    <path>/images/stephan.jpg</ path>
    <size>122K</size>
</img>
```

This is equivalent to the previous example, but shorter and more readable. When namespaces are used, they are often used to permit the mixing of elements that do not share namespace. In that case, this shortcut obviously cannot be used, and each element requires a namespace prefix or it will be assumed to not have a namespace. XSLT is one such case (it will be demonstrated shortly).

Validation

Given so much flexibility to invent your own markup (XML "dialect"), how can you enforce a format on your XML documents? You're probably familiar with the notion of *validation*: web forms get validated to ensure that they have all the required information, merchants validate credit card numbers to be sure that they are acceptable, and so on. To validate XML means to not just confirm well-formedness but also to confirm that it conforms to additional rules. These rules can include the names of elements and attributes, the number of children an element is allowed to have, or even the kind of content an attribute or element can contain.

Consider the previous XML example. This document could be fed to an XML parser and pass with flying colors   it is well-formed XML. However, no address book application could make heads or tails of it. It might make for a cute message to a friend, equivalent to saying this:

```
Name: Jim Brown
City: Minneapolis
```

But again, this information would not be particularly useful to an application because it doesn't know for certain what is being described. To provide data in a format that can be understood by an application, you need to know which *standards* it supports. For example, a prevalent standard for address book data is called vCard and is supported (or used natively) by most contact-management applications. vCard (and its XML version, RDF vCard) documents can be imported into an address book, and vCard would then know exactly what each field represented. The preceding example might look thus in the vCard format:

```
BEGIN:VCARD
VERSION:3.0
CLASS:PUBLIC
REV:2005-09-28 13:35:45
FN:Jim Brown
N:Brown;Jim;;;
ADR;TYPE=work:;;;Minneapolis;;;
END:VCARD
```

Address book applications understand this format because they have been written to process it. Similarly, address books by different developers running on different operating systems could export and import address books without loss of information. This is another benefit of a text-based format: no specific operating system software is necessary to read the file, as is true for binary data formats.

Credit card numbers are often validated before they are charged. For example, many online orders are emailed to the merchant, who then charges your card manually (instead of charging the card in real time as you place an order). To save the merchant the hassle of getting an erroneous credit card number (and to save you the hassle of getting a phone call to confirm it), credit card numbers are assigned to allow a simple computation to know whether the number is *valid*. Similarly, software that reads an XML document can quickly confirm whether it conforms to the expected format. If it doesn't, processing stops and an error is reported. This saves the software the expense of working on data that might be incomplete. In the case of software that generates the XML file, validation can be performed before the document is even saved.

Thus, validation is a process that a person or software must perform, and both require some formal description of the rules for this to happen. There are two popular ways to describe these rules: by using Document Type Definition (DTD) and XML schema. DTDs are older and less concise; schemas are concise, flexible, and are written with XML (making them easy to parse for XML software). If you are familiar with the idea of RDB schemas, the idea isn't too different: an RDB schema describes what the database (its tables and rows) looks like and what it is allowed to contain.

XML schemas do more than enforce the format of an XML file; they also explain to developers what a given XML document should look like in the form of documentation. It is important to understand that without some formal description of an XML format, even well-formed XML is useless for the storage or exchange of data. Sure, a human might be able to figure out what the document contains, but software has no point of reference. For this reason, XML is frequently referred to as "not very useful," and this assessment is correct. XML is simply some rules for formatting tags and their contents; it's the *schema* for the XML that makes the document intelligible to software and its *application* that makes it useful.

XML Schemas

I won't describe DTD here because it is a somewhat dated and unpopular format for describing rules. XML schema is the first schema language to be recommended by the World Wide Web Consortium (W3C) and is written in XML. Schema documents typically have the extension .xsd. The XML schema is a complicated subject all by itself, so I only introduce the topic here. Note that XML schemas are not completely necessary for using and understanding either XML or BDB XML.

XML schemas enable you to describe what constitutes a "valid" XML format for your data, with varying degrees in strictness. As was already discussed, well-formed XML is not necessarily intelligible to software. Consider that an XML element that you expect to contain a price for a product instead contains text or contains two prices instead of the expected single element. This is an error, even if the XML document is well-formed. Schemas give you a way to describe and enforce these rules.

Here again is the XML file person.xml:

```
<person>
    <name>
        <last>Brown</last>
        <first>Jim</first>
    </name>
    <age>24</age>
</person>
```

XML elements are *optionally ordered*, which means that some applications might depend on the order of tags, and that order must be retained to reproduce or write out the XML file. In the example, the <last/> tag comes before the <first/> tag. Although this placement is purely coincidental, you might want to enforce an order on these elements. Notice that these same two elements contain string content, whereas the <age/> element contains a number.

Note Of course, having an age field in any application makes little sense because you would want it incremented; given a birth date to do so, you could compute a person's age. Unless, of course, the list shows deceased persons. I digress.

Here is an XML schema document to accompany person.xml; it is called person.xsd:

```
<?xml version="1.0"?>
<xs:schema xmlns:xs="http://www.w3.org/2001/XMLSchema"
        xmlns="http://www.w3schools.com">
<xs:element name="person">
    <xs:complexType>
        <xs:sequence>
            <xs:element name="name">
                <xs:complexType>
                    <xs:all>
                        <xs:element name="first" type="xs:string"/>
                        <xs:element name="last" type="xs:string"/>
                    </xs:all>
                </xs:complexType>
            </xs:element>
            <xs:element name="age" type="xs:integer"/>
        </xs:sequence>
    </xs:complexType>
</xs:element>
</xs:schema>
```

The document is valid XML and uses namespaces. The root element is <xs:schema/>, indicating that this it a schema document. The same element defines the xs namespace and defines a default namespace. So far, the document is not saying anything about the "person" XML.

The bold sections in this schema example are the opening <xs:element/> tags that describe the "person" XML file. The first child element is <xs:element/> with an attribute "name" with value "person". This element describes the root element of this XML file   if the XML file did not begin with the <person/> element (which it does), an XML parser would fail right away with a validation error. Other <xs:element/> elements describe the <name/>, <first/>, <last/>, and <age/> elements.

Without delving too deeply, note that the <xs:element/> tags for the <first/> and <last/> elements have a type of "xs:string", meaning that any string value is valid for those tags. By contrast, the <age/> tags content is to an integer with the type "xs:integer". The <xs:complexType/> elements occur beneath elements that are allowed to contain other elements. In this case, there are the <person/> and <name/> elements; no others are allowed to have child elements. Finally, the <xs:sequence/> element requires that the children of <person/> occur in the order specified (having the <age/> tag before the <name/> tag would result in a validation error), and the <xs:all/> element tells the validator that <first/> and <last/> are required   but not necessarily in the order shown here. You can see that schemas give you a lot of control over what XML format you will consider legal.

■**Note** Most XML editors enable you to associate an XML document with a schema, performing validation as you type. Alternatively, shell tools such as the libxml2 xmllint enable validation, but they don't always do this by default. You can also pass it a path to an XSD for validation:

```
$ xmllint --schema people.xsd people.xml
```

This code outputs errors if the XML file does not conform to the specified schema.

Although an XML schema must be enforced, the XML document typically contains a reference to the XSD document. In the person.xml file, the xsi namespace is defined (the schema namespace), and the location of the schema document is specified:

```
<person xmlns:xsi="http://www.w3.org/2001/XMLSchema-instance"
        xsi:schemaLocation="person.xsd">
    <name>
        <last>Brown</last>
        <first>Jim</first>
    </name>
    <age>24</age>
</person>
```

Not all XML processors recognize this declaration or enforce it by default. Consult documentation for your XML parser or application to determine whether it is supported.

When should you use XML schemas? XML is pretty flexible, and schemas offer a lot of control. Even when you don't intend to validate all the XML you use, schemas can help you create well-designed XML and avoid some of the bloating and confusion that XML might otherwise cause when allowed to freely "evolve."

XPath: the Gist

As if this weren't enough fun already, it gets even better. Much of the power of XML becomes apparent when developers begin the process of searching and querying documents. In fact, XML querying technologies are the very reason why many shops opt to use XML in the first place: the ease of use, intuitive syntax, and standardized usage. This is certainly the case with BDB XML.

XPath is the original and most widely supported language for querying XML documents. It is now in version 2.0, which is fully supported by BDB XML. This section describes only XPath 1.0. But never fear   version 1.0 is a subset of 2.0 and is completely compatible with even the newest implementations.

Paths

I earlier compared an XML document to a file system. File directories have children in the form of other directories, attributes in the form of names and timestamps and permissions, and content in the form of files. Regardless of your choice of operating system, the syntax of a typical file path is familiar:

`/home/garron/documents/resume.pdf`

This example refers to a `resume.pdf` file, inside a `documents` directory, inside a `garron` directory, inside a `home` directory. The `home` directory could be considered the root (Unix mount points and nomenclature notwithstanding), the `garron` directory could be considered a child, and so on.

XPath uses a similar syntax to refer to nodes in an XML document. For these purposes, a node is any piece of data in the XML file: an element, an attribute, or even the content of an element can be considered a node. Using our person XML example, the following path refers to the node for the person's last name in that file:

`/person/name/last`

Executed against the XML document with an XPath interpreter, this query would match one node of our document: the element `<last/>`. It would return the value `<last>Brown</last>`, in this case. You can test this with several XPath command-line tools.

Nodes

It is important to understand why this example refers to the `<last/>` element instead of just giving the value `Brown`. Forget any notion you might have of a node as a tag. XPath (and other technologies, including the Document Object Model [DOM]   discussed next) view every part of an XML document as a node, any place in the document it can return some value   whether an element, an attribute, or text content. Each is a kind of node, and an XPath query sees it as such. Nodes can contain other nodes, as is the case with this example. The `<last/>` element contains a child text node with value `Brown`. If elements and attributes were object classes in a given programming language (as is the case with the XML DOM), they would be subclasses of a parent node class and would inherit its properties. Thus, a node is the most primitive piece of an XML document, and everything in an XML document is a node. XPath (and XQuery) operate on this data model view of a document instead of the text it contains. The differentiation is critical to understanding how technologies such as XPath view a document and is explored in more detail in the next section.

There are several ways to get the text value of an element. The most universal is to append the `text()` "node test" to the end of your XPath query:

`/person/name/last/`**`text()`**

In truth, every word in this expression is a node test. The string `person` is used by the processor to test the name of the top-level elements, as is `name` and `last`. The `text()` example is also a test, but in the form of an instruction to match text nodes (this is explained in the next section). Here, the XPath processor is told to return the text node children of the `<last/>` element, and you would get back the value `Brown`.

Some XPath processors enable you to query for a text value directly. For example, the Perl XML::LibXML module gives you a findvalue() method on node objects; this returns the literal value of the node, which means all child text it contains and no child elements (or text children of child elements).

Understanding how XPath and DOM processors (and everything that uses them) treat XML nodes will save you future headaches.

Document Object Model (DOM)

A discussion about the DOM is required to understand how XPath and other XML technologies "see" an XML document. The XML DOM is a W3C specification to give programming languages a consistent means of processing XML. When a program parses an XML file, it must give the file some internal representation to enable a program to browse it. Its this internal representation that an XPath processor uses to find requested nodes in the document.

The DOM defines a set of node types, which are typically defined as an object class in programming languages. (You dont need a solid understanding of all these node types to understand or use the DOM or XPath.) Each type might contain children nodes of the types listed in Table A-2. (This table is an abbreviated list of node types; I have omitted DocumentType, DocumentFragment, EntityReference, ProcessingInstruction, Entity, and Notation for clarity.)

Table A-2. *Abbreviated List of DOM Node Types*

Node Type	Description	Children
Document	The entire document, root node	Element (only one), Comment
Element	Element	Element, Text, Comment, CDATASection
Attr	Attribute	Text
Comment	Comment	None
Text	Text content (character data)	None
CDATASection	Block of CDATA text	None

Assume that youre working with this XML document:

```
<person>
    <!-- Record needs revision -->
    <name lang="en">
        Mr.
        <last>Brown</last>
        <first>Jim</first>
    </name>
    <age>24</age>
    <note><![CDATA[ 24 > 20 ]]></note>
</person>
```

Parsing it into a DOM tree will result in a code language similar to Table A-3, regardless of the language or DOM implementation you are using. Indents identify children, and parentheses contain the node name (if any) and value (if any). Compare this tree closely with the preceding XML; you will probably find that it does not match your expectations.

Table A-3. *Parsed DOM Node Tree and XPath for Each Node*

Node Tree	Corresponding XPath
Document ("#document", none)	/
Element ("person", "")	/person
Comment ("#comment", " Record needs revision ")	/person/comment()
Element ("name", "")	/person/name
Attr("lang", "en")	/person/name/@lang
Text("#text", " Mr. ")	/person/name/text()
Element ("last", "")	/person/name/last
Text("#text", "Brown")	/person/name/last/text()
Element ("first", "")	/person/name/first
Text("#text", "Brown")	/person/name/first/text()
Element ("age", "")	/person/age
Text ("#text", "24")	/person/age/text()
Element ("note", "")	/person/note
CDATASection (none, "24 > 20")	(none)

Note the following:

The top or root node is /, not /person. This node has no name or value; it has only children nodes. (Some processors report a name #document or no name.) This node can have only one element child because more than one would not be well-formed XML (in which every node needs a parent but one).

The /person element has five child nodes: a text node, a comment node, two element nodes, and a CDATA section.

The /person element has no obvious value, but /person/text() has a white space value. All the white space inside of <person/> but not contained in its children elements is counted as its value.

The /person/comment() node is addressed with the comment() function, much as text nodes need text(). Comment nodes have no given name. (Some processors report a name #comment or no name.)

The attribute node /person/name/@lang has a name and value. Getting values out of attributes is inexpensive.

The element /person/name/text() has a value that includes the white space in <name/>, including line breaks (not shown here). Text nodes have no given name. (Some processors report a name text or no name.)

White space throughout the document has been ignored by setting an option at parse time. Otherwise, the previous node tree would have many text nodes containing only white space, including each newline and leading white space. This often leads to confusion when querying and is expensive to both parse and store. (For this reason, prettily printed XML that retains all formatting does not store efficiently.)

The CDATA node is not addressable with XPath. These sections are treated as text blocks that occur as text within their parent element. In this case, even though `<note/>` contains no text other than the CDATA section, the processor expands the CDATA to text content. Calling `/person/note/text()` gives a value of `24 > 20`, even though the DOM tree contains no text child of `<note/>`. CDATA is simply a node type of convenience for enclosing character data that is not trusted to be well-formed XML. (Some processors report a name of `#cdata-section`, `cdata-section`, or no name.)

We will return to the DOM shortly to discuss the classes and their methods in more depth.

ELEMENTS OR ATTRIBUTES?

On multiple occasions I have been asked, "When should I use elements instead of attributes to store information?" This is really a matter of personal preference, with some obvious constraints. First, only one attribute of a given name can exist per element. If you require more than one piece of data by the same name, you need to use elements. Second, storing anything but relatively short text values in attributes makes for poor readability. If the value is anything else, an element is the better option.

In other cases, I do have a personal preference. The way you like to code can influence where you prefer to put simple values. When writing XPath predicates, I find it easier to query off of attributes than I do elements, mostly for the sake of XPath readability, so I tend to put oft-queried values in attributes. Also, in most DOM implementations, attribute lookups tend to be slightly faster than element values because element text value queries have to look at the text child nodes of that element to compare.

On the other hand, when working with DOM objects, I find it slightly easier to add and manipulate elements than to do so with attributes, partly because I do it more often. So I put data that changes frequently into elements.

XPath: the Details

With an understanding of how the XPath sees nodes in a tree of XML, XPath is easier to learn. Many developers opt to use XPath over the DOM because of its terseness and ease of use. To keep this introduction simple, I will cover only the most common operators, axes, and functions.

Contexts

All XPath expressions have *contexts*. If you were using a shell to browse a file system, you might find yourself several directories deep from the root directory. From there, you could `cd` to a parent directory, to a child directory, to a sibling directory, and so on. XPath is similar in that a statement carries varied meaning depending on the node in a node tree that is referenced. The XML analog of a *current working directory* on an operating system is a *current node*.

Path Operators

XPath provides the expressions shown in Table A-4 to select or navigate nodes. Each expression is actually a shortcut for a longer formal operation.

Table A-4. *Common Path Operators*

Expression	Description
/	Selects from the root node at the start of an expression; otherwise delimits parents and children
//	Unrestrained select operation from the current node that selects nodes anywhere in the document
.	Current node
..	Parent of the current node
@	Selects attributes
*	Element node wildcard; matches any element node
@*	Attribute node wildcard; matches any attribute node
node()	Matches any node of any kind

The period operators are used primarily in predicates, discussed in the next section. The others are fairly straightforward in their usage.

Table A-5 lists some example expressions.

Table A-5. *Example Paths*

Expression	Description
/	Selects the root document node
//age	Selects all nodes named age regardless of where they occur in the document
/person/name/*	Selects all child elements of /person/name
/person//last	Selects all elements named last that descend from /person
name/@lang	From the current node (this is the context), selects the lang attribute of any child nodes named name
//@*	Selects all attribute nodes in the document

Clearly, the use of the // operator incurs substantial overhead because the XPath processor must traverse the entire XML file (or all descendants if it comes after the current node) to determine all matches.

Predicates

A *predicate* is a conditional that gets placed in your query, enabling you to select nodes more specifically and use more criteria than a simple path. Predicates always occur inside of straight brackets within an XPath expression, after a node for which the query needs to be qualified. You'll examine the most common operators in a moment. For now, consider the examples of XPath queries that use simple predicates shown in Table A-6.

Table A-6. *Example Expressions Using Predicates*

Expression	Description
/person/age[1]	Selects the first element node named age that is a child of /person
//name[@lang]	Selects all nodes named name that have an attribute lang from anywhere in the document
/person[name/@lang = "en"]	Selects a node named person if it has a child name that in turn has an attribute lang with value "en"
/person[age > 20]	Selects a node person if it has a child element age with a value greater than 19
/person/name[last()]	Selects the last element name that is a child of /person

XPath statements are used to pull data out of a document and to determine a document match. Predicates are often used as if statements against an XML document. Take the following XPath query, for example:

```
/person[name/last = "Johnson"]
```

Knowing that you will be querying large collections of XML with XPath should make the intent of this statement obvious. You probably don't want to select the matching /person node as much as you want to find all documents about a person with the last name "Johnson". This expression can be used for both purposes.

■Note Many examples use the text() function appended to a path, but it does not do what many XPath programmers think it does. Instead of returning the string value of a query, it is a node test that returns all child text nodes. The function string() is more often what is intended; it returns the string result of a query, the path provided as argument to string(). Of course, this works only when the interface used to make the query accepts a return value as text instead of nodes.

Predicates supply only criteria for the processor to apply to the node selection. They don't select anything themselves; they provide tests that the select expression must accommodate. Each is evaluated in context, given the current node at that point in the expression. Consider this predicate-free expression:

```
string(/person/age)
```

This is the select statement that grabs the text content of the /person/age element. Adding a predicate might result in this expression:

```
string(/person[name/first = "Billy"]/age)
```

The predicate causes the processor to narrow the selection criteria. A natural language version of the original expression would read, "Give me the age of any person with the first name of Billy." Notice that the predicate starts with name; at the point in which the predicate is evaluated, the current node is /person. After the predicate, the selection path picks right up with a child age of /person. The predicate doesn't interrupt the selection; it merely qualifies the portion of the select statement that precedes it.

Note that predicates can be chained and even nested:

```
/person[name[@lang = "en"]/first = "Jim"]/age
```

This code selects the age element of a `/person/name` that has an attribute `lang` with value `"en"`, which in turn has a `/person/name/first` element with text value `"Jim"`.

Operators

The most common XPath operators are already familiar to you. Table A-7 shows an abbreviated listing.

Table A-7. *Common XPath Operators*

Operator	Description	Example
+	Addition	`20 + 4`
-	Subtraction	`20 - 4`
*	Multiplication	`5 * 4`
div	Division	`20 div 4`
=	Equal (test, *not* assign)	`age = 24`
!=	Not equal	`age != 23`
<	Less than	`age < 25`
>	Greater than	`age > 23`
<=	Less than or equal to	`age <= 30`
>=	Greater than or equal to	`age >= 24`
or	Logical or	`name/first = "Sue" or name/first = "Jim"`
and	Logical and	`age < 25 and age > 19`
|	Union of node sets	`/person/name/first | /person/name/last`

Operators used in XPath predicates do not make variable assignments; they stick around only long enough to determine selection criteria. XQuery greatly broadens the functional potential of XML queries, but were not there yet.

Axes

Things get a bit more complicated with XPath *axes*. (Do not worry if the concepts here dont register immediately; they will after you use them in real examples.)

An XPath axis defines directions that a query can take through an XML document. Axes have been in all the XPath examples thus far, but you have been using shortcuts. For example, each element and attribute name in the slash-delimited queries implies a child selection from the current node. More formally, each slash-delimited section of an XPath expression is referred to as a *step*. This is important for understanding the way a query is processed   starting at the left, evaluating each step in turn, taking the results from that step, and applying the next step to those results. In this way, an XPath expression is really a set of selection instructions given to the processor in the order of evaluation.

Recalling the file system analogy, simply typing **cd name** at a shell prompt will succeed only if the current working directory (whatever it might be) contains a directory named name. XPath also treats a single name in isolation as a child element. The explicit way to declare the child axis is to put the axis name in front of the element name by using double colons:

```
child::name
```

The name portion of this expression is referred to as the node test, with child as the axis. (Remember that the XPath processor uses the node test to test the node names and values as it crawls the node tree.)

When would you want to use such verbosity? The answer concerns contexts. When working with XML and related technologies such as XSLT and XQuery, you might want to know, for example, whether a given node descended from another node and how you can gain access to those nodes. Remember that nodes are represented within programs as class objects in the DOM model. Programs pass these objects around all by themselves, without the benefit (or overhead) of passing the entire XML tree. Having a way to know something about that node's context is useful in such cases.

The available axes used in XPath are listed in Table A-8.

Table A-8. *XPath Axes*

Axis	Description
ancestor	Ancestors of the current node
ancestor-or-self	Ancestors of the current node and the current node
attribute	Attributes of current node; the abbreviation is @
child	Children of current node; this is the default in the absence of an axis
descendant	Descendants of the current node
descendant-or-self	Descendants of the current node and the current node
following	Everything in the document after the current node (excluding descendants)
following-sibling	All siblings after the current node
namespace	All namespaces currently open at the current node
parent	Parent of the current node
preceding	All elements before the current node (excluding ancestors)
preceding-sibling	All sibling elements before the current node
self	Current node

■Note Seeing that @ is an abbreviation for the axis attribute, you might be tempted to declare . as an abbreviation for the axis self. In actuality, the proper basis expression for . is self::node() because an axis is not a selection itself; it is a direction for the selection to take place. Similarly, .. is an abbreviation for parent::node(), and // is an abbreviation for descendant-or-self::node().

With an axis placed before a node test (as with child::name), the expression is often referred to as a basis. A predicate that follows a basis further qualifies it (as with child::name[1]). Together they comprise a step, and a list of steps forms the location path.

■Caution Axes used with predicates can deliver unexpected results—unless, of course, your expectations are accurate. Although most basis expressions return matching nodes in order, some axes change that order. For example, the axis ancestor returns nodes in reverse order, which makes sense because you're looking "up" from the current node. This is important when using predicates that use ordering to apply select criteria. For example, ancestor::name[1] returns the closest ancestor element name, not the first ancestor name in the document.

Axes are a potentially confusing element of XPath, but you won't run in to them very often. When you do, they will make sense given their context.

Functions

The last aspect of XPath to be discussed is the XPath function. *Functions* introduce the missing functionality to XPath expressions. There are many standard functions in XPath 1.0 and many more in XPath 2.0, and most XPath implementations make it easy to write your own functions in a given programming language. Functions take on a life all their own with XQuery. Put simply, functions are where the interesting stuff happens.

■**Note** You have repeatedly seen the use of `comment()`, `node()`, and `text()` where a node name would normally be in a node test. They look like functions; they *are* functions because they return values to the processor. But where a node test of `age` in the path `/person/age` is used as a literal, comparing `age` with the names of each child element of `person` (and returning any nodes that match the node test), these function node tests tell the processor to return certain kinds of nodes. Because comment and text nodes do not have names, this is the only way to address them.

Functions in XPath statements occur anywhere   they can be in predicates or they can contain the entirety of the path expression. As an example of the latter, the following demonstrates the function `contains()` used in a predicate:

```
/person[contains(name/first, "Dan")]
```

This function takes two arguments and returns `true` if the second string is contained within the first. Thus, this query would select `/person` if the text value of `/person/name/first` contained the string "Dan". "Why isn't the first argument to the function `name/first` instead of `name/first/text()`,"you ask? It could be either, in fact. But because the `contains()` function expects text arguments, the XPath processor is smart enough to know that handing the node `first` to the function instead of its literal text value wouldn't achieve the desired result. Most XPath functions reflect a similar behavior, and you can cause your own custom functions to do the same.

Here is an example of a math function:

```
count(/person/name/*)
```

The function `count()` simply counts nodes passed to it. This is an example of an expression that doesn't select nodes. It returns a string instead.

Arguments to XPath functions can be fully qualified paths or they can use context:

```
/person[age > count(/person/shoesize)]/age
```

This expression selects the age element node, but only if that `age` value is greater than the person's shoe size. The expression could have been written this way:

```
/person[age > count(shoesize)]/age
```

The lack of a leading forward slash on the expression as argument to `count()` tells the processor that the note test is relative and not absolute.

More XPath functions are shown in Table A-9.

Table A-9. *Some XPath Functions*

Function	Description
ceiling()	Rounds a passed number to the smallest integer not smaller than the number
concat()	Concatenates all string arguments into one string
contains()	Returns true if the first string argument contains the second string argument
last()	Returns the index of the last node in the context note set
name()	Returns the name of the passed node
local-name()	Returns the local part of the name of the first node in the passed node set, minus a namespace
normalize-space()	Returns a white space.normalized copy of the passed string (leading and duplicate spaces removed)
not()	Returns the inverse of the passed value
position()	Returns the position of the current node in the context node set
starts-with()	Returns true if the first string argument starts with the second string argument
sum()	Sums the text values of all nodes in the passed node set

You will most often use functions within predicates to place conditions on your select. Here, too, you have already seen shortcuts for some of the functions:

`/person/age[1]`

This index syntax is a shortcut for the position() function:

`/person/age[`**`position() = 1`**`]`

The implication is that the node test before the predicate is an argument to the function itself. This is what is meant by the *context node set* in the function list descriptions. The node selection before the predicate comprises a node set, and functions such as position() and last() address this set as an array. This example selects the second-to-the-last age element that is a child of person:

`/person/age[`**`position() = last() - 1`**`]`

Finally, consider this multipredicate example:

`/person/name[@lang = "en"]/*[`**`position() = last()`**`]`

Here, everything before the position() = last() predicate determines the node set to be used to determine the set positions. This example selects the last child element of /person/name where name has an attribute lang with value "en".

In XML applications, custom XPath functions are frequently written and used to introduce external data into the evaluations. We won't look at the writing of custom XPath functions in this book, but most XPath implementations make it a relatively painless thing. You will likely find it unnecessary using BDB XML and XQuery because they provide better ways to move data between query processors and the application. A major exception is if you want to use BDB XML databases with XSLT.

This section has described XPath 1.0, which is more lightweight than XPath 2.0. Note that BDB XML uses XPath 2.0 and XQuery, which adopt XPath 1.0 as a subset (and therefore will understand examples in this section). The differences are outlined in Chapter 7, "XQuery with BDB XML."

XML DOM, Continued

This chapter already discussed the DOM in some detail; this section will look briefly at the DOM methods.

The whirlwind of buzz around the technologies dubbed *Asynchronous JavaScript and XML (Ajax)*   Google Maps is the showcase example   is really just excitement over a new approach to using tools that have been around for some time. Within a web browser, the DOM is the interface to change the HTML dynamically using JavaScript. The XML DOM is a specification for programming languages to navigate and manipulate XML. It specifies classes and methods that have been adapted to interfaces in most programming languages and makes fairly easy work of using XML within programs, as well as moving between programming languages.

The node tree example earlier in this chapter illustrated how an XML processor views a parsed XML document. The XML processor can be a command-line utility, a programming API, or a web browser. The Firefox web browser has a DOM Inspector window accessible via the Tools menu that shows this internal document representation and highlights within the web page a DOM node selected in the Inspector window (see Figure A-1).

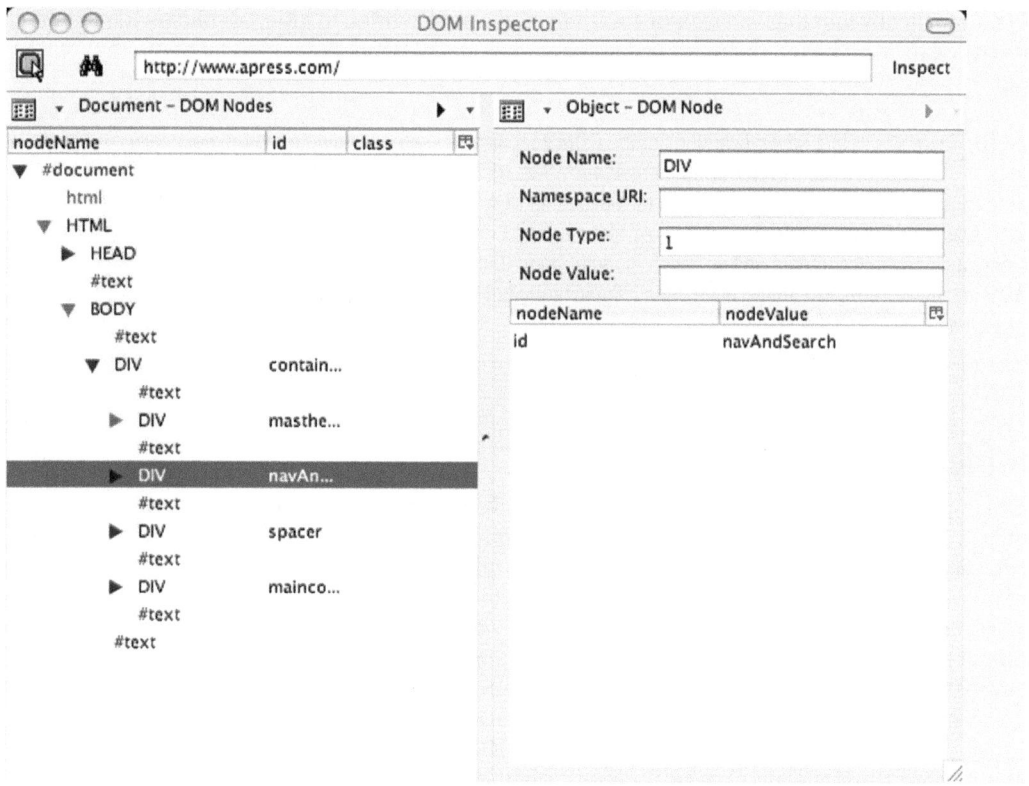

Figure A-1. *The Firefox DOM Inspector window*

DOM implementations do vary, but all share common (or at least similar) class and method organizations. The DOM defines the following interfaces that are implemented as classes. Table A-10 shows an abbreviated list.

Table A-10. *DOM Classes with Some Attribute and Method Examples*

Class	Attribute Example	Method Example
Node	nodeName, nodeValue, childNodes	replaceChild, appendChild, insertBefore
Document	doctype, documentElement	createElement, createComment
Attr	name, value	
Element	tagName	getAttribute, setAttribute
NodeList	length	item
Text		splitText
CharacterData	data, length	appendData, insertData, deleteData

The DOM interface enables both the reading and navigating of a parsed XML file, as well as the programmatic construction of an XML file. Writing XML using the DOM interface has the benefit that you never need to worry about properly formatting your elements, closing your tags, or escaping entities in text content because it is taken care of for you. Moreover, XML written with the DOM interface is assured to generate the same tree when parsed. Because XML is intended to be processed programmatically (not that you wouldn't want to read a book written in XML, of course), it makes the most sense to generate it programmatically, too.

Note There are in fact several versions of the DOM specification, each building upon the next: Level 1, Level 2, and Level 3. Level 1, which is referred to as *dynamic HTML*, defines the basic DOM structure, node types, and classes and methods. Level 2 adds support for Cascading Style Sheets (CSS) and events to the DOM, making the rich interaction of applications such as Google Maps easier. Level 3 adds a host of event modules that include loading and saving documents and an XPath module. Up to this point, XPath interfaces (not the query language, but the methods to execute them) have varied significantly between implementations. You won't deal with much that isn't defined in Level 1 in this book.

Implementation Considerations

DOM implementations are not always (or even usually) compatible—you cannot use two DOM libraries and pass documents or nodes between them. This isn't much of a problem unless you need to do very tight integration (for example, BDB XML with an XSLT processor). If so, your choice of programming language is more constrained. This is uncommon, however. XML makes it easy for incompatible programs to operate together with the same data, and not having compatible binary DOM objects is not much of a problem. In my own production environments, I use Python and Perl BDB XML interfaces to query and modify the database, but I use libxslt and Perl to perform XSLT transformations on an accompanying web site. Because BDB XML queries—whether returning lists of document matches or values—do not give you a DOM for that object without the overhead of rebuilding it, little is actually saved by operating on the same DOM object between applications.

In other words, don't worry about DOM compatibility when it comes to building applications that perform different operations with the same XML. You might choose to keep text copies of your XML files for use by processors other than BDB XML, treating them as authoritative and updating them to the database when they change, or treating the database as authoritative and getting XML source from your queries to parse.

Of course, if you are concerned with DOM compatibility, the Apache Xerces library should dictate your choice of processors and languages because BDB XML is built on it.

Reading and Writing XML

The uses of and differences between DOM implementations often reflect the styles of the programming language. We will explore a few parsing modules here, just to put the XML discussion into the context of actual code and provide a sense of XML processing with different languages.

Xerces C++

BDB XML uses (and includes) the Apache project's Xerces C++ XML parser. Xerces is a rather straightforward processor supporting the DOM specification, namespaces, and XML schema. It doesn't do XPath; it focuses instead on the core XML processing and lets related projects such as Apache Xalan tackle XPath. Xerces has parsers in Java as well, with Perl and COM bindings for the C++ libraries.

Listing A-1 omits declarations, includes, and error handling; it highlights the DOM method calls.

Listing A-1. *A C++ DOM Browse with Xerces*

```
static char* elementname = "Word";
static char* gXmlFile = "12.xml";

int main() {
    XMLPlatformUtils::Initialize();
    XercesDOMParser *parser = new XercesDOMParser;
    parser->parse(gXmlFile);

    // get the DOM representation
    DOMNode *doc     = parser->getDocument();
    DOMNode *element = doc->getFirstChild();
    DOMNodeList *nodelist = element->getChildNodes();

    for(int i=0; i < nodelist->getLength(); ++i) {
        DOMNode *child = nodelist->item(i);
        if (XMLString::compareString(child->getNodeName(),
                    XMLString::transcode(elementname)) == 0) {
            DOMNode *text = child->getFirstChild();
            printf ("%s: %s\n",
                        XMLString::transcode(child->getNodeName()),
                        XMLString::transcode(text->getNodeValue())
            );
        }
    }

    // clean up
    delete parser;
    XMLPlatformUtils::Terminate();
    return 0;
}
```

The file 12.xml has the following abbreviated content, which you might recognize from Chapter 2:

```
<Synset fileVersion="1.0" pos="n">
  <Id>12</Id>
  <WnOffset version="2.1" pos="n">00004576</WnOffset>
  <LexFileNum>03</LexFileNum>
  <SsType>n</SsType>
  <Word lexId="0">organism</Word>
  <Word lexId="0">being</Word>
</Synset>
```

Compiled (with the necessary header includes) and run, this listing outputs the following result:

```
Word: organism
Word: being
```

This is an example of a pure DOM parse without XPath. Of course, it can be cumbersome to navigate a document with the DOM if you don't know what it contains. It's made easier with Xerces filters that can be registered to act as node handlers.

Perl's XML::LibXML

The Perl XML::LibXML module, available from the Comprehensive Perl Archive Network (CPAN http://www.cpan.org), embeds the libxml2 C libraries. Its DOM classes are XML::LibXML::Document, XML::LibXML::Element, and so on. Given Perl's strength at parsing, it makes a good choice for converting data to XML. Its sister, XML::LibXSLT (embedding libsxlt), enables XSLT processing on the same DOM objects.

Chapter 2 discussed a conversion of the Wordnet database to XML files. Recall that the desired format looked like this:

```xml
<Synset fileVersion="1.0" pos="n">
    <Id>14861</Id>
    <WnOffset version="2.1" pos="n">02772480</WnOffset>
    <LexFileNum>06</LexFileNum>
    <SsType>n</SsType>
    <Word lexId="0">baseball</Word>
    <Pointers>
        <Hypernym>14746</Hypernym>
        <Hypernym>14866</Hypernym>
    </Pointers>
    <Gloss>a ball used in playing baseball</Gloss>
</Synset>
```

In the truncated script example shown in Listing A-2, the parsing functions are removed, and the document operations are highlighted. This listing should be fairly straightforward, assuming that the Perl method call operator (->) is familiar to you.

Listing A-2. *Building XML with the Perl Module XML::LibXML*

```perl
#!/usr/bin/perl -w
use strict;
use XML::LibXML;

open my $file, "data.noun";
my $id = 1;

# iterate each line (synset) in the file
while (my $line = <$file>) {

    # create the DOM object for the synset
    my $document = XML::LibXML::Document->new("1.0", "UTF8");

    # create a new element, set its attribute
    my $element = $document->createElement("Synset");
    $element->setAttribute("fileVersion", "1.0");
```

```
# read the offset and create an element for it
my $offset = extract_offset($line);
my $offset_element = $document->createElement("WnOffset");
$offset_element->appendText($offset);

# set attributes for version and pos ("part-of-speech")
my $wn_version = "2.1";
$offset_element->setAttribute("version", $wn_version);
my $pos = extract_pos($line);
$offset_element->setAttribute("pos", $pos);

# make the offset element a child of our synset element
$element->appendChild($offset_element);
...

# set the root element for the document
$document->setDocumentElement($element);

# increment the id, and write the file
open my $newfile, ">" . $id++ . ".xml";
print $newfile $document->toString();
close $newfile;
}
```

The result is a single XML file, starting with 1.xml, for each line in the data file. In this case, the result is about 120,000 XML files, each complying with the format created in this script. You could write an XML schema to describe this format and ensure that the DOM usage is correct. If you ran this script, you'd have a decent collection of XML documents containing interesting data. I use this data in examples throughout the rest of the book.

Parsing the file with XML::LibXML is simple, and it provides a full-featured XPath (1.0) implementation (see Listing A-3).

Listing A-3. *Parsing a File in Perl with XML::LibXML*

```
#!/usr/bin/perl -w
use strict;
use XML::LibXML;

my $parser    = new XML::LibXML;
my $document = $parser->parse_file("12.xml");
foreach my $node ($document->findnodes("/Synset/Word")) {
    print "Word: "  . $node->to_literal . "\n";
}
```

This listing outputs the following result:

```
Word: organism
Word: being
```

Recall that the resulting XML files contain pointers to the other files. These numbers are the incremented $id; the script created an index of offset-to-ID mappings. Most XPath implementations provide a standard document() function, which enables the processor to dynamically load XML files. For example, this XPath queried against a node takes the first /Synset/Pointers/Hyponym element,

concatenates it with ".xml" to get the filename for the record, opens the file with the document()
function, and selects the /Synset/Word node:

```
document(concat(/Synset/Pointers/Hyponym[1], ".xml"))/Synset/Word
```

This XPath expression placed in place of /Synset/Word in the previous code example causes the
script to output this result:

```
Word: benthos
```

Thus, the first hyponym or "kind of" organism type listed in the lexicon is benthos, which is
an organism at the bottom of the sea. Other hyponym pointers in 12.xml include plant, plankton,
parasite, mutant, and animal (the lexicon section in which human is located).

Other XML Technologies

XML dialects have been developed (and often standardized) for nearly every conceivable field,
including genealogy, astronomy research, and even music. Each dialect, although it is valid XML,
requires that applications know and understand that dialect   usually as it is described via an XML
schema.

XSLT

Translating from one XML dialect to another is useful in many situations, not least of all in trans-
forming XML to HTML. XSLT is a very popular technology for doing this. XSLT is actually written
in XML, meaning that it can process and output itself! XSLT templates are *declarative*. Instead of a
procedural language that tells the program what to do and in what order, declarative languages create functions with conditions. If you imagine that your entire program consists of procedural case
statements, you aren't far from declarative programming. Declarative programming can be especially
useful when dealing with semantically rich data such as XML. For example, here is the baseball XML
source, file 14861.xml:

```
<Synset fileVersion="1.0" pos="n">
    <Id>14861</Id>
    <WnOffset version="2.1" pos="n">02772480</WnOffset>
    <LexFileNum>06</LexFileNum>
    <SsType>n</SsType>
    <Word lexId="0">baseball</Word>
    <Pointers>
        <Hypernym>14746</Hypernym>
        <Hypernym>14866</Hypernym>
    </Pointers>
    <Gloss>a ball used in playing baseball</Gloss>
</Synset>
```

Note At this time. XSLT 2.0 is approaching a final recommendation. Note that this section describes XSLT 1.0,
and the specification is changing significantly in the new version.

An XSLT document could transform this into another XML dialect, as well as a non-XML format. Rules get created for each piece of data that needs to be transformed. For example, suppose

that you want to output an HTML page to display this and every other synset XML file. Each piece gets its own XSLT template in the following form:

```
<xsl:template match="/Synset">
    <p>This is synset number <xsl:value-of select="Id"/>.</p>
</xsl:template>
```

Notice that the HTML elements have no namespace, but the XSLT elements all use the xsl namespace prefix. All templates get enclosed in a single stylesheet element:

```
<xsl:stylesheet xmlns:xsl="http://www.w3.org/1999/XSL/Transform" version="1.0">
    <xsl:template match="/Synset">
        <p>This is synset number <xsl:value-of select="Id"/>.</p>
    </xsl:tempate>
</xsl:stylesheet>
```

If you save this stylesheet as synset.xsl and execute the transformation, it outputs this result:

```
<?xml version="1.0"?>
<p>This is synset number 14861.</p>
```

Note You can execute XSLT transformations from the command line with libxslt installed. The utility is called xsltproc and its syntax is as follows:

```
$ xsltproc synset.xsl 14861.xml
```

Notice the attributes on the <xsl:template/> and <xsl:value-of/> elements in the template. One has a match attribute, and the other has select both with an XPath expression for value. The match attribute registers the template with the XSLT engine and says, "As you parse the XML file, when you encounter a node that matches XPath /Synset, use this template." The select attribute on <xsl:value-of/> tells the engine to output the value of the selected node, using the current node as context. The current node within this template is /Synset, so the selected Id is its child element.

You could achieve the same output with two templates instead of one:

```
<xsl:template match="/Synset">
    <xsl:apply-templates select="Id"/>
</xsl:template>

<xsl:template match="Id">
    <p>This is synset number <xsl:value-of select="."/>.</p>
</xsl:tempate>
```

The <xsl:apply-templates/> element tells the processor to keep going to continue to apply templates to the children of the current node (or just the child indicated by its select attribute). All the Id template does here is output the value of the current node, which is the Id element in the second template.

Without explaining every XSLT element, Listing A-4 shows the file synset.xsl filled out with several templates. It also shows some of the power of XPath used within a stylesheet.

Listing A-4. *XSLT Stylesheet* synset.xsl

```
<xsl:template match="Gloss">
    <p><b>Gloss:</b> <xsl:value-of select="."/></p>
</xsl:template>
```

```
<xsl:template match="Pointers">
    <p>Synset has the following pointers:</p>
    <p><xsl:apply-templates/></p>
</xsl:template>

<xsl:template match="Hypernym">
    <p>This is a kind of
        <a href="{concat(., '.xml')}">
            <xsl:value-of select="document(concat(., '.xml'))/Synset/Word"/
>.
        </a>
    </p>
</xsl:template>

<xsl:template match="*">
    <!-- catch the rest of the elements and put them in comments -->
    <xsl:comment><xsl:value-of select="."/></xsl:comment>
</xsl:template>

</xsl:stylesheet>
```

Applied to 14861.xml, the output is the following:

```
<html><body>
  <p>This is synset number 14861.</p>
  <!--02772480-->
  <!--06-->
  <!--n-->
  <p><b>Word:</b>baseball</p>
  <p>Synset has the following pointers:</p>
    <p>This is a kind of
        <a href="14746.xml">ball.
        </a></p>
    <p>This is a kind of
        <a href="14866.xml">baseball equipment.
        </a></p>
  </p>
  <p><b>Gloss:</b>a ball used in playing baseball  </p>
</body></html>
```

Viewed in a web browser, this listing displays details on the synset and also enables the user to navigate to the hypernym synset files. Setting up a handler in your web server to apply stylesheets to an associated XSLT stylesheet is trivial, and some web browsers can do this transformation all on their own.

A Note on Current Node

Within applications such as XSLT and where processing is context-aware (for example, inside a predicate), it is often necessary to refer explicitly to the current node. The solution is to use the XSLT XPath function current(). In most cases, current() and . are equivalent:

```
<xsl:value-of select="current()"/>
<xsl:value-of select="."/>
```

However, the current node is usually different from the context node within a predicate. Consider the case when, inside a template, you want to select a node using a value from your context. For example, lets say that you are inside a template processing a Word element and you want to know whether the Gloss for this record contains that word:

```
<xsl:template match="Word">
    <xsl:value-of select="../Gloss[contains(., .)]"/>
</xsl:template>
```

Using . twice is obviously incorrect. In this case, the contains() function is getting Gloss as both arguments, meaning it will always be a true test (Gloss contains itself). You want Gloss to be the first argument, but the current node, Word, to be the second. The current() function does this, which always returns the current node:

```
<xsl:template match="Word">
    <xsl:value-of select="../Gloss[contains(., current())]"/>
</xsl:template>
```

Because current() returns a node set (albeit with only one member), it can precede a path (as with current()/Word/text()) or be used alone to get just the current node.

SAX

Simple API for XML (SAX) is a standard for parsing XML. A SAX processor does not have to parse the entire file or store it in memory. SAX is event-driven, so a parser triggers functions each time it encounters a new element, attribute, and so on. As it happens, most DOM implementations use a SAX parser to generate a node tree. Thus, SAX can be considered a lower-level parse interface, which is the reason why it is faster and more efficient than DOM.

RPC-XML and SOAP

Remote procedure calls (RPCs) enable software to request information and perform operations non-locally. If you arent familiar with RPCs and have the need to allow a clients website to submit orders to your website without human intervention, for example, you might write a script to run on the clients website that accepts a posted order form, connects to your website, fills in the form, and submits the form. Consider the problems with this process. If the web page or form input names ever change (which they are likely to do), your clients orders will no longer work and might get lost. And using a user interface from a program just to move data from one place to another is horribly inelegant.

A better way to move data to   and request actions from   another system is to use RPCs. Most programming languages have RPC-XML or Simple Object Access Protocol (SOAP) modules. If you will be providing the functionality, you write a response function to run on the server. If you need to access the server, you write a requestor function. Using one of these modules, you dont need to write any code to connect to the server, perform the request, or parse the response because it is all handled automatically. In fact, a developer working with an interface that uses RPC-XML or SOAP might have no idea that a given method call is occurring remotely at all. Functionality that is available via an RPC server is often referred to as a *Web Service* because it is accessed over HTTP and provides information or function services to other software programs.

RPC-XML is an example of a technology in which the XML is invisible to the developer. You might not even know that the function calls are exchanging XML. The point of RPCs is that you dont *need* to know how data is being moved between systems, enabling you to focus instead on the functionality. XML as a standard is the perfect format for transmitting RPC data because the methods are often operating between programs in different programming languages or operating systems.

Because all can process XML, they all understand the data. You will find this to be true with much of XML: after programs are enabled to process the data autonomously, developers can worry less about minutiae such as data formats. XML serves no end in and of itself; it simply makes the formatting and parsing of data transparent to software built on top of it.

Conclusion

From a simple foundation of tags built from greater-than and less-than signs, XML has standardized data formats, enabling dozens or hundreds of technologies to be designed and standardized. In many ways, Berkeley DB XML represents a major culmination of these technologies, providing everyone the capability to manage huge collections of XML files. The power of this capability won't be clear until you delve into BDB XML itself.

BDB XML API Reference

This appendix contains a slightly abbreviated reference of common API functions for C++, Python, Java, Perl, and PHP. Each class and method is first described generally; it is then accompanied by either header or pseudo-usage code for common method variants to illustrate the parameters accepted. Where the possible usages are lengthy, only several are included, illustrating the range of parameters. Remember that not all variants accept all parameters, and specific usage behavior might differ. Please refer to the BDB XML documentation at http://dev.sleepycat.com/documentation/ bdbxml.html for up-to-date and comprehensive descriptions of all API features. Documentation for most APIs is also included within the BDB XML distribution.

Throughout this section, parameters are defined only once for all languages unless they differ for a specific language's API. Perl and PHP usage examples add a dollar sign ($) before the parameters, but parameter lists omit the sign. Note that each API has slightly different prefix requirements for the flags; they are described in the language notes section that follows. The double colon (::) is used as a common convention in this appendix to separate methods and classes in their description.

Language Notes

This section describes some API-specific implementation details.

C++

C++ is the API used by all other language APIs, so it is authoritative. The other APIs attempt to provide idiomatic interfaces to many of the C++ functions. Exception handling is fully supported and described in Chapter 8, "BDB XML with C++." The main C++ classes implement a handle-body idiom, enabling objects to be copied while maintaining a reference to the same body; the exception to this rule is XmlInputStream. See the BDB XML documentation for details about which classes can be safely shared among threads in an application.

The C++ headers are included with the following:

```
#include "dbxml/DbXml.hpp"
```

Bitwise OR'd flags are supplied to methods, as shown in the flag tables in each method's section.

Java

Like C++, exception handling is supported (as described in Chapter 10, "BDB XML with Java"). Refer to the BDB XML documentation for details about which classes can be safely shared between threads. All Java packages can be loaded with the following:

```
import com.sleepycat.dbxml.*;
```

BDB XML objects must usually be explicitly deleted when using the Java API and they all include a delete() method for this purpose. Otherwise, garbage collection might not properly free them, resulting in memory issues and possible stale references to objects. The delete() method is also the proper way to close containers.

The main Java classes implement a handle-body idiom, enabling objects to be copied while maintaining a reference to the same body; the exception to this rule is XmlInputStream.

Finally, where the other APIs use flags to determine settings for most object methods, the Java API provides configuration objects that are described separate from the method sections. Refer to the class documentation for individual Config classes.

Python

The Python API does not yet provide exception handling. BDB XML and Berkeley DB modules are loaded with the following:

```
from bsddb3.db import *
from dbxml import *
```

The Python interface closes containers automatically when they leave scope.

Where used, method flags are supplied to methods as shown, bitwise OR'd as with the C++ interface.

Perl

The Perl API supports exception handling using eval { }; blocks, as described in Chapter 11, "BDB XML with Perl." The Perl packages are imported with the following, where 'simple' causes transaction objects to be optional where they might be provided:

```
use Sleepycat::DbXml 'simple';
```

In most places where XmlValue objects are used, the Perl interface enables scalars to be used instead.

The Perl API uses object scope to implicitly close open containers.

Finally, note that the Perl interface typically requires that flags passed to methods have a qualifying prefix: Db:: for Berkeley DB flags (for the environment object) and DbXml:: for BDB XML flags (for everything else). These are bitwise OR'd as with the C++ API.

PHP

The PHP interface does not yet implement exception handling. The BDB XML package is loaded into the processor using the php.ini configuration file.

The PHP unset() function is the proper way to close containers and free memory.

Where BDB XML methods accept setting flags, they are supplied as shown, bitwise OR'd as with the C++ API.

Where constants are used to identify types (such as XmlContainer::WholedocContainer) as arguments to methods, the PHP interface replaces the namespace delimiter with an underscore (as with XmlContainer_WholedocContainer).

DbEnv

DbEnv is the Berkeley DB database environment class and is not specific to BDB XML. It is passed to the XmlManager constructor and provides methods for opening, closing, creating, and removing environments (as well as low-level configuring of environment settings). This class differs greatly between the APIs, so each is described individually in the following sections.

DbEnv (Constructor)

See the BDB XML documentation for flag definitions; they are atypical for this constructor where a 0 can be passed.

C++

```
class DbEnv {
    public:
    DbEnv(u_int32 flags);
};
```

Java

Unlike the other APIs, the Java environment object gets the path to the environment with the constructor and uses a configuration object to set options that other APIs set with the open() method.

```
public Environment (File envHome, EnvironmentConfig envConfig)
```

Python

```
DBEnv(flags=0)
```

Perl

```
my $env = new DbEnv([$flags]);
```

PHP

The PHP API uses the Db4Env package as its interface to environments:

```
$env = new Db4Env($flags);
```

DbEnv::open

The open() method takes a directory path to the environment, a set of bitwise OR'd flags, and a Unix file mode (ignored on Windows). All parameters are optional. Following are some of the available environment flags:

Flag	Description
DB_CREATE	Creates the environment if it doesn't already exist.
DB_INIT_LOCK	Initializes the locking subsystem; used with concurrent reads and writes.

Continued

Flag	Description
DB_INIT_LOG	Initializes the logging subsystem; used for database recovery.
DB_INIT_MPOOL	Initializes the memory pool subsystem, providing a cache required for multithreaded applications.
DB_INIT_TXN	Initializes the transaction subsystem, permitting recovery in case of an error condition within a transaction.
DB_RECOVER	Initializes recovery, ensuring that the database files agree with the database logs.

C++

```
int DbEnv::open(const char *db_homedir, u_int32_t flags, int mode)
```

Java

The Java API does not provide an open() method; environments are opened using the constructor.

Python

```
DBEnv.open(homedir, flags=0, mode=0660)
```

Perl

Remember that the Perl interface here requires a Db:: prefix before bitwise OR'd flags.

```
$env->open($homedir, $flags, $mode);
```

PHP

The PHP environment object is unique in that its open() method has defaults for flags and mode. The flag default is DB_INIT_TXN|DB_INIT_LOG|DB_INIT_MPOOL|DB_INIT_LOCK|DB_CREATE, and the mode default is 0666.

```
$env->open([$homedir,] [$flags,] [$mode]);
```

DbEnv::close

Closes the environment and underlying subsystems; frees any allocated resources. The flags field is unused at this time and must be 0 unless defaulted for a particular language.

C++

```
DbEnv::close(u_int32_t flags)
```

Java

The delete() method is the proper way to close an environment, although this class provides a close() method.

```
public void close()
```

Python

```
DBEnv.close(flags=0)
```

Perl

```
$env->close($flags);
```

PHP

```
$env->close($flags=0);
```

DbXml

This constructor-less class provides some utility methods for setting logging options. It is also the namespace for all subclasses. Not all APIs provide this class, although most provide the same functionality with the XmlManager class.

DbXml::setLogCategory

Sets the category for logging. Log messages are categorized by subsystem and by importance. The messages are sent to the output stream that is configured in the Berkeley DB environment associated with the XmlManager generating the message. The output is sent to std::cerr if no environment is associated with the XmlManager.

Parameters

category

The log category to enable or disable. Possible values are shown in the following table.

Category	Description
DbXml::CATEGORY_MANAGER	Manager messages
DbXml::CATEGORY_CONTAINER	Container messages
DbXml::CATEGORY_INDEXER	Indexer messages
DbXml::CATEGORY_QUERY	Query messages
DbXml::CATEGORY_OPTIMIZER	Query optimizer messages
DbXml::CATEGORY_DICTIONARY	Dictionary messages
DbXml::CATEGORY_NODESTORE	Node storage messages
DbXml::CATEGORY_ALL	All BDB XML messages

enabled

Boolean flag that specifies whether to enable or disable the level or category.

C++

```
void DbXml::setLogCategory(LogCategory category, bool enabled)
```

Java

The Java API provides the corresponding method as `XmlManager.setLogCategory`.

```
public static void setLogCategory(int category, boolean enabled)
```

Python

The Python API exposes this functionality as class method `XmlManager.setLogCategory`.

```
XmlManager.setLogCategory(category, enabled)
```

Perl

```
DbXml::setLogCategory($category, $enabled);
```

PHP

```
dbxml_set_log_category($category, $enabled);
```

DbXml::setLogLevel

Berkeley DB XML can be configured to generate a stream of messages to help application debugging. The messages are categorized by subsystem and by importance. The messages are sent to the output stream that is configured in the Berkeley DB environment associated with the `XmlManager` generating the message. The output is sent to standard error if no environment is associated with the `XmlManager`.

Parameters

level

The log level to enable or disable; one of those shown in the following table:

Level	Description
DbXml::LEVEL_DEBUG	Execution tracing messages
DbXml::LEVEL_INFO	Informational messages
DbXml::LEVEL_WARNING	Warning messages
DbXml::LEVEL_ERROR	Fatal error messages
DbXml::LEVEL_ALL	All debug levels

enabled

Boolean flag that specifies whether to enable or disable the level or category.

C++

```
void DbXml::setLogLevel(LogLevel level, bool enabled)
```

Java

The Java class provides the corresponding method as XmlManager.setLogLevel.

```
public static void setLogLevel(int level, boolean enabled)
```

Python

The Python API exposes this functionality as class method XmlManager.setLogCategory.

```
XmlManager.setLogLevel(level, enabled)
```

Perl

```
DbXml::setLogLevel($level, $enabled);
```

PHP

```
dbxml_set_log_level($level, $enabled);
```

DbXml::dbxml_version

Returns the Berkeley DB XML release number. Each API has a slightly different interface to this information.

C++

```
void DbXml::dbxml_version(int *majorp, int *minorp, int *patchp)
```

Java

```
public static int get_version_major()
public static int get_version_minor()
public static int get_version_patch()
public static String get_version_string()
```

Python

```
DbXml.get_version_major()
DbXml.get_version_minor()
DbXml.get_version_patch()
DbXml.get_version_string()
```

Perl

```
my ($major, $minor, $patch);
DbXml::dbxml_version($major, $minor, $patch);
```

PHP

```
dbxml_version();
```

XmlContainer

The XmlContainer class encapsulates access to a database container its indexes and statistics. It provides methods for managing XmlDocument objects, manipulating indexes, and retrieving statistics for the container. You can use XmlManager::createContainer to instantiate an XmlContainer object for a container that does not exist or XmlManager::openContainer if it has already been created. XmlContainers are always open until the last referencing handle is destroyed.

A copy constructor and assignment operator are provided for this class, and used by passing an existing XmlContainer to this constructor. For most APIs, the class is implemented using a handle-body idiom. When a handle is copied, both handles maintain a reference to the same body.

XmlContainer::addAlias

Adds a new name alias to the list maintained by the containing XmlManager. The new alias can then be used as a parameter to the collection() function in an XQuery expression. Returns true if the alias is successfully added. If the alias is already used by the containing XmlManager object, false is returned.

C++

```
bool addAlias(const std::string &alias)
```

Java

```
public boolean addAlias(String alias)
```

Python

```
XmlContainer.addAlias(alias)
```

Perl

```
my $bool = $container->addAlias($alias);
```

PHP

```
$bool = $container->addAlias($alias);
```

XmlContainer::addIndex

XmlContainer::addIndex is a convenience method (see XmlIndexSpecification::addIndex) for adding to the container an index of the specified type for the named document node. Its various usages allow a transaction object, a Uniform Resource Identifier (URI), an index name, an index specification, and an update context to be passed.

Parameters

txn

If the operation is to be transaction-protected, the txn parameter is an XmlTransaction handle returned from XmlManager::createTransaction.

uri

The namespace of the node to be indexed. The default namespace is selected by passing an empty string for the namespace.

name

The name of the element or attribute node to be indexed.

index

A comma-separated list of strings that represent the indexing strategy. The strings must contain the following information:

```
unique-{path type}-{node type}-{key type}-{syntax}
```

These values are detailed in the following table; order is not important.

Value	Description
unique	Indicates that the indexed value is unique in the container. If this keyword does not appear on the index string, the indexed value is not required to be unique in the container.
{path type}	Either node or edge.
{node type}	One of element, attribute, or metadata. If metadata is specified, {path type} must be node.
{key type}	One of presence, equality, or substring.
{syntax}	Identifies the type of information being indexed. It must be one of the following values: none, anyURI, base64Binary, boolean, date, dateTime, dayTimeDuration, decimal, double, duration, float, gDay, gMonth, gMonthDay, gYear, gYearMonth, hexBinary, NOTATION, QName, string, time, yearMonthDuration, or untypedAtomic. See the BDB XML documentation for full descriptions of the types.

Note that if {key type} is present, {syntax} must be none or simply not specified. Some example index strings are as follows:

```
unique-node-element-presence
node-element-equality-string
edge-element-presence-none
node-metadata-equality-dateTime
node-attribute-equality-float
```

context

The update context (XmlUpdateContext) to use for the index insertion.

C++

```
void XmlContainer::addIndex(const std::string &uri, const std::string &name,
    const std::string &index, XmlUpdateContext &context)
XmlContainer::addIndex(XmlTransaction &txn, const std::string &uri,
    const std::string &name, const std::string &index, XmlUpdateContext &context)
```

Java

```
public void addIndex([XmlTransaction txn,] String uri, String name, String index,
    XmlUpdateContext context)
```

Python

```
XmlContainer.addIndex([txn,] uri, name, index [, context])
```

Perl

Remember that transaction objects are optional for the Perl interface only when simple is used to load the class package.

```
$container->addIndex([$txn,] $uri, $name, $index [, $context]);
```

PHP

```
$container->addIndex([$txn,] $uri, $name, $index [, $context]);
```

XmlContainer::addDefaultIndex

Adds a default index to the container. This method is for convenience; see XmlIndexSpecification::addDefaultIndex.

Parameters

txn

If the operation is to be transaction-protected, the txn parameter is an XmlTransaction handle returned from XmlManager::createTransaction.

index

A comma-separated list of strings that represent the indexing strategy. See the parameter description for XmlContainer::addIndex for the options and syntax.

context

The update context (XmlUpdateContext) to use for the index operation.

C++

```
void XmlContainer::addDefaultIndex(const std::string &index,
    XmlUpdateContext &context)
XmlContainer::addDefaultIndex(XmlTransaction &txn, const std::string &index,
    XmlUpdateContext &context)
```

Java

```
public void addDefaultIndex([XmlTransaction txn,] String index,
    XmlUpdateContext context)
```

Python

```
XmlContainer.addDefaultIndex([txn,] index, context)
```

Perl

```
$container->addDefaultIndex([$txn,] $index [, $context]);
```

PHP

```
$container->addDefaultIndex([$txn,] $index [, $context]);
```

XmlContainer::deleteDocument

The XmlContainer::deleteDocument method removes the specified XmlDocument from the XmlContainer. The document can be specified with a string name or an XmlDocument object. Note that the XmlDocument's name is used for this operation, and no check is performed on the document contents prior to deletion.

Parameters

txn

An XmlTransaction handle returned from XmlManager::createTransaction.

name

The name of the XmlDocument to be deleted from the container.

document

The XmlDocument to be deleted from the container.

context

The XmlUpdateContext object to use for this deletion.

C++

```
void XmlContainer::deleteDocument(const std::string name, XmlUpdateContext &context)
void XmlContainer::deleteDocument(XmlDocument &document, XmlUpdateContext &context)
void XmlContainer::deleteDocument(XmlTransaction &txn, const std::string name,
    XmlUpdateContext &context)
void XmlContainer::deleteDocument(XmlTransaction &txn,
    XmlDocument &document, XmlUpdateContext &context)
```

Java

```
public void deleteDocument([XmlTransaction txn,] String name,
    XmlUpdateContext context)
public void deleteDocument([XmlTransaction txn,] XmlDocument document,
    XmlUpdateContext context)
```

Python

```
XmlContainer.deleteDocument([txn,] name, context)
XmlContainer.deleteDocument([txn,] document, context)
```

Perl

```
$container->deleteDocument([$txn,] $name [, $context]);
$container->deleteDocument([$txn,] $document [, $context]);
```

PHP

```
$container->deleteDocument([$txn,] $name [, $context]);
$container->deleteDocument([$txn,] $document [, $context]);
```

XmlContainer::deleteIndex

Deletes an index of the specified type for the named document node. This method is for convenience; see XmlIndexSpecification::deleteIndex for more information. Note that an index description is always required to identify an index for the container.

Parameters

txn

An XmlTransaction handle returned from XmlManager::createTransaction.

uri

The namespace of the node to be indexed. The default namespace is selected by passing an empty string for the namespace.

name

The name of the element or attribute node to be indexed.

index

A comma-separated list of strings that represent the indexing strategy. See the index description in the parameter list for XmlContainer::addIndex for the full options and syntax.

content

The XmlUpdateContext to use for this operation.

C++

```
void XmlContainer::deleteIndex(const std::string &uri, const std::string &name,
    const std::string
    &index, XmlUpdateContext &context)

void XmlContainer::deleteIndex(XmlTransaction &txn, const std::string &uri,
    const std::string &name,
    const std::string &index, XmlUpdateContext &context)
```

Java

```
public void deleteIndex([XmlTransaction txn,] String uri, String name, String index,
    XmlUpdateContext context)
```

Python

```
XmlContainer.deleteIndex([txn,] uri, name, index, context)
```

Perl

```
$container->deleteIndex([$txn,] $uri, $name, $index [, $context]);
```

PHP

```
$container->deleteIndex([$txn,] $uri, $name, $index [, $context]);
```

XmlContainer::deleteDefaultIndex

Deletes the default index for the container. This method is for convenience; see XmlIndexSpecification::deleteDefaultIndex for more information.

Parameters

txn

An XmlTransaction handle returned from XmlManager::createTransaction.

index

A comma-separated list of strings that represent the indexing strategy. See the index description in the parameter list for XmlContainer::addIndex for the full options and syntax.

context

The XmlUpdateContext to use for this operation.

C++

```
void XmlContainer::deleteDefaultIndex(const std::string &index, XmlUpdateContext &
    context)
void XmlContainer::deleteDefaultIndex(XmlTransaction &txn, const std::string &index,
    XmlUpdateContext &context)
```

Java

```
public void deleteDefaultIndex([XmlTransaction txn,] String index, XmlUpdateContext
    context)
```

Python

```
XmlContainer.deleteDefaultIndex([txn,] index, context)
```

Perl

```
$container->deleteDefaultIndex([$txn,] $index [, $context]);
```

PHP

```
$container->deleteDefaultIndex([$txn,] $index [, $context]);
```

XmlContainer::getAllDocuments

Returns all documents in the container in a lazily evaluated XmlResult set.

Parameters

txn

An XmlTransaction handle returned from XmlManager::createTransaction.

flags

Possible flags are shown in the following table:

Flag	Description
DBXML_LAZY_DOCS	Retrieves the document lazily, copying document content and metadata to memory only as needed. Defaults to on with getAllDocuments.
DB_RMW	Acquires write locks instead of read locks, avoiding deadlocks during concurrent read-modify-write cycles.
DBXML_REVERSE_ORDER	Returns results in reverse order to the indexs sort.
DB_DEGREE_2	Returns results that might include items that have been deleted or modified by other transactions before this transaction completes; also known as "degree 2 isolation". In Berkeley DB 4.4 and later, this flag is called DB_READ_COMMITTED.
DB_DIRTY_READ	Returns result items that might be modified by other transactions, but that are not yet committed; also known as "degree 1 isolation". Starting with Berkeley DB 4.4 and later, this flag is called DB_READ_UNCOMMITTED. Requires that the underlying container be opened using the DB_DIRTY_READ flag.

C++

```
XmlResults XmlContainer::getAllDocuments(u_int32_t flags)
XmlResults XmlContainer::getAllDocuments(XmlTransaction &txn, u_int32_t flags)
```

Java

This and other Java methods use configuration objects instead of bitwise ORd flags; see the reference for XmlDocumentConfig.

```
public XmlResults getAllDocuments([XmlTransaction txn,] XmlDocumentConfig config)
```

Python

```
XmlContainer.getAllDocuments([txn,] flags)
```

Perl

```
my $results = $container->getAllDocuments([$txn,] $flags);
```

PHP

```
$results = $container->getAllDocuments([$txn,] $flags);
```

XmlContainer::getContainerType

Returns the container's type. Possible return values are XmlContainer::NodeContainer, where documents are broken down into their component nodes and these nodes are stored individually in the container; and XmlContainer::WholedocContainer, where documents are stored intact   all white space and formatting are preserved.

C++

```
ContainerType XmlContainer::getContainerType() const
```

Java

```
public int getContainerType()
```

Python

```
XmlContainer.getContainerType()
```

Perl

```
my $type = $container->getContainerType();
```

PHP

```
$type = $container->getContainerType();
```

XmlContainer::getDocument

Returns the XmlDocument with the specified name.

Parameters

txn

An XmlTransaction handle returned from XmlManager::createTransaction.

name

The name of the XmlDocument to be retrieved from the container.

flags

This parameter must be set to 0 or to one of the values shown in the following table:

Flag	Description
DBXML_LAZY_DOCS	Retrieves the document lazily, copying document content and metadata to memory only as needed.
DBXML_DIRTY_READ	Causes the operation to support "degree 1 isolation"; read operations can return data that has been modified but not committed by other transactions. Requires that the DB_DIRTY_READ flag be set when the container opens. This flag is renamed DB_READ_UNCOMMITTED in Berkeley DB 4.4 and later.
DB_DEGREE_2	Causes the operation to have "degree 2 isolation". Data items previous read by the transaction can be deleted or modified by other transactions before this one completes. This flag is renamed DB_READ_COMMITTED in Berkeley DB 4.4 and later.
DB_RMW	Acquires write locks instead of read locks, avoiding deadlocks during concurrent read-modify-write cycles.

C++

```
XmlDocument getDocument(const std::string &name, u_int32_t flags = 0)
XmlDocument getDocument(XmlTransaction &txn, const std::string &name,
    u_int32_t flags = 0)
```

Java

```
public XmlDocument getDocument([XmlTransaction txn,] String name,
    [XmlDocumentConfig config])
```

Python

```
XmlContainer.getDocument([txn,] name, flags = 0)
```

Perl

```
my $document = $container->getDocument([$txn,] $name [, $flags]);
```

PHP

```
$document = $container->getDocument([$txn,] $name [, $flags]);
```

XmlContainer::getIndexNodes

Returns true if the container is configured to create node indexes.

C++

```
bool XmlContainer::getIndexNodes() const
```

Java

```
public boolean getIndexNodes()
```

Python

```
XmlContainer.getIndexNodes()
```

Perl

```
my $bool = $container->getIndexNodes();
```

PHP

```
$bool = $container->getIndexNodes();
```

XmlContainer::getIndexSpecification

Retrieves the current indexing specification for the container. The indexing specification can be modified using XmlContainer::setIndexSpecification. See the XmlIndexSpecification class.

Parameters

txn

If the operation is to be transaction-protected, the txn parameter is an XmlTransaction handle returned from XmlManager::createTransaction.

flags

This parameter must be set to one of the values shown in the following table:

Flag	Description
DB_RMW	Acquires write locks instead of read locks when doing the retrieval. Setting this flag can eliminate deadlock during a read-modify-write cycle by acquiring the write lock during the read part of the cycle so that another thread of control acquiring a read lock for the same item, in its own read-modify-write cycle, will not result in deadlock.

C++

```
XmlIndexSpecification XmlContainer::getIndexSpecification()
XmlIndexSpecification XmlContainer::getIndexSpecification(XmlTransaction &txn,
    u_int32_t flags = 0)
```

Java

```
public XmlIndexSpecification getIndexSpecification([XmlTransaction txn,]
    [XmlDocumentConfig config])
```

Python

```
XmlContainer.getIndexSpecification([txn,] [flags=0])
```

Perl

```
my $indexSpec = $container->getIndexSpecification([$txn, [$flags]]);
```

PHP

```
$indexSpec = $container->getIndexSpecification([$txn, [$flags]]);
```

XmlContainer::getManager

Returns the XmlManager object for the XmlContainer.

C++

```
XmlManager &XmlContainer::getManager() const
```

Java

```
public XmlManager getManager()
```

Python

```
XmlContainer.getManager()
```

Perl

```
my $manager = $container->getManager();
```

PHP

```
$manager = $container->getManager();
```

XmlContainer::getName

The XmlContainer::getName method returns the name of the XmlContainer.

C++

```
const std::string &XmlContainer::getName() const
```

Java

```
public String getName()
```

Python

```
XmlContainer.getName()
```

Perl

```
my $name = $container->getName();
```

PHP

```
$name = $container->getName();
```

XmlContainer::getNumDocuments

Returns the number of documents in the XmlContainer.

C++

```
size_t XmlContainer::getNumDocuments() const
size_t XmlContainer::getNumDocuments(XmlTransaction &txn) const
```

Java

```
public int getNumDocuments([XmlTransaction txn])
```

Python

```
XmlContainer.getNumDocuments([txn])
```

Perl

```
my $count = $container->getNumDocuments([$txn]);
```

PHP

```
$count = $container->getNumDocuments([$txn]);
```

XmlContainer::getPageSize

Returns the actual database page size for the container.

C++

```
u_int32_t XmlContainer::getPageSize() const
```

Java

```
XmlContainer.getPageSize()
```

Python

```
XmlContainer.getPageSize()
```

Perl

The Perl API does not provide this method.

PHP

The PHP API does not provide this method.

XmlContainer::lookupIndex

This class is deprecated in favor of using `XmlManager::createIndexLookup` and `XmlIndexLookup::execute`.

XmlContainer::lookupStatistics

Returns an `XmlStatistics` object for the identified index. This object identifies the number of keys (both total and unique) maintained for the identified index. The variants of this method enable edge indexes to be retrieved when a `parent_name` parameter is supplied.

Parameters

txn

An `XmlTransaction` handle returned from `XmlManager::createTransaction`.

uri

The namespace of the node to which this index is applied.

name

The name of the node to which this index is applied.

parent_uri

The namespace of the parent node to which this edge index is applied.

parent_name

The name of the parent node to which this edge index is applied.

index

Identifies the index for which you want the statistics returned. The value supplied here must be a valid index. See `XmlContainer::addIndex` or `XmlIndexSpecification::addIndex` for a description of valid index specifications.

value

Provides the value to which equality indexes must be equal. This parameter is required when returning statistics on equality indexes and it is ignored for all other types of indexes.

C++

```
XmlStatistics XmlContainer::lookupStatistics(const std::string &uri,
    const std::string &name, const std::string &index,
    const XmlValue &value = XmlValue())

XmlStatistics XmlContainer::lookupStatistics(XmlTransaction &txn,
    const std::string &uri, const std::string &name,
    const std::string &parent_uri, const std::string &parent_name,
    const std::string &index, const XmlValue &value = XmlValue())
...
```

Java

```
public XmlStatistics lookupStatistics([XmlTransaction txn,] String uri, String name,
    [String parent_uri,] [String parent_name,] String index, XmlValue value)
```

Python

```
XmlContainer.lookupStatistics([txn,] uri, name, [parent_uri,] [parent_name,] index,
    value)
```

Perl

```
my $statistics = $container->lookupStatistics([$txn,] $uri, $name, $index [,$value]);
my $statistics = $container->lookupStatistics([$txn,] $uri, $name, $parent_uri,
    $parent_name, $index [,$value]);
```

PHP

```
$statistics = $container->lookupStatistics([$txn,] $uri, $name, $index [,$value]);
$statistics = $container->lookupStatistics([$txn,] $uri, $name, $parent_uri,
    $parent_name, $index [,$value]);
```

XmlContainer::putDocument

Inserts an XmlDocument into the container. The value returned by this method is dependent on the form of the method that you used to perform the insertion; where a string is returned, it is the document name.

Note that the name used for the document must be unique in the container. DBXML_GEN_NAME can be used to generate a name. In that case, the generated name is returned. To change a document that already exists in the container, use XmlContainer::updateDocument.

Parameters

txn

An XmlTransaction handle returned from XmlManager::createTransaction.

name

The name of the document to insert into the container.

stream

Identifies the input stream to use to read the document.

document

The XmlDocument to be inserted into the XmlContainer.

contents

The XML content to insert into the container in the form of a string. The content must be well-formed XML.

context

The update context to use for the document insertion.

flags

This parameter must be set to 0 or the following value:

Flag	Description
DBXML_GEN_NAME	Generates a unique name. If no name is set for this XmlDocument, a system-defined unique name is generated. If a name is specified, the unique string is appended to that name.

C++

```
void XmlContainer::putDocument(XmlDocument &document,
    XmlUpdateContext &context, u_int32_t flags = 0)

void XmlContainer::putDocument(XmlTransaction &txn, XmlDocument &document,
    XmlUpdateContext &context, u_int32_t flags = 0)

std::string XmlContainer::putDocument(const std::string &name,
    XmlInputStream *stream,
    XmlUpdateContext &context, u_int32_t flags = 0)

std::string XmlContainer::putDocument(XmlTransaction &txn, const std::string &name,
    const std::string &contents, XmlUpdateContext &context, u_int32_t flags = 0)
...
```

Java

```
public void putDocument([XmlTransaction txn,] XmlDocument document,
    XmlUpdateContext context, [XmlDocument config])

public String putDocument([XmlTransaction txn,] String name, XmlInputStream stream,
    XmlUpdateContext context, [XmlDocument config])

public String putDocument([XmlTransaction txn,] String name, String contents,
    XmlUpdateContext context, [XmlDocument config])
```

Python

```
XmlContainer.putDocument([txn,] document [, context [, flags=0]])
XmlContainer.putDocument([txn,] name, stream [, context [, flags=0]])
XmlContainer.putDocument([txn,] name, contents [, context [, flags=0]])
```

Perl

```
$container->putDocument([$txn,] $document [, $context [, $flags]]);
$container->putDocument([$txn,] $name, $stream [, $context [, $flags]]);
$container->putDocument([$txn,] $name, $contents [, $context [, $flags]]);
```

PHP

```
$container->putDocument([$txn,] $document [, $context [, $flags]]);
$container->putDocument([$txn,] $name, $stream [, $context [, $flags]]);
$container->putDocument([$txn,] $name, $contents [, $context [, $flags]]);
```

XmlContainer::removeAlias

Removes the named alias from the list maintained by the containing XmlManager. If the alias does not exist or matches a different XmlContainer, the call fails. Return value is true upon success and false upon failure.

C++

```
bool removeAlias(const std::string &alias)
```

Java

```
public boolean removeAlias(String alias)
```

Python

```
XmlContainer.removeAlias(alias)
```

Perl

```
$container->removeAlias($alias);
```

PHP

```
$container->removeAlias($alias);
```

XmlContainer::replaceIndex

Replaces an index of the specified type for the named document node. This method is for convenience; see XmlIndexSpecification::replaceIndex.

Parameters

txn

If the operation is to be transaction-protected, the txn parameter is an XmlTransaction handle returned from XmlManager::createTransaction.

uri

The namespace of the node to be indexed. The default namespace is selected by passing an empty string for the namespace.

name

The name of the element or attribute node to be indexed.

index

A comma-separated list of strings that represent the indexing strategy. See the index description in the parameter list for XmlContainer::addIndex for the full options and syntax.

context

The update context to use for this operation.

C++

```
void XmlContainer::replaceIndex(const std::string &uri, const std::string &name,
    const std::string &index, XmlUpdateContext &context)

XmlContainer::replaceIndex(XmlTransaction &txn, const std::string &uri,
    const std::string &name, const std::string &index, XmlUpdateContext &context)
```

Java

```
public void replaceIndex([XmlTransaction txn,] String uri, String name,
    String index, XmlUpdateContext context)
```

Python

```
XmlContainer.replaceIndex([txn,] uri, name, index, context)
```

Perl

```
$container->replaceIndex([$txn, ] $uri, $name, $index [, $context]);
```

PHP

```
$container->replaceIndex([$txn, ] $uri, $name, $index [, $context]);
```

XmlContainer::replaceDefaultIndex

Replaces the container's default index. This method is for convenience   see XmlIndexSpecification::replaceDefaultIndex for more information.

Parameters

txn

An XmlTransaction handle returned from XmlManager::createTransaction.

index

A comma-separated list of strings that represent the indexing strategy. See the index description in the parameter list for XmlContainer::addIndex for the full options and syntax.

context

The update context to use for the index replacement.

C++

```
void XmlContainer::replaceDefaultIndex( const std::string &uri, const std::string &name,
    const std::string &index, XmlUpdateContext &context)

XmlContainer::replaceDefaultIndex(XmlTransaction &txn, const std::string &uri,
    const std::string &name, const std::string &index, XmlUpdateContext &context)
```

Java

```
public void replaceDefaultIndex([XmlTransaction txn,] String index,
    XmlUpdateContext context)
```

Python

```
XmlContainer.replaceDefaultIndex([txn,] uri, name, index, context)
```

Perl

```
$container->replaceDefaultIndex([$txn, ] $uri, $name, $index [, $context]);
```

PHP

```
$container->replaceDefaultIndex([$txn, ] $uri, $name, $index [, $context]);
```

XmlContainer::setIndexSpecification

Defines the type of indexing to be maintained for a container of documents. The currently defined indexing specification can be retrieved with the XmlContainer::getIndexSpecification method.

If the container is not empty, the contained documents are incrementally indexed. Index keys for disabled index strategies are removed, and index keys for enabled index strategies are added. Note that the length of time taken to perform this reindexing operation is proportional to the size of the container.

Parameters

txn

An XmlTransaction handle returned from XmlManager::createTransaction.

index

The indexing specification for the container.

context

The update context to use for the index modification.

C++

```
void XmlContainer::setIndexSpecification(const XmlIndexSpecification &index,
    XmlUpdateContext &context)
```

```
void XmlContainer::setIndexSpecification(XmlTransaction &txn,
    const XmlIndexSpecification &index, XmlUpdateContext &context)
```

Java

```
public void setIndexSpecification([XmlTransaction txn,] XmlIndexSpecification index,
    XmlUpdateContext context)
```

Python

```
XmlContainer.setIndexSpecification([txn,] index, context)
```

Perl

```
$container->setIndexSpecification([$txn, ] $index [, $context]);
```

PHP

```
$container->setIndexSpecification([$txn, ] $index [, $context]);
```

XmlContainer::sync

Flushes database pages for the container to disk.

C++

```
void XmlContainer::sync() const
```

Java

```
public void sync()
```

Python

```
XmlContainer.sync()
```

Perl

```
$container->sync();
```

PHP

```
$container->sync();
```

XmlContainer::updateDocument

Updates an XmlDocument in the container. The document must have been retrieved from the container using XmlContainer::getDocument, XmlManager::query, or XmlQueryExpression::execute. It is possible to use a constructed XmlDocument object if its name is set to a valid name in the container. The document must still exist within the container. The document content is indexed according to the container-indexing specification, with index keys being removed for the previous document content and added for the updated document content. Note that the effect of updateDocument is to replace the document by name because its contents must be reindexed.

Parameters

txn

An XmlTransaction handle returned from XmlManager::createTransaction.

document

The XmlDocument to be updated in the XmlContainer.

context

The update context to use for the document insertion.

C++

```
void XmlContainer::updateDocument(XmlDocument &document,
    XmlUpdateContext &context)

void XmlContainer::updateDocument(XmlTransaction &txn,
    XmlDocument &document, XmlUpdateContext &context)
```

Java

```
public void updateDocument([XmlTransaction txn,] XmlDocument document,
    XmlUpdateContext context)
```

Python

```
XmlContainer.updateDocument([txn,] document, context)
```

Perl

```
$container->updateDocument([$txn, ] $document [, $context]);
```

PHP

```
$container->updateDocument([$txn, ] $document [, $context]);
```

XmlContainerConfig

This Java-only class replaces bitwise OR'd flags for container configuration. It extends the Berkeley DB DatabaseConfig, which performs the same function for databases. Each set method has a corresponding get method. This object is used as an argument to container instantiation. It is constructed with the class constructor.

XmlContainerConfig::setAllowValidation

Sets whether documents are validated when loaded   if they refer to a Document Type Definition (DTD) or XML schema.

Java

```
public XmlContainerConfig setAllowValidation(boolean value)
```

XmlContainerConfig::setNodeContainer

Sets whether documents• nodes are broken down and stored individually in the container or are stored intact with all white space and formatting. Storing nodes is preferred.

Java

```
public XmlContainerConfig setNodeContainer(boolean value)
```

XmlContainerConfig::setIndexNodes

Sets whether the indexer will create index targets that reference nodes rather than documents.

Java

```
public XmlContainerConfig setIndexNodes(boolean value)
```

XmlContainerConfig::setTransactional

Encloses the database open within a transaction.

Java

```
public void setTransactional(boolean transactional)
```

XmlDocument

XmlDocument is the storage unit within an XmlContainer. An XmlDocument has content, a name, and a set of metadata attributes. Only the name is not optional.

A documents content is a byte stream of XML and it can be get and set in multiple ways. It must be well formed XML, but need not be valid. The document name is a unique identifier for the document. The name is specified when the document is first placed in the container. It can either be explicitly specified by the user or autogenerated by Berkeley DB XML. See XmlContainer::putDocument for details.

The user can retrieve the document by name using XmlContainer::getDocument. In addition, the document name can be referenced in an XQuery expression using the doc() navigation function. Metadata attributes enable data to be associated with a document without storing that data within the document and are analogous to file attributes on a file system.

Empty XmlDocuments can be instantiated using the XmlManager::createDocument method.

XmlDocument::fetchAllData

If a document was retrieved using DBXML_LAZY_DOCS, document content and metadata are retrieved from the container only on an as-needed basis. This method causes all document data and metadata to be retrieved (but does not return anything). Note that documents in node storage containers are implicitly lazy.

If DBXML_LAZY_DOCS was not used to retrieve the document, use of this method has no significant performance impact. However, if the document was retrieved lazily, repeatedly calling this method on any given document might hurt your applications performance.

C++

```
void XmlDocument::fetchAllData()
```

Java

```
public void fetchAllData()
```

Python

```
XmlDocument.fetchAllData()
```

Perl

```
$document->fetchAllData();
```

PHP

```
$document->fetchAllData();
```

XmlDocument::getContent

Returns a reference to the document content. The returned value is owned by the XmlDocument and is destroyed when the document is destroyed.

C++

```
std::string &XmlDocument::getContent(std::string &content) const
XmlData XmlDocument::getContent() const
```

Java

```
public byte[] getContent()
```

Python

```
XmlDocument.getContent([content])
```

Perl

```
my $string = $document->getContent();
```

PHP

```
$xmldata = $document->getContent();
```

XmlDocument::getContentAsDOM

Returns the document content as a Xerces Document Object Model (DOM) object. If the document is from a node storage container, the nodes are live and retrieved on demand from the container database. This means that nodes will not be available if the transaction in which the document was retrieved is committed or aborted. Modifications to the DOM nodes will not be stored back to the document unless the XmlContainer::updateDocument method is called after the modifications have been made.

Not all Xerces DOM methods are supported by the implementation. This method is supported only by the Berkeley DB XML C++ API. See the BDB XML and Xerces documentation for more details.

C++

```
xercesc_2_7::DOMDocument *XmlDocument::getContentAsDOM() const
```

XmlDocument::getContentAsXmlInputStream

Returns the documents content as an XmlInputStream. The returned value is owned by the caller and must be explicitly deleted.

C++

```
XmlInputStream *XmlDocument::getContentAsXmlInputStream() const
```

Java

```
public XmlInputStream getContentAsXmlInputStream()
```

Python

```
XmlDocument.getContentAsXmlInputStream()
```

Perl

```
my $stream = $document->getContentAsXmlInputStream();
```

PHP

```
$stream = $document->getContentAsXmlInputStream();
```

XmlDocument::getMetaData

Returns the value of the specified metadata. The value of the metadata attribute can be retrieved as a typed or untyped value. Typed values are retrieved by passing an XmlValue to the API. Untyped values are retrieved by passing an XmlData object (Dbt) through the API.

This method returns true if metadata is found for the XmlDocument that matches the given URI and name; otherwise, it returns false.

C++

```
bool XmlDocument::getMetaData(const std::string &uri, const std::string &name,
    XmlValue &value)
bool XmlDocument::getMetaData(const std::string &uri,
    const std::string &name, XmlData &value) const
```

Java

```
public byte[] getMetaData(String uri, String name, [XmlValue value])
```

Python

```
XmlDocument.getMetaData(uri, name, value)
```

Perl

```
my $xmlvalue = new XmlValue(...);
$document->getMetaData($uri, $name, $xmlvalue);

my $string;
$document->getMetaData($uri, $name, $string);
```

PHP

```
$xmlvalue = getMetaData($uri, $name);
```

XmlDocument::getMetaDataIterator

Returns an XmlMetaDataIterator. Using this iterator, you can examine the individual metadata items set for the document by looping over them using XmlMetaDataIterator::next.

C++

```
XmlMetaDataIterator XmlDocument::getMetaDataIterator()
```

Java

```
public XmlMetaDataIterator getMetaDataIterator()
```

Python

```
XmlDocument.getMetaDataIterator()
```

Perl

```
$iterator = $document->getMetaDataIterator();
```

PHP

This method is not provided by the PHP API.

XmlDocument::getName

The XmlDocument::getName method returns the XmlDocument name.

C++

```
std::string XmlDocument::getName() const
```

Java

```
public String getName()
```

Python

```
XmlDocument.getName()
```

Perl

```
my $string = $document->getName();
```

PHP

```
$string = $document->getName();
```

XmlDocument::removeMetaData

Removes the identified metadata from the document.

C++

```
void XmlDocument::removeMetaData(const std::string &uri, const std::string &name)
```

Java

```
public void removeMetaData(String uri, String name)
```

Python

```
XmlDocument.removeMetaData(uri, name)
```

Perl

```
$document->removeMetaData($uri, $name);
```

PHP

This method is not supported by the PHP API.

XmlDocument::setContent

Sets the documents content to the provided content string. If this document is a new document (its name is new in the container), you can add it to a container using XmlContainer::putDocument. If you are updating (or replacing) an already existing document, you can update the document in the container using XmlContainer::updateDocument.

C++

```
void XmlDocument::setContent(const std::string &content)
void XmlDocument::setContent(const XmlData &content)
```

Java

```
public void setContent(byte [] content)
```

Python

```
XmlDocument.setContent(content)
```

Perl

```
$document->setContent($string);
```

PHP

```
$document->setContent($string);
$document->setContent($xmldata);
$document->setContent($inputstream);
```

XmlDocument::setContentAsDOM

Sets the documents content using the provided Xerces DOM object. If this document is a new document (its name is new in the container), you can add it to a container by using `XmlContainer::putDocument`. If you are updating (or replacing) an already existing document, you can update the document in the container using `XmlContainer::updateDocument`. Available only to the C++ API.

C++

```
void XmlDocument::setContentAsDOM(xercesc_2_7::DOMDocument *document)
```

XmlDocument::setContentAsXmlInputStream

Sets the documents content using the provided input stream. If this document is new, you can add it to a container using `XmlContainer::putDocument`. If you are updating an already existing document, you can update the document in the container using `XmlContainer::updateDocument`.

C++

```
void XmlDocument::setContentAsXmlInputStream(XmlInputStream *stream)
```

Java

```
public void setContentAsXmlInputStream(XmlInputStream stream)
```

Python

```
XmlDocument.setContentAsXmlInputStream(stream)
```

Perl

```
$document->setContentAsXmlInputStream($stream);
```

PHP

The PHP API does not provide this method as shown; instead, the `setContent()` function accepts an `XmlInputStream` object.

XmlDocument::setMetaData

Sets the value of the specified metadata attribute. A metadata attribute is a name-value pair, which is stored with the document, but not as part of the document content. The value of a metadata attribute can be typed or untyped.

A metadata attribute name consists of a namespace URI and a name. The namespace URI is optional, but it should be used to avoid naming collisions. Typed values are passed to the API as an instance of `XmlValue` and can be of any `XmlValue` type: `Number`, `String`, or `Boolean`.

C++ Usage

```
void XmlDocument::setMetaData(const std::string &uri, const std::string &name,
    const XmlValue &value)
```

```
void XmlDocument::setMetaData(const std::string &uri, const std::string &name,
    const XmlData &value)
```

Java Usage

```
public void setMetaData(String uri, String name, XmlValue value);
```

Python Usage

```
XmlDocument.setMetaData(uri, name, value);
XmlDocument.setMetaData(uri, name, string);
```

Perl Usage

```
$doc->setMetaData($uri, $name, $value);
$doc->setMetaData($uri, $name, $string);
```

PHP Usage

```
$doc->setMetaData($uri, $name, $value);
$doc->setMetaData($uri, $name, $string);
```

XmlDocument::setName

The XmlDocument::setName method sets the name of the document. Note that when the document is put in a container, the name that you specify must be unique; if not, you must use the DBXML_GEN_NAME flag, or else an exception is thrown.

C++ Usage

```
void XmlDocument::setName(const std::string &name)
```

Java Usage

```
public void setName(String name)
```

Python Usage

```
XmlDocument.setName(name)
```

Perl Usage

```
$document->setName($name);
```

PHP Usage

```
$document->setName($name);
```

XmlDocumentConfig

This Java-only class is used in place of bitwise OR'd flags to configure operations that function on `XmlDocument` objects.

XmlDocumentConfig::setGenerateName

Sets whether to automatically generate a name for the document.

Java Usage

```
public XmlDocumentConfig setGenerateName(boolean value)
```

XmlDocumentConfig::setReverseOrder

Sets whether to sort index lookups in reverse order.

Java Usage

```
public XmlDocumentConfig setReverseOrder(boolean value)
```

XmlDocumentConfig::setLockMode

Sets the lock mode for the operation. The modes are shown in the following table:

Mode	Description
DEFAULT	Acquires read locks for read operations and write locks for write operations.
DEGREE_2	"Degree 2 isolation" provides for cursor stability but not repeatable reads. In Berkeley DB 4.4 and later, this flag is named DB_READ_COMMITTED.
DIRTY_READ	Reads modified but not yet committed data. In Berkeley DB 4.4 and later, this flag is named DB_READ_UNCOMMITTED.
RMW	Acquires write locks instead of read locks when doing retrieval.

Java Usage

```
public XmlDocumentConfig setLockMode(LockMode lmode)
```

XmlException

Objects of this class represent a BDB XML error condition and get thrown when an API operation results in an error (when supported by the API). It supplies methods to retrieve error details. Refer to the API tutorial chapters (Chapters 8..12) for details on exception handling for each language. Note that the Python and PHP APIs do not yet support exception handling.

XmlException::what

Returns a description of the exception as a string.

XmlException::getExceptionCode

Returns the exception code (ExceptionCode).

XmlException::getDbError

Retrieves the underlying Berkeley DB error code as an integer for an XmlException with exception code DATABASE_ERROR.

XmlIndexLookup

The XmlIndexLookup class encapsulates the context within which an index lookup operation can be performed on an XmlContainer object. The lookup is performed by using an XmlIndexLookup object and a series of methods of that object that specify how the lookup is to be performed. Using these methods, it is possible to specify inequality lookups, range lookups, and simple value lookups (as well as the sort order of the results). By default, results are returned in the sort order of the index.

XmlIndexLookup objects are created using XmlManager::createIndexLookup. See the reference for that method for more details.

XmlIndexLookup::execute

Executes the index lookup operation specified by the configuration of the XmlIndexLookup object.

C++

```
XmlResults results = XmlIndexLookup::execute(XmlQueryContext &context,
    u_int32_t flags = 0) const

XmlResults results = XmlIndexLookup::execute(XmlTransaction &txn,
    XmlQueryContext &context, u_int32_t flags = 0) const
```

Java

```
public XmlResul ts execute([XmlTransaction txn,] XmlQueryContext context,
    [XmlDocumentConfig config])
```

Python

```
XmlIndexLookup.execute([txn,] context, flags=0)
```

Perl

```
$lookup->execute([$txn,] $context, $flags);
```

PHP

```
$lookup->execute([$txn,] [$context,] $flags);
```

XmlIndexLookup::setContainer

Sets the container to be used for the index lookup operation. The same XmlIndexLookup object can be used for lookup in multiple containers by changing this configuration. All APIs provide a corresponding getContainer method.

C++

```
void XmlIndexLookup::setContainer(XmlContainer &container)
const XmlContainer & XmlIndexLookup::getContainer() const
```

Java

```
public void setContainer(XmlContainer container)
```

Python

```
XmlIndexLookup.setContainer(container)
```

Perl

```
$lookup->setContainer($container);
```

PHP

```
$lookup->setContainer($container);
```

XmlIndexLookup::setHighBound

Sets the operation and value to be used for the upper bound for a range index lookup operation. The upper bound must be specified to indicate a range lookup. Each API provides an accompanying get method for the bound and operation.

Parameters

value

A value to be used for the upper bound of an index lookup. An empty value results in an inequality lookup.

op

The operation for the upper bound. The possible values are XmlIndexLookup::LT (less than) and XmlIndexLookup::LTE (less than or equal to).

C++

```
void XmlIndexLookup::setHighBound(const XmlValue &value,
    XmlIndexLookup::Operation op)
XmlIndexLookup::Operation XmlIndexLookup::getHighBoundOperation() const
const XmlValue &XmlIndexLookup::getHighBoundValue() const
```

Java

```
public void setHighBound(XmlValue value, int op)
```

Python

```
XmlIndexLookup.setHighBound(value, op)
```

Perl

```
$lookup->setHighBound($value, $op);
```

PHP

```
$lookup->setHighBound($value, $op);
```

XmlIndexLookup::setIndex

Sets the indexing strategy to be used for the index lookup operation. Only one index can be specified, and substring indexes are not supported. Each API provides an accompanying get method.

C++

```
void XmlIndexLookup::setIndex(const std::string &index)
const std::string &XmlIndexLookup::getIndex() const
```

Java

```
public void setIndex(String index)
```

Python

```
XmlIndexLookup.setIndex(index)
```

Perl

```
$lookup->setIndex($index);
```

PHP

```
$lookup->setIndex($index);
```

XmlIndexLookup::setLowBound

Sets the operation and value to be used for the index lookup operation. If the operation is a simple inequality lookup, the lower bound is used as the single value and operation for the lookup. If the operation is a range lookup, in which an upper bound is specified, the lower bound is used as the lower boundary value and operation for the lookup. Each API provides accompanying get methods for the value and the op.

Parameters

value

A value to be used for the lower bound of an index lookup. Use an uninitialized XmlValue object to specify an empty value.

op

The operation for the upper bound. The possible values are XmlIndexLookup::NONE, XmlIndexLookup:: EQ (equality), XmlIndexLookup::LT (less than), XmlIndexLookup::LTE (less than or equal to), XmlIndex:: Lookup::GT (greater than), and XmlIndexLookup::GTE (greater than or equal to).

C++

```
void XmlIndexLookup::setLowBound(const XmlValue &value, XmlIndexLookup::Operation op)
XmlIndexLookup::Operation XmlIndexLookup::getLowBoundOperation() const
const XmlValue &XmlIndexLookup::getLowBoundValue() const
```

Java

```
public void setLowBound(XmlValue value, int op)
```

Python

```
XmlIndexLookup.setLowBound(value, op)
```

Perl

```
$lookup->setLowBound($value, $op);
```

PHP

```
$lookup->setLowBound($value, $op);
```

XmlIndexLookup::setNode

Sets the name of the node to be used along with the indexing strategy for the index lookup operation. Each API provides get methods to retrieve the node URI and name.

C++

```
void XmlIndexLookup::setNode(const std::string &uri, const std::string &name)
const std::string &XmlIndexLookup::getNodeURI() const
const std::string &XmlIndexLookup::getNodeName() const
```

Java

```
public void setNode(String uri, String name)
```

Python

```
XmlIndexLookup.setNode(uri, name)
```

Perl

```
$lookup->setNode($uri, $name);
```

PHP

```
$lookup->setNode($uri, $name);
```

XmlIndexLookup::setParent

Sets the name of the parent node to be used for an edge index lookup operation. If the index is not an edge index, this configuration is ignored. Each API provides accompanying get methods to retrieve the parent node URI and name.

C++

```
void XmlIndexLookup::setParent(const std::string &uri, const std::string &name)
const std::string &XmlIndexLookup::getParentURI() const
const std::string &XmlIndexLookup::getParentName() const
```

Java

```
public void setParent(String uri, String name)
```

Python

```
XmlIndexLookup.setParent(uri, name)
```

Perl

```
$lookup->setParent($uri, $name);
```

PHP

```
$lookup->setParent($uri, $name);
```

XmlIndexSpecification

The XmlIndexSpecification class encapsulates the indexing specification of a container. An indexing specification can be retrieved with the XmlContainer::getIndexSpecification method and modified with the XmlContainer::setIndexSpecification method.

The XmlIndexSpecification class provides an interface for manipulating the indexing specification through the XmlIndexSpecification::addIndex, XmlIndexSpecification::deleteIndex, and XmlIndexSpecification::replaceIndex methods. The class interface also provides the XmlIndexSpecification::next and XmlIndexSpecification::reset methods for iterating through the specified indexes. The XmlIndexSpecification::find method can be used to search for the indexing strategy for a known node. Finally, XmlIndexSpecification::addDefaultIndex enables you to set a default indexing strategy for a container. You can replace and delete the default index using XmlIndexSpecification::replaceDefaultIndex and XmlIndexSpecification::deleteDefaultIndex. Note that adding an index to a container results in reindexing all the documents in that container, which can take a very long time. It is good practice to design an application to add useful indexes before populating a container.

An empty index specification object is constructed by using the class constructor.

XmlIndexSpecification::addIndex

Adds an index to the index specification. You then set the index specification using `XmlContainer::setIndexSpecification`.

Parameters

uri

The namespace of the node to be indexed. The default namespace is selected by passing an empty string for the namespace.

name

The name of the element or attribute node to be indexed.

index

A comma-separated list of strings that represent the indexing strategy. The strings must contain the following information:

`unique-{path type}-{node type}-{key type}-{syntax}`

These values are detailed in the following table; order is not important.

Value	Description
unique	Indicates that the indexed value is unique in the container. If this keyword does not appear on the index string, the indexed value is not required to be unique in the container.
{path type}	Either `node` or `edge`.
{node type}	One of `element`, `attribute`, or `metadata`. If `metadata` is specified, {path type} must be `node`.
{key type}	One of `presence`, `equality`, or `substring`.
{syntax}	Identifies the type of information being indexed. It must be one of the following values: `none`, `anyURI`, `base64Binary`, `boolean`, `date`, `dateTime`, `dayTimeDuration`, `decimal`, `double`, `duration`, `float`, `gDay`, `gMonth`, `gMonthDay`, `gYear`, `gYearMonth`, `hexBinary`, `NOTATION`, `QName`, `string`, `time`, `yearMonthDuration`, `untypedAtomic`. See the BDB XML documentation for full descriptions of the types.

Note that if {key type} is present, {syntax} must be `none` or simply not specified.

C++

```
void XmlIndexSpecification::addIndex(
    const std::string &uri, const std::string &name, const std::string &index)
```

Java

```
public void addIndex(String uri, String name, String index)
```

Python

```
XmlIndexSpecification.addIndex(uri, name, index)
```

Perl

```
$indexSpec->addIndex($uri, $name, $index);
```

PHP

```
$indexSpec->addIndex($uri, $name, $index);
```

XmlIndexSpecification::addDefaultIndex

Adds one or more indexing strategies to the default index specification. That is, the index provided on this method is applied to all nodes in a container, except for those for which an explicit index is already declared. For more information on specifying indexing strategies, see XmlIndexSpecification::addIndex.

C++

```
void XmlIndexSpecification::addDefaultIndex(const std::string &index)
```

Java

```
public void addDefaultIndex(String index)
```

Python

```
XmlIndexSpecification.addDefaultIndex(index)
```

Perl

```
$indexSpec->addDefaultIndex($index);
```

PHP

```
$indexSpec->addDefaultIndex($index);
```

XmlIndexSpecification::deleteIndex

Deletes one or more indexing strategies for a named document or metadata node. To delete an index set for metadata, specify the URI and name used when the metadata was added to the document.

C++

```
void XmlIndexSpecification::deleteIndex(const std::string &uri,
    const std::string &name, const std::string &index)
```

Java

```
public void deleteIndex(String uri, String name, String index)
```

Python

```
XmlIndexSpecification.deleteIndex(uri, name, index)
```

Perl

```
$indexSpec->deleteIndex($uri, $name, $index);
```

PHP

```
$indexSpec->deleteIndex($uri, $name, $index);
```

XmlIndexSpecification::deleteDefaultIndex

Deletes one or more indexing strategies from the default index specification. For more information on specifying indexes, see XmlIndexSpecification::addIndex.

C++

```
void XmlContainer::deleteDefaultIndex(const std::string &index)
void XmlContainer::deleteDefaultIndex(Type type, XmlValue::Type syntax)
```

Java

```
public void deleteDefaultIndex(String index)
```

Python

```
XmlContainer.deleteDefaultIndex(index)
```

Perl

```
$indexSpec->deleteDefaultIndex($index);
```

PHP

```
$indexSpec->deleteDefaultIndex($index);
```

XmlIndexSpecification::find

Returns the indexing strategies for a named document or metadata node. This method returns true if an index for the node is found; otherwise, it returns false. See XmlIndexSpecification::addIndex for more information on index strategies.

C++

```
bool XmlIndexSpecification::find(const std::string &uri, const std::string &name,
    std::string &index)
```

Java

```
public XmlIndexDeclaration find(String uri, String name)
```

Python

```
bool XmlIndexSpecification.find(uri, name, index)
```

Perl

```
my $bool = $indexSpec->find($uri, $name, $index);
```

PHP

```
$bool = $indexSpec->find($uri, $name);
```

XmlIndexSpecification::getDefaultIndex

Retrieves the default index. The default index is the index used by all nodes in the document in the absence of any other index.

C++

```
std::string XmlIndexSpecification::getDefaultIndex() const
```

Java

```
public String getDefaultIndex()
```

Python

```
XmlIndexSpecification.getDefaultIndex()
```

Perl

```
my $index = $indexSpec->getDefaultIndex();
```

PHP

```
$index = $indexSpec->getDefaultIndex();
```

XmlIndexSpecification::next

Obtains the next index in the XmlIndexSpecification. Use XmlIndexSpecification::reset to reset this iterator. Returns true if additional indexes exist in the index list; otherwise, it returns false.

C++

```
bool XmlIndexSpecification::next(std::string &uri, std::string &name,
    std::string &index)
```

Java

```
public XmlIndexDeclaration next()
```

Python

```
XmlIndexSpecification.next([uri, name, index])
```

Perl

```
my $index = $indexSpec->next();
```

PHP

```
$index = $indexSpec->next();
```

XmlIndexSpecification::replaceIndex

Identifies one or more indexing strategies to set for the identified document node or metadata node. All existing indexing strategies for that node are deleted, and the indexing strategy identified by this method is set for the node.

C++

```
void XmlIndexSpecification::replaceIndex(const std::string &uri,
    const std::string &name, const std::string &index)
```

Java

```
public void replaceIndex(String uri, String name, String index)
```

Python

```
XmlIndexSpecification.replaceIndex(uri, name, index)
```

Perl

```
$indexSpec->replaceIndex($uri, $name, $index);
```

PHP

```
$indexSpec->replaceIndex($uri, $name, $index);
```

XmlIndexSpecification::replaceDefaultIndex

Replaces the default indexing strategy for the container with one or more specified indexing strategies. The default index specification is used for all nodes in a document. You can add additional indexes for specific document nodes using XmlIndexSpecification::addIndex.

C++

```
void XmlIndexSpecification::replaceDefaultIndex(const std::string &index)
```

Java

```
public void replaceDefaultIndex(String index)
```

Python

```
XmlIndexSpecification.replaceDefaultIndex(index)
```

Perl

```
$indexSpec->replaceDefaultIndex($index);
```

PHP

```
$indexSpec->replaceDefaultIndex($index);
```

XmlIndexSpecification::reset

Resets the index specification iterator to the beginning of the index list. Use XmlIndexSpecification::next to iterate through the indexes contained in the index specification.

C++

```
void XmlIndexSpecification::reset()
```

Java

```
public void reset()
```

Python

```
XmlIndexSpecification.reset()
```

Perl

```
$indexSpec->reset();
```

PHP

```
$indexSpec->reset();
```

XmlInputStream

XmlInputStreams are used to read and write XML data; they are created by using one of the following: XmlManager::createLocalFileInputStream, XmlManager::createMemBufInputStream, XmlManager::createStdInInputStream, XmlManager::createURLInputStream, or XmlDocument::getContentAsXmlInputStream. Objects of this class are passed to XmlContainer::putDocument and XmlDocument::setContentAsXmlInputStream to set document content. You can manually retrieve the contents of the input stream by using XmlInputStream::readBytes and XmlInputStream::curPos.

For most APIs, XmlInputStream is a pure virtual interface and can be subclassed. This is useful for streaming XML from an application directly into Berkeley DB XML without first converting it to a string.

XmlInputStream::curPos

Returns the number of bytes currently read from the beginning of the input stream.

C++

```
virtual unsigned int XmlInputStream::curPos() const = 0
```

Java

```
public long curPos()
```

Python

```
XmlInputStream.curPos()
```

Perl

```
my $pos = $stream->curPos();
```

PHP

```
$pos = $stream->curPos();
```

XmlInputStream::readBytes

Reads maxToRead number of bytes from the input stream and places those bytes in toFill. Returns the number of bytes read or returns 0 if the end of the stream has been reached.

C++

```
virtual unsigned int XmlInputStream::readBytes(char *toFill,
    const unsigned int maxToRead)
```

Java

```
public long readBytes(byte[] toFill, long maxToRead)
```

Python

```
XmlInputStream.readBytes(toFill, maxToRead)
```

Perl

```
my $count = $stream->readBytes();
```

PHP

```
$count = $stream->readBytes();
```

XmlManager

XmlManager is a high-level object used to manage containers, prepare and execute queries, create transactions, create update contexts, create query contexts, and create input streams. The method list follows.

XmlManager (Constructor)

The XmlManager constructor. Some variants of this constructor take a provided DbEnv for the underlying environment. Subsystems (logging, transactions, and so on) enabled for that environment are then active for the constructed XmlManager and its operations. A convenience constructor takes no parameters and behaves as if a 0 were passed as flags.

Parameters

dbenv

The DbEnv to use for the underlying database environment. The environment provided here must be opened.

flags

This parameter must be set to 0 or by bitwise inclusively OR•ing together one or more of the following values:

Flag	Description
DBXML_ALLOW_EXTERNAL_ACCESS	Permits XQuery queries to access external data sources, including files on disk or network URIs. Disallowed by default.
DBXML_ALLOW_AUTO_OPEN	Automatically opens containers that query references and closes them when query references are released. Disallowed by default, causing queries that refer to unopened containers to fail.
DBXML_ADOPT_DBENV	Causes XmlManager to close and delete the underlying DbEnv object automatically. Applicable only when a DbEnv object is provided to the XmlManager constructor. This requires that the passed DbEnv be dynamically allocated and not be deleted by the caller.

C++

```
XmlManager::XmlManager(DbEnv *dbenv, u_int32_t flags = 0)
XmlManager::XmlManager(u_int32_t flags)
XmlManager::XmlManager()
XmlManager::XmlManager(const XmlManager &o)
XmlManager &operator = (const XmlManager &o)
XmlManager::~XmlManager()
```

Java

The Java API uses the XmlManagerConfig class in place of bitwise ORd flags.

```
public XmlManager([Environment dbenv,] [XmlManagerConfig config])
```

Python

```
XmlManager([dbenv,] [flags=0])
XmlManager([mgr,] [flags])
```

Perl

```
my $manager = new XmlManager([$dbenv,] [, $flags]);
```

PHP

```
$manager = new XmlManager([$dbenv,] [, $flags]);
```

XmlManager::createContainer

Creates and opens a container and then returns a handle to an XmlContainer object. If the container already exists at the time this method is called, an exception is thrown.

Use XmlManager::openContainer to open a container that has already been created. Containers always remain open until the last handle referencing the container is destroyed.

Variants of this method accept an XmlTransaction object, a string name for the container, and flags for container creation.

Parameters

txn

The XmlTransaction object to use for this container creation.

name

The containers name relative to the underlying environments home unless an absolute path is provided. Container names must be unique to their environment.

flags

The flags to use for this container creation. The parameter must be set to 0 or by bitwise inclusively OR•ing together one or more of the following values:

Flag	Description
DB_CREATE	Creates the container if it doesn•t exist; always used.
DB_EXCL	Returns an error if the container exists; always used.
DB_RDONLY	Opens the container for reading only.
DB_DIRTY_READ	Enables read operations on the container to support "degree 1 isolation", meaning that read data might have been modified by transactions but not committed. This flag is renamed to DB_READ_UNCOMMITTED in Berkeley DB 4.4 and later.
DB_NOMMAP	Causes Berkeley DB to not map the container into process memory.
DB_THREAD	Causes the container to be free-threaded; usable by multiple threads at once.
DB_XA_CREATE	Creates a database to be accessed under an X/Open-conformant Transaction Manager.
DB_TXN_NOT_DURABLE	Causes Berkeley DB to not write log records for the container, so that container integrity is maintained, but not after a system failure.
DBXML_CHKSUM	Causes BDB XML to perform checksum verification of pages read into the cache.
DBXML_ENCRYPT	Encrypts the database container using the password specified to DbEnv::set_encrypt().
DBXML_INDEX_NODES	When a container uses node storage, causes the indexer to reference nodes instead of documents so that XmlContainer::lookupIndex() can return individual nodes rather than whole documents.
DBXML_TRANSACTIONAL	Causes the container to support transactions, enabling XmlTransaction objects to be used. When this flag is specified, a transaction object is not required for createContainer.
DBXML_ALLOW_VALIDATION	Causes BDB XML to validate XML on database writes if an XML document refers to a DTD or XML schema.

Regardless of which flags you provide to this parameter, DB_CREATE | DB_EXCL are always used.

type

The type of container to create. The container type must be one of the following values:

Container Type	Description
XmlContainer::NodeContainer	Documents are stored in the container by individual nodes. Preferred storage type.
XmlContainer::WholedocContainer	Documents are stored in the container as whole documents, preserving white space and formatting.

mode

A Unix file mode. On Windows systems, the mode parameter is ignored.

C++

```
XmlContainer XmlManager::createContainer(const std::string &name)

XmlContainer XmlManager::createContainer(
    XmlTransaction &txn, const std::string &name)

XmlContainer XmlManager::createContainer(const std::string &name,
    u_int32_t flags, XmlContainer::ContainerType type, int mode = 0)

XmlContainer XmlManager::createContainer(XmlTransaction &txn,
    const std::string &name, u_int32_t flags,
    XmlContainer::ContainerType type, int mode = 0)
```

Java

```
public XmlContainer createContainer([XmlTransaction txn,] String name,
    [XmlContainerConfig config])
```

Python

```
XmlManager.createContainer([txn,] name, [flags,] [type,] [mode=0])
```

Perl

```
my $container = $manager->createContainer([$txn,] $name [, $flags, $type, $mode]);
```

PHP

```
$container = $manager->createContainer([$txn,] $name [, $flags, $type, $mode]);
```

XmlManager::createDocument

Instantiates a new XmlDocument object.

C++

```
XmlDocument XmlManager::createDocument()
```

Java

```
public XmlDocument createDocument()
```

Python

```
XmlManager.createDocument()
```

Perl

```
my $document = $manager->createDocument();
```

PHP

```
$document = $manager->createDocument();
```

XmlManager::createIndexLookup

Instantiates a new XmlIndexLookup object for performing index lookup operations. Only a single index can be specified, and substring indexes are not supported. As elsewhere, the uri, name, and index parameters identify the index, whereas op is one of the following possible operations:

Operation	Description
XmlIndexLookup::NONE	Test for existence
XmlIndexLookup::EQ	Test for equality
XmlIndexLookup::LT	Less-than range test
XmlIndexLookup::LTE	Less-than-or-equal-to range test
XmlIndexLookup::GT	Greater-than range test
XmlIndexLookup::GTE	Greater-then-or-equal-to range test

C++

```
XmlIndexLookup XmlManager::createIndexLookup(
    XmlContainer &container, const std::string &uri, const std::string &name,
    const std::string &index, const XmlValue &value = XmlValue(),
    XmlIndexLookup::Operation op = XmlIndexLookup::EQ)
```

Java

```
public XmlIndexLookup createIndexLookup(XmlContainer container, String uri,
    String name, String index, XmlValue value, int op)
```

Python

```
XmlManager.createIndexLookup(container, uri, name, index, value, op)
```

Perl

```
my $lookup = $manager->createIndexLookup($container, $uri, $name, $index, $value,
    $op);
```

PHP

```
$lookup = $manager->createIndexLookup($container, $uri, $name, $index, $value, $op);
```

XmlManager::createLocalFileInputStream

Returns an XmlInputStream to the file filename for use with XmlContainer::putDocument or XmlDocument::setContentAsXmlInputStream.

If the input stream is passed to either of these methods, it will be adopted and deleted. If it is not passed, it is the responsibility of the user to delete the object. No attempt is made to ensure that the file referenced contains well-formed or valid XML. Exceptions are thrown when the input stream is actually read if the stream does not contain well-formed or valid XML.

C++

```
XmlInputStream *XmlManager::createLocalFileInputStream(
    const std::string &filename) const
```

Java

```
public XmlInputStream createLocalFileInputStream(String filename)
```

Python

```
XmlManager.createLocalFileInputStream(filename)
```

Perl

```
my $stream = $manager->createLocalFileInputStream($filename);
```

PHP

This input stream is not supported by the PHP API.

XmlManager::createMemBufInputStream

Returns an XmlInputStream for the in-memory buffer srcDocBytes for use with XmlContainer::putDocument or XmlDocument::setContentAsXmlInputStream.

If the input stream is passed to either of these methods, it is adopted and deleted. If it is not passed, it is the responsibility of the user to delete the object. No attempt is made by this method to ensure that the memory referenced contains well-formed or valid XML. Exceptions are thrown at the time that this input stream is actually read if the stream does not contain well-formed or valid XML.

C++

```
XmlInputStream *XmlManager::createMemBufInputStream(const char *srcDocBytes,
    const unsigned int byteCount, const char *const bufId,
    const bool adoptBuffer = false) const

XmlInputStream *XmlManager::createMemBufInputStream(const char *srcDocBytes,
    const unsigned int byteCount, const bool copyBuffer) const
```

Java

```
public XmlInputStream createMemBufInputStream(String buffer, int bufLen,
    boolean copyBuf)
public XmlInputStream createMemBufInputStream(InputStream is)
```

Python

```
XmlManager.createMemBufInputStream(srcDocBytes, byteCount, bufId, adoptBuffer)
XmlManager.createMemBufInputStream(srcDocBytes, byteCount, copyBuffer)
```

Perl

```
my $stream = $manager->createMemBufInputStream($bytes, $count, $buffer);
```

PHP

```
$stream = $manager->createMemBufInputStream($bytes, $count, $buffer);
```

XmlManager::createModify

Instantiates an XmlModify object.

C++

```
XmlModify XmlManager::createModify()
```

Java

```
public XmlModify createModify()
```

Python

```
XmlManager.createModify()
```

Perl

```
my $modify = $manager->createModify();
```

PHP

```
$modify = $manager->createModify();
```

XmlManager::createQueryContext

Creates a new XmlQueryContext object.

Parameters

rt

The available return types are as follows:

Return Type	Description
XmlQueryContext::LiveValues	Query results are a reference to the data within the database. This is the default setting.
XmlQueryContext::DeadValues	Query results are a copy of the data from the database.

et

The two evaluation types are the following:

Evaluation Type	Description
XmlQueryContext::Eager	The query is executed, with resulting values determined and stored in memory before the query returns. This is the default.
XmlQueryContext::Lazy	The query is executed, but the resulting values are not determined or stored in memory until the API refers to them by iterating the result set. This means that a query uses less time and processing.

C++

```
XmlQueryContext XmlManager::createQueryContext(
    XmlQueryContext::ReturnType rt = XmlQueryContext::LiveValues,
    XmlQueryContext::EvaluationType et = XmlQueryContext::Eager)
```

Java

```
public XmlQueryContext createQueryContext(int rt, int et)
```

Python

```
XmlManager.createQueryContext(rt, et)
```

Perl

```
my $queryContext = $manager->createQueryContext($rt, $et);
```

PHP

```
$queryContext = $manager->createQueryContext($rt, $et);
```

XmlManager::createResults

Instantiates a new empty XmlResults object. XmlResults::add can be used to add XmlValue objects to this result set.

C++

```
XmlResults XmlManager::createResults()
```

Java

```
public XmlResults createResults()
```

Python

```
XmlManager.createResults()
```

Perl

```
my $results = $manager->createResults();
```

PHP

```
$results = $manager->createResults();
```

XmlManager::createStdInInputStream

Returns an XmlInputStream to the console. Use this input stream with XmlContainer::putDocument or XmlDocument::setContentAsXmlInputStream. If the input stream is passed to either of these methods, it will be adopted and deleted. If it is not passed, it is the responsibility of the user to delete the object.

C++

```
XmlInputStream *XmlManager::createStdInInputStream() const
```

Java

```
public XmlInputStream createStdInInputStream()
```

Python

```
XmlManager.createStdInInputStream()
```

Perl

```
my $stream = $manager->createStdInInputStream();
```

PHP

This stream type is not supported by the PHP API.

XmlManager::createTransaction

The XmlManager::createTransaction method creates a new XmlTransaction object. If a DbTxn object is not provided to this method, a new transaction begins (a DbTxn object is instantiated, and DbEnv::txn_begin is called).

Transactions must have been enabled when this XmlManager object was opened (DB_INIT_TXN specified), or else this method throws an exception.

Parameters

DbTxn

If a DbTxn parameter is passed to the XmlManager::createTransaction method, the new XmlTransaction is simply another handle for the DbTxn object. In this case, if the XmlTransaction object is destroyed or goes out of scope before XmlTransaction::commit or XmlTransaction::abort is called, the state of the underlying transaction is left unchanged. This enables a transaction to be controlled external to its XmlTransaction object. If no DbTxn is passed, and the XmlTransaction object is destroyed or goes out of scope, the transaction is implicitly aborted.

flags

This parameter must be set to 0 or by bitwise inclusively OR•ing together one or more of the following values:

Flag	Description
DB_DEGREE_2	The transaction will have "degree 2 isolation", meaning that previously read data items can be deleted or modified by other transactions during the transactions life span. In Berkeley DB 4.4, this flag was renamed to DB_READ_COMMITTED.
DB_DIRTY_READ	The transaction will have "degree 1 isolation", meaning that read data items can include data modified by other transactions, although not yet committed. Must be specified when the underlying container was opened to work. In Berkeley DB 4.4, this flag was renamed to DB_READ_UNCOMMITTED.
DB_TXN_NOSYNC	The transaction does not synchronously flush the log on commit or prepare. Database integrity will be maintained, but the transaction might be excluded if recovery is necessary.
DB_TXN_NOWAIT	Causes the transaction to not wait for a lock if one is unavailable. Instead of blocking, it will return DB_LOCK_DEADLOCK or throw an exception immediately.
DB_TXN_SYNC	The transaction will synchronously flush the log on commit or prepare. All atomic, consistent, isolated, durable (ACID) properties are exhibited. This is the default behavior.

C++

```
XmlTransaction XmlManager::createTransaction(DbTxn *toAdopt)
XmlTransaction XmlManager::createTransaction(u_int32_t flags = 0)
```

Java

```
public XmlTransaction createTransaction([XmlTransaction txn,] [Transaction Config config])
```

Python

```
XmlManager.createTransaction([txn,] [flags=0])
```

Perl

```
my $txn = $manager->createTransaction([$flags]);
```

PHP

```
$txn = $manager->createTransaction([$flags]);
```

XmlManager::createURLInputStream

Creates an input stream for the identified URL. URLs that require network access (for example, http://...) are supported only if Xerces was compiled with socket support. Use this input stream with `XmlContainer::putDocument` or `XmlDocument::setContentAsXmlInputStream`.

Parameters

baseId

The base ID to use for this URL.

systemId

The system ID to use for this URL.

publicId

The public ID to use for this URL.

C++

```
XmlInputStream *XmlManager::createURLInputStream(const std::string &base Id,
    const std::string &systemId, const std::string &publicId) const

XmlInputStream *XmlManager::createURLInputStream(
    const std::string &base Id, const std::string &systemId) const
```

Java

```
public XmlInputStream createURLInputStream(String baseId, String systemId
    [, String publicId])
```

Python

```
XmlManager.createURLInputStream(base Id, systemId [,publicId])
```

Perl

```
my $stream = $manager->createURLInputStream($baseID, $systemID [, $publicID]);
```

PHP

This method is not supported by the PHP API.

XmlManager::createUpdateContext

Instantiates a new `XmlUpdateContext` object with default settings. This object is used for `XmlContainer` and `XmlModify` operations that add, delete, and modify documents and also documents in containers.

C++

```
XmlUpdateContext XmlManager::createUpdateContext()
```

Java

```
public XmlUpdateContext createUpdateContext()
```

Python

```
XmlManager.createUpdateContext()
```

Perl

```
my $updateContext = $manager->createUpdateContext();
```

PHP

```
$updateContext = $manager->createUpdateContext();
```

XmlManager::dumpContainer

Dumps the contents of the container to the specified output stream. The result can be used to reconstruct a container with a call to XmlManager::loadContainer. The container must be closed and must have been opened at least once.

Parameters

name

The name of the container to be dumped.

out

The output stream to which the container is to be dumped.

C++

```
void XmlManager::dumpContainer(const std::string name, std::ostream *out)
```

Java

```
public void dumpContainer(String name, String out)
```

Python

```
XmlManager.dumpContainer(name, out)
```

Perl

```
$manager->dumpContainer($name, $out);
```

PHP

This method is not yet supported by the PHP API.

XmlManager::existsContainer

The XmlManager::existsContainer method examines the named file; if it is a container, it returns a nonzero database format version. If the file does not exist or is not a container, zero is returned. The container can be open or closed; no exceptions are thrown from this method.

C++

```
int XmlManager::existsContainer(const std::string &name)
```

Java

```
public int existsContainer(String name)
```

Python

```
XmlManager.existsContainer(name)
```

Perl

```
my $version = $manager->existsContainer($name);
```

PHP

```
$version = $manager->existsContainer($name);
```

XmlManager::getDbEnv

Returns a handle to the underlying database environment.

C++

```
DbEnv *XmlManager::getDbEnv()
```

Java

```
public Environment getEnvironment()
```

Python

```
XmlManager.getDBEnv()
```

Perl

```
my $env = $manager->getDbEnv();
```

PHP

This method is not supported in the PHP API.

XmlManager::getHome

Returns the home directory for the underlying database environment. XmlContainer files are placed relative to this directory unless an absolute path is used for the container name.

C++

```
const std::string &XmlManager::getHome() const
```

Java

```
public String getHome()
```

Python

```
XmlManager.getHome()
```

Perl

```
my $home = $manager->getHome();
```

PHP

This method is not supported in the PHP API.

XmlManager::loadContainer

Loads data from the specified stream into the container. The container's existing contents are discarded and replaced with the documents from the stream.

The specified input stream should contain data as created by XmlManager::dumpContainer. The container must be closed and must have been opened at least once.

Parameters

name

The name of the container to load.

in

The input stream from which the container is to be loaded.

lineno

Used by the application to specify the starting line number in the stream that is to be read. The system uses the same parameter to return the line number of the last line read from the stream.

context

The XmlUpdateContext object to use for the load.

C++

```
void XmlManager::loadContainer(const std::string name, std::istream *in,
    unsigned long *lineno, XmlUpdateContext &context)
```

Java

```
public void loadContainer(String name, String infile, XmlUpdateContext context)
```

Python

```
XmlManager.loadContainer(name, in, lineno, context)
```

Perl

```
$manager->loadContainer($name, $in_filename, [$lineno, [$context]]);
```

PHP

This method is not supported by the PHP API.

XmlManager::openContainer

Opens a container, returning a handle to an XmlContainer object. Unless DB_CREATE is specified, the container must already exist at the time that this method is called.

Use XmlManager::createContainer or provide DB_CREATE to the parameter on this method to create and open a new container   the effect is identical. Containers always remain open until the last handle referencing the container is destroyed. The name provided here must be unique for the environment.

Parameters

txn

The XmlTransaction object to use for this container open.

name

The container name. The container is created relative to the underlying environments home directory (see XmlManager for more information) unless an absolute path is used for the name; in that case, the container is created in the location identified by the path.

type

If the container is to be created, the type of the container. The container type must be one of the following values:

Type	Description
XmlContainer::NodeContainer	Documents are broken down into their component nodes; these nodes are stored individually in the container. This is the preferred container storage type.
XmlContainer::WholedocContainer	Documents are stored intact; all white space and formatting are preserved.

flags

The flags to use for this container open. The flags parameter must be set to 0 or by bitwise inclusively OR•ing together one or more of the following values:

Flag	Description
DB_CREATE	Creates the container if it does not currently exist.
DB_EXCL	Returns an error if the container already exists. The DB_EXCL flag is meaningful only when specified with the DB_CREATE flag.
DB_RDONLY	Opens the container for reading only. Any attempt to modify items in the container will fail, regardless of the actual permissions of any underlying files.
DB_THREAD	Causes the container handle to be free-threaded (concurrently usable by multiple threads in the address space).

Flag	Description
DBXML_CHKSUM	Performs checksum verification of pages read into the cache from the backing file store. Berkeley DB XML uses the Secure Hash Algorithm 1 (SHA1) if encryption is configured and uses a general hash algorithm if it is not.
DBXML_INDEX_NODES	Relevant for node storage containers only. Causes the indexer to create index targets that reference nodes rather than documents. Enables XmlContainer::lookupIndex to return individual nodes instead of whole documents.
DBXML_TRANSACTIONAL	Causes the container to support transactions. If this flag is set, an XmlTransaction object can be used with any method that supports transactional protection. Also, if this flag is used, and if an XmlTransaction object is not provided to a method that modifies an XmlContainer or XmlDocument object, autocommit is automatically used for the operation.
DBXML_ALLOW_VALIDATION	When loading documents into the container, validates the XML if it refers to a DTD or XML schema.

C++

```
XmlContainer XmlManager::openContainer(const std::string &name)

XmlContainer XmlManager::openContainer(
    XmlTransaction &txn, const std::string &name)

XmlContainer XmlManager::openContainer(
    XmlTransaction &txn, const std::string &name,
    u_int32_t flags, XmlContainer::ContainerType type, int mode)
...
```

Java

```
public XmlContainer openContainer([XmlTransaction txn,] String name,
    [XmlContainerConfig config])
```

Python

```
XmlManager.openContainer([txn,] name, [flags,] [type,] [mode])
```

Perl

```
my $container = $manager->openContainer([$txn,] $name [, $flags]);
```

PHP

```
$container = $manager->openContainer([$txn,] $name [, $flags]);
```

XmlManager::prepare

Compiles an XQuery expression into an XmlQueryExpression object. The XQuery expression can then be executed repeatedly by using XmlQueryExpression::execute.

Use this method to compile and evaluate XQuery expressions against your XmlContainer and XmlDocument objects any time you want to evaluate the expression more than once.

C++

```
XmlQueryExpression XmlManager::prepare(const std::string &xquery,
    XmlQueryContext &context)

XmlQueryExpression XmlManager::prepare(XmlTransaction &txn,
    const std::string &xquery, XmlQueryContext &context)
```

Java

```
public XmlQueryExpression prepare([XmlTransaction txn,] String query,
    XmlQueryContext context)
```

Python

```
XmlManager.prepare([txn,] xquery, context)
```

Perl

```
my $queryExpression = $manager->prepare([$txn,] $xquery, $context);
```

PHP

```
$queryExpression = $manager->prepare([$txn,] $xquery [, $context]);
```

XmlManager::query

Executes a query in the context of the XmlManager object. This method is the equivalent of calling XmlManager::prepare and then XmlQueryExpression::execute on the prepared query.

Parameters

txn

If the operation is to be transaction-protected, the txn parameter is an XmlTransaction handle returned from XmlManager::createTransaction.

xquery

The XQuery query string.

context

The XmlQueryContext to use for this query.

flags

This parameter must be set to 0 or by bitwise inclusively OR•ing together one or more of the following values:

Flag	Description
DBXML_LAZY_DOCS	Returns document content and/or metadata as needed; not retrieved (into memory) automatically at query time.
DB_DEGREE_2	Ensures that the query will have "degree 2 isolation", meaning that previously read data items can be deleted or modified by other transactions during the transactions lifespan. Renamed to DB_READ_UNCOMMITTED in Berkeley DB 4.4 and later.
DB_DIRTY_READ	Ensures that the query will have "degree 1 isolation", meaning that read data items can include data modified by other transactions, although not yet committed. Must be specified when the underlying container was opened. Renamed to DB_READ_UNCOMMITTED in Berkeley DB 4.4 and later.
DB_RMW	Forces the query to acquire a write lock instead of a read lock. This eliminates deadlock during a read-modify-write cycle by acquiring the write lock early, preventing a concurrent read-modify-write cycle from deadlocking.

C++

```
XmlResults XmlManager::query(const std::string &xquery,
    XmlQueryContext &context, u_int32_t flags = 0)

XmlResults XmlManager::query(XmlTransaction &txn,
    const std::string &xquery, XmlQueryContext &context, u_int32_t flags = 0)
```

Java

```
public XmlResults query([XmlTransaction txn,] String query, XmlQueryContext context,
    [XmlDocumentConfig config])
```

Python

```
XmlManager.query([txn,] xquery, context, flags=0)
```

Perl

```
my $results = $manager->query([$txn,] $xquery, $context, $flags);
```

PHP

```
$results = $manager->query([$txn,] $xquery [, $context] [, $flags]);
```

XmlManager::reindexContainer

Reindexes an entire container. The container should be backed up prior to using this method because it destroys existing indexes before reindexing. If the operation fails, and your container is not backed up, you might lose information.

Use this call to change the type of indexing used for a container between document-level indexes and node-level indexes. Depending on the size of the container, this method can take a very long time to execute and should not be used casually.

C++

```
void XmlManager::reindexContainer(
    const std::string &name, XmlUpdateContext &context, u_int32_t flags = 0)

void XmlManager::reindexContainer(
    XmlTransaction &txn, const std::string &name,
    XmlUpdateContext &context, u_int32_t flags = 0)
```

Java

```
public void reindexContainer([XmlTransaction txn,] String name,
    XmlUpdateContext context, [XmlContainerConfig config])
```

Python

```
XmlManager.reindexContainer([txn,] name, context, flags=0)
```

Perl

```
$manager->reindexContainer([$txn,] $name, $context, $flags);
```

PHP

This method is not supported by the PHP API.

XmlManager::removeContainer

The XmlManager::removeContainer method removes the underlying file for the container from the file system. The container must be closed and must have been opened at least once.

Parameters

txn

If the operation is to be transaction-protected, the txn parameter is an XmlTransaction handle returned from XmlManager::createTransaction.

name

The name of the container to be removed.

C++

```
void XmlManager::removeContainer(XmlTransaction &txn, const std::string &name)
```

Java

```
public void removeContainer([XmlTransaction txn,] String name)
```

Python

```
XmlManager.removeContainer([txn,] name)
```

Perl

```
$manager->removeContainer([$txn,] $name);
```

PHP

```
$manager->removeContainer([$txn,] $name);
```

XmlManager::renameContainer

The XmlManager::renameContainer method renames the container's underlying file. The container must be closed and must have been opened at least once.

Parameters

txn

If the operation is to be transaction-protected, the txn parameter is an XmlTransaction handle returned from XmlManager::createTransaction.

oldName

The name of the container whose name you want to change.

newName

The new container name.

C++

```
void XmlManager::renameContainer(XmlTransaction &txn, const std::string
    &oldName, const std::string &newName)
```

Java

```
public void renameContainer([XmlTransaction txn,] String oldName, String newName)
```

Python

```
XmlManager.renameContainer([txn,] oldName, newName)
```

Perl

```
$manager->renameContainer([$txn,] $oldName, $newName);
```

PHP

```
$manager->renameContainer([$txn,] $oldName, $newName);
```

XmlManager::setDefaultContainerFlags

Sets the default flags used for containers opened and created by this XmlManager object. If a form of XmlManager::createContainer or XmlManager::openContainer is used that takes a flags argument, the settings provided using this method are ignored. Each API provides a corresponding getDefaultContainerFlags method.

C++

```
void XmlManager::setDefaultContainerFlags(u_int32_t flags)
u_int32_t XmlManager::getDefaultContainerFlags()
```

Java

```
public void setDefaultContainerConfig(XmlContainerConfig config)
```

Python

```
XmlManager.setDefaultContainerFlags(flags)
```

Perl

```
$manager->setDefaultContainerFlags($flags);
```

PHP

```
$manager->setDefaultContainerFlags($flags);
```

XmlManager::setDefaultContainerType

Sets the default type used for containers opened and created by this XmlManager object. If a form of XmlManager::createContainer or XmlManager::openContainer is used that takes a type argument, the settings provided using this method are ignored. Each API provides an accompanying method: getDefaultContainerType.

C++

```
void XmlManager::setDefaultContainerType(XmlContainer::ContainerType type)
XmlContainer::ContainerType XmlManager::getDefaultContainerType()
```

Java

```
public void setDefaultContainerType(int type)
```

Python

```
XmlManager.setDefaultContainerType(type)
```

Perl

```
$manager->setDefaultContainerType($type);
```

PHP

```
$manager->setDefaultContainerType($type);
```

XmlManager::setDefaultPageSize

The XmlManager::setDefaultPageSize method sets the size of the pages used to store documents in the database. The size is specified in bytes in the range 512 bytes to 64 KB. The system selects a page size based on the underlying file system input/output (I/O) block size if one is not explicitly set by the application. The default page size has a lower limit of 512 bytes and an upper limit of 16 KB. Documents that are larger than a single page are stored on multiple pages. This method has no effect on existing containers.

Parameters

pagesize

The page size in bytes.

C++

```
void XmlManager::setDefaultPageSize(u_int32_t pageSize)
u_int32_t XmlManager::getDefaultPageSize()
```

Java

```
public void setDefaultPageSize(int pageSize)
```

Python

```
XmlManager.setDefaultPageSize(pageSize)
```

Perl

```
$manager->setDefaultPageSize($pagesize);
```

PHP

```
$manager->setDefaultPageSize($pagesize);
```

XmlManager::setLogCategory

Most APIs use this method as an alias for the C++ DbXml::setLogCategory. See its reference entry for details.

XmlManager.setLogLevel

This is an alias for the DbXml::setLogLevel method of the C++ API. See its reference entry for details.

XmlManager::upgradeContainer

Upgrades the container from a previous version of Berkeley DB XML or Berkeley DB to the current version. A Berkeley DB upgrade is first performed using the Db::upgrade method and then the Berkeley DB XML container is upgraded. If no upgrade is needed, no changes are made. Container upgrades are done in place and are destructive. For example, if pages need to be allocated, and no disk space is available, the container might be left corrupted. Backups should be made before containers are upgraded. The container must be closed.

Parameters

name

The name of the container to be upgraded.

context

The XmlUpdateContext object to be used for this operation.

C++

```
void XmlManager::upgradeContainer(const std::string &name, XmlUpdateContext &context)
```

Java

```
public void upgradeContainer(String name, XmlUpdateContext context)
```

Python

```
XmlManager.upgradeContainer(name, context)
```

Perl

```
$manager->upgradeContainer($name, $context);
```

PHP

```
$manager->upgradeContainer($name [, $context]);
```

XmlManager::verifyContainer

Checks to see that the container data files are not corrupt, and optionally writes the salvaged container data to the specified output stream. The container must be closed and must have been opened at least once.

Parameters

name

The name of the container to be verified.

out

The stream to which the salvaged container data is to be dumped.

flags

Must be set to 0, DB_SALVAGE, or DB_SALVAGE and DB_AGGRESSIVE. Please refer to the Berkeley DB reference manual for a full discussion of these values.

C++

```
void XmlManager::verifyContainer(const std::string &name, std::ostream *out,
    u_int32_t flags)
```

Java

```
public void verifyContainer(String name, String out, [VerifyConfig config])
```

Python

```
XmlManager.verifyContainer(name, out, flags)
```

Perl

```
$manager->verifyContainer($name, $out, $flags);
```

PHP

The PHP API does not provide this method.

XmlManagerConfig

This Java-only class is used to configure XmlManager objects in place of most APIs• bitwise OR•d flags. It provides corresponding get methods for each set method.

XmlManagerConfig.setAdoptEnvironment

Sets whether the XmlManager object will automatically close the environment handle at the end of the XmlManager life.

Java

```
public XmlManagerConfig setAdoptEnvironment(boolean value)
```

XmlManagerConfig.setAllowExternalAccess

Allows queries to access data sources external to a container, such as files on disk or network.

Java

```
public XmlManagerConfig setAllowExternalAccess(boolean value)
```

XmlManagerConfig.setAllowAutoOpen

Enables unopened containers to be automatically opened when queries reference them.

Java

```
public XmlManagerConfig setAllowAutoOpen(boolean value)
```

XmlMetaDataIterator

This class provides a simple iterator of the metadata for a document. Metadata is set on a document with XmlDocument::setMetaData. You can also use XmlDocument::getMetaData to return a specific metadata item. This object is instantiated using XmlDocument::getMetaDataIterator.

XmlMetaDataIterator::next

Returns the next item in the XmlDocument's metadata list. If there is no next item, this method returns false. Otherwise, it returns true.

C++

```
bool XmlMetaDataIterator::next(std::string &uri, std::string &name, XmlValue &value)
```

Java

```
public XmlMetaData next()
```

Python

```
XmlMetaDataIterator.next(uri, name, value)
```

Perl

```
$metadataIterator->next($uri, $name, $value);
```

PHP

This method is not supported by the PHP API.

XmlMetaDataIterator::reset

Sets the iterator to the beginning of the XmlDocument's metadata list.

C++

```
void XmlMetaDataIterator::reset()
```

Java

```
public void reset()
```

Python

```
XmlMetaDataIterator.reset()
```

Perl

```
$metadataIterator->reset();
```

PHP

This method is not supported by the PHP API.

XmlModify

The XmlModify class enables one or more documents to be modified in place. An object of this class provides methods to specify a series of changes to a document. The object is then executed and the steps performed in the order specified on one or many documents. The document set can be the result of an XQuery query. XmlModify objects are created using XmlManager::createModify.

XmlModify::addAppendStep

Appends the provided data to the selected node's child nodes. If the operation's target is an attribute node or the document root node, an exception is thrown at modification execution time.

If the content to be added is an attribute, the content is added to the targeted node's attribute list. If the content to add is an element node, text, comment, or processing instruction, its content is added immediately after the targeted node's last child node unless the location parameter is specified.

C++

```
void XmlModify::addAppendStep(const XmlQueryExpression &selectionExpr,
    XmlObject type, const std::string &name, const std::string &content,
    int location = -1)
```

Java

```
public void addAppendStep(XmlQueryExpression selectionExpr, int type, String name,
    String content)
```

Python

```
XmlModify.addAppendStep(selectionExpr, type, name, content)
```

Perl

```
$modify->addAppendStep($selectionExpr, $type, $name, $content [, $location]);
```

PHP

```
$modify->addAppendStep($selectionExpr, $type, $name, $content [, $location]);
```

XmlModify::addInsertAfterStep

Inserts the provided data into the document after the selected node. If the operation's target is an attribute node or the document root node, an exception is thrown at modification execution time.

   If the content to be added is an attribute, the content is added to the targeted node's parent node. For any other type of content, the content is inserted into the document immediately after the targeted node's end tag as its next sibling.

C++

```
void XmlModify::addInsertAfterStep(const XmlQueryExpression &selectionExpr,
    XmlObject type, const std::string &name, const std::string &content)
```

Java

```
public void addInsertAfterStep(XmlQueryExpression selectionExpr, int type,
    String name, String content)
```

Python

```
XmlModify.addInsertAfterStep(selectionExpr, type, name, content)
```

Perl

```
$modify->addInsertAfterStep($selectionExpr, $type, $name, $content);
```

PHP

```
$modify->addInsertAfterStep($selectionExpr, $type, $name, $content);
```

XmlModify::addInsertBeforeStep

Inserts the provided data into the document before the selected node as a previous sibling. If the operations target is an attribute node or the document root node, an exception is thrown at modification execution time.

    If the content to be added is an attribute, the content is added to the targeted nodes parent node. For any other type of content, the content is inserted into the document immediately before the targeted nodes start tag.

C++

```
void XmlModify::addInsertBeforeStep(const XmlQueryExpression &selectionExpr,
    XmlObject type, const std::string &name, const std::string &content)
```

Java

```
public void addInsertBeforeStep(XmlQueryExpression selectionExpr, int type,
    String name, String content)
```

Python

```
XmlModify.addInsertBeforeStep(selectionExpr, type, name, content)
```

Perl

```
$modify->addInsertBeforeStep($selectionExpr, $type, $name, $content);
```

PHP

```
$modify->addInsertBeforeStep($selectionExpr, $type, $name, $content);
```

XmlModify::addRemoveStep

Removes the node targeted by the selection expression. If the operations target is the document root node, an exception is thrown at modification execution time.

C++

```
void XmlModify::addRemoveStep(const XmlQueryExpression &selectionExpr)
```

Java

```
public void addRemoveStep(XmlQueryExpression selectionExpr)
```

Python

```
XmlModify.addRemoveStep(selectionExpr)
```

Perl

```
$modify->addRemoveStep($selectionExpr);
```

PHP

```
$modify->addRemoveStep($selectionExpr);
```

XmlModify::addRenameStep

Renames an element node, attribute node, or processing instruction. If the document content targeted by selectionExpr is any other type of content, an exception is thrown at modification execution time.

C++

```
void XmlModify::addRenameStep(const XmlQueryExpression &selectionExpr,
    const std::string &newName)
```

Java

```
public void addRenameStep(XmlQueryExpression selectionExpr, String newName)
```

Python

```
XmlModify.addRenameStep(selectionExpr, newName)
```

Perl

```
$modify->addRenameStep($selectionExpr, $newName);
```

PHP

```
$modify->addRenameStep($selectionExpr, $newName);
```

XmlModify::addUpdateStep

Replaces the targeted node's content with text. If the targeted node is an element node, all the element node's children and text nodes are replaced with text. If the targeted node is an attribute node, the attribute's value is replaced by text. The purpose of this interface is primarily to replace text content. Note that text is treated as a text node. If it contains markup, that markup is escaped to make it legal text.

C++

```
void XmlModify::addUpdateStep(const XmlQueryExpression &selectionExpr,
    const std::string &text)
```

Java

```
public void addUpdateStep(XmlQueryExpression selectionExpr, String text)
```

Python

```
XmlModify.addUpdateStep(selectionExpr, text)
```

Perl

```
$modify->addUpdateStep($selectionExpr, $content);
```

PHP

```
$modify->addUpdateStep($selectionExpr, $content);
```

XmlModify::execute

Executes one or more document modification operations (or steps) against an XmlResults or XmlValue object. Upon completing the modification, the modified document is optionally updated in the backing XmlContainer for you. Returns the number of nodes modified.

If the XmlUpdateContext object state is set to apply changes to the backing container (the default), modifications are automatically written back to the container. This state is controlled by using XmlUpdateContext::setApplyChangesToContainers.

Note that the modification steps are executed in the order in which they were specified to this object. Modification steps are specified using XmlModify::add*Step methods.

See the BDB XML documentation for details on the variant uses of this method.

Parameters

txn

If the operation is to be transaction-protected, the txn parameter is an XmlTransaction handle returned from XmlManager::createTransaction.

toModify

The `XmlValue` or `XmlResults` object to modify using this collection of modification steps from the current position in the result set.

context

The `XmlQueryContext` to use for this modification.

uc

The `XmlUpdateContext` to use for this modification.

C++

```
unsigned int XmlModify::execute(XmlValue &toModify,
    XmlQueryContext &context, XmlUpdateContext &uc) const

unsigned int XmlModify::execute(XmlResults &toModify,
    XmlQueryContext &context, XmlUpdateContext &uc) const

unsigned int XmlModify::execute(XmlTransaction &txn,
    XmlValue &toModify, XmlQueryContext &context, XmlUpdateContext &uc) const

unsigned int XmlModify::execute(XmlTransaction &txn,
    XmlResults &toModify, XmlQueryContext &context, XmlUpdateContext &uc) const
```

Java

```
public void execute([XmlTransaction txn,] XmlResults toModify,
    XmlQueryContext context, XmlUpdateContext uc)
```

Python

```
XmlModify.execute([txn,] toModify, context, uc)
```

Perl

```
$modify->execute([$txn,] $toModify, $context, $uc);
```

PHP

```
$modify->execute([$txn,] $toModify, $context [, $uc]);
```

XmlQueryContext

This class encapsulates the context within which a query is performed against a container, including namespace mappings, variable bindings, and flags that indicate how the query result set should be determined and returned.

XmlQueryContext objects are instantiated using XmlManager::createQueryContext. XmlQueryContext enables you to define whether queries executed within the context are to be evaluated lazily or eagerly, and whether the query is to return live or dead values. For detailed descriptions of these parameters, see XmlQueryContext::setReturnType and XmlQueryContext::setEvaluationType. Note that these values are also set when you create a query context using XmlManager::createQueryContext.

XmlQueryContext::clearNamespaces

The XmlQueryContext::clearNamespaces method removes all namespace mappings from the query context.

C++

```
void XmlQueryContext::clearNamespaces()
```

Java

```
public void clearNamespaces()
```

Python

```
XmlQueryContext.clearNamespaces()
```

Perl

```
$queryContext->clearNamespaces();
```

PHP

```
$queryContext->clearNamespaces;
```

XmlQueryContext::removeNamespace

The XmlQueryContext::removeNamespace method removes the namespace prefix to URI mapping for the specified prefix. A call to this method with a prefix that has no existing mapping is ignored.

C++

```
void XmlQueryContext::removeNamespace(const std::string &prefix)
```

Java

```
public void removeNamespaces(String prefix)
```

Python

```
XmlQueryContext.removeNamespace(prefix)
```

Perl

```
$queryContext->removeNamespace($prefix);
```

PHP

```
$queryContext->removeNamespace($prefix);
```

XmlQueryContext::setDefaultCollection

Sets the default collection to be used when `fn:collection()` is called without any arguments in an XQuery expression. You can discover the name of the default collection used by `fn:collection()` with no arguments in an XQuery expression. Returns the URI of the default collection.

Parameters

uri

A URI specifying the name of the collection.

C++

```
void XmlQueryContext::setDefaultCollection(const std::string &uri)
std::string XmlQueryContext::getDefaultCollection() const
```

Java

```
public void setDefaultCollection(String uri)
```

Python

```
$queryContext->setDefaultCollection($uri);
```

Perl

```
$queryContext->setDefaultCollection($uri);
```

PHP

```
$queryContext->setDefaultCollection($uri);
```

XmlQueryContext::setNamespace

Maps the specified URI to the specified namespace prefix. Each API provides a corresponding getNamespace method.

Parameters

prefix

The namespace prefix.

uri

The namespace URI.

C++

```
void XmlQueryContext::setNamespace(const std::string &prefix, const std::string &uri);
std::string XmlQueryContext::getNamespace(const std::string &prefix)
```

Java

```
public void setNamespace(String prefix, String uri)
```

Python

```
XmlQueryContext.setNamespace(prefix, uri)
```

Perl

```
$queryContext->setNamespace($prefix, $uri);
```

PHP

```
$queryContext->setNamespace($prefix, $uri);
```

XmlQueryContext::setBaseURI

Sets/gets the base URI used for relative paths in query expressions. For example, a base URI of file:///export/expression and a relative path of ../another/expression resolve to file:///export/another/expression.

Parameters

baseURI

The base URI as a string.

C++

```
void XmlQueryContext::setBaseURI(const std::string &baseURI)
std::string XmlQueryContext::getBaseURI()
```

Java

```
public void setBaseURI(String baseURI)
```

Python

```
XmlQueryContext.setBaseURI(baseURI)
```

Perl

```
$queryContext->setBaseURI($string);
```

PHP

```
$queryContext->setBaseURI($string);
```

XmlQueryContext::setEvaluationType

Enables the application to set the query evaluation type to eager or lazy. Eager evaluation means that the whole query is executed and its resultant values derived and stored in memory before evaluation of the query is completed. Lazy evaluation means that minimal processing is performed before the query is completed, and the remaining processing is deferred until the result set is enumerated. As each call to XmlResults::next is called, the next resultant value is determined. Each API provides a corresponding getEvaluationType method.

Parameters

type

The evaluation type must be specified as either of the following:

Type	Description
XmlQueryContext::Eager	The query is executed with resulting values determined and stored in memory before the query returns. This is the default.
XmlQueryContext::Lazy	The values resulting from a query are not determined or stored in memory until the API refers to them by iterating the result set. This means that a query uses less time and processing.

C++

```
void XmlQueryContext::setEvaluationType(EvaluationType type)
EvaluationType XmlQueryContext::getEvaluationType()
```

Java

```
public void setEvaluationType(int type)
```

Python

```
XmlQueryContext.setEvaluationType(type)
```

Perl

```
$queryContext->setEvaluationType($type);
```

PHP

```
$queryContext->setEvaluationType($type);
```

XmlQueryContext::setReturnType

The XmlQueryContext::setReturnType method enables the application to define whether the query should return live or dead document values. Each API provides an accompanying getReturnType method.

Parameters

type

The type parameter specifies which documents or values to return and must be set to one of the following values:

Type	Description
XmlQueryContext::LiveValues	Query results are a reference to the data within the database.
XmlQueryContext::DeadValues	Query results are a copy of the data from the database.

C++

```
void XmlQueryContext::setReturnType(ReturnType type)
ReturnType XmlQueryContext::getReturnType()
```

Java

```
public void setReturnType(int type)
```

Python

```
XmlQueryContext.setReturnType(type)
```

Perl

```
$queryContext->setReturnType($type);
```

PHP

```
$queryContext->setReturnType($type);
```

XmlQueryContext::setVariableValue

Creates an externally declared XQuery variable by binding the specified value or sequence of values to the specified variable name. The XmlQueryContext::setVariableValue method can be called at any time during the life of the application. Each API provides a corresponding getVariableValue method.

Parameters

name

The name of the variable to bind. Within the XQuery query, the variable can be referenced by using the normal $name syntax.

value

The value to bind to the named variable. If value is an XmlResults object, a sequence of values is bound to the variable.

C++

```
void XmlQueryContext::setVariableValue(const std::string &name,
    const XmlValue &value)
bool XmlQueryContext::getVariableValue(const std::string &name, XmlValue &value)
void XmlQueryContext::setVariableValue(const std::string &name,
    const XmlResults &value)
bool XmlQueryContext::getVariableValue(const std::string &name, XmlResults &value)
```

Java

```
public void setVariableValue(String name, XmlValue value)
```

Python

```
XmlQueryContext.setVariableValue(name, value)
```

Perl

```
$queryContext->setVariableValue($name, $value);
```

PHP

```
$queryContext->setVariableValue($name, $value);
```

XmlQueryExpression

An XmlQueryExpression represents a parsed XQuery expression, enabling the cost of query parsing and optimization to be amortized over many evaluations. An XmlQueryExpression is created by a call to XmlManager::prepare.

XmlQueryExpression::execute

Evaluates (runs) an XQuery query that was previously prepared by XmlManager::prepare and returns an XmlResults set.

There are two basic forms of this method: one that takes an XmlValue object and another that does not. For methods that do not take an XmlValue, the XQuery must restrict the scope of the query by using either the collection() or the doc() XQuery navigation functions, or else an exception is thrown. For those forms of this method that take an XmlValue, the query is applied against that object.

Parameters

txn

If the operation is to be transaction-protected, the txn parameter is an XmlTransaction handle returned from XmlManager::createTransaction.

queryContext

The XmlQueryContext to use for this evaluation.

contextItem

The XmlValue object to perform the query against.

flags

This parameter must be set to 0 or by bitwise inclusively OR•ing together one or more of the following values:

Flag	Description
DBXML_LAZY_DOCS	Retrieves the document lazily. That is, it retrieves document content and document metadata only on an as-needed basis when reading the document.
DB_DIRTY_READ	This operation supports "degree 1 isolation"; that is, read operations can return data that has been modified by other transactions but has not yet been committed. Silently ignored if the DB_DIRTY_READ flag was not specified when the underlying container was opened. This flag is renamed to DB_READ_UNCOMMITTED in Berkeley DB 4.4 and later.
DB_DEGREE_2	This operation has "degree 2 isolation". It provides for cursor stability but not repeatable reads. Data items that have been previously read by this transaction can be deleted or modified by other transactions before this transaction completes. Silently ignored if the DB_DEGREE_2 flag was not specified when the underlying container was opened. This flag is renamed to DB_READ_COMMITTED in Berkeley DB 4.4 and later.
DB_RMW	Acquires write locks instead of read locks when doing the retrieval. Setting this flag can eliminate deadlock during a read-modify-write cycle by acquiring the write lock during the read part of the cycle so that another thread of control acquiring a read lock for the same item, in its own read-modify-write cycle, will not result in deadlock.

C++

```
XmlResults XmlQueryExpression::execute(XmlQueryContext &queryContext,
    u_int32_t flags = 0)
XmlResults XmlQueryExpression::execute(const XmlValue &contextItem,
    XmlQueryContext &queryContext, u_int32_t flags = 0)
XmlResults XmlQueryExpression::execute(XmlTransaction &txn,
    XmlQueryContext &queryContext, u_int32_t flags = 0)
XmlResults XmlQueryExpression::execute(XmlTransaction &txn,
    const XmlValue &contextItem,
    XmlQueryContext &queryContext, u_int32_t flags = 0)
```

Java

```
public XmlResults execute([XmlTransaction txn,] [XmlValue contextItem,]
    XmlQueryContext queryContext, [XmlDocumentConfig config])
```

Python

```
XmlQueryExpression.execute([txn,] [contextItem,] queryContext, flags=0)
```

Perl

```
$expression->execute([$txn,] [$contextItem,] $context [, $flags]);
```

PHP

```
$expression->execute([$txn,] [$contextItem,] $context [, $flags]);
```

XmlQueryExpression::getQuery

Returns the query as a string.

C++

```
std::string XmlQueryExpression::getQuery() const
```

Java

```
public String getQuery()
```

Python

```
XmlQueryExpression.getQuery()
```

Perl

```
my $query = $expression->getQuery();
```

PHP

```
$query = $expression->getQuery();
```

XmlQueryExpression::getQueryPlan

Returns the query plan for the expression as a string.

C++

```
std:string XmlQueryExpression::getQueryPlan() const
```

Java

```
public String getQueryPlan()
```

Python

```
XmlQueryExpression.getQueryPlan()
```

Perl

```
my $plan = $expression->getQueryPlan();
```

PHP

```
$plan = $expression->getQueryPlan();
```

XmlResults

The XmlResults class encapsulates the results of a query or other lookup operation as a collection of XmlValue objects.

An XmlResults object is created by executing a query or calling XmlIndexLookup::execute. A query is performed in several ways: XmlManager::query can be used for one-shot queries, and XmlManager::prepare can be used to create an XmlQueryExpression object for use in repeated queries. The class provides an iteration interface through the XmlResults::next method.

XmlResults::add

Adds the specified XmlValue to the end of the result set. Note that if the XmlResults object was created as the result of a lazy evaluation, this method throws an exception. This method is used primarily for application resolution of collections in queries (see XmlResolver and XmlManager::createResults).

C++

```
void XmlResults::add(const XmlValue &value)
```

Java

```
public void add(XmlValue value)
```

Python

```
XmlResults.add(value)
```

Perl

```
$results->add($value);
```

PHP

The PHP interface does not support this method.

XmlResults::hasNext

Returns true if there is another element in the result set.

C++

```
bool XmlResults::hasNext()
```

Java

```
public boolean hasNext()
```

Python

```
XmlResults.hasNext()
```

Perl

```
my $bool = $results->hasNext();
```

PHP

```
$bool = $results->hasNext();
```

XmlResults::hasPrevious

Returns true if there is a previous element in the result set.

C++

```
bool XmlResults::hasPrevious()
```

Java

```
public boolean hasPrevious()
```

Python

```
XmlResults.hasPrevious()
```

Perl

```
my $bool = $results->hasPrevious();
```

PHP

```
$bool = $results->hasPrevious();
```

XmlResults::next

Retrieves (and returns, for some APIs) the next value in the result set. When no more values remain in the result set, the XmlResults::next method returns false.

Parameters

value

The XmlValue into which the previous value in the result set is to be placed.

document

The XmlDocument into which the previous document in the result set is to be placed.

C++

```
bool XmlResults::next(XmlValue &value)
bool XmlResults::next(XmlDocument &document)
```

Java

```
public XmlValue next()
```

Python

```
XmlResults.next(value)
XmlResults.next(document)
```

Perl

```
my $value = new XmlValue;
$results->next($value);

my $value = new XmlValue ;
while ($results->next($value)) { ... }
```

PHP

```
$value = $results->next();
while ($results->hasNext()) { ... }
```

XmlResults::peek

Retrieves (and returns, for some APIs) the current element in the result set without moving the internal iterator. If the provided object is successfully populated, this method returns true; otherwise, false is returned.

C++

```
bool XmlResults::peek(XmlValue &value)
bool XmlResults::peek(XmlDocument &document)
```

Java

```
public XmlValue peek()
```

Python

```
XmlResults.peek(value)
XmlResults.peek(document)
```

Perl

```
$results->peek($xmlvalue);
```

```
$results->peek($document);
```

PHP

```
$value = $results->peek($xmlvalue);
```

XmlResults::previous

Retrieves the previous value in the result set (and returns it, in the case of some APIs). When the first value in the result set has been reached, the XmlResults::previous method returns false. This method does not work for lazily evaluated results.

C++

```
bool XmlResults::previous(XmlValue &value)
bool XmlResults::previous(XmlDocument &document)
```

Java

```
public XmlValue previous()
```

Python

```
XmlResults.previous(value)
XmlResults.previous(document)
```

Perl

```
$results->previous($value);
```

PHP

```
$value = $results->previous();
```

XmlResults::reset

If a query was processed with eager evaluation, a call to the XmlResults::reset method resets the result set iterator, so that a subsequent call to XmlResults::next method returns the first value in the result set. If the query was processed with lazy evaluation, a call to XmlResults::reset method throws an exception.

C++

```
void XmlResults::reset()
```

Java

```
public void reset()
```

Python

```
XmlResults.reset()
```

Perl

```
$results->reset();
```

PHP

```
$results->reset();
```

XmlResults::size

If a query was processed with eager evaluation, a call to the XmlResults::size method returns
the number of values in the result set. If the query was processed with lazy evaluation, a call to
XmlResults::size throws an exception.

C++

```
size_t XmlResults::size()
```

Java

```
public int size()
```

Python

```
XmlResults.size()
```

Perl

```
my $size = $results->size();
```

PHP

```
$size = $results->size();
```

XmlStatistics

This class provides access to statistics for keys in a given index. Statistics are available for the total
number of keys currently in use by the specified index, as well as the total number of unique keys in
use by the index. The number of keys maintained for an index is a function of the number and size
of documents stored in the container, as well as of the type of index being examined.

XmlStatistics objects are instantiated by XmlContainer::lookupStatistics.

XmlStatistics::getNumberOfIndexedKeys

Returns the total number of keys contained by the index for which statistics are being reported.

C++

```
double XmlStatistics::getNumberOfIndexedKeys() const
```

Java

```
public double getNumberOfIndexedKeys()
```

Python

```
XmlStatistics.getNumberOfIndexedKeys()
```

Perl

```
my $numkeys = $statistics->getNumberOfIndexKeys();
```

PHP

```
$numkeys = $statistics->getNumberOfIndexKeys();
```

XmlStatistics::getNumberOfUniqueKeys

Returns the number of unique keys contained in the index for which statistics are being reported. Keys do not equate to documents; there are likely to be many more keys than unique keys in the index because a given key can appear multiple times   once for each document feature on each document that it is referencing.

C++

```
double XmlStatistics::getNumberOfUniqueKeys() const
```

Java

```
public double getNumberOfUniqueKeys()
```

Python

```
XmlStatistics.getNumberOfUniqueKeys()
```

Perl

```
my $numkeys = $statistics->getNumberOfUniqueKeys();
```

PHP

```
$numkeys = $statistics->getNumberOfUniqueKeys();
```

XmlTransaction

This class provides a transaction handle, encapsulating a Berkeley DB DbTxn object. Methods of the XmlTransaction class are used to abort and commit the transaction. XmlTransaction handles are provided to XmlContainer, XmlManager, and other objects that query and modify documents and containers to transactionally protect those database operations. XmlTransaction objects that go out of scope (or are otherwise deleted) without a commit or abort are implicitly aborted.

XmlTransaction objects are instantiated using XmlManager::createTransaction.

XmlTransaction::abort

Causes an abnormal termination of the transaction. All write operations previously performed within the scope of the transaction are undone. Before this method returns, any locks held by the transaction will have been released. In the case of nested transactions, aborting a parent transaction causes all children (unresolved or not) of the parent transaction to be aborted. The handle cannot be accessed again after an abort, regardless of its return.

C++

```
void XmlTransaction::abort()
```

Java

```
public void abort()
```

Python

```
XmlTransaction.abort()
```

Perl

```
$txn->abort();
```

PHP

```
$txn->abort();
```

XmlTransaction::commit

Ends the transaction. Container and document modifications made within the scope of the transaction are by default written to stable storage. The handle cannot be accessed after a commit, regardless of its return. If the operation encounters an error, the transaction and all child transactions are aborted.

Parameters

flags

This parameter must be set to 0 or to one of the following values:

Flag	Description
DB_TXN_NOSYNC	Does not synchronously flush the log. The transaction exhibits the atomicity, consistency, and isolation (ACI) properties, but not durability (D). Database integrity is maintained, but this transaction can be undone during recovery.
DB_TXN_SYNC	Synchronously flushes the log. The transaction exhibits all the ACID properties. This is the default.

C++

```
void XmlTransaction::commit(u_int32_t flags = 0)
```

Java

```
public void commit()
```

Python

```
XmlTransaction.commit(flags=0)
```

Perl

```
$txn->commit([$flags]);
```

PHP

```
$txn->commit();
```

XmlTransaction::createChild

The XmlTransaction::createChild method creates a child transaction of this transaction. Although this child transaction is active (has been neither committed nor aborted), the parent transaction cannot issue any operations except for XmlTransaction::commit or XmlTransaction::abort.

C++

```
XmlTransaction XmlTransaction::createChild(u_int32_t flags = 0)
```

Java

The Java API does not support this method.

Python

```
XmlTransaction.createChild(flags=0)
```

Perl

```
my $txn2 = $txn->createChild([$flags]);
```

PHP

The PHP API does not support this method.

XmlTransaction::getDbTxn

The XmlTransaction::getDbTxn method returns a pointer to the DbTxn object encapsulated by this XmlTransaction.

C++

```
DbTxn *XmlTransaction::getDbTxn()
```

Java

```
public Transaction getTransaction()
```

Python

```
XmlTransaction.getDbTxn()
```

Perl

```
$dbtxn = $txn->getDbTxn();
```

PHP

This method is not yet supported by the PHP API.

XmlUpdateContext

This class encapsulates the context data used by update operations performed against a container. XmlUpdateContext objects are instantiated using XmlManager::createUpdateContext.

XmlUpdateContext::setApplyChangesToContainers

This setting controls whether modifications made during an update caused by `XmlModify::execute` are written to the corresponding `XmlContainer`. When `true` (the default), changes are written to the container. This allows modifications to be grouped before being written, as well as modifications that are not written to a container at all.

C++

```
void XmlUpdateContext::setApplyChangesToContainers(bool applyChanges)
bool XmlUpdateContext::getApplyChangesToContainers()
```

Java

```
public void setApplyChangesToContainers(boolean applyChanges)
```

Python

```
XmlUpdateContext.setApplyChangesToContainers([applyChanges])
```

Perl

```
$context->setApplyChangesToContainers($bool);
```

PHP

```
$context->setApplyChangesToContainers($bool);
```

XmlValue

`XmlValue` is a broad value class, storing the value of a node in an XML document. Because the class encapsulates many value types, methods enable testing and conversion of data types. The class also provides some DOM-like navigation methods for retrieving subsequent values from nodes.

The value type returned by the constructor (`XmlValue::Type`) is determined by the type of value passed (`STRING` for `std::string` or `const char*`, `BOOLEAN` for `bool`, and so on) as well as an `XmlDocument`.

The `XmlValue::is*` methods permit type tests, whereas `XmlValue::as*` methods allow type conversion. For `XmlValue::Type` of `NODE`, `XmlValue::get*` methods permit retrieval of node names; values, namespace URIs and prefixes; and parent, child, and sibling nodes.

Parameters

value

The value for the `XmlValue` object.

document

An XmlDocument object to be used as the value.

type

Any of the XmlValue types. They are listed as follows, and most correspond to the XML schema data types (several are added by XQuery):

Data Type	Description
XmlValue::NONE	No type.
XmlValue::NODE	A general node type.
XmlValue::ANY_SIMPLE_TYPE	Any of the primitive datatypes.
XmlValue::ANY_URI	An absolute or relative URI.
XmlValue::BASE_64_BINARY	Base 64_encoded binary data.
XmlValue::BINARY	Binary data.
XmlValue::BOOLEAN	An XML schema boolean value.
XmlValue::DATE	A date in dateTime format (ISO 8601), specifying a day (without a time of day).
XmlValue::DATE_TIME	A dateTime value.
XmlValue::DAY_TIME_DURATION	A time duration in PnYnMnDTnHnMnS format (ISO 8601).
XmlValue::DECIMAL	A decimal number (arbitrary precision); this is the primitive number type within BDB XML.
XmlValue::DOUBLE	A 64-bit float.
XmlValue::DURATION	A duration value, either of dates or times.
XmlValue::FLOAT	A 32-bit float.
XmlValue::G_DAY	A recurring Gregorian day value, such as "5th of the month," in the ---DD format (ISO 8601).
XmlValue::G_MONTH	A recurring Gregorian day of the year, such as an annual holiday, in the --MM format.
XmlValue::G_MONTH_DAY	A day recurring on a specific day of the year, such as May 3rd, in the --MM-DD format.
XmlValue::G_YEAR	A Gregorian calendar year in the CCYY format.
XmlValue::G_YEAR_MONTH	A specific month in a specific Gregorian year, specified as CCYY-MM.
XmlValue::HEX_BINARY	Hex-encoded binary data (octets).
XmlValue::NOTATION	A notation XML attribute type.
XmlValue::QNAME	An XML qualified name (one that includes a namespace and a local part).
XmlValue::STRING	A character string.
XmlValue::TIME	A daily-recurring instant of time, specified hh:mm:ss.sss.
XmlValue::YEAR_MONTH_DURATION	A duration with year and month parts only.
XmlValue::UNTYPED_ATOMIC	A pseudo-type for all untyped (via a schema) XML data.

C++

```
#include <DbXml.hpp>

class DbXml::XmlValue {
    public:
    XmlValue();
    XmlValue(const std::string &value);
    XmlValue(const char *value);
    XmlValue(double value);
    XmlValue(bool value);
    XmlValue(XmlDocument &value);
    XmlValue(Type type,const std::string &value);
    XmlValue(Type type,const XmlData &data);

    virtual ~XmlValue();
    XmlValue(const XmlValue &);
    XmlValue &operator=(const XmlValue &);

    Type getType() const;

    bool isType(XmlValue::Type type) const
    bool isNumber() const;
    bool isString() const;
    bool isBoolean() const;
    bool isBinary() const;
    bool isNode() const;

    bool isNull() const;

    double asNumber() const;
    std::string asString() const;
    bool asBoolean() const;
    bool asBinary() const;
    DOMNode *asNode() const;
    const XmlDocument &asDocument() const;

    bool operator==(const XmlValue &v) const
    bool equals(const XmlValue &v) const;

    std::string getNodeName() const
    std::string getNodeValue() const
    std::string getNamespaceURI() const
    std::string getPrefix() const
    std::string getLocalName() const
    short getNodeType() const
    XmlValue getParentNode() const
    XmlValue getFirstChild() const
    XmlValue getLastChild() const
    XmlValue getPreviousSibling() const
    XmlValue getNextSibling() const
    XmlResults getAttributes() const
    XmlValue getOwnerElement() const
    ...
};
```

Java

```
public XmlValue([int type,] [XmlValue value])
public XmlValue([int type,] [String value])
public XmlValue([XmlDocument document])
...

public int getType()
public boolean isNumber()
public boolean isString()
public boolean isNode()
...

public String asString()
public boolean asBoolean()
public String getNodeName()
public String getNodeValue()
public String getNamespaceURI()
public String getPrefix()
public String getLocalName()
public short getNodeType()
public XmlValue getParentNode()
public XmlValue getFirstChild()
public XmlValue getLastChild()
public XmlValue getPreviousSibling()
public XmlValue getNextSibling()
public XmlResults getAttributes()
public XmlValue getOwnerElement()
...
```

Python

```
XmlValue([type,] [value])
XmlValue([document])
...

XmlValue.getType()
XmlValue.isNumber()
XmlValue.isString()
XmlValue.isNode()
...

XmlValue.asString()
XmlValue.asBoolean()
XmlValue.getNodeName()
XmlValue.getNodeValue()
XmlValue.getNamespaceURI()
XmlValue.getPrefix()
XmlValue.getLocalName()
XmlValue.getNodeType()
XmlValue.getParentNode()
XmlValue.getFirstChild()
XmlValue.getLastChild()
XmlValue.getPreviousSibling()
```

```
XmlValue.getNextSibling()
XmlValue.getAttributes()
XmlValue.getOwnerElement()
...
```

Perl

```
my $v = new XmlValue()
my $v = new XmlValue(value);
my $v = new XmlValue(type, value);
my $v = new XmlValue(document);

my $type = $v->getType();
my $type = $v->getTypeName();

my $boolean  = $v->isType(type);
my $boolean  = $v->isBoolean();
my $boolean  = $v->isNumber();
my $boolean  = $v->isString();
my $boolean  = $v->isNode();

my $number   = $v->asNumber();
my $string   = $v->asString();
my $document = $v->asDocument();

...

my $string    = $v->getNodeName() ;
my $string    = $v->getNodeValue() ;
my $string    = $v->getNamespaceURI() ;
my $string    = $v->getPrefix() ;
my $string    = $v->getLocalName() ;
my $type      = $v->getNodeType() ;
my $xmlvalue  = $v->getParentNode() ;
my $xmlvalue  = $v->getFirstChild() ;
...
```

PHP

```
$v = new XmlValue()
$v = new XmlValue(value);
$v = new XmlValue(type, value);
$v = new XmlValue(document);

$type = $v->getType();
$type = $v->getTypeName();

$boolean  = $v->isType(type);
$boolean  = $v->isBoolean();
$boolean  = $v->isNumber();
$boolean  = $v->isString();
$boolean  = $v->isNode();
```

```
$number   = $v->asNumber();
$string   = $v->asString();
$document = $v->asDocument();

...

$string   = $v->getNodeName() ;
$string   = $v->getNodeValue() ;
$string   = $v->getNamespaceURI() ;
$string   = $v->getPrefix() ;
$string   = $v->getLocalName() ;
$type     = $v->getNodeType() ;
$xmlvalue = $v->getParentNode() ;
$xmlvalue = $v->getFirstChild() ;
...
```

XQuery Reference

This brief XQuery reference includes alphabetical tables for expression keywords and operators, built-in functions, and data types. Please see the XQuery candidate recommendation at http://www.w3.org/TR/xquery/ for more details.

Expressions

Table C-1 contains an alphabetical listing of mode XQuery operators and keywords. Each entry includes a brief (and general) usage syntax and description of the behavior. Not included are built-in character references (&, <, and so on), rare keywords, alternate forms, examples, special cases, operation function definitions that back up operators, or varying behaviors based on context and data types. Where a sample usage is redundant and lengthy (such as with prolog declarations), no column value is included. Where operators take sequences as context, remember that a sequence can be one item (a singleton).

Table C-1. *XQuery Expression Operators, Keywords, and Symbols*

Expression	Usage	Description and Notes
'	'characters'	Apostrophe; surrounds string literals; double it to escape; can contain newlines
-	expr - expr	Subtraction operator
!=	seq != seq	General inequality comparison; tests whether values in either sequence are unequal
"	"characters"	Quotation mark; surrounds string literals; double it to escape; can contain newlines
$	$variable	Denotes a variable where variable names are a QName value (see Table C-3)
&#	&#N;	Decimal character reference; the integer specifying a Unicode code value
&#x	&#xH;	Hexadecimal character reference; the number specifying a Unicode code value
( )	(expr)	Parentheses; group expressions denote function arguments; empty parentheses denote empty sequences
(: :)	(:characters:)	XQuery comment (not an XML comment)
*	expr * expr	Multiplication operator

Continued

Table C-1. *Continued*

Expression	Usage	Description and Notes
*	*	Wildcard name test; tests a node name within a path expression, matching any
,	*expr, expr*	Comma; separates items in a sequence and some expression parts
.	.	Current context item
..	..	Parent node; navigation shortcut for `parent::node()`
/	/ *step*	Navigation step separator in a path; root when at the start of a path (`fn:root()`)
//	// *step*	Navigation step operator in a path; shortcut for `/descendant-or-self::node()`
:	:	Colon; separates local and namespace in names
::	*axis::nodetest*	Axis separator; separates axis from node test in navigation steps
:=	let $*var* := *expr*	Assignment operator used with the `let` keyword
?	*type*?	Cardinality indicator for type of a sequence; indicates zero or one values
@	@*nodetest*	Shortcut for the attribute axis, `attribute`
[ ]	*step*[*expr*]	Predicate symbol; encloses a filter expression for a test in a path
{ }	{ *expr* }	Subexpression symbol; encloses a subexpression for some keywords (declarations, node constructors); double up to escape
|	*node** | *node**	Union operator; shortcut for `union`
+	*expr* + *expr*	Addition operator
+	*type*+	Cardinality indicator; indicates one or more values after a type name (as in parameters in a function declaration)
<	*seq* < *seq*	General less-than comparison; tests whether any value on left is less than any value on right
< />	<*name attributes*> *content*</*name*>	XML element constructor; the only difference from real XML is that curly braces ({ }) enclose an XQuery expression; see `element`
<!-- -->	<!-- *chars* -->	XML comment constructor
<![CDATA[ ]]>	<![CDATA[*chars*]]>	CDATA section constructor
<<	*expr* << *expr*	"Before" node order test; tests whether one node is before another in document order
<=	*seq* <= *seq*	General less-than-or-equal-to comparison; tests whether any value on the left is less than or equal to any value on the right
=	*seq* = *seq*	General equality comparison; tests whether any value on the left is equal to any value on the right
>	*seq* > *seq*	General greater-than comparison; tests whether any value on the left is greater than any value on the right
>=	*seq* >= *seq*	General greater-than-or-equal-to comparison; tests whether any value on the left is greater than or equal to any value on the right

Expression	Usage	Description and Notes
>>	*expr* >> *expr*	"After" node order test; tests whether one node is after another in document order
ancestor	ancestor::*nodetest*	Ancestor navigation axis
ancestor-or-self	ancestor-or-self::*nodetest*	Navigation axis matching the current context node and its ancestors
and	*expr* and *expr*	Logical and operator; tests whether both expressions evaluate to true
as	as	Used where variables are declared (FLWOR, declare variable, and so on) to give it a type
ascending	ascending	Ascending order order by keyword in FLWOR expressions
at	at	Creates a variable for keeping position in FLWOR expressions
attribute	attribute::*nodetest*	Attribute navigation axis
attribute()	attribute *name* { *expr* }	XML attribute constructor
case	case	Used by typeswitch
cast as	*expr* cast as *type*	Attempts to cast an expression as a type
castable as	*expr* castable as *type*	Tests whether an expression can be cast as a type
child	child::*nodetest*	Child navigation axis
comment	comment { *expr* }	XML comment constructor
declare base-uri		Sets the base Uniform Resource Identifier (URI); used in the prolog
declare default element namespace		Sets the default element namespace; used in the prolog
declare default function namespace		Sets the default namespace for all functions
declare function		Declares a user-defined function; used at the end of the prolog
declare namespace		Sets a namespace; used in the prolog
declare validation		Declares a validation mode for the validate operator and XML constructors
declare variable		Declares a global variable; can specify an external parameter with external keyword
declare xmlspace		Sets behavior for outer white space to strip or preserve
descendant	descendant::*nodetest*	Descendant navigation axis
descendant-or-self	descendant-or-self::*nodetest*	Navigation axis matching the current context node and all its descendants
descending	descending	Descending order order by keyword in FLWOR expressions
div	*expr* div *expr*	Division operator; the slash (/) is a separator for paths only
document	document { *expr* }	XML document node constructor

Continued

Table C-1. *Continued*

Expression	Usage	Description and Notes
element	element *name* { *expr* }	XML element constructor
empty greatest	empty greatest	Used as keyword for order by in FLWOR expressions; treats the empty sequence as greatest
empty least	empty least	Used as keyword for order by in FLWOR expressions; treats the empty sequence as least
eq	*expr* eq *expr*	Value equality comparison
every	every $*var* in *expr* satisfies *expr*	Quantification condition test; true if every item satisfies the condition
except	*node** except *node**	Difference set operator; computes the difference between two node sequences
following	following::*nodetest*	"After" navigation axis; matches all nodes in the same document that come after it in document order
following-sibling	following-sibling::*nodetest*	Navigation axis matching all siblings that follow the current node in document order
for	for $*var* in *expr* at $*pos*	Iteration clause in a FLWOR expression; introduces one or more iterated variables
ge	*expr* ge *expr*	Greater-than-or-equal-to value comparison
gt	*expr* gt *expr*	Greater-than value comparison
idiv	*expr* idiv *expr*	Integer division operator
if	if (*expr*) then *expr* else *expr*	Constructs a conditional expression; else if is a nested conditional
import module		Imports an external module; used in the prolog
import schema		Imports an external schema; used in the prolog
instance of	*expr* instance of *type*	Tests whether an expression matches a type
intersect	*node** intersect *node**	Set intersection operator; returns all nodes that are in both sequences
is	*node* is *node*	Node equality; tests whether two nodes are equal (using node identity)
le	*expr* le *expr*	Less-than-or-equal-to value comparison
let	let $*var* := *expr*	Variable declaration clause in a FLWOR expression
lt	*expr* lt *expr*	Less-than value comparison
mod	*expr* mod *expr*	Modulo operator (modulo is the "remainder" after a division operation); useful for result alternation
module	module namespace *prefix* = "*namespace*";	Begins a library module
namespace	namespace *prefix* { *expr* }	XML namespace constructor

Expression	Usage	Description and Notes
ne	*expr* ne *expr*	Not-equal value comparison
or	*expr* or *expr*	Logical or operator; tests whether either value is true
order by	order by *sortkey modifier*	Sorts the results of a FLWOR expression given one or more sort keys and sort modifiers
parent	parent::*nodetest*	Parent navigation axis; matches the parent node of the current context node
preceding	prededing::*nodetest*	Navigation axis matching all nodes before the current context node in the same document
preceding-sibling	preceding-sibling::*nodetest*	Navigation axis matching all siblings before the current node
return	return *expr*	Sets the result for each iteration of a FLWOR expression
self	self::*nodetest*	Current node navigation axis; same as the period (.)
some	some $*var* in *expr* satisfies *expr*	A quantification condition test; true if any value satisfies the condition
text	text { *expr* }	XML text node constructor
to	*expr* to *expr*	Integer range operator; similar to integer .. integer in other languages
treat as	*expr* treat as *type*	Casts an expressions type without changing its value
typeswitch	typeswitch (*expr*) case ...	Sets a value based on type of an expression
union	*node** union *node**	Set union operator; returns nodes in both sequences without duplicates
where	where *condition*	Specifies a condition expression in FLWOR expressions
validate	validate *mode context* { *node* }	Validates a node expression against an XML schema

Functions

This section provides an alphabetical list of the XQuery built-in functions. All standard XQuery/XPath 2.0 functions exist in the namespace fn, which is omitted in Table C-2. Because what precedes a function does not affect its operation, the first column names the function and provides its sample usage. Example usages are brief (and general) and do not reflect all usages, returned data types, or behavior based on different data types. Many functions have a zero argument usage that operates on current context items (as when used in path predicates such as string()) or empty arguments that default to a static value. Please see the XQuery specification for mode details and see the XPath function reference at http://www.w3.org/TR/xpath-functions.

Table C-2. *XQuery Built-In Functions*

Function/Usage	Description
abs(*number*)	Computes the absolute value of the argument
adjust-dateTime-to-timezone(*dateTime, time zone*)	Returns the date (xs:dateTime) adjusted to a time zone
adjust-date-to-timezone(*date, time zone*)	Returns the date (xs:date) adjusted to a time zone (xdt:dayTimeDuration)
adjust-time-to-timezone(*time, time zone*)	Returns the time adjusted to a time zone
avg(*seq*)	Computes the average value for the sequence
base-uri(*node*)	Returns the base URI for a node
boolean(*seq*)	Returns the boolean value for its argument
ceiling(*number*)	Returns the value rounded to the least integer greater than the number
codepoints-to-string(*sequence*)	Returns a string of Unicode characters for the provided integer code points
collection(*string*)	Sets input to a collection of nodes; sets input to read from a container in BDB XML
compare(*string1, string2*)	Compares equality of strings
concat(*string1, ...*)	Returns strings concatenated
contains(*string1, string2*)	Tests whether the first string contains the second string
count(*seq*)	Returns the number of items in a sequence
current-date()	Returns the current date
current-dateTime()	Returns the current date and time
current-time()	Returns the current time
data(*seq*)	Converts nodes in a sequence to atomic values (atomization)
day-from-date(*date*)	Returns the day for the provided xs:date value
day-from-dateTime(*dateTime*)	Returns the day for the provided xs:dateTime value
days-from-duration(*duration*)	Returns the days in an xdt:dayTimeDuration value
deep-equal(*seq, seq*)	Tests sequences for deep equality; every item equal in the same order
default-collation()	Returns the default collation definition; used for string order
distinct-values(*seq*)	Removes duplicate (atomic) values from a sequence
doc(*string*)	Opens an XML document and returns its document node
document-uri(*node*)	Returns the document URI of a node

Function/Usage	Description
empty(*seq*)	Tests whether a sequence contains zero items
ends-with(*string1*, *string2*)	Tests whether the first string ends with the second string
error(*item*)	Terminates the query processing and sets an error
escape-uri(*string*, *boolean*)	URI-escapes the string; the boolean sets whether to escape special characters
exactly-one(*seq*)	Causes an error if a sequence is not a singleton
exists(*seq*)	Tests whether a sequence contains at least one item
false()	Boolean false
floor(*number*)	Returns the greatest integer less than the number
hours-from-dateTime(*dateTime*)	Returns the hours for an xs:dateTime value
hours-from-duration(*duration*)	Returns the hours for an xdt:dayTimeDuration value
hours-from-time(*time*)	Returns the hours for an xs:time value
id(string)	Returns the element with a given ID value; unsupported in BDB XML
idref(string)	Returns the node with the given IDREF value; unsupported in BDB XML
implicit-timezone()	Returns the default time zone
index-of(*seq*, *item*)	Finds the position of the item in the sequence
in-scope-prefixes(*element*)	Returns a sequence of namespace prefixes for the element
insert-before(*seq1*, *position*, *seq2*)	Constructs a new sequence with the first sequence inserted into the second sequence at the position (as an integer)
lang(*string*)	Tests the current context node for the given language (specified by an xml:lang attribute)
last()	Returns the position of the last item in the current context sequence (its length)
local-name(*node*)	Returns the local-name of a node
local-name-from-QName(*stringQName*)	Returns the local-name part of a QName
lower-case(*string*)	Converts a string to lowercase
matches(*string*, *pattern*)	Tests the string using the regular expression pattern
max(*seq*)	Returns the maximum numeric value in a sequence
min(*seq*)	Returns the minimum numeric value in a sequence
minutes-from-dateTime(*dateTime*)	Returns the minutes for an xs:dateTime value
minutes-from-duration(*duration*)	Returns the minutes for an xdt:dayTimeDuration value
minutes-from-time(*time*)	Returns the minutes for an xs:time value
month-from-date(*date*)	Returns the months for an xs:date value
month-from-dateTime(*dateTime*)	Returns the months for an xs:dateTime value
months-from-duration(*duration*)	Returns the months for an xdt:yearMonthDuration value
name(*node*)	Returns a nodes name as a string

Continued

Table C-2. *Continued*

Function/Usage	Description
namespace-uri(*node*)	Returns a node's namespace URI
namespace-uri-for-prefix(*element, string*)	Gets the namespace URI for an element provided a prefix
namespace-uri-from-QName(*QName*)	Returns the namespace URI part of the xs:QName
node-name(*node*)	Returns a node's name as an xs:QName value
normalize-space(*string*)	Returns a string with outer white space removed and consecutive white space consolidated
normalize-unicode(*string*)	Returns a string after Unicode normalization
not(*expr*)	Logical negation; returns the inverse of the boolean result of the expression
number(*expr*)	Converts an expression to an xs:double
one-or-more(*seq*)	Causes an error on an empty sequence; otherwise, returns the sequence
position()	Returns the position of the current context item within its sequence
QName(*namespace, local name*)	Returns a QName provided with a namespace and local name
remove(*seq, position*)	Removes an item from a sequence and returns the sequence
replace(*string, pattern1, pattern2*)	Returns a string with the first pattern replaced with the second pattern
resolve-QName(*string, element*)	Returns an xs:QName using the qualified name and element for namespaces
resolve-uri(*string*)	Returns the absolute URI given a URI
reverse(*seq*)	Returns the sequence reversed
root(*node*)	Returns the root node for the tree to which the node belongs
round(*number*)	Returns the number rounded to the closest integer, half rounded up
round-half-to-even(*number*)	Returns the number rounded to the closest integer, half rounded even; a second argument allows for decimal precision
seconds-from-dateTime(*date*)	Returns the seconds part of an xs:dateTime value
seconds-from-duration(*duration*)	Returns the seconds for an xdt:dayTimeDuration value
seconds-from-time(*time*)	Returns the seconds for an xs:time value
starts-with(*string1, string2*)	Tests whether the first string starts with the second string
string(*item*)	Converts the item to xs:string
string-join(*seq, delim*)	Returns a string with the sequence of strings joined with the delimiter
string-length(*string*)	Returns the length of a string
string-to-codepoints(*string*)	Returns a sequence of integers for each Unicode code point in a string

Function/Usage	Description
subsequence(*seq, position1, position2*)	Returns the subsequence of a sequence, by using a start and end position, to the sequences end if no second position is provided
substring(*string, position1, position2*)	Returns a substring of a string, by using a start and end position, or to the end of the string if no second position is provided
substring-after(*string1, string2*)	Returns the substring of the first string that occurs after the first occurrence of the second string
substring-before(*string1, string2*)	Returns the substring of the first string that occurs before the first occurrence of the second string
sum(*seq*)	Returns the sum of all values in a sequence
timezone-from-date(*date*)	Returns the time zone for the xs:date value
timezone-from-dateTime(*dateTime*)	Returns the time zone part of an xs:dateTime value
timezone-from-time(*time*)	Returns the time zone for the xs:time value
tokenize(*string1, string2*)	Returns a sequence of the first string split using the second string
trace(*seq*, string)	Calls a debugging routine; the sequence is a return value; the second is a trace message
translate(*string1, string2, string3*)	Replaces in the first string the characters in the second string with the corresponding characters in the third string
true()	Boolean true
unordered(seq)	Gives to the query processor a hint that the sequence does not need to be maintained
upper-case(string)	Returns the string with all characters converted to uppercase
year-from-date(*date*)	Returns the year part of an xs:date value
year-from-dateTime(*dateTime*)	Returns the year for an xs:dateTime value
years-from-duration(*duration*)	Returns the years for an xdt:yearMonthDuration value
zero-or-one(seq)	Causes an error if a sequence contains more than one item

Data Types

XQuery data types belong to a type hierarchy described briefly in Chapter 7, "XQuery with BDB XML." They are listed in Table C-3 with a brief description. Types that have parentheses after their names have corresponding type tests that can usually be used with arguments (to test an item) or as void (as a context test). All types (except abstracts and where noted) can be constructed; node types use the expression keyword of the same name (that is, element *name* { *expr* }) using the function of the same name as the type, and atomic types have corresponding constructor functions of the same name as the type that take an item (some with restricted atomic types; most with any) as argument. Types in the xs namespace are XML schema types used by XQuery, and xdt types are those introduced by XQuery/XPath 2.0 (XPath Data Types). Abstract types are listed first, node types are listed next, and then atomic types are listed in postprefix alphabetical order.

Note BDB XML optionally validates data types for XML that use an XML schema or Data Type Definition (DTD), but type information is not stored within the database. Explicit casting is required within XQuery expressions to use types, and indexes for a container need to be given proper types for those expressions to yield timely results.

Table C-3. *XQuery Data Types*

Type	Description
item()	Abstract; the basic XQuery type; all values are items; a sequence is zero or more items
node()	Abstract; any XML node; all node types descend from this type
xdt:anyAtomicType	Abstract; any atomic type; all atomic types descend from this type
attribute()	Attribute node
comment()	Comment node
document-node()	Document node
element()	Element node
namespace()	Namespace node
processing-instruction()	Processing instruction node
text()	Text node
xs:anyURI	URI value
xs:base64Binary	Base 64.encoded value
xs:boolean	Boolean value; true or false
xs:byte	Signed byte value (-128 to 127)
xs:date	Calendar date value with year, month, day, and time zone
xs:dateTime	Calendar time value with year, month, day, hour, minute, second, and time zone
xdt:dayTimeDuration	Duration value with day and time granularity (permits duration comparisons)
xs:decimal	Numeric fixed-point decimal value (128-bit)
xs:double	Numeric double-precision floating point value (8-byte)
xs:duration	Duration value with years, months, days, hours, minutes, and seconds
xs:float	Numeric single-precision floating-point value (4-byte)
xs:gDay	Day in the Gregorian calendar
xs:gMonth	Month in the Gregorian calendar
xs:gMonthDay	Month and day in the Gregorian calendar
xs:gYear	Year in the Gregorian calendar
xs:gYearMonth	Month and year in the Gregorian calendar
xs:hexBinary	Hex-encoded value
xs:ID	XML ID value
xs:IDREF	XML IDREF value
xs:IDREFS	List of XML IDREF values
xs:int	Signed 4-byte integer value

Type	Description
xs:integer	Signed integer value
xs:language	XML language value (represents an xml:lang attribute)
xs:long	Signed 8-byte integer value
xs:Name	Valid XML name value (prefix, colon, and local-name)
xs:NCName	Nonqualified XML name; colons illegal
xs:negativeInteger	Negative integer value
xs:nonNegativeInteger	Zero or positive integer value
xs:nonPositiveInteger	Zero or negative integer value
xs:normalizedString	String with normalized white space
xs:NOTATION	XML notation value
xs:positiveInteger	Positive integer value
xs:QName	Qualified XML name value (QName)
xs:short	Signed 2-byte integer value
xs:string	String value
xs:time	Time value with hour, minute, second, and time zone
xs:token	Token value (no spaces)
xs:unsignedByte	Unsigned byte value (0 to 255)
xs:unsignedInt	Unsigned integer value
xs:unsignedLong	Unsigned long value
xs:unsignedShort	Unsigned short value
xdt:untypedAtomic	Untyped value given to all untyped XML data
xdt:yearMonthDuration	Duration value with year and month (permits duration comparisons)

Index

Numbers and symbols

You Need the Companion eBook

Your purchase of this book entitles you to its companion eBook for only $10.

We believe this Apress title will prove so indispensable that you'll want to carry it with you everywhere, which is why we are offering the companion eBook for $10 to customers who purchase this book now. Convenient and fully searchable, the eBook version of any content-rich, page-heavy Apress book makes a valuable addition to your programming library. You can easily find, copy, and apply code—and then perform examples by quickly toggling between instructions and the application. Even simultaneously tackling a donut, diet soda, and complex code becomes simplified with hands-free eBooks!

Once you purchase this book, getting the $10 companion eBook is simple:

❶ Visit **www.apress.com/promo/tendollars/**.

❷ Complete a basic registration form to receive a randomly generated question about this title.

❸ Answer the question correctly in 60 seconds and you will receive a promotional code to redeem for the $10 eBook.

2560 Ninth Street • Suite 219 • Berkeley, CA 94710

Offer valid through 2/07.